Seeds of Destiny

A Devotional Study of Genesis

By Warren Henderson

All Scripture quotations in this book are taken from the
King James Version of the Bible unless otherwise noted.

Seeds of Destiny
By Warren Henderson
Copyright ©2004

Published by Gospel Folio Press
304 Killaly Street West
Port Colborne, ON L3K 6A6, Canada
ISBN 1-897117-01-9

ORDERING INFORMATION
Gospel Folio Press
Phone 1-905-835-9166
E-mail: orders@gospelfolio.com

Printed in the United States of America

Acknowledgments

"...those members of the body, which we think to be less honorable, upon these we bestow more abundant honor" (1 Cor. 12:22-23). The author greatly appreciates the abilities and the sacrificial attitude of those members in the body of Christ who have assisted me in publishing *Seeds of Destiny*. A special thanks to Colin Anderson who labored much with me in the technical editing of this work. Thanks also to: David Dunlap, and Will Webber for technical editing inputs; Caroline Cairns, and Jane Biberstein for general editing; Karen Cyborski and David Lindstrom for proofreading assistance.

Preface

The Christian community sits upon a vast resource of vintage exposition, exegetic, and apologetic writings from a host of writers who have long since been ushered into the Lord's presence. Most of these books are out of print, and some are difficult to obtain. In general, these writings sustain a devotional depth and a Christ-centered attraction that is void in much of today's Christian literature. I have endeavored to include some of the best gleanings from these writers in this book. *Seeds of Destiny* is a "commentary style" devotional which upholds the glories of Christ while exploring Genesis from the whole of Scripture. *Seeds of Destiny* contains over 100 brief devotions. This allows the reader to use the book as either a daily devotional or a reference source for deeper study.

Warren Henderson

Why is Genesis so Important?

Genesis, more than any other book of the Bible, provides an overview of God's immense purpose for humanity – His ultimate plan to redeem, restore and bless the only portion of creation bearing His image. This fountainhead of Holy Scripture stretches from the dawn of time, past the birth pangs of the world, the fall of man, and beyond to the restoration of mankind to God. Yes, even God's plan of redemption is displayed through dazzling allegory in Genesis. Genesis spans time from creation to a new creation. Beyond these bounds, time is meaningless. The climax of Genesis is the exaltation of the Son of God, and redeemed souls receive eternal bliss and communion with Him.

The revelation in Genesis concerning the "blueprint" for human affairs is immense. However, most of this information is in "seed form." The word "seed" is a key word in Genesis. It occurs 56 times – over twice as many references as any other book in the Bible. What does the phrase "seed form" mean? As Paul explains in 1 Corinthians 15:37-38, a plant derives its features from the seed that died in the ground. All living plants and creatures today derive their features from a seed contribution from the previous generation. Likewise, the main teachings of the Bible derive their heritage and features from Genesis seeds. The New Testament draws approximately 200 direct references from the book of Genesis. As God is sovereign over creation there is nothing that can thwart His plans for mankind. Hence the seeds of Genesis are nothing less than "seeds of destiny."

Genesis is full of "initial seeds" which give evidence to realities not yet complete. Genesis is a book of beginnings – the "seed plot of the Bible." God could not divulge the details of His redemption plan so early in human history; however, He did reveal glimpses of His plan in "seed form." If the wicked ones of this world had understood what God would accomplish by Christ's death, the Lord Jesus would have never been crucified (1 Cor. 2:8-9). John Darby writes concerning the character of Genesis:

> Genesis has a character of its own; and, as the beginning of the Holy Book, presents to us all the great elementary principles which find their development in the history of the relationships of God with man, which is recorded in the following books. The germ of each of these principles will be found here...[1]

This awesome disclosure in itself invites every believer to drink deeper and more abundantly each time he or she reads Genesis. It should be a passion of every Christian to affectionately pursue God and to know His heart. It is a passionate plea for extended and closer intimacy. This book invites the reader to *"drink, yea drink abundantly, O beloved"* (Song of Sol. 5:1). Herein taste of the Lord; taste the sweetness of the Savior again and again.

Aided by keys contained in New Testament Scripture, we will unlock the hidden meaning of numerous types, shadows, symbols, and analogies in Genesis. We seek to see the Savior! C.H. Mackintosh writes, "Whether we turn to Genesis or to Ephesians – to the prophets of the Old or those of the New Testament – we learn the same truths. 'All Scripture is given by inspiration of God.'" Divine unity pervades Holy Scripture!

What should a devotional study contain besides the visage of the Savior? In his writings, the Apostle Paul demonstrates a fundamental link between doctrine and practice. He lays a firm foundation of doctrinal truth, then implores the reader to obey it – to walk circumspectly upon it. Examples: The first three chapters of Ephesians expound doctrine; the last three exhort practice. The first eleven chapters of Romans express God's plan of redemption; the final five chapters appeal to godly conduct. Colossians devotes the first two chapters to doctrine; the last two chapters to proper living. Paul first informs the believer what God has done; he then teaches what the Christian should do in response. In other words, given our *position* in Christ what should be our *practice*?

The only true motive for holy living and for Christian service is unrestrained affection for the Savior. Imposing *guilt trips* and *heavy-handed accountability* upon those struggling in their faith may bring temporary change, but without heart alteration the desired effect will be short lived. A believer must ever be expanding his or her heart's capacity for devotion to Christ. This is the only true motive for serving God! H.A. Ironside explains this discovery in his book *Holiness – The False and the True*:

> I have been learning all along my pilgrim journey that the more my heart is taken up with Christ, the more do I enjoy practical deliverance from sin's power, and the more do I realize what it is to have the love of God shed abroad in that heart by the Holy Spirit given to me, as the earnest of the glory to come.[2]

This is the true purpose of a devotional study – learning Christ and proper doctrine to promote healthy life. Paul instructs his protégé Titus to *"speak of the things which become sound doctrine"* (Tit. 2:1). Doctrine should be learned and lived. Learning about God's holy character and His tender mercies and sacrificial love towards us should lead us to humbly bow in worship and to burst forth in service to show appreciation.

One of our goals in this study is to uncover hidden treasures of Christ veiled away in abstract symbols, reclusive personal portraits and mysterious names. Though these Old Testament gems were once concealed from human comprehension, they glisten Christ when illuminated by the light of New Testament revelation. A.W. Pink writes:

> As we read thoughtfully the books of the Old Testament our study of them is but superficial if they fail to show us that in divers ways and by various means God was preparing the way for the coming of His Son. The central purpose in the Divine Incarnation, the great outstanding object in the life and death of the Lord Jesus, were prefigured beforehand, and ought to have been rendered familiar to the minds of men. Among the means thus used of God was the history of different persons through whom the life and character of Christ were to a remarkable degree made manifest beforehand. Thus Adam represented His Headship, Abel His death, Noah His work in providing a refuge for His people. Melchizedek pointed to Him as priest, Moses as prophet, David as King. But the fullest and most striking of all these typical personages was Joseph, for between his history and that of Christ we may trace fully a hundred points of analogy![3]

Seeds of Destiny

Many of the topics introduced to us in Genesis are not encountered again until they appear in the Gospels followed by their explanation in the epistles. Through a series of concealed patterns and analogies, Genesis reveals God's awesome plan of redemption, the glories of His Son, the future aspects of His kingdom, the institution of marriage, the justification of the believer, the conflict of that which is spiritual with the flesh, and the pilgrim status of God's people; just to name a few.

J. Boyd Nicholson elaborates on why God employs such splendid forms of communication throughout Scripture.

> God Himself understands our limitations, especially when it comes to things divine and eternal that are not naturally discerned. So in grace He has revealed Himself in many graphic ways. He has declared His might, power and supreme intelligence in the vastness of the universe. He has shown his wisdom in the wonders of nature. But all the revelations of God in the material universe must fade before the greatest of all, the revelation of Himself in His Son. This is a revelation of His matchless love.
>
> As a Father, God is delighted to show forth the excellence and beauty of His Son by many revelations in His Word, if by any means he might call forth our worship, love and praise. In His Word, He utilizes every device of human language to present in countless word-pictures the wonders of the Lord Jesus. He uses statements of plain language; proclamations of predictive prophecy; types and shadows, parables and allegories, figures and emblems to show to us the "mystery of godliness" – God manifest in the flesh. God the Father plunders every realm of His universe to show these beautiful pictures of His dear Son.[4]

It is Jesus Christ whom we will endeavor to behold and contemplate as we expose "seeds of destiny" in God's inspired seed plot of Scripture.

Devotions from Genesis

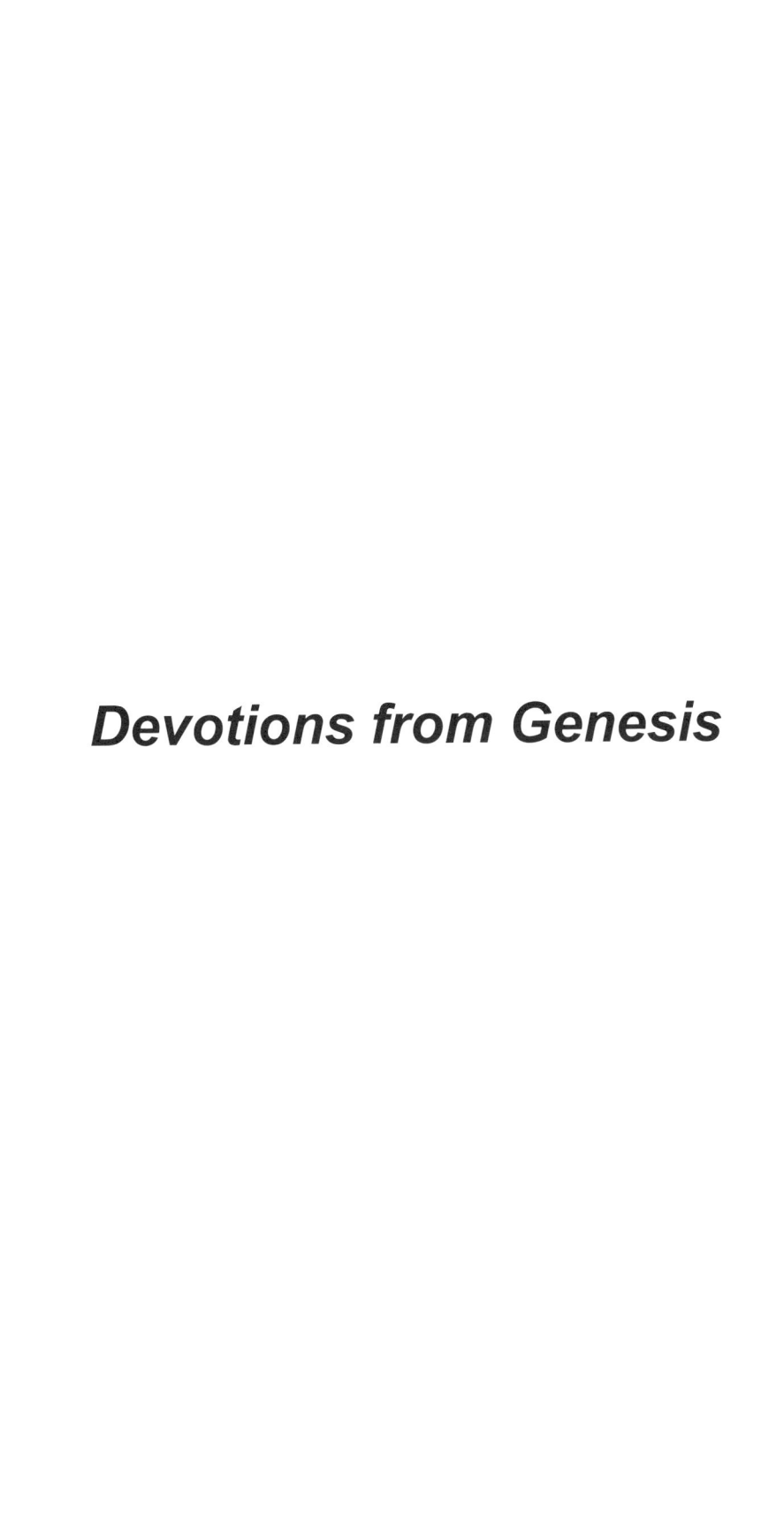

A Book of Beginnings
Genesis 1:1-3

"In the beginning." There are four "beginnings" in the Bible that are of great importance to every human being. In John 1:1, we learn that in the beginning there was only God. The beginning of creation is wonderfully described in Genesis 1:1. Thirdly, 1 John 1:1 records the beginning of the Lord Jesus' ministry on earth. Finally, 2 Corinthians 5:17 declares that God promises a new spiritual beginning to all those seeking salvation solely through His Son Jesus Christ. The first beginning speaks of God's eternal existence. The second beginning demonstrates His wisdom and power over creation when He brought space, matter and time into existence. God's third beginning speaks of His immense love and righteous justice. God's fourth beginning demonstrates His power to righteously seek and save repentant sinners and then give them a new life and identity in Christ.

The beginning described in John 1:1-3 is especially important to understand in reference to the Lord Jesus. In the first verse, the Greek imperfect tense is better translated *already was* instead of *was*. John was emphatically declaring that the Son of God already was existing before creation. Then in verse 3, the Greek aorist tense is used in contrast with the earlier imperfect tense to show that *"All things were made [became] by Him...."* John was literally saying in these first three verses of his Gospel account that the Word (the Son of God) was already existing before He created all things. Paul declares that the Son of God was the Creator of all things, *"...all things were created by Him, and for Him; and He is before all things, and by Him all things consist, and He is the head of the body, the church; ..."* (Col. 1:16-18). The writer of Hebrews, speaking of the Son states, *"Thou, Lord, in the beginning hast laid the foundation of the earth; and the heavens are the works of Thine hands"* (Heb. 1:10). When the Word became flesh (Jn.

Seeds of Destiny

1:14), the eternal Creator became a man. Paul refers to the incarnation of the Son of God as a great mystery – *"the mystery of godliness"* (1 Tim. 3:16).

Through this supernatural act, God prepared for Himself the only suitable sacrifice for the judgment of mankind's offenses against Him. The judgment of all human sin occurred some 2000 years ago when the Lord Jesus was publicly crucified. The Lord had been deserted by His disciples and rejected by his family (excluding His mother – Mary). The wicked swarmed about Him with insults and mocking torment. The Lord Jesus bore our sin in solitary agony – there was no human or divine solace to comfort His anguish. He was engulfed by the horror of pestilent darkness as the billows and waves of divine wrath broke upon Him (Ps. 42:7). At last, emotionally consumed and physically exhausted, He drew His last breath to declare victory: *"It is finished."* Three days later, His Father, fully satisfied with His work at Calvary, raised Him up from the dead and highly exalted Him to His right hand.

Those who trust the Lord Jesus alone for salvation get a "new beginning." They become a new creation (2 Cor. 5:17) and possess eternal life with Christ (Jn. 5:24). Spiritually speaking, they shall never die (Jn. 10:28). This is the principal message of the Bible. Creation itself is God's grand stage to accomplish His plan of redemption for mankind. The redeemed will ultimately enjoy Jehovah's self-expression of all that He is and forever bask in His glory.

Viewing God's overall plan for humanity aids our understanding as to the brief narrative concerning *"the beginning"* of Genesis 1. The focus of Genesis quickly turns from origin to God's relationship with His creation called man. J. W. Ferguson explains:

> While the expression "the heaven and earth" may safely be taken as a synonym for "the universe," or perhaps for "everything," the focus shifts abruptly in v.2 to earth; and from v.2 onward anything outside the earth is viewed from earth's standpoint. This sentence in v.1 is not merely the introduction to Genesis, it is the basic foundation on which rests the whole of Scripture. Scripture as a whole is God's revelation to mankind, bringing God within human ken and telling how man can be brought to God. This accounts for both inclusions and omissions in Scripture, and specifically in Genesis. Earth must

be central in a story, which deals basically with God and His relations with the human race.[1]

In the beginning, a triune God was already here. God created the spiritual realm of powers, principalities and angels. We read in Job 38:4-7 that the angels shouted for joy when God laid the foundations of the world. God then brought time and space into existence to form the beginning of everything we see, hear, smell, taste and touch. God, foreknowing man's rebellion and failures, arranged the ministry of His own Son on earth, ultimately resulting in His substitutional death for mankind's sin. Now, He can justly offer a new spiritual beginning to those who will receive Him (the Son). How wonderful our God is! He truly is a God of new beginnings.

> Once far from God and dead in sin, No light my heart could see;
> But in God's Word the light I found, Now Christ liveth in me.
>
> Daniel Whittle

Seeds of Destiny

Perfect Communication
Genesis 1:4-19

Have you had past difficulties communicating your thoughts and words properly to others? God doesn't have this problem. Our God is a God of perfect communication: *"Let there be light"* (Gen. 1:3), *"Let there be a firmament"* (Gen. 1:6), and *"Let the waters under the heaven be gathered"* (Gen. 1:9), etc. God could have just thought creation into existence, or spoken it into being with one word, but He chose to declare creation order, that we might understand His purposes. Before there was creation, there was communication. God is an articulating God who wants us to comprehend what He reveals to us (Deut. 29:29). We understand, by faith, that creation was spoken into existence (Ps. 33:6-10; Heb. 11:3).

God intimately converses with us throughout the Bible. Psalm 100:3 reads, *"Know ye that the Lord, He is God; it is He who hath made us, and not we ourselves; we are His people, and the sheep of His pasture."* God not only wants us to understand that He created us, but He created us to be His people and His sheep. The terms *"His people"* and *"His sheep"* speak of relationship and fellowship. God desires communion and fellowship with us in a personal way. In the New Testament, the Lord Jesus is called the "Word" (Jn. 1:1; 1 Jn. 1:1), which is derived from the Greek word *logos*. *Logos* is far more than the act of expressing words (speaking); it also includes the aspirations of the mind. God wanted us to know His Son intimately and thereby know Him. He yearns for us to understand His eternal love for us – a love so infinite that He was not willing to withhold His Son from suffering and dying for us.

God discloses the first Ten Commandments in Genesis 1. Ten times it is recorded *"And God said...."* All these commands relate to creating or ordering creation, and all ten continue to this day. In contrast to God's faithfulness is man's rebellion against another Ten

Commandments given to Israel at Mt. Sinai (Ex. 20). In both cases we see that God is faithful to man, even when man is not faithful to God. *"If we believe not, yet He abideth faithful; He cannot deny Himself"* (2 Tim. 2:13).

The Hebrew text of Genesis 1:1 declares creation perfection. The verse is composed of seven Hebrew words. The number "seven" in Scripture is the number of God, a number of perfection and completeness. Genesis 1 contains seven creative acts and seven expressions of God's satisfaction with creation "...and God saw that it was good."

The Hebrew text of 1:1 also contains twenty-eight letters. The number "four" is the number for creation or the created world. There are four seasons, four elements (earth, air, fire, and water), four regions, (north, south, east, and west), four divisions of day (morning, noon, evening, and night), four phases of the moon, four winds (from the four directions of the earth), and four regions in which creatures dwell (upon the earth, under the earth, in the heaven, or in the sea). In the Hebrew language, this statement is made up of seven Hebrew words, comprising twenty-eight letters. The text states literally *"In the beginning God created the heavens and the earth"* and metaphorically, by utilizing the numbers "four" and "seven," it is declared a perfect creation.

Through plain statements and symbols God has proclaimed to us in Genesis 1 that His creative acts were accomplished in perfection and with purpose.

> I need not shout my faith.
> Thrice eloquent are the trees and the green listening sod;
> Hushed are the stars, whose power is never spent;
> The hills are mute: yet how they speak of God!
>
> Charles Hanson Towne

The First Workweek
Genesis 1:20-25

Seven times during that first workweek God declared that what He had accomplished was perfect *"...and God saw that it was good."* Because God is perfect, He can only do and create that which is perfect in purpose. Even Lucifer, prior to his rebellion, was acknowledged as being a perfect creation (Ezek. 28:12-15). The fact that creation was formed by God in perfection is foundational to the Christian faith. John Darby summarizes the first six days of God's laboring to bring about this perfect creation:

> The first four days, God brings light and order out of darkness and confusion: light, the first day, the expanse as a scene of heavenly power over the earth, the second day; then He divided what was formed and orderly, on the one hand, from the moving powerful but shapeless mass of waters, on the other, and then ornamented the ordered habitable scene with beauty and fruitfulness on the third. The symbols of directing power were set visibly in their places on the fourth.
>
> The scene of man's display and dominion was formed, but man was not yet there. But before He formed man, God created living energies of every kind in the seas, and earth, and air, which, instinct with life, should propagate and multiply, the proof of God's life-giving power, that to matter He could communicate living energy; and thus, not only a scene was formed, where His purposes in man should be displayed, but that existence, which man should rule so as to display his energies and rights according to the will of God, and as holding his place as vicegerent over the earth, apart, and distinct from all, the centre of all, the ruler of all, as interested in them as his; living in his own sphere of blessedness according to his nature, and as to others,

ordering all in blessing and subjection. In the midst of all the prepared creation, in a word, man is set.[1]

The personal narratives contained in Genesis provide natural divisions in the book. Within the first major division pertaining to Adam, two distinct sections are observed: God's work and rest (Gen. 1:1-2:3), and His relationship with the creature He created (Gen. 2:4-25).

Genesis 1:1-2:3 records the first workweek and may be further divided into three sections with the first two sections being a double parallel series. On day one God labors with "light," day two with "water," and day three with "earth." This series of three is repeated again in days four through six. God orders light on day four, water on day five, and earth on day six. On day seven He rested, thus, ending the first workweek.

Genesis 2:4-25 acknowledges the special relationship of God with man, man with creation, and man with his wife. It is in Chapter 2, that God, for the first time, intimately identifies Himself by His personal name *Jehovah*. Adam's union with his wife wonderfully typifies the spiritual relationship of Christ, the second Adam, and His bride the Church. In this portion of Scripture, two great principles of the Bible are introduced: First, man's responsibility for obedience to God. Secondly, that God is the sovereign source of all life – apart from Him there is no life, only death. John said of the Lord Jesus, *"All things were made by Him; and without Him was not anything made that was made. In Him was life..."* (Jn. 1:3-4).

On the seventh day God rested. The workweek concluded with rest. The text conveys a sense of satisfaction in that all that God created was found good – perfect! Man was innocent, in fellowship with his Creator, and living in paradise; Eden means "pleasure."

> Open, ye heavens, your living doors; let in
> The great Creator from His work returned
> Magnificent, His six days' work, a world!
>
> John Milton

Three in One
Genesis 1:26

"In the beginning, God created the heavens and the earth." This first sentence of the sacred page affixes humanity in the presence of the infinite Creator. There is no argument put forth to prove His existence since creation itself testifies of a Creator (Rom. 1:20). Before there was anything, God eternally existed harmoniously in three Persons. God is not creation, as some teach, for creation came subsequent to the eternal God. However, God does permeate all His creation (Ps. 139:7; Acts 17:27-28) and maintains it in perfect order (Col. 1:17). Consequently, the first and second of the Ten Commandments demand that the Creator, not creation, be worshipped.

God's tri-unity in creation is distinctly seen in the pronouns "Us," "Our," and "Their" employed to describe man's creation (Gen. 1:26), events after the fall of mankind (Gen. 3:22), and again when God confounded mankind's language (Gen. 11:4-7). God introduces Himself to us as *Elohim* in Genesis 1:1 and continues to refer to Himself as such throughout the chapter. *Elohim* speaks of God's majesty, power, and omnipotence as the Creator. The *im* suffix is the Hebrew ending to denote plurality (*Elohim* is plural of *Eloah*). *Elohim* may be translated literally as *gods*, but clearly in the context of the passage, it is used in the singular – the name of the mighty Creator. Thus, *Elohim* is a plural name with a singular meaning. Nearly ninety percent of the references to *"God"* in the Old Testament are *Elohim* (*Elohim* is employed in the Hebrew text approximately 2700 times).

In Genesis 2:4, God first identifies Himself to mankind as *Jehovah*, the self-existent and eternal One. *Jehovah* is used over 6850 times in the Old Testament and expresses God's moral and personal relationship with the intelligent creation bearing His image.

Later in Genesis, God identifies Himself to the Patriarchs as *El Elyon*, the Most High God or Almighty God. As *El Elyon*, He alone would be their sustaining power through adversity and the only source of hope for their faith to confide in.

There is one unique God consisting of three individual Persons, each having the same divine attributes and characteristics. Each is perfect in grace, mercy, and love and is all-powerful, all-knowing and all-present (dwelling everywhere). The unity of the Godhead concerning the plan of salvation for mankind is recorded in Isaiah 48:16-17.

Throughout Scripture, their roles are consistent: God the Father declares the will of God (He chooses), God the Son executes the will of God, and the Holy Spirit enables and ratifies the will of God to be done, usually through the Son. Each Person of the Godhead acts to affect praise of God's glory (Eph. 1:6, 12, 14). The fact that the Father chooses does not imply that the Son and the Holy Spirit do not have individual wills – for They do – but They always align with the Father's (Jn. 6:38; 1 Cor. 12:11). The fact that the Holy Spirit issues power to ratify God's will does not mean that the Son does not have power to invoke miracles – He does. On some occasions the Son did miracles by His own power and not through the direct power of the Holy Spirit (Lk. 5:17, 8:46).

It is by the Son that we know God, for *"He has spoken unto us by His Son"* (Heb. 1:2). One cannot constrain what is mysterious and beyond human comprehension into a formula of operation; yet, Scripture does portray the Trinity in a consistent way and with distinct roles. For what we do not understand, let us simply remove our shoes and not trespass upon holy ground. The following are a few examples of triune operation within the Godhead:

The Plan of Salvation
The Father purposes to save souls through His Son's sacrifice (Jn. 3:16; 1 Pet. 1:2). Jesus Christ gave Himself freely to accomplish the will of the Father (Jn. 10:17-18). The Holy Spirit makes effectual the work of the Son by convicting mankind of sin and wooing sinners to the Savior (Jn. 16:8).

Creation
The Father directed (Isa. 40:12-14; Acts 17:24), the Son created, perhaps spoke it into being (Heb. 1:2, 11:3; Jn. 1:3; 1 Cor. 8:6; Col. 1:16-17), and the power of the Spirit formed it (Gen. 1:2; Ps. 104:30; Job 26:13 and 33:4).

The Son of God's Incarnation
Power from the Father through the Spirit accomplished the incarnation of Jesus (Lk. 1:35).

The Lord's Baptism
The Father baptized the Son with the Holy Spirit to initiate His ministry (Lk. 3:22; Acts 10:38).

The Lord's Death
The Son offered Himself for our sins (2 Cor. 5:21; Gal. 2:20) through the power of the Eternal Spirit (Heb. 9:14), while also addressing His God who was judging Him for human sin (Matt. 27:46).

Giving of the Spirit to the Church
The Father sent the Holy Spirit after Christ's ascension (Jn. 14:16, 26). The Son told His disciples that He would pray for and later send the Holy Spirit from the Father (Jn. 15:26, 16:7; Acts 2:33).

The roles within the Godhead (Trinity) are seen also in biblical typology. By the word *type*, we simply mean a picture, figure, or pattern that reflects something or someone in reality. The word "type" or "print" comes from the Greek word *tupos*. It is used to speak of the nail "print" in the Lord's hand (Jn. 20:25) and of the tabernacle furniture which was to be fashioned according to the "pattern" given Moses in the mount (Heb. 8:5). Thomas said he would not believe that the Lord had been raised up unless he felt the print of the nail in the Lord's hand. In other words, the pattern left in the Lord's hand would match the nail, but yet it was not the nail. However, the print gave evidence of what the nail was like (size and shape). Likewise, Scripture is saturated with "types" of Christ. These give evidence of Christ, but are not Christ.

There is no perfect "type" or "pattern," or it would be the real thing. Therefore, all types, foreshadows, symbols, analogies, and patterns are inadequate to express fully and completely every aspect of His person and work.

In the Bible, a type of God the Father is seen in father Abraham (Gen. 22). Abraham is willing to offer his only son Isaac for a sacrifice, just as God the Father would in the future offer His Son for a sin sacrifice. Types of Christ in the OT are usually seen in both *people* and *objects*: the ark, a rock, a rod, a door, an arm, a shepherd, a veil, etc. Objects or people are used to accomplish a work, which pictures Christ performing the Father's will. The Holy Spirit is generally depicted in *active* fluids: flowing olive oil (Zech. 4), blowing wind (Jn. 3), seven flames of fire (Rev. 4), and rushing water (Jn 7). The Holy Spirit, in these types, is not visibly seen doing the Father's will, but rather enabling and accomplishing the task at hand in a powerful and invisible fashion.

This operation of the Holy Spirit is clearly seen in Genesis 1:2, *"The Spirit of God moved upon the face of the waters."* Here the Holy Spirit is described as "moving" in the presence of the formless water. The Hebrew word translated "moving" is *rachaph*. *Rachaph* occurs only three times in the Old Testament. It is translated "shake" in Jeremiah 23:9 and "fluttereth" in Deuteronomy 32:11. In today's scientific vernacular we might say that the Holy Spirit vibrated or energized basic elements to put them into prescribed order. B. H. Carroll comments to the "quickening" work of the Holy Spirit in creation:

> The doctrine is that matter is inert of itself. It had no inherent potentiality. In itself was no capacity to become a world of order and beauty. The quickening of matter by the Holy Spirit was therefore the second creative activity. Given matter alone, and we have chaos alone; but given also an extraneous power, intelligent, beneficent and omnipotent, to impart capacity to matter and to direct its movements, and we will have a well-ordered and beautiful world.[1]

A triune God created all that was created. Paul often writes of the Trinity, *"But to us there is but one God, the Father, of whom are all things, and we in Him; and one Lord Jesus Christ, by Whom are all things, and we by Him [we exist by Him]"* (1 Cor. 8:6). *"The grace of*

Seeds of Destiny

the Lord Jesus Christ, and the love of God, and the communion of the Holy Spirit be with you all" (2 Cor. 13:14). Paul understood that our existence, our salvation and our fellowship is integrally connected with a triune God. In the same way, the Lord Jesus commanded that all those who had believed His Gospel message to be baptized *"in the name of the Father, and of the Son and of the Holy Spirit"* (Matt. 28:19). God is three individuals in one entity. All three are God, eternal, and equal, though Scripture does reveal a distinction in personality (not holy character) and roles. God the Father could not be the Eternal Father (Isa. 9:6) without an Eternal Son!

> Holy, Holy, Holy! Tho' the darkness hide Thee,
> Tho' the eye of sinful man Thy glory many not see,
> Only Thou art holy; there is none beside Thee
> Perfect in power, in love and purity.
> Holy, Holy, Holy! Lord God Almighty!
> All Thy works shall praise Thy name in earth, and sky and sea,
> Holy, Holy, Holy! Merciful and Mighty!
> God in Three Persons, blessed Trinity!
>
> Reginald Heber

God's Icon
Genesis 1:26

The creation of man was the grand finale and crowning moment of God's ingenious work. God's connection with mankind would be distinctly different than to the fish of the sea and beasts of the field – man was to be created in God's image. *"Let us make man in our **image**, after our **likeness**..."* (Gen. 1:26). *"So God created man in his own **image** ..."* (Gen. 1:27). Though mankind would be the apex of organic life, there would be an impassable chasm between him and the next highest order of beast. Man was to bear God's image and represent Him by ruling over God's creation.

So man was created in God's image, but what does the word "image" imply? How do the meanings of "image" and "likeness" differ in Scripture? Someone might say of a newborn babe, "he is the spitting image of his father," implying that the baby "looks like" his dad. However, the word "likeness" relates more to character and behavior and must be proven out in time. When the baby grows up and walks in the footsteps of his father, it might then be said, "he is just like his father."

In what form does man possess the image of God? First it is noted that *"God is a spirit"* (Jn. 4:24) and *"the Father of spirits"* (Heb. 12:9). Man is also a spiritual being. *"The Lord...formeth the spirit of man within him"* (Zech. 12:1). The human spirit possesses God consciousness (Prov. 20:27; Job. 32:8). It is thus apparent that the spirituality of man's nature is in the image of God. Man's spiritual nature is seen in other ways:

1. Intuitive knowledge and cognitive abilities (Col. 3:10; Isa. 1:18).
2. Moral consciousness (Rom. 2:15).
3. Initially innocent and upright (Eccl. 7:29).
4. Immortality of soul (Rev. 14:10-11; Jn. 5:24).

Seeds of Destiny

5. A will – free moral agent (Matt. 16:25; Rev. 22:17).
6. Capacity to labor apart from struggling for existence (Eph. 4:28).
7. Capacity for marriage vs. the mating of beasts (Gen. 2:22-24).
8. Communication and distinct speech (Gen. 2:23).
9. Communion and worship of God (Gen. 4:4, 22:5).
10. Distinct dignity of presence (Gen. 9:5-6; 1 Cor. 11:7).

The Greek word for "image" in 1 Corinthians 11:7 is *eikon*. The root meaning of *eikon* is derived from the word *eiko,* which means "be like or to resemble." In the figurative sense *eikon* means "a representation." Our English word "icon" is derived from *eikon*. Icons have become a common part of computer operating systems. The user is able to "click" on an icon to initiate or open a desired program or file. The icon is not the program or file but is an image that "represents" the program or file. Paul implies by the use of *eikon* in 1 Corinthians 11:7 that man was fashioned in the moral likeness of God and that man figuratively "represents" God. Adam was not God, but he was an icon representing Him. He represented the glory of God – man was God's crown to creation (Heb. 2:7).

*For a man indeed ought not to cover his head, forasmuch as he is the **image** and **glory** of God: but the woman is the **glory** of the man. For the man is not of the woman; but the woman of the man* (1 Cor. 11:7-8).

Woman was drawn from man's side and thus became Adam's glory. Because woman came from man she would also bear God's likeness but would not symbolically represent God. The male gender alone would be God's icon. Woman would be Adam's glory, not God's from a representation point of view. Equality and God-likeness would characterize both genders, but representation would not. This is why Paul instructs the sisters to cover themselves while intimately in God's presence for prayer and teaching (1 Cor. 11:5-6). The man's glory (the woman) and the woman's glory (her long hair – 1 Cor. 11:15) should be veiled, so that God's glory, represented in the uncovered man, is clearly seen. In this manner, a visible salute is given to God's order and no competing glories will rival God's glory in representation.

Matthew Henry comments the following, concerning the creation of mankind and man's obligation to represent God in both holy behavior and by presiding over creation:

> Man was made last of all the creatures: this was both an honour and a favour to him. Yet man was made the same day that the beasts were; his body was made of the same earth with theirs; and while he is in the body, he inhabits the same earth with them. God forbid that by indulging the body, and the desires of it, we should make ourselves like the beasts that perish! Man was to be a creature different from all that had been hitherto made. Flesh and spirit, heaven and earth, must be put together in him. God said, *"Let us make man."* Man, when he was made, was to glorify the Father, Son, and Holy Ghost. Into that great name we are baptized, for to that great name we owe our being. It is the soul of man that especially bears God's image. Man was made upright, Ecclesiastes 7:29. His understanding saw Divine things clearly and truly; there were no errors or mistakes in his knowledge; his will consented at once, and in all things, to the will of God. His affections were all regular, and he had no bad appetites or passions. His thoughts were easily brought and fixed to the best subjects. Thus holy, thus happy, were our first parents in having the image of God upon them. But how is this image of God upon man defaced! May the Lord renew it upon our souls by his grace![1]

In Genesis 3, mankind failed to represent God and was consequently cursed. God could not have a fallen head to preside over a perfect creation so He was constrained to curse the earth upon which man would live. Man fell and creation was brought down. How would God restore unto Himself a degraded icon and a cursed creation? He would venture to earth from enthroned glory to become a man and suffer the very curse of death He pronounced upon mankind.

> A man's true value consists in his likeness to God. What gives value to his thoughts, his feelings, and his actions is the extent to which they are inspired by God, the extent to which they express the thought, the will, and the acts of God.
>
> Paul Tournier

Creating or Making?
Genesis 1:27-31

Before discussing the Genesis 1 creation account, let us review what God has revealed from other passages of Scripture concerning creation. God is a God of order and not confusion (1 Cor. 14:33); therefore, He creates with exact purpose. God created the world by His power, wisdom, and understanding (Jer. 10:12).

We know that only God can create life. The Hebrew word *bara* is translated *created* in verse 1. Interestingly, this word is always used in connection with God's creative handiwork; it does not speak of human productivity. Only God can call into existence that which had no previous existence. This was Satan's limiting problem in mimicking the plagues God brought on Egypt through Moses. God caused lice to materialize from the dust of the earth – life came from what was not living (Ex. 8:16-19). Satan cannot create life for the essence of all life is in God (Jn. 1:4). Thus, Pharaoh's baffled magicians rightly spoke, *"This is the finger of God."*

We know from Isaiah 40:22 that the earth was circular in original construction. This is a fact that was not widely held by the western world until some 500 years ago. Unfortunately, some that proclaimed that the world was not flat, as popular opinion dictated, but round were put to death. But God declared the world was round to mankind nearly 2600 years ago through the prophet Isaiah.

From Genesis 1, we learn that God created life in the order of sophistication – from the more simple to the more complex. He originally created something out of nothing (Gen. 1:1), then unconscious life – vegetation (Gen. 1:11), then conscious life – sea life, birds, land creatures (Gen. 1:20-21, 25), and lastly human life (Gen. 1:26-27).

There are three prevalent views (each having several variations) of when the Genesis 1 account of creation occurred: *Young Earth*

Creationism, Old Earth Creationism, and Theistic Evolution. As not to distract from our devotional study with pure academics, an evaluation of these views are contained in Appendix A. Two summary thoughts from Appendix A are mentioned here. First, insertion of any form of evolution in Genesis 1 is flatly rejected by the whole of Scripture. Secondly, Scripture does not confirm either an *old earth* or *young earth* viewpoint – these are theories derived from human reasoning and not direct biblical revelation. Unfortunately, embracing theories divide God's people, while adherence to God's Word binds believers together.

The word for *created* in verse 1, *bara*, can support either an *old* or *young earth* creation view. *Bara* may speak of an initial creative act or of a new activity upon something already in existence. The synonymous parallelism poetry style of Psalm 51:10 demonstrates this fact, *"Create [bara] in me a new heart, O God, and renew [hadas] a right spirit within me."* Here the paralleled meaning of *create* is to *renew* or *restore*, not to initially create. Exodus 20:11 seems to substantiate a re-creation or remaking of the earth, *"For in six days the Lord made **heaven and earth**...."* Moses reviews what God accomplished in the six days of Genesis 1: He *made* (meaning fashioned or formed) the heaven and the earth. *Creating* the *heavens* and the earth (Gen. 1:1) is not spoken of. John Darby comments on why the historical revelation is partial:

> It [Genesis 1] communicates what is for the conscience and spiritual affections of man. The created world therefore is taken up as it subsists before the eyes of man, and he is the midst of it, and in so bringing it forward Genesis gives God's work as the author of it. What is here said is true of the whole Bible. Here it is evident in this, that nothing is said of the creation, but what places man in the position which God had made for him in the creation itself, or presents to him this sphere of his existence as being the work of God. Thus no mention is made of any heavenly beings. Nothing is said of their creation. We find them as soon as they are in the relationship with men; although afterwards, as a truth, it is fully recognized of course that they are so created.
>
> Thus also, as regards this earth, except the fact of its creation, nothing is said of it beyond what relates to the present form of it. The fact is stated that God created all things, all man sees, all the material

Seeds of Destiny

universe. "In the beginning God created the heavens and the earth." What may have taken place between that time and the moment when the earth (for it only is then spoken of) was without form and void, is left in entire obscurity.[1]

William Kelly approaches this matter of textual silence with reverence:

> God *made* heaven and earth in six days: it is never said He *created* heaven and earth in six days. When it is no question of these, creating, making and forming may be freely used, as in Isa. 45:18. The reason is plain when we look at Genesis 1. He created the heaven and earth at the beginning. Then another state of things is mentioned in verse 2, not for the heaven, but for the earth. "The earth was without form and void." The heavens were in no such state of chaos: the earth was. As to how, when, and why it was, there is silence. Others have spoken – spoken rashly and wrongly. The wisdom of the inspired writer's silence will be evident to a spiritual mind, and the more, the more it is reflected on.[2]

Given the silence of Scripture, it seems prudent and God honoring to accept the Genesis 1 creation account as a relative beginning, which pertains to mankind, and not as an absolute beginning of all things. Origen (185-255 AD), a pupil of Clement of Alexandria, who later directed the school of Alexandria after Clement's departure held this viewpoint. "This is also part of the church's teaching: that the world was made and took its beginning at a certain time and that it is to be destroyed on account of its wickedness. But there is no clear statement in the teaching of the church regarding what existed before this world or what will exist after it."[3]

Perhaps Genesis 1:1 does refer to God's universal creation, but more likely, it relates to that creation which directly affects man – creation, as man would know it. Why would God reveal more information to us than we need to know? Since creation, that in which we operate, is God's stage to act out His great plan of redemption, do we need to know what is backstage? Might we do better to focus our attentions center stage on the One who is the center of all human existence?

Our God labored at creation and still is laboring in human affairs to renew what has been confounded or lost by sin. All restoration effectively will be accomplished through the Lord Jesus. He provides spiritual restoration now to those trusting His gospel message. Physical restoration (glorification) will be enjoyed when He returns for His church. Creation restoration will occur in the future when He purges all creation of the damages of sin and brings forth a new heaven and earth without sin.

None of us were present at the creation of the world to say categorically how it all took place. Science can only theorize what happened in the past and, thus, will be prone to constant change as technological advancements are achieved and lofty speculations are composed and ratified by the human mind. God's Word does not change. Therefore, we must simply trust the concise biblical record and not allow science and human philosophy to force details to the contrary. Let us be careful and not speak where God is silent!

Neither the creation account or "high-sounding theories" should divide God's people. On the contrary, our lack of understanding should unite us on bent knee before a magnificent God – a God who created such wonders that we might have proof of His existence (Rom. 1:19-20). God's Word is sharper than any two-edged sword (Heb. 4:12); let it, and not the intellect of man, divide asunder what is false and true!

> O Lord my God! When I in awesome wonder
> Consider all the worlds Thy hands have made,
> I see the stars, I hear the rolling thunder,
> Thy power throughout the universe displayed,
> Then sings my soul, my Saviour God to Thee,
> How great Thou art, how great Thou art!
> Then sings my soul, my Saviour God to Thee,
> How great Thou art, how great Thou art!
>
> Carl Boberg

Seeds of Destiny

Is Seeing Believing?
Genesis 2:1

When was the world, as we know it, created? Archbishop James Ussher (1581-1656) developed one of the best known Biblical chronological systems. Ussher assumed completeness of the genealogies in Genesis 5 and 11 and established a creation date of 4004 B.C. Henry Morris notes, "In addition to Ussher's date of 4004 B.C. for the creation, many other dates have been computed, some of which are as follows (all in years B.C.): Jewish, 3760; Septuagint, 5270; Josephus, 5555; Kepler, 3993; Melanchthon, 3964; Luther, 3961; Lighfoot, 3960; Hales, 5402; Playfair, 4008; Lipman, 3916; ...,"[1] while Sir Robert Anderson places the date at 4141 B.C.[2] Some scholars have inserted gaps of different magnitudes in the genealogies of Genesis 5 and 11. Yet, it is generally agreed that no more than 5000 years could possibly be inserted without rendering the biblical record irrelevant and absurd. Consequently, the Bible will not support a creation date of mankind prior to 10,000 B.C.

Many have, with some success, harmonized scientific discoveries with the Genesis account of creation. However, it must be plainly stated that the biblical and scientific approaches to studying creation are vastly different and have different goals. The scientific approach peers backward in time to theorize how the world came into being. This method is accomplished by extracting and evaluating *observable* information and then extrapolating backwards through the darkness of unknown history. The Biblical approach assumes a Creator and looks forward to understand the *invisible* connection that man has with his Creator.

The Lord Jesus stated that it was the unrighteous who wanted to see a "sign or a wonder" in order to believe in Him. He called these "sign seekers" an evil generation and spiritually adulterous (Matt. 12:38-39). Even those people that witnessed the miracle of the feeding of the 5000 were pestering the Lord the very next day: *"What sign showest Thou,* *then, that we **may see and believe** Thee"* (Jn. 6:30)? Had they not recalled the miracle the day before? Did they not fill their bellies with a boy's multiplied sack lunch? The Israelites saw miracles every day in the wilderness for forty years, yet it did not increase their spirituality – for they constantly murmured against God and His leadership.

Peter shows us that true faith in God opens our eyes to understand the things of God. When the Lord asked His twelve disciples if they, too, would turn away from Him, as many had done, Peter responded, *"Lord to whom shall we go? Thou hast the words of eternal life. And we **believe and are sure** that Thou art that Christ, the Son of the living God"* (Jn. 6:68-69). The unrighteous want a sign to believe, but the righteous believe, then understand. Thus, until we exercise faith we will not understand from where we came. *"Through faith we understand that the worlds were framed by the Word of God, so that things which are seen were not made of things which do appear"* (Heb. 11:3).

The Bible also addresses why some will not believe in a Creator. *"For this they [the scoffers who say the Christ will not return again] willingly are ignorant of, that by the Word of God the heavens were of old, and the earth standing out of the water and in the water, by which the world that then was, being overflowed with water, perished"* (2 Pet. 3:5-6). Willful ignorance of God's Word brings blindness, while faith in God's Word confers sight and assurance.

So let us lay hold of what God has revealed concerning creation and leave the remaining missing details with God. Alfred Edersheim summarizes this point well:

> As for the exact date of the *first* creation, it may be safely affirmed that we have not yet the knowledge sufficient to arrive at any really trustworthy conclusion. It is of far greater importance for us, however, to know that God "created all things by Jesus Christ" (Eph. 3:9); and further, that "all things were created by Him, and for Him" (Col. 1:16), and that "of Him, and through Him, and to Him are all things" (Rom. 11:36). Thus all creation has something in common, its living connection with our Lord Jesus Christ.[3]

It is only by faith in the Lord Jesus that we understand how creation came about. *"So then faith cometh by hearing, and hearing by the word of God"* (Rom 10:17). Faith comes by hearing not seeing! Faith is

Seeds of Destiny

founded on the Word of God, which is immutable and eternal. Sight sees only the temporal and what is briefly tangible. The Lord Jesus strongly declares this truth in the narrative of Luke 16. After the rich man realized that there was no escape from the torment of Hades, he made the following request of father Abraham:

> *Then he said, I pray thee therefore, father* [Abraham], *that thou wouldest send him* [Lazarus] *to my father's house: For I have five brethren; that he may testify unto them, lest they also come into this place of torment. Abraham saith unto him, They have Moses and the prophets;* **let them hear them**. *And he said, Nay, father Abraham: but if one went unto them from the dead, they will repent. And he said unto him,* **If they hear not Moses and the prophets, neither will they be persuaded, though one rose from the dead** (Lk. 16:27-31).

Abraham's response to the rich man clearly testifies to the "faith by hearing" principle we are exploring. So then, seeing only will never lead to believing, for faith comes by hearing the Word of God.

I love to think of nature as an unlimited broadcasting station, through which God speaks to us every hour, if we will only tune in.

George Washington Carver

Devotions in Genesis

The Gift of Rest
Genesis 2:2-3

Let us apply the principle of "first mention" to Genesis 2. This rule of hermeneutic implies that the first mention of a particular "key word" in the Bible establishes that word's general application throughout Scripture. For example, the words "love," "worship," and "lamb" first occur in Genesis 22. The initial meanings of love, worship, and selfless sacrifice are there defined and then developed throughout the remainder of the Bible.

The key words in Genesis 2:1-3 are "seven" and "sanctified." The number seven is God's number and a fundamental building block throughout Scripture. God speaks of completeness or perfection through the number seven. The word "sanctified" means "set apart" or "holy." The week of creation ended with a day of rest for the Lord. This was not a divine response to weariness, but to satisfaction (Isa. 40:28). Although God did not command mankind to keep the Sabbath at this time, He taught, through example, the principle of resting one day in seven. Later, He would command that the seventh day be "set apart" by the children of Israel (Ex. 20:8-11, 23:10-12, 31:13-17) although they would miserably fail to do so.

We never read of God resting again in all of Scripture, but to the contrary, God is laboring for the redemption and restoration of man throughout the biblical account until final rest is again achieved in Revelation 21 and 22. The Lord Jesus said, *"My Father worketh hitherto, and I work"* (Jn. 5:17). There are only two Sabbaths that God could truly call a day of rest – the seventh day of creation and the eternal rest after the new creation (i.e. the eternal state, Rev. 21:1-2). Only then may He finally cease from laboring. The Son finished His laboring on earth at Calvary, but in heaven He continues even now to make intercession for the Church. A Greek scholar, Dudley Sherwood, paraphrased John 5:17 in this manner, "My Father has been working up till now and I am continuing His work to bring it to completion." This is a tremendous claim, asserting His oneness with the Father. Likewise, the Holy Spirit is laboring to convict the world of sin and to woo a bride for the Son. God is still working today!

The number seven becomes a building block of order for man, but especially so for the future Jewish nation. The Jews were commanded to rest on the seventh day – the Sabbath day; not to plant on the (seventh) Sabbath Year; to keep seven "Feasts of Jehovah;" and to return purchased land to the original owners after seven times seven years, the year of Jubilee. They were told by the prophet Jeremiah that they would have seventy years of captivity by the King of Babylon because of their idolatry (Jer. 25:11, 29:10) and that, ultimately, God would deal with Israel's rebellion as spoken of by the Prophet Daniel through fulfillment of a seventy week prophecy (i.e 70 weeks of years – Dan. 9:25-27).

How else is the number seven used in Scripture? It would require a book the size of which you hold in your hands to describe all the ways, but here are just a few from John's Gospel account: There were seven direct "I AM" statements which declared the Lord's deity, and there were also seven specific statements made by Jesus from the cross. Apparently, seven of the disciples were fishermen (Jn. 21:2), and John recorded in detail seven specific miracles that Jesus performed. In the synoptic gospel accounts, we read of the Lord's "Seven Woes" message to the Pharisees. In the book of the Revelation, there are seven stars (messengers) sent to seven churches, seven beatitudes, seven seal judgments, seven trump judgments, and seven bowl judgments. There are seven main characters in the book, seven lampstands (representing seven church testimonies), and the beast of Revelation 13 has seven heads representing world empires controlled by Satan.

Once symbols are understood from the Old Testament, the book of Revelation becomes a spectacular testimony concerning the person of the Lord Jesus. For example: the horn in Scripture represents "power" (It is the strength of an animal), and an eye represents "seeing." So, in Revelation 5 when the Lord Jesus is spoken of having seven eyes and seven horns, we understand that these symbolically represent the

Lord's perfect power and wisdom. The revelation of God to John would be less literal and more symbolic (Rev. 1:1).

The question may arise whether a Christian should observe the seventh day of the week as a day of rest? The Sabbath is first mentioned in Genesis 2:1-3. It can be practically seen in the Israelite instructions for gathering manna in Exodus 16. It became a strict observance for Israel with the giving of the law at Sinai (Ex. 20:8-11). William MacDonald summarizes the significance of the Sabbath for the believer:

> It is a picture of the rest which believers now enjoy in Christ and which a redeemed creation will enjoy in the Millennium. The Sabbath is the seventh day of the week, from sundown on Friday to sundown on Saturday. Nowhere in the NT are Christians commanded to keep the Sabbath.[1]

God has displayed a pattern in which we should rest one day in seven, yet this is not commanded. It seems logical that periodic rest would help remedy physical fatigue and emotional strain. But concerning religious appointment, the Lord Jesus reaffirmed all of the Ten Commandments except "keep the Sabbath day holy." The writer of Hebrews instructs the believer to *"go forth, therefore, to Him outside the camp, bearing His reproach"* (Heb. 13:13). The writer is informing the Jews that they are no longer under the law but under a new covenant of grace established by Christ. The law showed sin but could not save (Rom. 3:20). What the law could not do, God's grace found a way – *"for the just shall live by faith"* (Gal. 3:10-12).

The Law commanded the Jews to keep the Sabbath, which they miserably failed to do. The Lord issued no such command to the church, as individual believers can worship God any time and anywhere as believer priests (Jn. 4:23-24). The early Church did not gather corporately on Saturday, but Sunday – the first day of the week – Christ's resurrection day (1 Cor. 16:2; Acts 20:7). The believers then gathered to worship their Savior, not to keep the law. This is why John refers to Sunday as the Lord's day (Rev. 1:10).

Paul strictly forbids Christians from legislating special days, feast days or sabbath days and forcing their personal convictions on others (Col. 2:16, Rom. 14:5). To the contrary Paul says, *"Let every man be fully persuaded in his own mind"* about such things. In principle, it

Seeds of Destiny

seems wise to rest the body one in seven days and follow the pattern of the early church, which dedicated the first day of the week for corporate worship and service. We continue doing this on earth until the church enters God's final gift of rest in glory.

> No man has a right to lead such a life of contemplation as to forget in his own ease the service due to his neighbor; nor has any man a right to be so immersed in active life as to neglect the contemplation of God.
>
> Augustine

The Gift of Work
Genesis 2:4-14

Adam was a real man that God fashioned on the sixth day of creation. He is not some fairy tale character or mythological person. The New Testament speaks of Adam as the first created man and as such is the basis for several salvation doctrines. The genealogy of Mary, Christ's mother, is traced back to Adam (Lk. 3:23-38). In Romans 5, Paul explains the consequences to humanity because of Adam's sin and then shows how through the obedience of the last Adam (Christ) the damages of disobedience by the first Adam can be repaired (1 Cor. 15). The Lord Jesus spoke of Adam and Eve when addressing the Pharisees about God's plan for marriage in Matthew 19. Those who deny that there was a real Adam are denying the fall of man and the consequent need of a Savior. In effect, they call God a liar!

After God created man, He planted a garden and placed man in it. Genesis 2:15 states that Adam had the opportunity to please God by tilling and keeping the garden. As this work setting is prior to God cursing the ground in Genesis 3, it is hard to comprehend what exactly Adam's work consisted of. The Hebrew word translated *"to dress"* (KJV) or *"to tend"* (NKJV) is *abad*, which means "to serve." Whatever work Adam did do, it was his assigned service to God and his opportunity to demonstrate his love for his Creator.

Perhaps there is a lesson to be gleaned concerning rest and work from the river that flowed out of Eden – the river of God. When God rested from His work, the whole world enjoyed the blessing and refreshment of God's presence and blessing. There is a connection between the river and God's rest. Consequently, a river is used throughout Scripture to convey the truth that all peace and blessing originates with God then flows out to others. Moses smote a rock to provide flowing water to the children of Israel in the desert to save their lives. The Lord likened the blessings of the Holy Spirit in a believer's life to a river of flowing water (Jn. 7:37-39). Then when the Lord returns to earth at the end of the Tribulation Period, He will split the Mount of Olives, and a river of living water will flow towards the east and the west symbolizing that world peace and rest has come (Zech. 14:8). Finally, in the eternal state, after the present earth has been destroyed, there shall be a *"pure river of water of life"* flowing out from the throne of God forever and ever (Rev. 22:1). Until man sinned, God rested, and His peace flowed out of His presence upon the whole earth.

God labored six days and then rested the seventh. He continued to rest until man created work for Him through sin. God will restore His peace to creation, and He will finally rest in the age to come when all wickedness is vanquished and the redeemed of mankind are again with Him in Paradise. Until that time the church should be laboring diligently. Why? Because man again has the privilege to demonstrate love for the Creator through working the revealed will of God. He in turn labors with us for the cause of righteousness and to affect His Own glory (1 Cor. 3:9; Eph. 2:10).

> *And **whatsoever ye do, do it heartily, as to the Lord**, and not unto men; knowing that of the Lord ye shall receive the reward of the inheritance: for **ye serve the Lord Christ*** (Col. 3:23-24).

The Church exists to train its members through the practice of the presence of God to be servants of others, to the end that Christlikeness may become common property.

William Adams Brown

A Price to Be Paid
Genesis 2:15-22

The Bible begins and ends with a wedding. Both weddings occur in a beautiful garden and in the presence of God. In Genesis 2, the first wedding is of Adam and Even in the garden of Eden. The last wedding is recorded in Revelation 20-22 – it is the marriage of the Lamb and His bride before the tree of life and at the very throne of God.

The man, Adam, that God had created from the dust of the earth and into whom He breathed an eternal spirit, began serving God by naming the animals. The task assignment demonstrated God had delegated authority over the animals to Adam (Gen. 1:28). Yet, something was missing in Adam's life; there was loneliness in his existence. No beast could be man's consort; he required a special creation that would pertain directly to him. To ensure that this creation would pertain to Adam and also bear characteristics of God's image, God drew raw building materials from Adam's side and created a helper and companion for him. This new creation became his wife. It was an ideal marriage situation – Adam never heard the woman talk about all the men she could have married, and the woman never heard Adam boast about his mother's cooking.

The word "rib" (Gen. 2:22) is not the best translation of the Hebrew word *tsela*. *Tsela* appears forty-four times in the Old Testament. It is translated only here as "rib;" most commonly it is translated "side." God took part of Adam's side to create woman and then closed up the remaining flesh. There would be flesh, bone, and blood associated with this "operation," as both bone and flesh are sustained by blood flow. Why did God create woman from a portion of Adam's side? If God had created the woman from Adam's foot, he might think he could trample her over with heavy-handed leadership. If she had been created from Adam's head, he might think she should rule over him. But, since the woman was created from Adam's side, a picture of equality is presented. As the man and woman shared companionship and followed God's order, the woman would naturally find joy and protection under her husband's arm. She would return to the "one" and "the place" from where she came. Adam's first words to his wife confirm that more than a rib was taken *"This is now bone of my bones, and flesh of my flesh; she shall be called Woman, because she was taken out of Man"* (Gen. 2:23).

In Adam's sacrifice for his bride, God foretells of a time when His Son, Jesus Christ, would freely and unselfishly suffer to obtain a bride (the Church). Adam entered into a deep sleep just prior to God opening his side to fashion him a wife. Soon after the Lord Jesus yielded up His spirit unto death a Roman spear opened His side where upon blood and water poured out. Adam awoke to enjoy a new and satisfying relationship with his wife. Likewise Christ was raised up again and will enjoy His bride, once removed from the earth (1 Thess. 4:13-17) and forevermore in heaven (Jn. 14:1-3; Rev. 19:7-9, 21:1-4).

The first Adam was presented a wife, but the last Adam shall *"present it to Himself, a glorious Church, not having spot, or wrinkle or any such thing"* (Eph. 5:27). Adam named his wife Woman; a name that directly represented her origin – himself. After arriving in heaven, Christ will give every believer a special name relating to Himself (Rev. 2:17, 3:12). In heaven, every Christian will be able to relate to the Lord Jesus in a unique and special way. In this way, individual companionship with the Lord will be ensured and relished even among the throngs of heaven's court. The Church will be ever present with the Lord in glory! C. H. Mackintosh writes in his commentary on the Pentateuch:

> Looking at Adam and Eve as a type of Christ and the Church, as Scripture fully warrants us to do, we see how that the death of Christ needed to be an accomplished fact ere the Church could be set up; though, in the purpose of God, she was looked at and chosen in Christ before the foundation of the world.[1]

In the same way the Church finds her significance and security in Christ even as the woman found her beginning, purpose, and dignity in Adam. It only cost Adam his side for his bride, but the price of Christ's bride was much higher – it cost Him His life. Yet, both the first Adam and the last Adam (Christ) were pleased with what their personal sacri-

Devotions in Genesis

fices obtained for them, the former a woman and the latter a multitude of redeemed souls (Isa. 53:11). Both the first marriage of the Bible and the last marriage of the Bible convey God's importance on integrity and permanence of the union. Henry Morris writes on this subject:

> It is true, of course, that with marriage as well as with all other human activities, *"God hath made man upright; but they have sought out many inventions"* (Eccl. 7:29). Polygamy, concubinage, polyandry, easy divorce, adultery, promiscuity, and other distortions of the marriage covenant have permeated many cultures; but, as the Lord Jesus said: *"From the beginning it was not so"* (Matt. 19:8).[2]

Our union with Christ came at great cost to the Savior. May we endeavor to delight in Him and honor Him through adhering to His plan for marriage and demonstrating His sacrificial love for each other.

> A successful marriage demands a divorce; a divorce from your own self-love.
>
> Paul Frost

A Companion for Adam
Genesis 2:23-25

God instituted marriage between one man and one woman; therefore, only His rules for marriage apply. Homosexuality is an abomination to the Lord and is revolting against His order (Lev. 18:22, 20:13; Rom. 1:24–32). Polygamy was the result of either man's lust, lack of faith, or trickery but was never approved of by God (Matt. 19:5-6; Deut. 17:17) except to allow a Jewish brother's widow to conceive and bear up children in the name of her dead husband. This was of necessity to protect the woman's inheritance and not lust motivated. God intended one man and one woman to become a one-person reality through a marriage covenant, which would protect and sanctify their sexual relationship.

God wanted a deep sense of oneness to develop from the elaborate intertwining of two companions who would freely and openly mingle in every aspect. After Adam and his wife sinned, the beautiful oneness that had been enjoyed was spoiled with the sense of isolation and guilt. A new individuality was realized. Their sin not only made them uncomfortable with God, but also with each other, for they knew that they were naked. Before sinning, not even clothes separated them, but after their rebellion, they sought to cover up and limit self-disclosure. This is the nature of human sin – it seeks what we are not and hides the reality of who we are. It is only through Christ and the indwelling Spirit of God that this damage can be repaired and a real sense of unity can be developed in the marriage relationship again. With Christ at the helm, there is no reason for love deprivation within the Christian marriage or family.

The oneness the man and woman shared in the garden is clearly seen when God only called out Adam's name to arouse the hiding sinners from their recluse. Genesis 5:2 reads, *"male and female created he them; and blessed them, and called their name Adam, in the day when they were created."* The man was created first and named Adam. When the woman was created from Adam, she received no name except "woman," speaking of her origin – "from man." She needed no private name for she already had one in Adam. Therefore, the garden experience of the woman in relationship to the man can be summed up as follows: She was made **for** Adam **from** Adam, **brought to** Adam, **led** Adam into sin (1 Tim. 2:13-15), then ultimately was **named by** Adam after their fall, which demonstrated his authority over her. Until the fall of mankind, the peacefulness of God-ordered headship governed family life in the garden. Satan's temptation brought disorder and chaos into a perfect marital relationship. After the fall of man, God reaffirmed order by declaring proper headship in the marriage relationship. However, the yearnings of self and the lusts of fallen flesh would forever rival the order God prescribed for marital bliss.

The spiritual resources of love, grace, and longsuffering are available for every believer to draw upon to repair the inherent damage that two people with sin natures will cause to any marriage. Ephesians 1:3 reads, *"Blessed be the God and Father of our Lord Jesus Christ, who hath blessed us with all spiritual blessings in heavenly places in Christ."* Marriages need Christ to mend the damage of sin and to nurture and equip mates to love each other unselfishly in order to survive and thrive in today's immoral self-seeking culture.

There can be absolutely no doubt that God created woman in His divine wisdom to satisfy Adam's need for companionship: *"And the Lord God said, 'It is not good that the man should be alone; I will make him an help meet* (suitable helper) *for him'"* (Gen. 2:18). However, while creating the perfect partner for Adam, He also was planning for the perfect mate for the new creature (woman).

Everything that the woman became (spirit, soul, and body) was derived from Adam. When his companion was presented to him, he uttered *Isha*, or "woman," meaning "derived from man." The woman was as much a descendant of Adam as you and I are. By human procreation, everything that we are (body, soul and spirit) is derived from the dust of the earth and the original breath of God into Adam. Adam was created as an innocent living soul, but became degraded by personal sin. We in him are also depraved (Rom. 5:12). Depravity is hereditary and requires regeneration by the Holy Spirit to resolve. Satan initially tempted the woman to eat the forbidden fruit, but the ultimate target was Adam, as recorded in Genesis 3. Eve as a descendant of Adam was not responsible for the human race. Her sin would bring death to her, but to her only, whereas Adam's sin would usher in death to all that would be derived from him.

Before the surgical procedure, Adam had likely seen most, if not all, the animals because of his naming task. How insignificant everything on earth must have seemed after one glimpse of his new helper. The experience for the woman was different; when she opened her eyes for the first time, it was the Lord she saw, for it was God who brought her to Adam. She knew nothing of her new world before meeting her companion. This allowed Adam to show his wife God's handiwork and to have the opportunity to appreciate it with her. Man has escorted woman ever since. Life's special moments are more exceptional when there is someone to share them with!

I like to think that as Adam showed the woman God's creation his appreciation for her increased – she was a special creature, a gift from God to him. Instead of awe and appreciation, many men today tend to continually compare their wives to other women instead of accepting them as a gift from God. Where there are areas of growth husbands should seize the responsibility to encourage their wives to mature in Christ and reach their full potential as a wife and mother. A wife is a special gift from God (Prov. 18:22) and, as Solomon says, the virtuous wife is worth more than rubies (Prov. 31:10). Men, don't be bitter towards your wives (Col. 3:19), just love and cherish them (Eph. 5:28-29).

Though God desires godly children through the marriage union of a man and a woman (Mal. 2:15), His overshadowing marital aspiration was for intimate companionship. A man and a woman after entering a marriage covenant become companions for life in God's best plan. What a finale to the week of creation! Stars were spoken into existence, oceans were puddled up, and dust of the earth burst forth life. But, it is the gift of companionship (the woman) to God's crowning creation, the man, which concluded His workweek!

Since it is the marriage covenant that initiates this blessed camaraderie between a man and a woman as husband and wife, we pause to examine Malachi 2:11-14 and Proverbs 2:17 to identify the root meanings of companionship as it relates to the marriage covenant.

The prophet Malachi rebuked the men of Israel for divorcing their wives (Mal. 2:11-14). He informs them of God's anger over the matter, for "God hates divorce" (Mal. 2:16), and that God would punish them for their negligent behavior. Malachi 2:14 reads *"Yet ye say, Why? Because the LORD hath been witness between thee and the wife of thy youth, against whom thou hast dealt treacherously; yet is she thy **companion**, and the wife of thy covenant."* The Hebrew word for companion is *chabereth*, which means "a consort or wife," but the root word *chaber* means "to be associated with or united to," or as Strong's Concordance states "to be knit together." We conclude that one aspect of companionship is a sense of duty and a commitment to stay knitted together. It is interesting that the modern Hebrew word for marriage is *kiddushin*, which means "sanctification" (being set apart). The marriage bond "sets apart" a husband and wife to fulfill a lifetime covenant of intimate and committed companionship before God. A marriage must be based on a forged commitment of both parties to stay together no matter what. Not only is the mindset of staying together a necessity for a marriage to thrive, but it is one of the greatest gifts to pass along to your children.

Solomon rebukes an adulterous wife in Proverbs 2:17, *"Which forsaketh the guide (companion or partner) of her youth, and forgetteth the covenant of her God."* The Hebrew word for guide is *alluwph*, which means "to be familiar and intimate, with a foremost friend." Another key aspect of the marriage covenant is intimacy, a deep desire to disclose and be familiar with one another. If your spouse is not your best friend, you are missing God's design for marriage.

Biblical companionship consists of an unwavering duty of **commitment** and open disclosure that promotes **intimacy**. When will a marriage relationship be the most satisfying? When total commitment leads to open disclosure. Full disclosure promotes exuberant passion to be shared between a husband and wife. Jehovah's passion for Israel – his wife through covenant is poetically described in Ezekiel 16:8. *"Now when I passed by thee, and looked upon thee, behold, thy time was the time of **love**; and I spread my skirt over thee, and covered thy nakedness. Yea, I swore unto thee, and entered into a covenant with thee,* *saith the Lord God, and thou becamest mine."* The Hebrew word for "love" in this verse is *dowd*, which means "to boil" (i.e. figuratively: "to love" and, by implication, "a lover"). This word is rendered "love" seven times in the Old Testament and always gives the sense of a boiling pot of fervent passion between masculine and feminine individuals (not necessarily sexually).

If a marriage relationship is pursued and obtained on the basis of romantic love instead of obligation and disclosure, there will be no foundation to weather life's storms. However, a marriage based on commitment and intimacy will be joyfully romantic. This was God's intention for marital companionship! There is no reason for a Christian marriage not to achieve biblical companionship.

> Duty does not have to be dull. Love can make it beautiful and fill it with life.
>
> Thomas Merton

> Erotic and philia love are emotional. Christian love [agape] is an attitude, not feeling.
>
> Joseph Fletcher

The First Question
Genesis 3:1-6

No doubt God enjoyed walking with Adam in the cool of the day (perhaps morning and night). Have you ever wondered about what they talk about? "Rhinoceros – what caused you to think of that name Adam?" Who started the conversation each morning? How long did they walk together? Our imaginations are left to ponder the matter in the absence of scriptural narrative.

This communion was tragically broken on the day man ignored God's only restriction of continued life in Eden. On that sad day man ate from the prohibited tree of the knowledge of good and evil. The cost of savoring one bite of the forbidden fruit was immensely high, for our first parents traded a refreshing continuous life with God for a sorrow-filled and brief existence.

There were two notable trees in the Garden of Eden: the Tree of Life and the Tree of Knowledge of Good and Evil, which for mankind was a Tree of Death. Apparently (based on the narrative in Genesis 3), as one exercised faith in the partaking of the Tree of Life, rather than the Tree of Death, immortality of the body was maintained. Both trees likely presented low-hanging branches laden with accessible fruit. There was nothing magical in the fruit, but grace was imputed through an operation of faith in God's Word to do what was right instead of what was unlawful.

The first rebel led an angelic revolt against God and now assisted man in his rebellion. Satan side-stepped Adam's authority and directed his assault on the unprotected woman. Fueled by his own jealousy of God and His glory, Satan beguiled her through a barrage of deceptive tactics. His goal was to stir up self-focus and to diminish her perceived need for God. Although his evil operations used today are often more high-tech, his core strategies against mankind have not changed since the dreadful day sin intruded humanity. With these he has been successful in causing some to err from the faith or embrace some Christ-defaming doctrine. Paul writes, *"Lest Satan should get an advantage of us: for we are not ignorant of his devices"* (2 Cor. 2:11). The believer must be wise to Satan's deceit. A study of his offensive against the woman will aid in highlighting many of his evil strategies today.

First, mark the miracle – the serpent spoke. So crafty was Satan's communication to Eve that she thought nothing unusual about the serpent being able to form human speech. Didn't she know that she was talking to a serpent? Until now, only God had communicated to mankind through speech. Beware dear believer of clever words uttered by those following Satan. Children of the devil are pernicious to the children of God – one must always expect malicious behavior (Jn. 15:18-19). A serpent is a serpent – don't be deceived by crafty speech or the conjuring of some unusual sign. Those looking for signs and wonders to substantiate their faith invariably fall in the trap of ignoring God's immutable Word. Paul acknowledges that same dark practice when he walked upon the earth:

> *For such are false apostles, deceitful workers, transforming themselves into the apostles of Christ. And no marvel; for Satan himself is transformed into an angel of light. Therefore it is no great thing if his ministers also be transformed as the ministers of righteousness; whose end shall be according to their works* (2 Cor. 11:13-15).

Secondly, note that Satan projected doubt on what God actually said: *"Yea, hath God said, Ye shall not eat of every tree of the garden"* (Gen. 3:1)? Until this point, Scripture accounts God's creative acts and statements of truth. The first question in Scripture belongs to Satan. It was a leading question for its purpose was not to provoke rational thought but to instill doubt and invoke rebellion. The tactic worked on the woman, who quickly slid from the ground of faith into human reasoning. Satan's question to the woman has a flavor of unfairness: "Could God be good and limit you in such an unfair way?" "Surely a good God would not keep you from all that is good." "Are you sure that you recalled exactly what God said?"

A third satanic strategy is seen in the focusing upon the negative rather than the positive. Man was invited to eat from every tree in the garden, save one. Yet, the serpent beckoned mankind to focus upon the only one off limits. Satan enjoys sowing dissatisfaction. When embraced, dissatisfaction stirs up doubts concerning God's goodness and wisdom. Dear believer, the next time Satan tempts you not to be content, train your eye upon all the blessings in Christ and not what, in your own mind, you lack or deserve.

Eve's reply to the serpent demonstrates a diminished God in her thinking. F. W. Grant writes concerning the woman's reply to the serpent:

> But here God and the dragon had changed places. Thus she adds to the prohibition, as if to justify herself against One who has lost His sovereignty for her heart, "Ye shall not eat of it, *neither shall ye touch it*" –which He had not said. A mere touch, as she expressed it to herself, was death; and why, then, had He put it before them only to prohibit it? What was it He was guarding from them with such jealous care? Must it not be indeed something that He valued highly? She first adds to the prohibition, then she weakens the penalty. Instead of "ye shall surely die," it is for her only "*lest* [for fear] ye die." There is no real certainty that death would be the result. Thus the question of God's love becomes a question of His truth also. I do not want upon the throne a being I cannot trust; hence comes the tampering with His word. The heart deceives the head. If I do not want it to be true, I soon learn to question if it be so.[1]

Fourthly, notice Satan added to what God had said; *"And the serpent said unto the woman, Ye shall not surely die"* (Gen 3:4): The addition of one-three letter word changed God's intended meaning completely. God said, *"when you eat you shall surely die,"* but Satan said, *"you shall **not** surely die."* Satan was referring to physical death while ignoring the subject of spiritual life with God completely. God warned of immediate spiritual death, though physical death would naturally come to those apart from God. Every cemetery is proof that God told the full truth and that Satan is a liar. The Lord declared that Satan is the father of lies and that there is no truth in him (Jn. 8:44). John Darby once declared, "The devil is never more satanic than when he has a Bible in his hands." Be careful when the enemy is quoting Scripture, the whole truth will never be presented!

A fifth tactic employed was the breaking down of Scripture into small pieces to obscure the contextual meaning of what God said. The truth of

Seeds of Destiny

God's Word is found in the whole of Scripture. Browsing over minute portions alone can result in doctrines that are inconsistent with the remainder of Scripture. It has been said that there are three rules in selling real-estate – "location, location, location." Likewise, there are three rules to determining what Scripture is saying – "context, context, context." The Bible as a whole presents a specific truth about God's plan of redemption for mankind. No passage of Scripture should be interpreted to contradict this central theme of the Bible, as summarized in John 3:16. There is also a specific subject that each book of the Bible is addressing, so the understanding of a passage within that book should be in the context of the main theme. Finally, specific portions of Scripture must be interpreted by the encompassing verses to ensure correct understanding. Satan cast doubt on what God said, changed what God said, and only referred to select portions of what God said when speaking to the woman. Beware of those reducing divine revelation into obscurity.

Lastly, the "sales pitch" Satan used on the woman is no different than the one he is using today through the "New Age" movement. It is a "repackaged old lie," and it has worked on man since the beginning. Satan told the woman that she could improve her position, that she was in control of her destiny, that she could gain knowledge and understanding and be like God. How man scrambles at the chance to become like God and to have His power and might. Yet, the best man can do is bow in humility, accept God's plan of salvation, and become a child of God.

When God is shut out and man no longer allows God's love and truth to be recognized in his life, *"the lust of the flesh, the lust of the eyes, and the pride of life"* then become the controlling influences in that person's life. This is what happened to woman – she doubted God's love and truth. It is these three agencies that comprehend that which is of the world (1 Jn. 2:16) and that Satan consequently stimulates to work his will. "The lust of the flesh, the lust of the eyes, and the pride of life" describe giving over one's flesh, mind and will to secular reasoning and influences instead of resting upon divine truth. Temptations thus may be directed against the body, the soul, or the spirit or at all three at once, as was the case with Eve.

It is obvious that Satan communicates throughout the Bible, but his actual voice is recorded only three times. In Genesis 3, he spoke to undermine and cast doubt on the Word of God. In Job 1, Satan spoke to undermine and cause the child of God to doubt. Lastly, in Matthew 4 the devil spoke to cause doubt concerning the Son of God. The summary of Satan's recorded communication in the Bible – three verbal attempts to cast doubt on what is righteous. Let us be wise to his deceit.

When Satan externally solicited Christ to sin in the wilderness (Matt. 4), he utilized these three avenues because they had worked so well on mankind previously. Satan solicited the Lord Jesus to sin by an appeal to His body to satisfy its appetite. Satan's second attempt to solicit the Lord to sin was through an appeal to human spiritual pride. If the Lord would have thrown Himself off the top of the temple and the angels did scramble to save Him, it would have been a demonstration to the world that He was approved of God and would bring worldwide recognition and spiritual preeminence. The last fiendish attempt was aimed at the soul level – an appeal was made to stir up covetous and emotional desires for fame and prestige that the authority over kingdoms would ensure. Yet, Satan failed to cause Christ to sin because the Lord Jesus did not have the fallen human element that would respond to these solicitations – for Christ is God in the flesh. He was not merely innocent as was Adam, but absolutely holy (Lk. 1:35). It was His nature to loath sin, He could not respond to such ill appeals.

The aggressive assault on the bulwark of divine character was completely thwarted by the use of exact and complete quotations from God's Word. Let the child of God follow the Lord's example and lift up the shield of faith and appropriate the instruction and promises of God's Word to deflect the incoming fiery darts of temptation. For our first parents the temptation came in the form of a single question! Be alert; the devil won't inform you of his battle tactics.

Tempters seek to lure astray, Storms obscure the light of day:
But in Christ I can be bold, I've an anchor that shall hold.

W. C. Martin

Be on guard today that the tree of knowledge does not keep you from the tree of life.

C. H. Spurgeon

Seeds of Destiny

Lost in Eden
Genesis 3:7-13

The woman sinned when she ate from the forbidden tree. Unfortunately, the woman didn't stop with her own ruin. *"The woman gave to Adam and he did eat."* Satan knew that directly tempting the man to sin would prove to be ineffective, but if he could deceive the woman he might well get the man. The plan worked! The Apostle Paul states that the woman was deceived, tricked if you will, into sin, but Adam sinned with his eyes open (1 Tim. 2:13-14). Adam knew it was wrong, but apparently was willing to stand by his wife even if it meant following her into a grave! Adam forfeited his leadership and followed his wife. It is the same passive masculine bent that has plagued humanity ever since. Men fail to be men, and women seeing the void assume a wrongful role. In God's eyes Adam's sin was greater than the sin of the woman, for the death that has reigned over the world since that time was not a result of the woman's sin but of Adam's.

Did God know man would fall in the garden? He certainly did because the plan of redemption was masterminded before creation occurred (1 Pet. 1:19-20). Could not God have avoided the disaster in the garden by making man a robot? Yes. Then why did God give man a "free will" that could choose "bad" if He could have prevented man from making bad choices? God gave man a free will because a "will" that cannot choose "bad" cannot choose "good" either. God only wants those who will love Him to be with Him. Commanding affection is not love, but brutality – this is not God. God gives us the opportunity to say "yes" to His offer of salvation. A seeking God and a seeking sinner through the wooing of the Holy Spirit will find each other.

It is important to understand that Adam's test was not the choice between a good tree that God had made and an evil tree that God had made. God does not make evil things or test mankind through evil means (Jas. 1:13). God is holy (1 Pet. 1:16). Adam's choice was to do that which would please God or to do that which would not please God. To validate man, as a true representative made in His image, God gave man freedom of choice. Without choice, demonstrating love is impossible. God had allowed the possibility of evil but had not actualized it; man did. God warned against the consequences of evil but did not prevent it from occurring. William Kelly comments about the choice and the responsibility God had given man:

> It is of great interest and importance to observe that God distinguished from the first between responsibility on the one hand, and life-giving on the other, in the two trees [Gen. 2:9]. Even for Adam, innocent as he was, life did not depend on abstinence from eating of the tree of the knowledge of good and evil. Death followed if he disobeyed God in eating of this tree (v.17); but, walking in obedience, he was free to eat of the tree of life. He fell in partaking of the forbidden fruit; and God took care that he should not eat of the tree of life. But the two trees, representing the two principles, which man is ever confounding or obliterating one for the other, are in the Scripture as in truth wholly distinct.[1]

After eating of the forbidden tree, Adam and the woman were suddenly awakened to a harsh reality. Their eyes were opened to understand good, but they had no power to do it. Likewise they knew evil without the wherewithal to shun it. They were stuck in a huge chasm between knowing divine righteousness and not being able to perform it. In the sense they did become like God, as the Lord admits at the end of the chapter, for they now knew good and evil. But they didn't know right and wrong like God does, for He does not know evil experientially.

Adam and his wife immediately sought to hide their nakedness from each other by sewing fig leaves together as clothes. Yet, this did not resolve the "cover up" feelings of guilt their consciences were inflicting upon them for the first time. So many new thoughts and feelings swarmed their minds. So what did Adam and his wife do when their Creator called for them? They sought seclusion in their darkened state and hid themselves in the shadows of trees. Their response to God's call essentially demonstrated that the "fig clothes" which they had made were insufficient to deal with their guilt before God. How did

Seeds of Destiny

God respond? God did what He continues to do today; He came looking and seeking that which was lost. When God's voice resounded in the garden, the fig-leaf apron availed nothing; man feared and hid from God.

Psalm 104:2 speaks of God's attire *"...coverest thyself with light as with a garment;...."* Man could not hide from God. His presence penetrates the deepest slumber of the human conscience and the vastness of all creation. David understood the difficulty of hiding from God: *"Where shall I go from thy Spirit? Or where shall I flee from thy presence?"* (Ps. 139:7). Yet, to this very day, men, encompassed by the darkness of sin still scurry into the shadows of self-misery when the Creator comes seeking that which is lost. He beckons them to face the shame of their condition by venturing out into the light of divine truth and grace. Unfortunately, many still hide from finding Him and peace.

The deafening silence, which had unfortunately permeated the garden that day, was broken by God's longing words, *"Where art thou?"* This is the second question of the Bible and addresses the spiritual state of man apart from God. The significance of this question to Adam still sounds in the ear of every sinner today. Ambrose puts the matter this way, "As in paradise, God walks in the Holy Scriptures, seeking man." God is calling out to every lost soul with a loving offer of redemption. Every one of us must admit we are *lost* before we can call out to God and be *found*. Dear reader, "where are you today?" Hiding in the shadows of guilty despair or walking in blissful fellowship with Holy God?

Why is there a moral code that is nearly consistent around the world? Why is it wrong to murder, steal, commit adultery, and lie worldwide? Romans 2:14-15 states that God has written His laws instinctively in the depths of our being to teach us right and wrong. The conscience is a warning system to monitor our moral programming. A uniform code of ethics worldwide is a natural fallout of the human conscience. Adam and the woman could not ignore the guilt they felt. Many today ignore their conscience until it becomes seared.

When our human conscience becomes active, we feel guilt and impending judgment although we do not understand from where, so we naturally try to do good deeds to get the clanging bell out of our heads. Thus, all religions, except Christianity, have a basis of good works to secure heavenly bliss or a higher ranking in earthly existence during the next lifetime. But Christianity is different. Isaiah 64:6 reminds us that *"...all our righteousnesses are as filthy rags ...."* The human conscience was given to prove that we fall short of perfection and deserve judgment for rebelling against perfection (the standard of the Creator). As Paul summarizes in Romans 2, the guilt we feel is proof that we are sinners and that the God who made us is perfect.

Interestingly, when the trial began, both the man and the woman told the simple truth of the matter. God's first question was an appeal for Adam to reckon his spiritual condition, "Where art thou?" God's next three questions would focus man upon the sins committed and his resultant lost state. "What have you done?" Both the fallen position of a sinner and the associated practice of the sin are indicated. Adam answered, *"The woman whom Thou gavest to be with me, she gave me of the tree, and I did eat"* (Gen. 3:12). God then questioned the woman, *"What is this that thou hast done?"* And the woman said, *"The serpent beguiled me, and I did eat"* (Gen. 3:13). God did not bother to question the serpent for he is the father of lies and there is no truth within him – he is a liar and always lies. Satan had already been found guilty of the sin of pride and cast off the holy mount of God (Isa. 14). Some have accused our first parents of shifting blame for personal behavior when answering the Lord's questions. From the narrative we conclude that they stated the plain truth. They both honored God by admitting their sin and how it happened. When standing before the Judge of the universe, one should do no less than to be honest about sin and admit guilt.

What does the child of God have now compared to what Adam had in the garden? Adam had fellowship with God and was well taken care of. But, considering the Christian is indwelt by God's Spirit (1 Cor. 6:19), possesses all spiritual blessings in heaven (Eph. 1:3), becomes a part of the bride of Christ (Rev. 19:7-8; Eph. 5:24-33), and is destined to rule and reign with Christ (1 Cor. 4:8; 2 Tim. 2:12) and to become joint heirs of everything created (Rom. 8:17), we have much more in Christ now than Adam ever had in Eden.

> Jehovah lifted up His rod – O Christ, it fell on Thee;
> Thou wast sore stricken of Thy God; There's not one stroke for me.
> Thy blood beneath that rod has flowed; Thy bruising healeth me.
>
> Ann Ross Cousin

Curses
Genesis 3:14-19

God told Adam that he would die if he ate of the tree of knowledge of good and evil. Adam was created as a dependent being but had acted independently, and God would honor his choice. Adam learned that man dies apart from God – thus "in Adam all die" (Rom. 5:12, 18). Not only would mankind now experience physical and spiritual death, but he would also suffer under the curses of God – rightful judgments upon man and the earth which man had been given dominion over. Just as God had formed the world through audible commands, He speaks once more to curse the earth and radically change it. Then, God put Adam and the woman out of the garden to prevent them from eating of the tree of life. Immortality cannot be enjoyed when one is dead in trespasses and sins. Men are seduced to sin in the hope that they may escape or delay its judgment, but Adam soon learned that the penalty of sin was immediate and unbearable.

Now everyone that is naturally born through parents has Adam's rebellious nature, which opposes God. Even King David acknowledged he was born a sinner *"Behold, I was shaped in iniquity, and in sin did my mother conceive me"* (Ps. 51:5). King Solomon, after receiving a great gift of wisdom from God declared, *"For there is not a just man upon earth, that doeth good and sinneth not"* (Eccl. 7:20). The Apostle Paul acknowledged in Romans 3:23 that we all fall short of God's sinless perfection. In Romans 6:23, he speaks of the consequence (the wage) of our sin and God's solution for mankind's fallen condition: *"For the wages of sin is death, but the gift of God is eternal life through Jesus Christ, our Lord."* God pays a fair wage for sin – eternal death, but gives eternal life to those who will trust Christ for salvation and not trying to **earn** heaven by doing good works (Rom. 4:4-5). Christ finished the work for human salvation at Calvary. There is nothing more that can be done to appease God's wrath over human sin! The Father is fully satisfied with His Son's sacrifice (Heb. 10:14).

Although several types of death are spoken of in Scripture there are three deaths or "separations" that are most significant to all mankind. We are all born **spiritually dead**; we are spiritually separated from God. Then, when **physical death** occurs, our soul separates from our body. If physical death occurs while still being spiritually dead, **eternal death** is assured (eternal judgment in hell). Hebrews 9:27 proclaims, *"it is appointed unto men once to die, but after this the judgment."* The only exception to the above is that, perhaps, God will demonstrate His grace by applying the blood of Christ to the mentally handicapped and those wee souls who died in the womb or early in life before they understood the moral law within them and God's solution to their sin problem. But as adults and older children, the unsaved are just one heartbeat, one breath away from sealing an eternal destiny of woe.

It is not God's desire for us to experience eternal death, but on the contrary, *"He ... is long suffering toward us, not willing that any should perish, but that all should come to repentance"* (2 Pet. 3:9). Everlasting fire (hell) was not originally prepared for mankind but for Satan and rebellious angels (Matt. 25:41). However, God will use this place of torment to also punish those who would rebel against His solution for restoration (His Son's substitutionary death for their sin).

God pronounced curses upon Adam and the woman and upon the ground. The woman's ability to conceive was enhanced, along with the pain and travail she would experience in bearing children. Because she had overstepped the bounds of creation order in the marital union, she would now be directly accountable to God for undermining her husband's authority over her. The soil's capability of bearing food was diminished, meaning Adam would have to toil hard to obtain enough food to sustain his family. Before this time Adam had known work, for he was put into the garden of Eden *"to dress* (till) *it and to keep it"* (Gen. 2:15), but now he would know "toiling" and difficulties in growing food for his family. Commenting on the curses upon the earth recorded in Genesis 3:18, Francis Schaeffer writes:

> "Thorns and thistles shall it bring forth to thee." The word thistles here means luxuriously growing but useless plants. The phrase it shall bring forth to thee has in the Hebrew the sense of "it shall be

Seeds of Destiny

> caused to bud." This phrase, therefore, suggests that here, too, the change was wrought by fiat. Furthermore, the phrase suggests the modern biological term mutation, a non-sterile sort. That is, the plants had been one kind of thing and were reproducing likewise, and then God spoke and the plants began to bring forth something else and continue to reproduce likewise, and then God spoke and the plants began to bring forth something else and continued to reproduce in that new and different form.[1]

Lastly, they would experience death and return to the dust. Yet, in pronouncing judgment, God does not directly speak again (as He did in Gen. 2:17) of the ultimate consequence of their disobedience, the very thing most dreaded – death. God was not leaving them without hope. He extended them one bright ray of sunshine, on this, the darkest of days. God spoke of a future day, a day of restoration for mankind.

Lest we forget the serpent, he was cursed also. *"And the Lord God said, 'Because thou hast done this, thou art cursed above all cattle, and above every beast of the field; upon thy belly shalt thou go, and dust shalt thou eat all the days of thy life'"* (Gen. 3:14). F. W. Grant comments concerning the serpent's punishment:

> Thus the victory of evil is in reality the degradation of the victor: he is degraded necessarily by his own success. How plainly is this an eternal principle, illustrated in every career of villany under the sun! By virtue of it, Satan will not be the highest in hell, and prince of it, as men have feigned, but lowest and most miserable of all the miserable there. "Dust shall be the serpent's meat."[2]

From verse 15, we understand that the seed of the woman (a "he" or a "son") would bruise the head of the serpent (Satan per Rev. 12:9). However, the bruising of his head would require the bruising of the son's heel. Obviously, this is the first prophecy in Scripture to point to the future suffering of the Savior and the defeat of Satan at Calvary (Jn. 12:31-32). By the woman came sin to the man, and by the seed of a woman would come the Savior to save man. Adam understood by faith God's promise through the woman. Though death had been introduced through her, she would not be the mother of the *dying*, but *Eve*, "the mother of all living." Humanity would spring forth from Eve, including the future Savior.

The "seed of the woman," by implication the human race, would continue to suffer by Satanic and demonic influences in the world. The virgin birth of a Son is the literal meaning of "he" (the One bruising Satan's head) in this prophecy, as the Lord Jesus came not from the seed of man but of a woman who never knew a man. Mary conceived by the power of the Holy Spirit in her womb (not in the fallopian tubes, which is the normal location of natural human conception). In other words, it was an unnatural conception in location and origin (her seed through the Spirit).

From an *allegory vantage point* the woman represents the nation of Israel who was yet in the loins of Adam. Revelation 12:1-4 pictures Israel as the woman who gave birth to a Son (the Lord Jesus) who escaped the fury of the Dragon at his birth (Herod the Great's attempt to murder Christ as a baby). This Son would later rule and reign over all the nations with a rod of iron. It will be at this future time that the nation of Israel acknowledges Jesus Christ as their Messiah (Zech. 12:10). He will deliver a Jewish remnant from the annihilation efforts of the anti-Christ (who kills two-thirds of the Jewish population – Zech. 13:8) at the culmination of the tribulation period. But until then, suffer they will, for "war and desolations" are determined against them until their deliverance (Dan. 9:26).

Scientists tell us that there are 8,600 birds, 5,500 reptiles and amphibians, and 3,500 mammals – Adam named them all. Adam knew a lot of words, but there were seven words missing from his vocabulary before the fall of mankind. These seven words express the sum of man's suffering because of sin. Each of these consequences of sin were experienced and borne by the Son of Man, as He suffered for mankind.

Results of the Sin	Reference	Experienced by Christ	Reference
Death	Gen. 3:19	Death for every man	Heb. 2:9
Nakedness	Gen. 3:7	Naked	Jn. 19:23
Curse	Gen. 3:14	Cursed	Gal. 3:13
Sorrow	Gen. 3:17	Man of Sorrows	Isa. 53:3
Thorns	Gen. 3:18	Crowned with Thorns	Jn. 19:5
Sweat	Gen. 3:19	Sweat … drops of blood	Lk. 22:44
Sword	Gen. 3:24	Centurion's sword/spear	Jn. 19:34

Seeds of Destiny

Crown Him the Lord of life: Who triumphed o'er the grave,
Who rose victorious in the strife for those He came to save,
His glories now we sing, Who died and rose on high,
Who died eternal life to bring and lives that death may die.

Matthew Bridges

A Covering for Man
Genesis 3:20-21

In the Garden of Eden, God exchanged Adam and the woman's garments of fig leaves for that of animal skins. The fig leaves were man's attempt to fix his condition of nakedness. In general, the fig tree is a type of "religion apart from God" and is most often applied to "religious Israel" (Lk. 13:6-9). A fig tree was the only thing that the Lord directly cursed during His first advent – it withered up immediately. How God hates the traditions of men and the doctrines of demons. In Genesis 3, the fig leaves symbolized a bloodless religion that provided no atonement for sin. That is, there was no appropriate covering for sin that reflected Christ's future dealing with sin by the sacrifice of Himself. The fact that Adam and the woman still hid from God demonstrates that the fig leaves did not clear man's conscience of the guilt resulting from his sin. In the mind of God, fig leaves would never do, so He killed innocent animals, removed their hides, and fashioned clothes for Adam and the woman.

Let us understand that immediately after the fall of mankind, God's grace intervened. God labored to provide man an appropriate covering that would reflect His righteous solution to man's spiritual nakedness. Why were the skins of animals considered righteous attire? Because the skins pictured the future work of God's Son. His Son, like the animals, would be innocent of wrongdoing but would be sacrificed to resolve man's spiritual nakedness before God. The skin clothing would serve as a reminder to mankind of God's resolution concerning man's nakedness. Through Christ's efficacy a gift of divine righteousness is accredited personally to those trusting Christ as Savior. This is called "justification." Although we are not righteous, we are declared righteous. This is why a repentant sinner can enter into God's presence in heaven with-

Seeds of Destiny

out fear. God sees the believer with a perfect standing because of our perfect union with His perfect Son.

Adam's conscience would never save him – actually, it drove him to hide from God. Paul logically concludes in Romans 2 that, because man cannot continue in well-doing, his own conscience bears witness to him that he is a sinner. The reality of man's natural depravity must be confronted by God's supernatural righteousness for salvation to be possible. The Savior was stripped naked of all His covering at Calvary that we might be fully clothed with the righteousness of God. In the animal skins was God's revelation of redemption truth – a righteous covering for sin that allowed Adam to venture into the presence of God without the fear of immediate death. It would be the pattern throughout Scripture. Whether on Mount Sinai for the nation of Israel just out of Egypt, or mankind just put out of Eden, God expediently seeks to restore lost fellowship with man through redemption. By shedding the blood of an innocent animal, atonement is accomplished (a temporary covering for sin until that sin would be fully put away by Christ's sacrifice).

The Old Testament is full of portraits of God's substitutionary death of His Son for the sinner and the imputation of divine righteousness to the offerer of the sacrifice. For example, the offering priest kept the skin of the animal given by another for a burnt offering (Lev. 7:8). The priest would likely make coverings for himself with the skin, such as shoes, clothes or a hat. Thus, when the priest walked to the tabernacle to perform his priestly service, the sacrifice (his covering) and not the priest would be seen.

What is the application for the believer? *"Put ye on the Lord Jesus Christ, and make not provision for the flesh, to fulfil the lusts thereof"* (Rom 13:14). The position of righteousness we have in Christ should practically cause us to "shine out" Christ during daily service to Him. Others should not see us in daily living, but the "sacrifice" – the Lord Jesus. The inherent beauty of the bride of Christ in Revelation 19:7-9 is the glory of Christ seen in the bride. Not only does she have a position of righteousness, but the works of righteousness Christ has done through her are spectacular.

Done is the work that saves, Once and forever done;
Finished the righteousness that clothes th' unrighteous one.
The love that blesses us below is flowing freely to us now.
The sacrifice is over, the veil is rent in twain,
The mercy-seat is red, with blood of Victim slain.
Why stand we then without, in fear?
The blood of Christ invites us near.

Horatius Bonar

Eden Lost
Genesis 3:22-24

So He drove out the man; and He placed at the east of the garden of Eden Cherubim, and a flaming sword which turned every way, to keep the way of the tree of life (Gen. 3:24).

The Hebrew word *haphak* is translated "way" in this verse. It means to "turn about" and by implication to "return." Cherubim and a flaming sword guarded Eden to ensure every possible *return* route would be met with judgment. There is only one way to the tree of life. It would be by Calvary's Road. The Lord Jesus declared, *"I am **the way,** the truth, and the life: no man cometh to the Father but by Me"* (Jn. 14:6). Consequently there is only one street in heaven leading to the tree of life (Rev. 22:2). The way to God was not man venturing in, but God coming out. The Son of God took the judgment of the flaming sword that we might have entrance to the tree of life.

Eviction from the Garden of Eden was a major blow to Adam and Eve, but this was only the beginning of woes for now cursed humanity. The Bible commences and ends with the Creator in fellowship with man in a garden paradise (Rev. 22:1-6). However, the journey man travels between these two gardens is a difficult one, but thankfully this journey is bridged by a third garden – *"Now in the place where He was crucified there was a garden; and in the garden a new sepulcher."* (Jn. 19:41). Both the first Adam and last Adam (Christ – 1 Cor. 15:45) died in a garden. The first Adam changed the first garden into a spiritual graveyard, but the Lord Jesus raised from His garden tomb to offer spiritual life. Those who receive this provision will be restored to their Creator and be returned to an eternal garden paradise. Only through the center garden of Calvary may a connection between bliss and eternity be obtained.

Devotions in Genesis

God has imposed many such objects (seeds) in the preamble chapters of Genesis that we might know who is the center of human affairs. The crown of creation was man according to Hebrews 2:7, but the center of Scripture calls us reverently to view a crown of thorns upon the Savior's brow and then peer forward; nearly to the close of time, to rejoice in the triumph of the Lord Jesus, the One crowned with royal diadems (Rev. 19:12).

God calls our attention to three trees in Scripture. The fruit from the tree of knowledge of good and evil was forbidden but tasted by human desire. The center of Scripture has us again kneel before the suffering Savior nailed to a tree at Golgotha. Those who do, are able to freely eat of the Tree of Life, which will be available in Heaven forever (Rev. 22:2).

There are also three thieves God would have us contemplate. Adam may have been a crown to creation, but he was also a thief; he ate what was forbidden to him to taste. Yet, the center of Scripture unveils another thief suffering next to the One bearing the crown of thorns at Calvary. Although this thief disdained the Lord at first, he later repented, embraced the suffering Savior by faith and inherited Paradise! Now, this repentant thief is forever invited, by the One wearing royal diadems, to freely take of the Tree of Life forever. But beyond this scene is a terrible sight: Suffering in eternal fire with Satan, the great thief of human souls (Jn. 10:10), are all those who would not embrace the middle tree of Calvary. Whether gardens, crowns, trees, or thieves, the center garden, the center crown, the center tree, the center thief show the best God has to offer humanity.

Genesis 3 concludes with one of the harshest statements in Scripture: *"He drove out the man."* Speaking to God, Cain laments, *"Thou has driven me out...from Thy face"* (Gen. 4:14). By blood atonement a degree of divine fellowship would be possible, but the blood of beasts would never attain full communion with the Creator. Though our first parents found themselves homeless and cursed, the promise of future restoration and God's provision of redemption ignited a spark of hope within them; they would live and obey God's command to procreate, despite past sorrows and ever-present suffering. The seed of a woman, the Son of God, would bear the very curses levied on man. "Thorns" would be beaten into His brow to feel (Jn. 19:2) and the "bitter herbs of the field" would be pressed to His lips to taste (Matt. 27:34). The Lord Jesus knows deep distress, anguish so chilling that droplets of sweat

Seeds of Destiny

beaded upon His brow and trickled down His cheeks (Lk. 22:44). He knows all about being the man of sorrows (Isa. 53:3) and accursed of God (Gal. 3:13)

> "Man of Sorrows," what a name for the Son of God who came,
> Ruined sinners to reclaim! Hallelujah! What a Saviour!
> Bearing shame and scoffing rude, In my place condemned He stood;
> Sealed my pardon with His blood; Hallelujah! What a Saviour!
>
> Philip P. Bliss

The Way of Cain
Genesis 4:1-7

God blessed the marriage union of Adam and Eve with children. After Cain's birth, Eve is recorded speaking for the third and last time in the Bible. All three statements are tied with the serpent in one way or another. In Genesis 2, she recounted God's instruction concerning the tree of the knowledge of good and evil to the serpent. In Genesis 3, she blamed the serpent for causing her to sin. In Genesis 4:1, she proclaims *"I have gotten a man from the Lord"* thus acknowledging God's prophetic statement to the serpent concerning mankind's future deliverance from His grip, for it would be by "her seed" a Son would come and bruise the serpent's head. Although she did not understand the prophecy referred to Christ at Calvary, we applaud her simple appropriation of God's promises in a personal way. It must have brought delight and joy to her soul to think God was fulfilling His word that very day. Might all Christians lay hold of the promises of God in Christ which await them and enjoy the same elation Eve did. *"For all the promises of God in Him [Christ] are yea, and in him Amen, unto the glory of God by us"* (2 Cor. 1:20). Are you delighting in the promise of the Lord's coming? It might be today (2 Tim. 4:8)!

Two boys were born to our first parents: Cain and Abel. There were other children also; certainly there were daughters that later became wives for the sons. It is noted that in these early days of humanity there were no mutant genes in the genetic system of any of Adam and Eve's children so that no genetic harm could have resulted from brother-sister marriages. Later, after the human population was established, God would forbid such inter-family marriages (Lev. 18).

Scripture does not specifically state that Cain was the first child born, though he may well have been. The Bible records Cain's birth and that of his younger brother Abel because the progression of the narrative is connected with them. In general, the Bible does not give a detailed world history or complete biographies of individuals. Scripture only records such persons and events that directly relate to God's working in human affairs to accomplish His great plan of redemption. Rarely are the births of daughters or even their existence recorded in the Bible, unless they are associated with some significant event, such as Dinah in Genesis 34 and Jephthah's daughter in Judges 11.

These two boys were not born innocent, as their parents had been created, but as sinners with a fallen nature. Eve rejoiced at Cain's birth, but she would soon learn that nothing born of the sinful flesh would continue to please God. Cain in the process of time developed a "green thumb" and became a gardener. His younger brother Abel matured and became a shepherd of sheep. There is little doubt that mom and dad explained the horrible events that had tragically transpired in the Garden of Eden to their sons and daughters. Certainly, Adam explained to his children God's means of satisfying their need of clothing by killing and taking the hides of innocent animals, a practice they continued doing to provide clothing for themselves and their family.

Scripture is brief in describing the occupations of these two sons of Adam: Cain a "tiller of the ground" and Abel the "keeper of sheep." Yet, it becomes obvious that the choice of their professions depended not on accidental circumstances, but according to their character and views of life. Alfred Edersheim writes:

> Abel chose the pilgrim-life, Cain that of settled possession and enjoyment of the earth. The nearer their history lay to the terrible event which had led to the loss of Paradise, and to the first giving of the promise, the more significant would this their choice of life appear. Quite in accordance with this, we afterwards find Cain, not only building a city, but calling it after the name of his own son, to indicate settled proprietorship and enjoyment of the world as it was.[1]

The Christian should note and follow the examples of Abel and Abraham in living a pilgrim lifestyle. Our days upon the earth are few; we are just passing through. Let us not get settled down and invest or delight in a world that is cursed, under judgment, and shall some day be destroyed.

Abel was a "keeper of sheep." He took the best sheep of his flock and approached God by offering a burnt sacrifice. God had respect for Abel's offering because it pictured the future means in which He would reconcile mankind to Himself – through the death of His beloved Son the Lord Jesus. Abel did not know about His future Savior or how He would be judged for his sins. He simply did what pleased God and knew, by faith, that God would accept him. Because Abel demonstrated faith in accordance to what had been revealed to him, God could justly declare him righteous (accredit divine righteousness to his account). Abel lived up to his name, which means "exhalation." His life of faith exhaled worship unto God.

His brother Cain, however, was a "tiller of the ground" and brought to God what he had labored for – the fruit from a cursed ground. There is nothing naturally originating from that which is cursed that can please God. The fruit Cain offered to God represented his accomplishments (his good works) and not an innocent substitute to bear judgment in his place – there was no life in the fruit. Cain chose to worship God his way or, as the New Testament puts it, "the way of Cain." In the way of Cain, we have the first system of theology apart from atonement of sin through blood sacrifice. Cain's way denied the guilt of man and his need for a Savior (as pictured by the required animal sacrifices). Cain hated divine truth. In short, Cain's way is the wide way to hell!

The acceptance of Abel's sacrifice and the rejection of Cain's offering clearly demonstrate that God had appointed a practice and means of worship. God spoke to Cain and pleaded with him to approach his Creator through prescribed worship. It was a solemn warning to mortify his religious pride and hatred toward those who were approaching God properly. The first reference to a "door" in Scripture is found in Genesis 4:7. A door describes "an entrance" or an "opening" and for Cain the door spoke of a choice. Behind Cain's door, sin crouched like a lion poised to pounce victoriously upon its victim. Cain had to choose to squelch his pride and turn away from the door, or open it and embrace sin. The choice was to repent and enjoy acceptance and fellowship with his Creator, or to rebel against his Creator and be judged. This same choice confronts all of humanity today. To receive Jesus Christ as Savior is to open the door to God's way of salvation, or man may choose to rebel against God and seek another way.

Seeds of Destiny

 Consequently, the next Genesis reference to a "door" is used to speak of the pathway of faith by which Noah and his family entered the ark. God provided a life and death choice for Noah. He could enter through the one door, the only way to life, or turn away and perish. Man, in his fallen state, has a natural propensity for religious pride (i.e. to make choices that neither show faith in God nor turn us from a path of sin). Nadab and Abihu, two sons of Aaron the High Priest of Israel, offered strange incense to God in worship just after God had given specific instructions as to the proper way for priests to offer sacrifices to Him. God struck them both dead for their arrogance, and their father was not permitted to mourn their deaths for they had offended God (Lev. 10:1-6).

 Likewise, the Christian should make a special effort to worship God in the way God has deemed appropriate. The Lord Jesus instituted the "Lord's Supper" as a time for the corporate worship for the local church (1 Cor. 11:17, 20). He said to do it often, understanding our tendency to forget Him and His work. Yet the command set down no rules for how frequently Christians should gather to remember the Lord; our love for Him will determine this matter. The early church transitioned from "breaking bread" daily in Acts 2 to the established pattern of remembering the Lord once a week on Sunday (Acts 20:7). Every believer should confess their sins before partaking of the Lord's Supper (1 Cor. 11:23-32), just as the Levitical priests washed their hands and feet at the bronze laver before entering into the tabernacle with their offerings to worship God (Ex. 30:17-21). If a Levitical priest did not prepare properly to offer worship he was in danger of dying, and Paul acknowledges that the Christian – a believer priest (1 Pet. 2:5, 9) faces the same peril if approaching God in worship with unconfessed sin. God has appointed a way for the churches to offer corporate worship to Him. Let us not follow in the "way of Cain" and seek our own method.

 When believers assemble for worship, they should do so in the beauty of holiness (sins humbly confessed) and with a spiritual offering ready to present to the Lord (1 Chron. 16:29). The audible ministry should be done by Spirit-led men, as the man represents God when speaking (1 Cor. 11:7) and per the speaking instructions given for church order (1 Cor. 14). The women should attend to the visual ministry in the assembly of revealing God's glory by covering all competing glories (herself being man's glory and her hair which is her glory –1 Cor. 11:7, 15). In this way, only God's glory, as represented by uncovered men, is seen by God and the angels overlooking the assembly. This pictures the scene in heaven as seraphim and cherubim cover their own intrinsic glories with their wings in the presence of God, so only God's glory is preeminent (Isa. 6:2, Ezek. 1:11). Satan was a covering cherub (Ezek. 28:14-16) who rebelled against God's creation. He didn't want to conceal his own glories any more, but wanted to have the position of God. Thus, Satan continually opposes God's order, whether it be civil, church or family order. May the church do what Satan failed to do – show submission to God's order by obeying scriptural practices.

> Not all the blood of beasts, on Jewish altars slain,
> Could give the guilty conscience peace, or wash away its stain.
> But Christ, the heavenly Lamb, took all our sins away,
> A sacrifice of nobler name and richer blood than they.
>
> Issac Watts

The Second Murder
Genesis 4:8-15

Pride swelled in Cain's heart, and he further rebelled against God. There is a trail of bloody rebels through the Bible. Like Cain, the religious leaders and the brutal mob in Christ's day cried out to Pilate, *"Crucify Him." "His blood be on us, and on our children"* (Matt. 27:25). The way to please God had been shown, but, like Cain, they would rather see innocent blood shed than trust in it. Not much has changed, even today, as the unrighteous seek religious form apart from God's revealed truth, then try to convince those of righteous standing of its merit. As evil loathes God's truth, unceasing strife between good and evil have plagued the world since the fall of man.

Beyond the world about us is the unseen world within. For the believer this sphere of individual experience is a conflict of two natures. F. W. Grant likens the struggle of Cain and Abel with the internal struggle of the spiritual nature and the flesh nature of a believer:

> The conflict is between two natures – the one which is ours as born naturally; the other, as born of God supernaturally; and here, evidently, the order is, "first, that which is natural, and afterwards that which is spiritual." The law of Genesis is thus that the elder gives place to the younger. Cain represents, therefore, that in us which we rightly and necessarily call "the old nature." His name signifies "acquisition, possession;" Abel's "vapor, exhalation." The contrast between them cannot be questioned, and was prophetic of their lives; Cain possessing himself of that earth on which for man's sake the curse rested, while Abel's life exhaled to God like vapor drawn up by the sun.[1]

Like spiritual Abel, the believer must have the sentence of death within and the stench of death without. He must not trust in flesh at all; it must die, and the Spirit of God must reign within our mortal bodies.

When it comes to the desires of the flesh, these must be mortified or satisfied. There is no middle ground, for if we satisfy the flesh a little, it will only want more in time. The flesh is never satisfied! The flesh strives for self-gratification, while the spiritual man yearns for Christlikeness. The internal battle rages on and our only hope is to fully trust and rest in the God that raises the dead.

There was nothing inherently evil in Cain's offering of thanksgiving to the Lord, for later the Mosaic Law incorporated such offerings. But the Law would teach that any offering of thanksgiving to God which disregards the blood sacrifice or is disassociated from it is completely void of value. The basis of acceptance of all offerings indirectly or directly is by blood, thus symbolizing that there could be no fellowship with God or thanksgiving to Him without dealing with sin through substitutional death.

How did Cain respond to God's request to do what was right and His warning of the consequences of wrongdoing? Cain sought out righteous Abel instead of right doing. We are not informed of the conversation between Cain and Abel on that dreadful day, but Abel apparently did not listen to Cain. Abel knew that the Lord had accepted both him and his offering (Gen. 4:4). He had overwhelming assurance of divine acceptance for *"By faith Abel offered unto God a more excellent sacrifice than Cain"* (Heb. 11:4). It is liberating for believers to know that they are secure in Christ and what is unselfishly done for Christ is fully accepted. Cain, on the other hand, did not enjoy this sense of security and significance. Cain could not direct his anger to God for rejecting him, so he vented his rage upon his brother Abel and slew him. So it has been since that time that the religious "Cains" of the world have slain faithful "Abels." Even after Cain saw the blood of his brother spill on the ground, his conscience was still repressed. God questioned Cain about his heinous crime. Cain's lying response to His "all-seeing" and "all-knowing" Creator shows he had no shame and no idea to Whom he spoke.

Cain was the second murderer of the Bible. His father, the devil, was the first. The Lord Jesus told the Pharisees, *"Ye are of your father the devil, and the lusts of your father ye will do. He was a murderer from the beginning, and abode not in the truth, because there is no truth in him. When he speaketh a lie, he speaketh of his own; for he is a liar, and the father of it"* (Jn. 8:44). Satan was the father or "originator" of murder and of lying. Through lies and deceit, Satan caused Adam and the woman to trade their full life with God in the garden for spiritual and physical death. The ungodly descendants of Cain will be prone to mimic the evil activities of their fathers Cain and Satan.

God told Cain that his brother's blood was crying unto Himself from the ground. Though His brother's body lay silent and still upon the ground, screams for justice from his pooled blood sounded in the ears of Almighty God with stinging clarity. Righteous Abel was innocent in God's eyes because he had sacrificed the best of his animals to please God. Four thousand years later, there would be another innocent man, Jesus, who would also utterly seek to please God. Like Abel, He would be silent before His accusers. And though found innocent by two civil authorities in order to avoid a Jewish riot, He would be sentenced to death. His words were few, but His actions and His blood yet speak infinite volumes of God's love and justice.

The Lord said to His disciples, *"But **that the world may know** that I love the Father; and as the Father gave Me commandment, even so I do"* (Jn. 14:31). Jesus was going to prove to the whole world that love and obedience were inseparable qualities when relating to God. At Calvary, Jesus scarcely uttered a word while blood trickled from His swollen body, but within celestial realms, His blood sprang forth eternal anthems of loving-kindness. The Creator was suffering for His creation. Hebrews 12:24 reads, *"Jesus, the mediator of the new covenant, and to the blood of sprinkling, that speaketh better things than that of Abel."* Abel's blood cried out for vengeance and justice. Christ's blood satisfied the need of divine justice; therefore, it cried out God's mercy and grace to a fallen human race!

God cursed Cain and condemned him to be a wanderer. We find out that he dwelled in the land of Nod, which means "wandering" or "unrest." So Cain was condemned to wander in a land of restless wandering. Cain's conscience was seared, but his sense of recompense for his crimes was very rational and selfish; *"My punishment is greater than I can bear"* (Gen. 4:13) and *"every one that findeth shall slay me"* (Gen. 4:14). Derek Kidner notes this concerning God's dealing with Cain's plea:

> God's concern of the innocent (v.10) is matched only by His care for the sinner [v.15]. Even the querulous prayer of Cain had contained a germ of entreaty; God's answering pledge, together with His mark or

sign (the same word as in 9:13; 17:11) – not a stigma but a safe-conduct – is almost a covenant, making Him virtually Cain's…protector…. It is the utmost that mercy can do for the unrepentant.[2]

Cain worried only about his future not about his past doings. As an act of mercy to the sinner, God satisfied Cain's selfish concern. He set a mark on Cain to protect him from being slain by others. All men should realize Cain's fear of judgment, for none of us can bear the judgment of our own sins. Arthur Pink summarizes this chapter well:

Abel was accepted because he offered to God a bleeding lamb. Cain was rejected because he refused to offer such. Here, then we have traced back to their fountain head the two streams which empty themselves in Heaven and Hell, namely, the saved and the lost, and the dividing line between them is a line of blood.[3]

It was the same line between Egyptian and Israelite on the eve of Passover – applied blood on the door brought life, and no blood brought death. Thank God that He sent His beloved Son to be the bearer of our sin (2 Cor. 5:21), to taste death for all men (Heb. 2:9), and to redeem us once and for all by His blood (1 Pet. 1:18-19). Throughout human history, God has called every individual to spiritually step from the doomed line of Cain to the line of faithful Abel and receive eternal life. He still calls today.

"Some day," you say, "I will seek the Lord, Some day I will make my choice;
Some day, some day, I will heed His Word, and answer the Spirit's voice."
God's time is now, for the days fly fast, and swiftly the seasons roll;
Today is yours, it may be your last; Choose life for your priceless soul!
Choose now, just now! There's a soul at stake! O what will your answer be?
'Tis life or death; and the choice you make is made for eternity.

Harriet Fithian

Death Without Living
Genesis 4:16-5:20

It has been said that there are two types of people walking on planet Earth today "saints and ain'ts" – those who are saved and those who are unsaved. Similarly, two types of people are represented in Genesis Chapters 4 and 5. Genesis 4:16-24 lists the ungodly line of Cain (destined to be destroyed in the flood), while Genesis 5 records the godly genealogy of Seth, Adam and Eve's third son. Biblical and Church history have shown that, when the unrighteous are allowed to murder the righteous, God conveys a greater blessing to man, brings glory to Himself and then provides a replacement to continue His Sovereign plan. Seth was faithful Abel's replacement to carry on the godly messianic line.

Genesis 5:1-3 expresses a sharp contrast between the words "image" and "likeness." Adam was originally created in the "likeness" and "image" of God, but, after the fall, man would only bear God's "image," for moral "likeness" had been lost. Man was still God's representative on earth. Genesis 5:3 states that Adam begot children *"in his own likeness, after his image."* Image is not likeness; these are distinctly different ideas. Likeness is similitude, being like; image is representation, whether alike or not. The Lord Jesus is never spoken of as "being in the likeness of God." He cannot be "like" God since He is God. Adam's descendants, though still representing God, would be like their father Adam in moral likeness.

Adam was 130 years old when he begot Seth (Gen. 5:3). Apparently, it did not take long from the creation of man to his sin in Eden. Seth is at least the fourth child of Adam and Eve and perhaps the fifth or sixth, given Cain had a wife (Gen. 4:17) and that Abel may have had a sister for a wife also. From the biblical record of Noah's sons and their sons, the average duration between a child's birth at that time is estimated at 28 years, assuming equal births of the genders.

Note the contrast in accomplishments between the genealogies of Cain and Seth. Cain's line represents those who live for the world. Cain's ancestors dwelled in a land of Nod (They wandered through life.); they built cities, raised cattle, were musicians, had skilled craftsmen, and were afflicted by social crime. Genesis 4:16 reads, *"Cain went out from the presence of the Lord...."* After Cain left God's presence, he built the first city recorded in the Bible (Gen. 4:17) – a society apart from God. Cain's descendants exemplify the accomplishments that a world system under the influence of Satan would seek for self-significance: industry, commerce, science, and the arts. These things are not inherently wicked, but in the absence of God, possessions, careers, and abilities become idols. These idols derail man from his intended purpose – to bring God glory (Rev. 4:11).

It is noted that all the elements which evolutionary archaeologists and anthropologists identify as necessary characteristics to declare the emergence of evolving mankind from the Stone Age are apparent in the civilization of Adam's earliest descendants. It did not take hundreds of thousands of years for man to learn to tie his shoes. Commonsense declares the same conclusion when reviewing man's achievements just in the last few centuries. Medically we have progressed from bleeding sick people to death 200 years ago to developing powerful antibiotics and surgical procedures that do not cut the skin. Two centuries ago it took months to cross the North American continent, now it requires but a few hours. Man has progressed from cannon balls to atomic bombs and from merely gazing at the moon to walking upon it. But man is just as incapable of ruling himself wisely now as he was in the beginning.

Cain's descendants are not mentioned as living or even dying. In the sight of eternity, their lives did not count for anything. It was as if they never lived – their lives had no benefit to God on earth. They lived for the day and were "earthy" in focus. Lamech was the first to rebel against God's established order of monogamy (Gen. 4:19). He was evidently a powerful and prosperous man who understood that having more wives meant more children and more children brought more power in a society functioning on a patriarchal basis. One of his wives was Adah meaning "beauty" or "adornment," and the other was Zillah meaning "shade," perhaps referring to flowing locks of hair. His daughter's name was Naamah meaning "pleasant" or "lovely." The meaning of these women's names illustrates the propensity of the Cainites to lust with their eyes and with their flesh.

Seth's line, however, has several noticeable differences. First, there is only one accomplishment mentioned in Seth's descendants – Enoch walked with God. Enoch is only one of two men of whom it is said in Scripture that he *"walked with God"* (Noah being the other). He is also only one of two men in Scripture of whom it is said, *"he pleased God"* (the Lord Jesus is the other).

Secondly, the names bear witness of a different mentality. Seth had a son and named him Enos, meaning "a mortal man," which speaks of man's frailty. Genesis 4:26 records, *"And to Seth, to him also there was born a son; and he called his name Enosh: then began men to call upon the name of the Lord."* This does not mean that sacrifices and praise to God had not been offered up before on an individual basis, but that now the vital spiritual differences between these two lines were outwardly professed. The Sethites praised God openly, while Cainites lived for self and pursued temporal satisfaction. Culture used or abused offers no hope of restoration with God.

Thirdly, missing in Seth's line are secular accomplishments and achievements and the mention of violence. Genesis 5 records that Seth's ancestors obeyed God in populating the earth with godly children. They simply lived and died and walked with God. Dear Christian, invest in eternity. Do not squander your life away accumulating titles, degrees, trophies, money and pleasure for yourself. Live for God! Everything on earth rusts, rots or decays. Only those things you invest into the kingdom of God will bring you a heavenly reward and the appreciation of God Himself (Matt. 25:20-21).

It is relevant to note that Genesis 4:21 is the first mention of "music" in the Bible; however, this was not the first occurrence of music in the history of creation. According to Ezekiel 28:13, Lucifer was created with every precious stone as a covering and had a provision of timbrels and flutes to make music before God. In the celestial realms, worship (accompanied by music) was being offered by spiritual beings to their Creator, even before man was created. But Satan's inflated pride motivated a desire to be worshipped, thus God cast him off His holy mount. The "light bearer" became the "father of darkness."

Why did the descendants of Cain, and not Seth, become musicians? There are many avenues of expressing what is in one's heart: musical composition, painting, speaking, and facial expressions are but a few. Music can settle the soul (as when David played for King Saul), or it can afflict the soul (as with David and Jeremiah, see Psalm 69:12 and Lam. 3:14, respectively). Music can be used to affect pagan worship (Dan. 3:4-6) or to worship God (Ps. 150). If one is full of Christ, acceptable music reflecting humility on our part and adoration towards God will be enjoyed by all (see Rev. 14:2-3, 18:22). The Lord Jesus, who had a heart that swelled with love for His Father, sang hymns of praise unto His God (Mk. 14:26).

Jubal was the originator of music on earth, *"the father of all such that handled* (literally manipulated) *the harp and pipe"* (Gen. 4:21). What kind of music do you think precipitated from Jubal's heart towards God? Worship, praise, or perhaps a spiritual song? Probably not. Jubal's name is derived from the Hebrew word *yuwbal*, which means "stream." His name is rooted in the word *yabal*, which means "to flow," or by implication, "to carry or bring with pomp." Jubal was the son of three murderers. His father, Lamech, was the third murderer recorded in the Bible; his great-great-great-grandfather, Cain, was the second, and his father, the devil murdered (took life away from) Adam and Eve in the garden (Jn. 8:44). Jubal's name, his ungodly ancestors, and the stimulation of demonic forces controlling the line of Cain suggest his music displayed the inherent rebellion and depraved heart of his family and his father Satan, the devil.

Like Jubal, Enoch was also seventh from Adam in generations. The number "seven," as stated earlier is "God's number of perfection and completeness." Its place in the genealogy of Seth announced the appearance of a just and godly man – Enoch. However, the number "six" is man's number (Rev. 13:18); thus, a prodigy of Cain, Lamech, is given as a representative of the "natural man" and his wherewithal apart from God. Lamech was Jubal's father and reaffirms the natural propensity man possesses to follow the path of the devil and Cain, both murderers.

Seeds of Destiny

Reviewing the early genealogies of Cain we conclude that it is possible to physically die without ever truly living, as pictured in the line of Cain. They lived for the moment, for selfish gratification, and apart from God. In the sight of eternity, their lives counted for nothing – it was as if they never lived. But in Seth's descendants we see the abundant life, for they lived to please God.

Death is more universal than life; everyone dies, but not everyone lives.
A. Sachs

Walking With God
Genesis 5:21-5:24

What do you think led to Enoch's conversion? Perhaps Enoch's great-great-great-great-grandfather Adam had something to do with Enoch's decision and desire to walk with God. Adam was only 622 years old when Enoch was born. Perchance Adam told Enoch how he and his wife walked with God in the cool of the day. Perhaps Enoch, after learning of the intimate fellowship that Adam and God enjoyed in the Garden of Eden, longed for that intimacy too.

Walking with God starts with a desire. Enoch had that desire, and he enjoyed 300 years of closeness with God before God took him home. I like to think that one day God and Enoch were just strolling across a meadow together when God turned to his friend Enoch and said, "I have enjoyed walking with you, Enoch, these last 300 years. Instead of us saying goodbye today, would you like to come home with Me? Then we will always be together." I think Enoch smiled ear to ear, then in a blink of an eye, he was gone.

What does it mean to walk with God? First, walking with God requires faith. A quick review of Enoch's testimony per Heb. 11:5-6 reveals that he pleased God, for it is impossible to please God without faith in God. Therefore, Enoch had faith in God. He believed what God had revealed to him and trusted God for all that had not been disclosed to him. Paul writes in Rom. 1:17, *"the righteousness of God revealed from faith to faith, as it is written; the just shall live by faith."* Both the Old and New Testament declare this truth – one must have faith in God's revealed word to be saved. A believer then seeks to live by faith in order to be sanctified for God's good use and glory.

Secondly, we read in 1 John 1:5-7 that walking with God requires walking in the light of divine truth. A willingness to walk according to revealed truth brings happy fellowship with God and with other believers. We must have light to walk safely. When we choose to walk in the dark, we are inviting injury – the chastening hand of God. Listen to Paul's medley of exhortation concerning the walk of the believer from the book of Ephesians: walk not as fools (Eph. 5:15), or as we formerly did (Eph. 5:8), or the way the Gentiles walk – in the vanity of their minds (Eph. 4:17), but walk as children of light. In other words, "Don't be fools, walk according to truth, not in the darkness you once did." The Lord Jesus promised that, if we obey His commandments, He will manifest Himself to us in deeper fellowship (Jn. 14:21). Enoch could walk with God because he was in agreement with God about the matter of sin. For *"can two walk together except they be agreed?"* (Amos 3:3). Surely, light has no communion with darkness; thus Enoch walked with God according to divine truth and in moral integrity.

Thirdly, we read these words from the prayer of Jabez in 1 Chron. 4:10: *"that thine hand might be with me."* Like Jabez, Enoch wanted intimacy and close fellowship with God. And, wherever there is a man that desires a closer fellowship with God, the Creator will be eager to reveal Himself in new and meaningful ways. Since Enoch walked with God, he was the benefactor of God's companionship and protection.

Enoch enjoyed intimacy with God because he desired it and was willing to walk by faith and according to revealed truth. Does your heart yearn for that type of communion with God? What does it mean to walk with God? Micah 6:8 declares, *"He hath shown thee, O man, what is good; and what doth the Lord require of thee, but to do justly, and to love mercy, and to walk humbly with thy God?"* Walking with God in this way benefits us, and ensures that others will see Him in us.

> Hold Thou my hand, and closer, closer draw me
>   to Thy dear self – my hope, my joy, my all,
> Hold Thou my hand, lest haply I should wander,
>   and missing Thee, my trembling feet shall fall.
> Hold Thou my hand; the way is dark before me
>   without the sunlight of Thy face divine;
> Hold Thou my hand, that when I reach the margin
>   of that lone river Thou didst cross for me,
> A heavenly light may flash along its waters,
>   and every wave like crystal bright shall be.
>
>   Fanny J. Crosby

Unnatural Unions
Genesis 5:25-6:7

After the translation of Enoch, a new era in human existence occurred on earth, and a strongly-marked division in the book of Genesis is noticed. In Genesis 6:1-2, we read: *"And it came to pass, when men began to multiply on the face of the earth, and daughters were born unto them, that the sons of God saw the daughters of men that they were fair; and they took them wives of all which they chose."* The *"daughters of men"* are generally understood to be either be "women of natural humanity" or possibly "the ungodly line of Cain." *"The sons of God"* is from the Hebrew phrase *bene elohim* used to describe angels in Job 1:6, 2:1, and 38:7. Excluding the latter reference, Satan (also a spiritual being) is accompanying these other angels as they report to God. A similar Hebrew phrase *bene elim* is employed in Psalm 29:1 and 89:6 to refer to angels. Thus, combining the teaching of Jude 6 many see that "the sons of God" (Gen. 6:2) are fallen angels who left their first estate (position in creation) and habitation (heaven) and took on a human form. These evil entities then mated with normal women to bring about supernatural and evil beings in human form on the earth.

Others simply see Satan corrupting the godly line of Seth (the sons of God) by intermarriage with the ungodly descendants of Cain (the daughters of men). H. C. Leupold supplies a lengthy argument for this position then summarizes: "the Sethites had grown indifferent to their heritage; the Cainites had developed high-handed violence [asserting that "giants" of Genesis 6:4 refer to "powerful attackers"]. When Yahweh regards this, He sees that it constitutes 'great wickedness'."[1] However, this naturalistic interpretation would allow only the selective marriages of the sons of Seth with the daughters of Cain, and not vice versa. It also diminishes the full intensity of the expression "mighty men" used to describe the wicked offspring, whereas, some sort of demonically derived monstrosity of humanity or at least demon possessed and controlled humans would better fit the description. Those in rebellion become easy targets of demonic possession or obsession. This is the general sense of J. W. Ferguson's conclusion:

> Each of these lines of explanation [speaking of various views of the sons of God intermarrying with the daughters of men] runs into some kind of difficulty, but, on balance, some form of the first interpretation [fallen angels or similar beings = sons of God] seems to fit the context best. Briefly, it takes the title, "sons of God," in its usual sense, it presents a monstrous intrusion into human society, it fits into the following picture of open rebellion against God calling for His judgment and for the cleansing of human society from this pollution."[2]

Whatever corruption is spoken of, the result was rampant sexual perversion that caused a population explosion of powerful and vile people, which were successful in thoroughly influencing all humanity to rebel against God (excluding Noah and his family).

Some have used the Lord's statement in Matthew 22:30 to teach against the possibility of creating offspring from the union of woman and an angel. *"For in the resurrection they neither marry, nor are given in marriage, but are as the angels of God in heaven."* Henry Morris writes concerning the Lord's statement:

> ...this is not equivalent to saying that angels are "sexless," since people who share in the resurrection will surely retain their own personal identity, whether male or female. Furthermore, angels are always described, when they appear, as "men," and the pronoun "he" is always used in reference to them. Somehow they have been given by God the capacity of materializing themselves in masculine human form when occasion warrants, even though their bodies are not under the control of the gravitational and electromagnetic forces which limit our own bodies in the present life.

> When Jesus said that the angels of God in heaven do not marry, this did not necessarily mean that those who have been cast out of heaven were incapable of doing so. It clearly was not God's will or intention that angels mix in such a way with human women, but these wicked

angels were not concerned with obedience to God's will. In fact, it was probably precisely for the purpose of attempting to thwart God's will that this particular battalion of the "sons of God" engaged in this illegal invasion of the bodies of the daughters of men.[3]

Practically speaking, it does not really matter who these "sons of God" were as they were all destroyed in the flood. Although Satan's global assault on humanity through sexual perversions of one sort or another failed, we should not be ignorant of his insidious devices (2 Cor. 2:11). We must recognize his despicable goal – to mar the testimony to Christ on earth. His depraved strategy is to mingle "that which is of God" with "that which is of man." Satan attempted to pollute the godly line of Seth, from which the Messiah would ultimately come. He was not successful. There seems to be two fronts of this compromising agenda: (1) corrupt God's people through close association with children of the devil (unbelievers – worldliness), and (2) undermine God's truth by embracing the doctrines of demons. Paul states that the children of God should not be *"tossed to and fro, and carried about with every wind of doctrine, by the sleight of men, and cunning craftiness, by whereby they lie in wait to deceive"* (Eph 4:14).

It is a human tendency to forge unnatural spiritual unions for the sake of reaching some desired end result. The end does not justify the means if God's truth has been compromised. In the case of Genesis 6, "the end," from a human prospective, seemed more than adequate to justify "the means" as "mighty men" and "men of renown" were created from the unions of the sons of God and daughters of men. But from God's point of view, holiness and truth had been compromised.

Certainly, one of Satan's main strategies to confront God's people throughout time is the use of "unnatural unions." C. H. Mackintosh wrote regarding this in the mid 19th century:

> There is great danger, at the present day, of compromising truth for the sake of union. This should be carefully guarded against. There can be no true union attained at the expense of truth. The true Christian's motto should be, "Maintain truth at all cost, if union can be promoted in this way, so much the better, but maintain the truth." The principle of expediency, on the contrary, may be thus enunciated: "Promote union at all cost; if truth can be maintained as well, so much the better, but promote union." This latter principle can only be

carried out at the expense of all that is divine in the way of testimony.[4]

Satan has used this tactic of "unnatural unions" on many throughout Biblical history. After the Jews returned from Babylonian exile and began to rebuild the temple, the scheme was tried on Zerubbabel. The enemy tried to forge a union with the people of God to frustrate the work of God. *"Let us build with you; for we seek your God, as ye do"* (Ezra 4:2). Joshua fell prey to the Gibeonites trickery in Canaan: "we are your servants ... we know your God ... make a peace treaty with us" (Josh. 9). He listened to the enemy, did not seek God's counsel on the matter, and paid a high price for submitting to the deception.

Nehemiah, however, would not listen to the continued solicitations of the enemy while building the wall at Jerusalem. The enemy wanted to visit with Nehemiah about the rebuilding of the wall – *"come let us meet together"* – but they only wanted to lure Nehemiah into seclusion to kill him. Stop the leader, stop the work. Dear beloved, pray for your church leaders for they are under reoccurring attacks and constant solicitation to do evil. Satan knows that, if he can cause the undershepherds of the local assembly to fall, he can divide and devour the scattering sheep – like a raging wolf.

Genesis 5:29 is a blunt reminder of what happens when we listen and follow Satan, *"... Noah...shall comfort us concerning our work and toil of our hands, because of the ground which the Lord hath cursed."* Satan had successfully solicited mankind to sin in Eden over 1500 years earlier. Scripture records that in the days of Noah mankind was still suffering the righteous judgment of God upon a cursed earth.

What was God's attitude about the unnatural unions Satan had brought about in an attempt to corrupt the godly messianic line of Christ? *"The Lord said, I will destroy man"* (Gen. 6:7). God's judgment is sure for all things that have been corrupted by evil.

> Lord, take my life and make it wholly Thine;
> Fill my poor heart with Thy great love divine.
> Take all my will, my passion, self and pride;
> I now surrender, Lord – in me abide.
>
> J. Edwin Orr

When it Comes
Genesis 6:8-13

Enoch's conversion seems to be about the time of his son Methuselah's birth. Enoch was 65 years old when Methuselah was born. In a mysterious way, the birth of his son was a prophecy in itself – Methuselah's name means "when it comes." God was telling Enoch that as long as his son lived the world would live, but, when his son died, the world would die. How do you think this knowledge affected Enoch's life? He did not know when his son would die, so he had to live in constant anticipation of suddenly being ushered into the presence of God. Likewise, the Church operates today with the anticipation of suddenly being ushered into the presence of God. This is the hope of the Church: *"Looking for that blessed hope, and the glorious appearing of the great God and our Savior, Jesus Christ"* (Tit. 2:13). The Lord's return may not be immediate, but it is imminent!

So, when did Methuselah die? Methuselah was 187 years old when his son Lamech was born, and Lamech was 182 years old when Noah was born. Noah was 600 years old when the flood came (Gen. 7:6). Consequently, Methuselah was 969 years old when the flood came, and Scripture records that he lived 969 years – he died the year the flood occurred. Literally, the prophecy of his name was fulfilled "when it came."

God was greatly grieved over the wickedness of mankind – the behavior of man had sunk into the miry depths of his depraved heart. So God told a righteous man named Noah that He was pronouncing judgment upon mankind: *"The end of all flesh is come before me...I will destroy them (wicked man) with the earth...make thee an ark of gopher wood"* (Gen. 6:13-14). The far reaching scope of the cross is thus pre-witnessed – in that by one act, God could judge all that was wicked and at the same time bestow a marvelous provision of grace on the right-

Seeds of Destiny

eous, for *"Noah found grace in the eyes of the Lord"* (Gen. 6:8). Those with a humble heart choosing to obey God's truth receive the undeserved favor of heaven.

The fact that Methuselah lived longer than any other man in the Bible illustrates God's long suffering nature. 2 Peter 3:9 reads, *"The Lord is not slack concerning His promise, as some men count slackness, but is longsuffering toward us, not willing that any should perish, but that all should come to repentance."* The Lord was longsuffering because a righteous man was preaching repentance to the people. Who was this righteous preacher? Noah. We learn from 1 Peter 3:18-20 and 2 Peter 2:5 that Christ was preaching through Noah to the wicked men of earth. This preaching lasted until the ark was completed. Every gopher tree felled, every sound of wood being gnawed by a saw or chopped by ax, and pound of the hammer was a call to repentance and gave testimony that judgment was coming. B. H. Carroll comments concerning the preaching of Noah and the unavoidable judgment which came despite his preaching.

> There is a reference to him [Noah] in Ezekiel 14:14, where he speaks about a certain wicked city, and he says, "Though Noah, Job, and Daniel were in this city they could save only themselves by their righteousness." Whenever the number of righteous men gets so small that the salt cannot preserve the world, or whenever the testimony of the righteous becomes so low that it cease to conserve, then doom comes and the doom is irretrievable.[1]

It is my opinion that we do not know exactly how long it took Noah to build the ark. However, if you play "Bible Trivia" and this question is read, the right answer will be 120 years. This is based on Genesis 6:3, the only timing given when torrential rain was in the extended weather forecast. However, Noah was 500 years old when his first son was born (Gen. 5:32). This was probably Japheth as he is spoken of as being Shem's older brother (Gen. 10:21) and Ham is identified as the youngest son of Noah (Gen. 9:24). Thus, the order of Noah's sons in Genesis 5:32 does not reflect their birth order. Genesis 6 states that Noah's sons were old enough to help Noah build the ark and to each have a wife. Perhaps Noah built the ark alone for a large portion of that 120 years, but it is more likely that the ark was built as a family effort

Devotions in Genesis

in much less time. Scripture does not inform us of the duration of the building project, but that Noah was 600 years old when it was completed (Gen. 7:6).

Three days before Christ's crucifixion His disciples asked Him, *"What shall be the sign of thy coming, and of the end of the age?"* (Matt. 24:3). The Lord responded to their question by describing several escalating signs of the coming Tribulation Period and detailing chronologically events that would occur during those seven years. The Lord concluded by giving the following warning.

> *But of that day and hour knoweth no man ... but as the days of Noah were so shall also the coming of the Son of man be. For as in the days that were before the flood they were eating and drinking, marrying and giving in marriage, until the day that Noah entered into the ark. And knew not until the flood came, and took them all away, so shall also the coming of the Son of man be* (Matt. 24:36-39).

The days prior to the Lord's Second Coming will be similar to the behavior of man in Noah's day. Sexual perversion and unceasing wickedness will characterize the days just prior to judgment. Man will be living for all the pleasure life can offer and have no remorse for the Creator's grieving heart. Noah's contemporaries lived like they had flood insurance, but the only insurance was the ark. Likewise today, in our post-Christian society, man lives for the day, not realizing that judgment is coming and that the good news of Jesus Christ is the only means of escape.

In all, eight souls were saved from God's wrath because they entered the ark that they had built by faith. Their faith was based solely on the Word of God – no signs were given to Noah to believe. He simply took God at His word, and it was accounted to Him as righteousness. Noah must have had tremendous faith in God, considering the enormous task of building a 450 foot by 75 foot by 45 foot triple deck ship out of wood with archaic tools on dry land. Can you imagine how Noah was laughed at for building a giant ship far away from water? How would he get it to water? Well, God's plan was to bring the water to the ark, but the Bible informs us that, until the time of the flood, there had not been rain upon the earth (Gen. 2:5-6 and Heb. 11:7). What faith Noah had and what mercy God demonstrated by not destroying every-

Seeds of Destiny

thing because of man's continual wickedness. But Noah was a righteous man and walked with God (Gen. 6:9), and he found grace in the eyes of the Lord (Gen. 6:8).

This was not just a local flood as some have wrongly speculated. If this judgment had been via a local flood, God could have caused Noah, his family and the animals to go to an elevated location elsewhere to preserve them. However, if they could have found sanctuary by scurrying to higher ground, so could the wicked. The waters rose above the 17,000-foot peaks of Mt. Ararat (Gen. 7:19-20). How do you keep a three mile high pile of water localized to one area? Waters broke up from within the earth, and the thick atmospheric mist that had watered the whole earth for at least 1600 years condensed into turbulent rain (Gen. 7:11). This was a worldwide flood that would wipe out everything that lived on land. This is why the ark was so huge (over 1.5 million cubic feet – equivalent to 800 railroad boxcars) – it had to hold a lot of animals and a lot of food safely in the midst of a horrendous upheaval from below and a fierce storm with global ramifications above.

The Lord's future coming to the earth to judge the wicked and to rule the nations will surprise all those who are not looking for Him. "When it comes" the judgment will be severe and global. Every eye shall see Him and every man will reckon with Him (Matt. 24:30; Rev. 1:7).

> Lo! He comes, with clouds descending, Once for our salvation slain;
> Thousand thousand saints attending, Swell the triumph of His train:
> Alleluia! Alleluia! God appears on earth to reign.
> Every eye shall now behold Him, Robed in dreadful majesty;
> Those who set at naught and sold Him, Pierced and nailed Him to the tree,
> Deeply wailing, deeply wailing, Shall the true Messiah see.
> Yea, Amen! Let all adore Thee, High on Thine eternal throne;
> Savior, take the power and glory, Claim the kingdom for Thine own:
> O come quickly, O come quickly, Alleluia! Come, Lord, come!
>
> Charles Wesley

The Ark
Genesis 6:14-22

There are several wonderful prophetic pictures in the ark, for the ark itself is a type of Christ. In the broad sense, the ark pictures the safety that Christ offers all who will "enter in" His own body the Church by faith. Before the ark could be constructed, building materials were needed – gopher trees had to be cut down. The death of these trees pictured the humanity of Christ in that only through His sacrifice could spiritual life for man be secured. But since trees don't have blood, God is careful to apply some to the ark that we not miss the "type." The word *"pitch"* in Genesis 6:14 is most often translated "atonement" (nearly 75 times in the Old Testament). Prior to Calvary, man's sin could only be atoned (covered) by the blood of animals through sacrifices. The fact that the ark was pitched from within and without further shadows the future suffering and sacrifice of Christ. From His wounds redemptive blood would rudely and profusely coat his outer skin and then drip and splatter upon the ground. The word usage and the typology of Genesis 6 both convey the visage of a bleeding ark, thus picturing the suffering Savior at Calvary.

There was only one door into the ark (Gen. 6:16), and only God could shut it (Gen. 7:16) once all those who entered by faith were within. It would be God who judged the earth for man's wickedness (Gen. 6:7); thus, the very ark that Noah had built would know God's wrath. However, while the ark bore the judgment of almighty God, all the souls that were in the ark were kept safe from judgment. The Lord Jesus said He was the only door (Jn. 10:1) and the only way (Jn. 14:6), and He bore the judgment of God for man's sin once and for all (Heb. 9:26-28, 10:9-18). The Lord said, *"whosoever liveth and believeth in Me shall never die"* (Jn. 11:26). Our soul's security rests in the hand (Jn. 10:28-29) and the sealing power of God (Eph. 1:13). We never

Seeds of Destiny

read of water pouring through the door to despair Noah's family or that any family member was lost at sea. When God sealed the door shut, it was securely closed, and when God seals the believer in Christ, he or she is maintained securely within.

As a note of application, the ark lifted up eight faithful souls off the face of the earth by the judgment of water. Likewise, seeing that by judgment our old man was crucified with Christ (Gal. 2:20; Rom. 6:6) and that we were raised up with Him into heavenly citizenship (Eph. 2:6, Phil. 3:20), we should be desiring to live a separated life from the world (This is not however a secluded life.). Paul describes this attitude in Ephesians 4:22-24: *"That ye put off concerning the former manner of life the old man, which is corrupt according to the deceitful lusts, and be renewed in the spirit of your mind and that ye put on the new man, which after God is created in righteousness and true holiness."*

There also exists a second prophetic picture concerning the ark. In this perspective we must relate back to Enoch, who pictures the Church living by faith, walking with God, then being translated before the wrath of God on the wicked. God has promised the Church that it will be delivered from His future wrath upon the world (1 Thess. 1:10, 5:9, Rom. 5:9-10, and Rev. 3:10). We read in Hebrews 11:5 that Enoch was translated without seeing death. What a beautiful picture of the rapture of the Church (1 Thess. 4:13-18; 1 Cor. 15:51-52). The ark, in this perspective, still represents a safe haven for the faithful, but only a remnant of the Jews (pictured in Noah) are promised safety during the Tribulation Period, according to Revelation 12:6, 12:13-17. Everyone else not worshipping the beast during the Tribulation Period will face death (Rev. 13:15, 20:4), and, according to Revelation 13:7, many Gentiles turning to Christ during that time will die. Then, after this period, there will again be radical changes on the earth (just as after the flood) as a time of peace under the global rule of Christ is realized.

> O Christ, what burdens bowed Thy head! Our load was laid on Thee;
> Thou stoodest in the sinner's stead – To bear all ill for me.
> A Victim led, Thy blood was shed; Now there's no load for me.
> The tempest's awful voice was heard, O Christ, it broke on Thee;
> Thy open bosom was my ward; It bore the storm for me.
> Thy form was scarred, Thy visage marred; Now cloudless peace for me.
>
>   Ann Ross Cousin

The Flood
Genesis 7:1-24

The last verse of Genesis 6 reads, *"Thus did Noah; according to all that God commanded him, so did he."* It is hard to have a much better testimony than that. The evening before the Lord Jesus was crucified He reminded His disciples four times of the importance of obedience (Jn. 14:15, 14:21, 14:23-24, 15:10). And, four times He also tied obedience to His commands as a practical demonstration of their love. Love and obedience cannot be separated from one another. To prove it, Jesus was going to give them and the world an example they would never forget – Calvary. The Lord declared, *"But **that the world may know** that I love the Father; and as the Father gave Me commandment, even so I do"* (Jn. 14:31).

The first verse of Genesis 7 contains the first command of God to *"come"* in the Bible. It is the first gospel invitation – come into the ark and find security and safety from the wrath to come. It is evident by God's communication that He was already in the ark and waiting for Noah to come in, otherwise He would have commanded Noah to "go into the ark." Then, once in the ark, what words in Scripture could possibly describe the security of the believer in Christ more clearly than the words *"the Lord shut him in"* (Gen. 7:16). There was one door, and the hand of God closed it and sealed Noah's family safely within. The opportunity for salvation had come to a close, and only those choosing to come through the door were saved. The Lord Jesus said, *"I am the door, by Me if any man enter in, he shall be saved"* (Jn. 10:9). In verses 28 and 29 of the same chapter, He describes the security of the believer's soul as being in both the hand of His Father and of Himself. It all began with an invitation to "come." Philip used the same invitation to attract Nathanael to the Savior, *"come and see"* (Jn. 1:46). It worked. Nathanael became a disciple of Jesus Christ. On the last page

Seeds of Destiny

of God's Oracle, the Lord uses the word "come" three times to urge all Christians to eagerly look for Him while living for Him, *"Behold I come quickly."* Noah, being warned of God, came!

Do not think that, because Noah and his family were saved from judgment, their lives were easy. There was a lot of work to be done. Since the ark only had one 18-inch window, most of their activities were performed in obscure and gloomy conditions. Why only one small window for such a big ark? Genesis 6:16 directs that the window was to be made "above" – "top side." Perhaps God did not want Noah and his family focusing their attention on the judgment below. He wanted their eyes fixed heavenward as they served day in and day out in the ark that was dimly lit and certainly reeked with various foul odors.

In application for the Christian, God does His work in bringing salvation to us, then we have a charge to work out our salvation (Phil. 2:12). It requires us to make our *"calling and election sure"* so that we do not fall (2 Pet. 1:10). We must practically *"seek those things which are above...set [our] affection on things above"* because we presently *"sit together in heavenly places in Christ Jesus"* (Col. 3:1-2; Eph. 2:6). In light of what God has done and who we are in Christ, we should live radically different from the world even during the darkest of times. Spiritually speaking, this planet is dark, but Christ within the believer is to shine through in order to illuminate and reveal His truth to others (Matt. 5:14-16).

How long were Noah and his family within that stinky, smelly ark anyway? There are slight disagreements separating some events from others, but the following summation will put us in the ballpark of 377 days (over a year). Noah waited in the ark 7 days before the rain. It then rained 40 days, and then the waters receded for 110 days, which allowed the ark to rest on Mt. Ararat. After another 74 days, mountaintops were visible. 40 days later, a raven and a dove were sent out on a reconnaissance mission, then the dove was sent again 7 days later, and again a final time another 7 days later. For another 22 days, the waters receded, and the land dried for another 70 days for a total of 377 days.

Modern man describes his present condition as insignificant and unfallen, but God has shown through judging man in the garden and in the flood that man is indeed fallen, yet loved and thus significant. Certainly a terminal judgment of mankind for rebellion against the

Creator would have been justified, but God's mercy found a way to save man from divine wrath and God's grace offered mankind a new opportunity to please his Creator.

> Grace, grace, God's grace, Grace that will pardon and cleanse within;
> Grace, grace, God's grace, Grace that is greater than all our sin!
>
> Julia Johnston

The Gift of Hope
Genesis 8:1-14

In Genesis 8, man has opportunity to contemplate a time of future ease. The ark finally settled on Mt. Ararat in verse 4, signaling God's rest was near, but not yet attained for *"the dove found no rest for the sole of her foot"* (Gen. 8:9). Then, in the midst of their deliverance, God sent Noah an extraordinary message of hope. It was delivered in the mouth of a dove, which Noah had sent out to fly a reconnaissance mission over the earth. Noah and his family had been tucked away in their gigantic wood box for 278 days. Do you think that they were getting discouraged? Perhaps they were wondering if they would ever walk on dry land again. God knew just what to do. He guided that seeking dove to an olive tree (growing again on resurrection ground) and directed her to bring a message of "resurrected life" back to Noah. It was a message from a tree, and the little olive branch is still used today as an emblem of peace. The Lord Jesus' first words to His disciples after He was raised from the grave were *"peace be unto you"* (Jn. 20:19). No doubt this tiny twig gave Noah and his family hope that their ordeal would be over soon.

In this way, the ark reaches beyond the symbolized judgment of our Lord at Calvary to the blessings of His resurrection. William Lincoln summarizes:

> There seems no reason to doubt that the day the ark rested on the mountain of Ararat is identical with the day on which the Lord rose from the dead. It rested "on the seventeenth day of the seventh month." But by the commandment of the Lord, given at the time of the institution of the feast of the Passover, the seventh month was changed into the first month. Then three days after the Passover, which was on the fourteenth day of the month, the Lord, having passed quite through the waters of judgment, stood in resurrection in

the midst of His disciples, saying "Peace be unto you." They, as well as Himself, had reached the haven of everlasting rest.[1]

There are many such messages of peace and of hope communicated through the use of a tree in Scripture – each speaking of some aspect of the Lord's character or work. In Genesis 22, the wood that Isaac, the beloved son of Abraham, bore up Mt. Moriah gives a glimpse of the Lord, the beloved Son of God, bearing His cross at Calvary. The budding and fruitfulness of Aaron's "dead" rod declared Christ's resurrection from the dead and the newness of life the believer can have in Him. The acacia wood of the Ark of the Covenant reveals the humanity of Christ, while the overlaid gold speaks of His deity. Moses found that, through a tree, the bitter waters of Marah could be made sweet and enjoyed. Likewise, the Christian finds the bitter cup of life's circumstances becomes sweet through the cross of Christ.

Lastly, we are told that God curses everyone that is hung on a tree, and the only Jewish King to ever hang on a tree was Jesus Christ. He hung there on our behalf (Gal. 3:13). Hebrews 9:14 informs us that Christ's offering was accomplished through the power of the Eternal Spirit. Is it a coincidence that the Holy Spirit descended upon the Lord Jesus to commission His ministry in the form of a dove? No. The dove and the olive branch are symbols of peace, and God was using both to picture the peace He would offer mankind through the sacrifice of His Son through the Holy Spirit.

A Christian can only properly proclaim how to have peace with God (Rom. 5:1) if his new nature (as pictured in the clean bird – the dove) is controlling him. Then, he will also experience the peace of God (Phil. 4:9). Our flesh nature (pictured in the raven – an unclean bird) has nothing within itself that can please God (Rom. 7:18) or be used of God for personal benefit. Just as the Holy Spirit in the form of a dove anointed the Lord for ministry to proclaim the truth (Acts 10:38), let us through the power of the Spirit carry the message of peace to others.

Finally, the great day arrived when God spoke unto Noah, *"Go forth of the ark"* (Gen. 8:16), and Noah and his family went forth (Gen. 8:18). The whole of John 10:9 reads, *"I am the door: by Me if any man enter in, he shall be saved, and shall go in and out, and find pasture."*

Seeds of Destiny

The Good Shepherd had guided His sheep to green pasture, and now it was time to "go out" and enjoy the goodness of God.

> Yes, Jesus is the Truth, the Way, that leads you into rest;
> Believe in Him without delay and you are fully blessed.
>
> John Stockton

An Offering and a Promise
Genesis 8:15-22

Noah's world would be radically different than the world he once knew. Oceans were now more extensive than before, while visible land would be less prominent. The first direct visible sunlight and unfiltered solar radiation would now invade man's world. With the thick vapor blanket covering the earth gone, polar caps would form, and seasons would be noticed. This also allowed the present hydrologic system to be established. Solar energy would now draw up water from oceans through evaporation, the wind would transfer this life-sustaining moisture inland to where it would condense into clouds, rain and snow. Now mankind would experience hurricanes, tornadoes, typhoons, and fierce storms of all types.

In Noah's "new world" not much vegetation would be visible at first until sprouting seeds could again bring forth plant life. With the weight of the vaporous canopy that once surrounded the earth now condensed on the earth's surface, the conservation of angular energy would suggest that the earth's rotational speed was slightly increased. Perhaps this explains why a prophetic year throughout the Bible is 360 days, but the earth presently rotates 365.26 times each year. Certainly, many subterranean and volcanic instabilities characterized the early days of Noah's new world.

The day finally came to breathe some fresh air, and God directed Noah and his family to disembark the ark and to lead the animals out of their "hibernation" unto "full life." What would be your first inclination if you had been cooped up with a bunch of smelly animals for a year in a big floating barn? The first order of business would probably be a shower, then perhaps a walk with your spouse to enjoy the abundant life the earth was now boasting.

Seeds of Destiny

That is not what Noah did. His first order of business was to build an altar and worship God. This is the first occurrence of the word "altar" in the Bible and thus presents the appropriate use of an altar throughout Scripture. In Genesis 7, Noah was commanded to bring a pair of animals (male and female) of all the creeping creatures and seven pairs of "clean" beasts and fowls, which would be used for food and sacrifice once their journey was over. Why did Noah erect an altar? What was the purpose? He was thanking God for keeping His word and delivering him and his family from judgment. Noah led his family in worshipping the One who was righteous in judging wickedness, gracious to the faithful, and trustworthy to fulfill His promises.

What did Noah offer to God as a sacrifice? He took of "every" clean animal and bird and offered burnt sacrifices. The Scripture tells us that the ascending smoke was a sweet savor in the nostrils of God. Why? Because, it was an offering that cost Noah something, and the bird and animal sacrifices, as before in the book of Genesis, portrayed God's future sacrifice of His Son on man's behalf. By virtue of God's full satisfaction with Christ's future substitutional sacrifice at Calvary (Isa. 53:10-11), God could also enjoy the offerings of Noah.

Today, we do not offer animals to God as burnt sacrifices because that economy has been put away by the finished work of Christ. There are very few commandments under the new covenant that Christ accomplished and established for the Church. God has given us a great deal of freedom to work out the questionable things of our salvation (Phil. 2:12) and the liberty to praise and worship Him to the extent to which we desire. The Christian should be laboring to give back to God according to the measure of his heart's adoration of the Savior.

Man is required to give God his first fruits: time, finances, and energy. Yet, God desires another sacrifice, it requires labor in Scripture, learning of the beauties of His Son. We carefully arrange what we have learned throughout the week for a sacrifice of adoration to be laid at His feet when the assembly gathers for the Lord's Supper. This is a spiritual activity that every man, woman, and child should engage in, though not all will share audibly. In this way, the spiritual worship of all God's people, who have come in the beauty of holiness and with an offering, mingles together and ascends to the nostrils of God. One brother, guided by the Spirit of God, leads the assembly audibly to align and center everyone's thoughts on one thing at a time. This verbal role has been given to the men in the assembly (1 Cor. 14:34, 11:7; 1 Tim. 2:8-12) as part of God's order for the Church. Yet, the Christian assembly joins together in offering sacrifices of praise and in song (Heb. 13:15).

Noah kept those animals alive for over a year only to sacrifice them to God. Truly it was an offering that cost Noah and his family something. Then, God responded by giving Noah a visible sign to accompany His new covenant with him. The rainbow would be a token of God's promise never to judge the earth again by a flood.

After the flood, many things in man's world changed. It would rain regularly, there would be direct sunlight, and man would eat meat (but not the blood). The earth would have seasons and polar caps. The flood explains why mammals, including great mammoths, have been found in what are now Arctic regions, some of which were frozen so fast that plants from warmer climates were still in their mouths. The flood had radically changed the earth!

The aftermath of the flood brought changes to mankind, too. God made man responsible for ensuring those who murdered others would be put to death. Civil authority and human government were commenced. The life span of man became much shorter. Instead of living 900 years, man's time upon the earth was brought to approximately 200 years in length in just five generations.

Not only was human life dynamically changed, but the animal kingdom realized its own changes also. Henry Morris comments on these radical changes:

> Lack of competition permitted animal populations to multiply very rapidly; so there was much incentive for the different groups to keep pressing forward until they found an ecological niche for which they were more suited than other groups. These conditions (rapid multiplication, small inbreeding populations, rapidly changing environments) were ideal to permit rapid variation to take place in each kind (not evolution, but rather opportunity for the originally created variational potential latent in the genetic system of each kind to become expressed openly in distinct varieties). Consequently, different varieties (or even species, and perhaps genera, in some

Seeds of Destiny

cases, as arbitrarily defined by modern taxonomists) could rapidly develop and become established in appropriate environments.[1]

Noah must have felt much like 15th and 16th century explorers setting foot on uncharted soil for the first time. Noah stepped off the ark into a new creation – a world very different than the one he knew. He was witnessing God's resurrection power. Every budding tree and blooming flower would testify of God's covenant with Noah and indeed be a "shadow" of the new life a believer has in Christ – a life to be lived out for Christ, for it is His very life. Vibrant color and divine splendor now sprang forth from what was old and dead. *"Therefore, if any man be in Christ, he is a new creature* [creation]*; old things are passed away; behold, all things are become new"* (2 Cor. 5:17).

> Only one life to offer – take it, dear Lord, I pray;
> Nothing from Thee withholding, Thy will I now obey;
>
> Avis Christiansen

Human Government
Genesis 9:1-19

Chapter 9 initiates another major section in Genesis. We will diverge from the narrative for a moment to highlight some of these important divisions in Genesis. Covenants, dispensational truths, deaths of key people, and the identification of "new generations" all cluster homogeneously to create distinct divisions within the book of Genesis. These divisions often begin with a covenant, which is defined as "a promise or vow of the strongest nature," to form a dispensation. "Dispensation" is defined as an economy of revealed truth that God reveals to man and holds him accountable to. Man eventually rebels against what God requires and, therefore, earns God's righteous judgment. Yet, God uses the very failures of men to offer a wider blessing to humanity. In this way, God is shown to be holy and gracious, and He obtains all the glory for man's salvation. A covenant in which God's blessing is contingent upon man's obedience is called a **conditional** covenant, whereas a covenant in which God would bless despite man's failures is called an **unconditional** covenant. Both are contained in the book of Genesis. These major divisions normally begin after the death of a key person and with the announcement phrase *"These are the generations ..."* signifying that God is working with a new group of people and in a new and different way.

Four major divisions are noted in Genesis:
Innocence: Began through the Edenic Covenant (Gen. 1:28-30, 2:16-17), which was a conditional covenant – man was given one command – he could not eat of the "tree of the knowledge of good and evil" or else he would die. If he obeyed, he would live in fellowship with God in the garden. Man was created "innocent" (Eccl. 7:29). He disobeyed the command, so spiritual and

Seeds of Destiny

physical death came upon him. Note this division begins with the phrase *"These are the generations of the heavens and the earth when they* (Adam and the woman) *were created"* (Gen. 2:4) and closes with the spiritual death of mankind and the physical death of righteous Abel.

Moral Responsibility: Began through a covenant with Adam (Gen. 3:14-19). Although there were curses placed on the man and woman as a result of their fall, God promised that the seed of the woman (Christ) would defeat the serpent (Satan) – the one that had caused man to fall. This covenant is unconditional, and the curses would be lifted when completed. During this interval of human history (from the fall to the flood), man's conscience had been invoked for the first time at the fall (Gen. 3:7, 22; Rom. 2:15) and would continue to reveal right and wrong to him. But, man did not obey his conscience, the world became more and more wicked, and God had to judge the world through a flood. This division begins with the phrase "the generations of Adam" and ends with the death of the wicked Antediluvians destroyed in the flood.

Human Government: God made an unconditional covenant with Noah. God promised not destroy the earth again with water and gave man the power of government. Man was allowed to eat meat, told to repopulate the earth, and given the authority to impose capital punish (Gen. 9:5-6). In the dispensation of Moral Responsibility, no instruction for capital punishment was issued; thus Cain was not put to death for his murder of Abel. Instructions for one dispensation cannot be brought into another dispensation without marring God's program for that dispensation (unless permitted by Scripture). Until now, man was not permitted to judge deeds of the flesh. Previously, there had been violence without constraint, but no civil law to mediate. God intervened and imposed justice through one stroke of judgment – the flood. Murders in the previous dispensation were not punished. Cain was not put to death for his crime but marked by God and sentenced to wandering aimlessly in the world. Now, God would require mankind to put to death those murdering another. Would man be capable of ruling himself? No, man gathered together instead of obeying God's command to spread out and repopulate the earth and, in further rebellion, made a tower to reach heaven because they desired to be like God. God responded by confounding their languages. This division begins by the phrase "These are the generations of Noah" and ends with the overthrow of the tower of Babel in Genesis 11. This chapter also records the births and deaths of Shem's descendants and the death of Terah, Abraham's father.

Promise: God made an unconditional covenant with Abraham, which had conditional personal blessings with Abraham (Gen. 12:1-3, 13:14-17, 15:1-5, 17:1-8): He promised to give Abraham a special son of promise, to make a nation from him, to give him a land, and to bless all families of the earth. He also pledged to curse his enemies, to bless his friends, and to have a special relationship with him. God called Abraham out of idolatry to be the father of a nation – His own people. Although Abraham would have a few lapses of faith, which brought personal consequences, he was, in general, a great man of faith, obeyed God's call, and obtained His promise. This division begins with the phrase "these are the generations of Terah," who also left Ur with Abram his son, and ends with the giving of the Law in the book of Exodus.

If God makes an unconditional promise to man, He is bound by the power of His name to keep it. In this chapter, He gave man a token of His covenant with Noah, the rainbow. It is a product of both storm and light and is hung in heaven for all to see and appreciate. Thus, the rainbow is a portrait of God's unfailing grace. To the believer God's grace and peace settles our hearts during life's storms – for He will not test us above what we are able to bear without providing the way of escape (1 Cor. 10:13). To the unbeliever, the rainbow is an invitation to find peace with God and escape the wrath to come. *"For the grace of God that bringeth salvation hath appeared to all men"* (Tit. 2:11).

Seeds of Destiny

The rainbow is a symbol that the believer will enjoy for eternity, for we read in Revelation 4:3 that one encircles the throne of God in heaven. The circle, or a ring, represents eternity – it continues without end. Therefore, the circular rainbow about God's throne is an eternal testimony that God always keeps His word and fulfills His promises! Truly God is faithful! How faithful is God? Despite knowing that *"the imagination of man's heart is evil from his youth"* He promised, *"neither will I again smite any more every thing living, as I have done"* (Gen. 8:21). And, though we have grieved Him severely throughout human history, He has kept that promise even to this day.

> Fill all my vision, Saviour, I pray,
> Let me see only Jesus today;
> Though thro' the valley Thou leadest me,
> Thy fadeless glory encompasseth me.
> Fill all my vision, let naught of sin,
> Shadow the brightness shining within.
> Let me see only Thy blessed face,
> Feasting my soul on Thy infinite grace.
>
> Avis Christiansen

Two More Sins
Genesis 9:20-29

Just as the sin of Adam affected all of humanity, so did the sin of Noah in Genesis 9. *"He planted a vineyard, and he drank of the wine and was drunken, and he was uncovered within his tent"* (Gen. 9:20-21). The abuse of alcohol is forbidden throughout Scripture (Deut. 21:20-21; 1 Cor. 6:10; Eph. 5:18). Man is not to be subdued by creation but to have dominion over it (Gen. 1:28). Through substance abuse, man allows creation to control him. In drunkenness, man loses control of rational thinking and commits offensive acts against his conscience and his God. Genesis records several testimonies of the ills of drunkenness: Noah's nakedness, Lot's cave experience in which he fathered two nations from his own daughters, and likely, Jacob's wedding feast which led him to marry the wrong girl.

It should be noted that, if man had written the Bible, the record of "heroes of the faith" would not have included such blunders as we have before us in the life of Noah. But, the Holy Spirit moved men of old to record such failures for at least two purposes. First, *"For whatsoever things were written aforetime (in earlier times) were written for our learning"* (Rom. 15:4). We need to learn from others' past mistakes, then seek not to repeat such errors in judgment. Secondly, the tendency of the human heart is toward hero worship. Biographers and autobiographers often gloss over the behavioral defects and failures of their subject characters. This is not so in the Bible – God wants the true disposition of the human heart revealed so that all may see there is none perfect, no not one!

We never read of Noah having a drinking problem before the flood. Why is that? Because Noah was engrossed in pleasing the Lord by building Him an ark. *"By much slothfulness the building decayeth; and*

Seeds of Destiny

through idleness of the hands the house droppeth through" (Eccl. 10:18).

Many of God's people have fallen into sin because their hands were idle. King David had acquired enormous prosperity and had nearly vanquished all his enemies. It was now springtime, the appropriate time to capture the last Ammonite stronghold of Rabbah and have total control of the kingdom. But, instead of engaging God's enemy in battle, David tarried in Jerusalem (2 Sam. 11:1). His idleness made him restless – he wasn't sleeping well. One evening he arose from bed, took a casual stroll on his roof, and per chance beheld beautiful Bathsheba bathing. He was given over to his own lusts and took her (Uriah's wife), and committed adultery. If David had been attending to the Lord's business, he would have been tired and enjoyed a good night's rest; Bathsheba would have been nowhere in the vicinity to view. He was tempted because he chose to be idle.

The Prophet Ezekiel informs us that the perverse city of Sodom had an *"abundance of idleness"* (Ezek. 16:49). Let God's people be busy about the Lord's work and escape temptation. Solomon eloquently warns of this evil, *"Whatsoever thy hand findeth to do, do it with thy might; for there is no work, nor device, nor knowledge, nor wisdom, in the grave, whither thou goest"* (Eccl. 9:10).

Noah was granted a clean start and a new creation to govern, but he failed. Thankfully, failures are never final unless we make them so – God wants us to succeed. *"For a just man falleth seven times and riseth up again, but the wicked shall fall into mischief"* (Prov. 24:16). It is not falling that makes one a failure; it is remaining submersed in your failures that makes you a failure (staying down). The Prophet Ezekiel records twice that Noah was a righteous man (Ezek. 14:14, 20), and the writer of Hebrews describes him as a man of faith (Heb. 11:7). Thankfully for Noah, God did not see his nakedness, for divine grace had covered all his sins, and clothed his body with a clean white linen robe of righteousness – the positional righteousness of the future Savior. Noah was a righteous man that found grace in the sight of the Lord and was accredited a righteous standing before God. Ham, however, like Cain, would follow his own way and never know the blessings of being forgiven and declared righteous by a Holy God.

In the case of Noah, his youngest son Ham (Gen. 9:24) thought that dad's nakedness was somewhat amusing and sought to use the circumstance to demean the authority of his father (an authority whom God had placed over Ham). It is "fools" who *"make a mock of sin"* (Prov. 14:9). However, Noah's other two sons, Shem and Japheth, acted righteously and covered their father's nakedness in his drunken stupor. After Noah recovered and understood what had happened, he spoke a prophecy concerning his sons. Ham's son, Canaan, would be a servant of his brothers; Japheth would be greatly enlarged and enjoy fellowship with Shem, and Shem would enjoy a close relationship (religious privileges) with his Creator the Lord God.

This prophecy has already been fulfilled. The descendants of Ham's son were the Canaanites. They were an immoral and perverse people (Lev. 18:3, 27) who were greatly destroyed by the Israelites (the descendants of Shem) under the leadership of Joshua (Deut. 20:17-18). Some, like the Gibeonites, became slaves to the Israelites as a result of their trickery (Josh. 9:16-27). Those who survived the Canaan Conquest were levied a tribute of bond service by King Solomon, according to 1 Kings 9:20-21. In general, Japheth settled to the north and greatly expanded. Shem located in the midpoint of the globe, and Ham in the south. As Noah acknowledged, it would be through the line of Shem that God's Messiah would come. This is one of hundreds of prophecies concerning the Lord Jesus spoken to us by dozens of prophets over the span of several millennia. God's Word is sure! Doctor Luke documents the fact that Jesus Christ was born of the line of Shem (Lk. 3:36).

> Come, Holy Ghost, for moved by Thee
> The prophets wrote and spoke;
> Unlock the truth, Thyself the key,
> Unseal the sacred book – [Christ to see].
>
> John Calvin

Seeds of Destiny

A Rebel
Genesis 10:1-11:9

We pause within the genealogies of Ham to make mention of a man named "Nimrod," whose name means "rebel." One particular ancient legend records that Nimrod was conceived by a sunbeam, and therefore was obliged to marry his mother. It is from Nimrod that false religion and pagan worship can be traced. Even the 1st century BC Jewish Historian Josephus regarded Nimrod as the father of heathenism. He is accredited with being the father of Babylonian and Assyrian pagan cultures which began to oppose God in Genesis 10 and will continue to do so through Revelation 18 when Babylon – the mother of harlots – is finally destroyed. This is the great day for which all the hallelujahs in heaven have been reserved according to Revelation 19:1-6. For it is upon this day that all anti-God humanistic agendas will be eradicated. Nimrod foreshadows the last great world ruler – the anti-Christ who during the Tribulation Period leads the world in vehement rebellion against God. Yet, the Lord Jesus at His Second Advent to the earth will destroy this vicious enemy of humanity and of God personally (Rev. 17:14, 19:20).

Genesis 10:10 records that the Babylonians called their new kingdom *Babel*, which meant in their estimation they were "the gate of God." Through human achievement, they believed they could obtain divinity, could reach God and could be as gods. Nimrod's rebellious quest for divinity would hinge on his success in constructing a tower to bridge earth and heaven and close the eminence gap between man and God. Obviously, such a tower would be an affront against God, who is holy and separated from sinful man. Any attempt to bridge the distance between a Holy God and fallen mankind must be righteous in nature and God-ordained. Only the cross of Christ can bridge the gap between fallen humanity and holy deity.

Man was disobeying God's command to spread out and repopulate the earth. Instead, a large part of humanity was dwelling together in Shinar to erect a huge tower to mock God. Notice in mankind's declaration of pride in Genesis 11:3-4 that there are six "us" and "we" terms to describe what man will do by his own power and intellect. The number "six" represents "man's number" throughout Scripture (Rev. 13:18). God intervened in this human effort to help them refocus on repopulating the earth as He had commanded. This was accomplished by confounding the one and only language that mankind had at that time for until then *"the whole earth was of one language and of one speech"* (Gen. 11:1). Perhaps this was the Hebrew language as the names recorded earlier in Genesis are Hebrew in origin. If this is true, it is likely that the descendants of Shem, or at least some of Shem's descendants, were not involved with the Shinar rebellion. In Genesis 10, Shem was identified as the father of *Eber*. It is likely that the term *Hebrew*, which is applied to Abram in Genesis 14:13, is derived from *Eber*.

James G. Murphy notes that God utilized two terms to emphasize that all the known world spoke only one language:

> *Of one lip, and one stock of words.* In the table of nations the term "tongue" was used to signify what is here expressed by two terms. This is not undesigned. The two terms are not synonymous or parallel, as they form the parts of one compound predicate. "One stock of words," then, we conceive, naturally indicates the matter, the substance, or material of language. This was one and the same to the whole race. The term "lip," which is properly one of the organs of articulation, is on the other hand, used to denote the form, that is, the manner, of speaking; the mode of using and connecting the matter of speech; the system of laws by which the inflections and derivations of a language are conducted. This also was one throughout the human family. Thus the sacred writer has expressed the unity of language among mankind, not by a single term as before, but, with a view to his present purpose, by a combination of terms expressing the two elements which go to constitute every organic reality.[1]

Seeds of Destiny

With one mighty act God stifled the noise and commotion of the building program and dispersed the nations. This event had been previously prophesied by the birth of Peleg, in the same fashion Methuselah's birth announced the forthcoming flood. The Bible references the meaning of Peleg's name "for in his days was the earth divided" (Gen. 10:25). Peleg, was born to Eber 101 years after the flood (assuming no gaps in the Genesis 11 genealogies). Peleg's name literally means "division." The division of the people occurred in Peleg's lifetime and, thus, no sooner than 101 years after the flood.

In Genesis 11:9, a play on words is noted in the Hebrew language. The word *babal* is alluded to which means "confusion." What the Babylonians had previously called "the gate to God" the Hebrews referred to as "confusion." Nothing less than a deceived mind embedded with "the lie" of Satan (Jn. 8:44) would cause man to think he could become as God. Paganism finds its roots in Nimrod at Babel. It is noted that our English word *Babylon* is simply the word *Babel* with a Greek ending. After humanity was dispersed, each nation possessed their own borders and language (Gen. 10:5, 20, and 31). In all, Genesis 10 identifies the birth of fifty-eight individual nations through Shem, Ham and Japheth.

God confused man's languages because of their rebellion, but three millennia later, He would give the ability of speaking different languages to obedient believers who were waiting in Jerusalem, as instructed by Christ, for the coming of the Holy Spirit. On the Feast of Pentecost, the awaiting believers were baptized into Christ to form His body the Church and were filled and gifted to declare the good news of Christ in ten distinct languages (Acts 2:4-11). The foreigners visiting Jerusalem for the feast were able to hear the gospel message in their own tongue. For the Jews, the tongues signaled that forthcoming judgment was near (Isa. 28:11-12; Deut. 28:49; Jer. 5:15). In both these situations, "the confusion of" or "understanding of" languages caused the message of God's greatness to be carried over all the earth!

Concerning languages, a testimony of God's abundant grace is foreseen in Revelation 7:9. People speaking *every* known tongue will be about the throne praising God forever and ever.

So, as with the judgment of the flood, we see God using another punishment for man's rebellious actions in Genesis 11, which serves to propagate His name and message and, in the end, bring Him greater glory. It is God's way – aren't you glad!

> Love brought my Savior here to die on Calvary,
> For such a sinful wretch as I, How can it be?
> Love bridged the gulf between me and heaven, Taught me to pray;
> I am redeemed, set free, forgiven – Love found a way.
>
> > Avis B. Christiansen

A Pagan Named Abram
Genesis 11:10-30

The Book of Genesis may be divided into two equal parts, with the juncture of the two divisions meshing at Genesis 12. The first portion begins with God's perfectly ordered creation and concludes with the righteous judgment of a responsible race that has disordered creation through sin. These judgments include the curses upon our first parents, the destruction of a thoroughly wicked society by the flood and the confusion of human language at Babel. Instead of man responding to God's discipline in a positive way, the vast majority remained rebellious. But, praise be to God; He always leaves Himself a witness on earth to be a testimony of His grace and goodness (Acts 14:17; Rom. 11:5; 1 Kings 19:18). Abel, Enoch, Noah, Melchizedek, and Job, to name a few, were faithful to this calling.

For over 400 years, God suffered a pagan world in silence. Then suddenly the God of glory appeared to a man named Abram. Until Genesis 12, God had been dealing with mankind as a whole, now He would focus His sovereign dealings in the life of one man. Through Abram would come both the written Word of God and the Living Word of life. Despite mankind's overall propensity to rebel, God would bestow mercy again to humanity by making another covenant. On this occasion, it would not be made with humanity in general, but with one man named Abram and his seed. In Genesis 9, God made a conditional pledge to all humanity. However, human conscience and government were insufficient agents to ensure morality; thus, mankind forfeited the blessings of God. Now God would bring an unconditional promise of blessing through one man to all the families of the earth (Gen. 12:3). The blessing would ultimately come through Christ and would be imparted to all those who would embrace God's revealed truth by faith.

Devotions in Genesis

Genesis 12 marks the chronological halfway point through the Old Testament (This assumes connectivity of genealogies in Genesis 5 and 11.). Sir Robert Anderson's calculations place God's covenant with Abram at 2055 BC, exactly in the center between "creation" in 4141 BC and the crucifixion of Christ in 32 AD.[1] He further notes that there is also 430 years symmetry on either side of the covenant with Abram, which spans to the flood (2485 BC) and the giving of the law to Moses on Mt. Sinai (1625 BC). Whether these dates are exact or not, only God knows, but the dates are good approximations in the least. What these dates do illustrate is that the divine covenant with Abram is the center hub of the Old Testament that all other human activities in accordance with God's purpose in time rotate about.

What do we know about Abram? From Joshua 24:2, we learn that Abram's family were idol worshippers. Consequently, Abram is described in Deuteronomy 26:5 as *"a Syrian ready to perish."* Though an idol worshipper ready to perish, Stephen informs us in Acts 7, that the *"God of Glory"* appeared to Abram in Ur and called Abram away from Ur to a land He would give him. The reference to the Lord being the *"God of Glory"* is stated only twice in Scripture. Once speaking of God's authority over creation (Ps. 29:3) and once when God spoke to Abram. Why did God pick a man tainted by idol worship for His covenant? God had to choose somebody – He chose Abram (Isa. 51:1-2). God rules over His creation in whatever way He deems to be the best. God made a sovereign choice to bring forth the Messiah through Abram. Thus far in the book of Genesis, we have had the beginning of the world through creation, the beginning of man through Adam, the new beginning for man after the flood through Noah, and now we have the beginning of a chosen nation (Israel) in Abram. So, God called a pagan named Abram to leave his country, to separate from his kindred, and to go forth to inherit a land he had never seen.

Did Abram have any choice in the covenant God made with him? Yes. God did not force him to separate from his kindred and to leave Ur or Haran. God did not physically constrain Abram from worshipping his false gods. It is, therefore, possible to have human choice and human responsibility "within" sovereign choice, which already foreknows the human choice. It is through God's foreknowledge and sovereign control that He then brings the greatest blessing despite human choice.

111

Seeds of Destiny

Passengers may have freedom to move about an ocean liner steaming across the Atlantic Ocean, but they have no control of the ship's destination. Yet, they have freedom to purchase a ticket and board the ship or to jump overboard if they desire.

God's end plan cannot be changed. His great plan of redemption shall not be spoiled, for it was completely and thoroughly fashioned before the foundation of the world with all future failures of man known to God and with the end result of "son placing" of the faithful guaranteed for eternity.

God made an unconditional covenant to bring blessing to the world and for Abram to be an instrument of salvation, without making a covenant of salvation with him. Because Abram believed God – God could use him as a fit and faithful example of a pilgrim, elevate his name among men, forge a nation from him, and award him a land of his own. The mystery here lies in the recesses of God's mind, for certainly He foreknew of Abram's faith and proper choice, yet chose him as a vessel of mercy and a tool of righteousness. The choice of Abram to believe God's revealed truth and to reject the social pull of Ur accomplished for him what it does for an individual today when they believe the gospel and reject the wisdom and toxic influence of the world. Namely, it makes him a worshipper of God and a citizen of heaven and, thus, a pilgrim and a stranger on earth as God's witness. Abram's life characterizes that of a Christian who embraces and enjoys the cross but loathes the world.

Did Abram have a choice in obeying God in order to receive God's blessing personally? Consider the following references:

Get thee out of thy country...and I will make thee a great nation (Gen. 12:1-2).

God told Abram to *walk before Him and be thou perfect* (Gen. 17:1).

God told Abraham (name is changed from Abram) and his children to keep his covenant (Gen. 17:9)

For I know him, that he will command his children and his household after him, and they shall keep the way of the Lord, to do [righteousness and justice]; that the Lord may bring upon Abraham that which he hath spoken of him (Gen. 18:19).

Would the Messiah come from Abram's line? Absolutely. Would Abram be blessed? If he demonstrated faith in God's Word by obedience, God would bestow favor upon him. God made an unconditional covenant with conditional blessing to Abram. We step softly now, for we are nearing the sacred and mysterious realm of God's sovereignty over creation and human responsibility to God. Both doctrines are clearly taught in Scripture, yet the human mind cannot fully harmonize these truths. To us these truths are like two parallel rails of train track, yet in the distance these seemingly distinct realities converge with God. The lack of our complete understanding of these two tenets should not divide God's people, but unify them in reverential awe.

The Christian's existence is marked by this same mysterious contrast. We are commanded to be filled with the Holy Spirit (Eph. 5:18), but Spirit filling is clearly a sovereign act of God. Spirit filling of believers occurs while they are submitting to God's revealed will, thereby ensuring he or she is an available vessel to be filled (see Acts 1:4-14 with 2:1-4, Acts 4:29 with 4:31-32). We are commanded to walk in the good deeds that God has ordained (Eph. 2:10). For these good works to be accomplished, which God has already planned for us, we must continue walking in the light of revealed truth (1 Jn. 1:5-7). Peter acknowledges this apparent mystery: *"Elect according to the foreknowledge of God the Father, through sanctification of the Spirit, unto obedience and sprinkling of the blood of Jesus Christ: Grace unto you, and peace, be multiplied"* (1 Pet. 1:2) and *"Wherefore the rather, brethren, give diligence to make your calling and election sure: for if ye do these things, ye shall never fall"* (2 Pet. 1:10). The Apostle Paul echoes the same message in 2 Timothy 1:9. Not only has God saved us, but also He has called us; it is *"a holy calling ... according to His own purpose."* God "designs," but man is presented a choice in "doing." The conclusion: Let us be trusting, obedient, and available. The Master has an intended purpose, and He will, as already determined, use our availability to further His glory.

> Dear Lord and Father of mankind, Forgive our foolish way!
> Reclothe us in our rightful mind; In purer lives Thy service find,
> In deeper reverence, praise.
>
> John Whittier

Seeds of Destiny

No More Delays
Genesis 11:31-32

It took tremendous faith for Abram to leave his home, land, inheritance, friends and family and seek a God who revealed Himself only once. Yet, that one exposure to the God of Glory compelled Abram to seek God his entire life. Abram is spoken of as a friend of God (Isa. 41:8; Jas. 2:23), the Father of all spiritual seed (Rom. 4:11-12, 9:6-7), a great man of faith (Heb. 11:8), and a stranger and pilgrim while on earth (Heb. 11:13). F. W. Grant observes the connection of Abram's faith to his lifelong pilgrimage:

> The life of Abraham is the well-known pattern-life of faith, as far as the Old Testament could furnish this. It connects, as already noticed, in the closest way, with the story of Noah which precedes it, and alone makes it possible. For the essential characteristic of the life of faith is strangership, but this founded upon citizenship elsewhere. Faith dwells in the unseen, substantiating to itself things hoped for. This is exemplified in Abram, called to Canaan, his possession in hope alone. He dwells there, but in tabernacles, the bringing together of two things typically – the heavenly calling and its earthly consequence.[1]

Abram is recognized for exchanging the known for the unknown, but he was not a perfect man and, in fact, suffered, like we all do, as a result of wrong personal choices. God used him despite his failures – no one is perfect but God. So let us be encouraged by his faith and learn too from his mistakes.

Though Abram obeyed God and left his country, he did not obey God's command to separate from his kindred. This was Abram's first mistake – partial obedience necessitates **disobedience in part**. There would be repercussions for bringing family members other than his

Devotions in Genesis

wife along with him. There was a reason God commanded Abram to come alone. First of all, His covenant was with Abram. Secondly, he did not want other pagans along to influence His chosen man to return to idolatry or pagan thinking. Thirdly, God did not want Abram to rely on human strength during his "wilderness experience." This would be counter-productive in maturing Abram's faith in the God of Glory.

Apparently, Terah, Abram's father assumed the leadership position in the family's departure from Ur as Genesis 11:31 informs us that *"Terah took Abram, his son, and Lot,...and they went forth...and they came unto Haran, and dwelt there."* Relevant also is that somehow Terah knew that he had been chosen to keep the patriarchal records received from Shem. God would use these records to document the Messianic line of Christ through Seth, Shem, and Abram. He completes this assignment in Genesis 11:27. *"These are the generations of Terah."* Previously, the Bible has signalled the dawning of a new dispensation by recording a father's age at the time of his first son's birth and then the names of all his sons. Genesis 5:32 records the age of Noah and his three son's names. Likewise Terah's age and the names of his three sons are recorded in Genesis 11:26.

Abram's second mistake was **delayed** obedience, which in effect is "disobedience." God had called Abram to a land and to leave his kindred, yet his father and his nephew Lot and his wife Sarai traveled with him some 600 miles from Ur to Haran. His father was too old to travel any further, so their movement was checked. It is noted that Nahor, the older brother of Abram, seems to have later followed to this same point and settled. Based on Sir Robert Anderson's chronology, Abram likely lived in Haran four to five years (accounting 430 years between flood and the Abrahamic covenant). Matthew Henry calculates Abram dwelled five years in Haran and then summarizes the practical lesson of Haran for us all.

> Haran [Terah's son] died in Ur, before the happy removal of the family out of that idolatrous country. It concerns us to hasten out of our natural state, lest death surprise us in it. We here read of Abram's departure out of Ur of the Chaldees, with his father Terah, his nephew Lot, and the rest of his family, in obedience to the call of God. This chapter leaves them about mid-way between Ur and Canaan, where they dwelt till Terah's death. Many reach to Charran, and yet fall

Seeds of Destiny

short of Canaan; they are not far from the kingdom of God, and yet never come thither.[2]

Oddly enough, Terah's name (Abram's father) means "delay," and "Haran" means "parched." The message from the names is a simple one – when a believer has "delayed" obedience, he suffers the loss of spiritual satisfaction, and his soul is left "parched." Abram got delayed in the world because of the pull of human relationships.

The Lord Jesus once rebuked a man who wanted to bury his father before leaving home and following Him (Matt. 8:21-22). Perhaps, God's second call to Abram (in Haran) was to admonish His servant in the same way.

Interestingly, God did not reveal himself to Abram again until he had obeyed Him and had journeyed to the land God had promised him (Gen. 12:7). God spoke to Abram a second time at Haran, but did not appear to him again until his faith had been proven by complete obedience. Faith without works is dead being alone (Jas. 2:17). We are saved by grace through faith alone (Eph. 2:8), but faith never stands alone (Jas. 2:20). This faith aspect of man's obedience and God's disclosure is seen throughout Scripture. On this subject Herbert Taylor offers the following warning to Christians:

> One of the great mistakes of this age is the endeavor to worship God by those who have never seen Him by faith; such must of necessity worship an unknown God, and try to serve One whose blessings they have never opened their hearts to receive. It is certain we can only give out praise to God, and testify for Him, when He has first given to us; otherwise all must be from ourselves, and being ourselves corrupt, all must be corruption, death, and sin. It is like pumping at a dry well; the spring must be there; then the clear sparkling water will flow freely enough.[3]

The timing of God's appearance to Abram was in direct response to Abram's obedience. Abram discovered that there were Canaanites in the land that God had given him (Gen. 12:6). God appeared to Abram to ensure his focus remained on Him and not on the difficulties ahead. Let the Christian walk by faith in full obedience to Christ, and let Christ be the only vision through the difficult course of life.

The Lord Jesus made this promise to His disciples the night before He was crucified, *"He that hath My commandments, and keepeth them, he it is that loveth Me; and he that loveth Me shall be loved of My Father, and I will love him, and will manifest Myself to him"* (Jn. 14:21). If we love the Lord, we should show Him so by trusting in His word and obeying it, knowing full well that He will show us more of Himself in our lives. Do you want to know God more deeply and His plan for your life? "Trust and obey for there is no other way!" Let us not languish between submission and having things our own way.

    When it is good vs. evil or right vs. wrong, neutrality is a sin.

                              Whitson Seaman

Seeds of Destiny

The Promise of a New World
Genesis 12:1-5

The call of Abram was a separating call. *"Get thee out of thy country, and from thy kindred, and from thy father's house."* He was commanded to forsake the political world – *"thy country,"* the social world – *"thy kindred,"* and perhaps the most endearing, the domestic world – *"thy father's house."* Certainly, he had forsaken his country, most of his kindred, but his father's house had been an unfortunate snare to his spiritual journey. Would Abram trust God and leave Haran? Or would he be delayed longer still? After the death of his father, Terah, Abram resumes his pilgrimage to Canaan. Though Abram had tarried in Haran without God's consent, Abram had not been totally idle there, for he had gained "souls" (Gen. 12:5). Abram had new converts! These individuals, most likely servants, would follow him to a new land and embrace the one true God, Abram's God. Wherever you find yourself believer, be a lampstand for the Lord, so others may be freed from darkness. Abram "brought" or "bought" others, so they too might know the "God of Glory."

What was Abram promised if He trusted God and left Haran? First, that He would father a great nation – incredible considering he had no children. Secondly, though he would be a total stranger in Canaan, God would exalt His name there, and thirdly, God would bestow him the title deed to the whole territory. But most importantly, Abram was promised that he would be a blessing to all families of the earth. This promise was not explained to Abram, but we now know from Luke 3:23-38 that God had plotted an ancestry route through the corridors of time that would connect Abram and the Messiah.

Most of this covenant has been fulfilled. The Jewish people today give testimony of a nation God raised up through the miraculous birth of Isaac. The story of Abraham (as Abram is later called) offering Isaac

Devotions in Genesis

is a well-known children's story today within Jewish and Christian spheres and even some secular circles. Was his name made great? God inspired the prophets of old to record his name in twenty-seven books of the Bible. Today, approximately 0.2 percent of the world population is Jewish, nearly 20 percent is Islamic, and about 33 percent profess Christianity. Thus, more than half of the present world population would both recognize and respect Abram (Abraham) as a man of faith.

Are all families of the world blessed through Abram? Through the finished work of Christ, a descendent of Abraham, the opportunity for salvation is offered to all mankind (Jn. 3:16; 1 Jn. 2:2; 2 Pet. 3:9), and indeed John acknowledges that there will be some saved of every nation, people, kindred (extend family) and tongue (Rev. 7:9).

But what about the land, has that portion of the covenant been accomplished? The land promised to Abram and his descendants has never been fully realized. Even during the glorious reigns of Kings David and Solomon, Israel never occupied more than about a tenth (approx. 30,000 square miles) of the land that God gave Abram according to Genesis 15:18-21. The eastern boundary of this land is the river Euphrates, which runs through central Iraq today. So, although the nation of Israel is partially back in the Promised Land that has been brought back by a sword (Ezek. 38:8), they do not inhabit the full portion God issued Abram. We understand the "literal" fulfillment of this to be future, after the Jews have turned back to Jesus Christ whom they crucified and received Him as their Messiah (Zech. 12:10; Rom. 11:26-32). So, in the figurative sense of future fulfillment, Abram did obtain *"the land."*

The very call of Abram separated him from the present world unto another world. The God of Glory had brought Abram into the glory of God – a world of fellowship far beyond the temporal reality. Stephen acknowledges this citizenship transition in his sermon to the Sanhedrin (Acts 7). The journey between worlds commences with the God of Glory appearing to man (Acts 7:2) and ends with a Man – the Lord Jesus – present in the glory of God (Acts 7:55). It is to this world mankind is beckoned. And like Abram, those responding to the "call" must forsake the political, social, and domestic links with that which is corrupt and temporary in exchange for that which is spiritual and eternal. Of this world, Abram tasted while on earth and inherited in death.

Seeds of Destiny

God promised His preserving care while Abram dwelled in this outside place. Hamilton Smith comments, "He [Abraham] may indeed have to face opposition and trial, for it is often true that *'he that departeth from evil maketh himself a prey'* (Isa. 59:15). But God says to the separated man, *'I will...curse him that curseth thee.'* The separated man is preserved from many a trial that overtakes the believer who remains in association with the world." [1]

> There's a land that is fairer than day, and by faith we can see it afar;
> For the Father waits over the way to prepare us a dwelling place there.
> We shall sing on that beautiful shore the melodious songs of the blest,
> And our spirits shall sorrow no more, not a sigh for the blessing of rest.
>
> Sanford Bennett

The Tent and the Altar
Genesis 12:6-9

Abram had a work associated with the land God had given him – for there were Canaanites living there (Gen. 12:6). God cursed Canaan, the son of Ham because of his disrespect to his father, Noah (Gen. 9:25). God was to bless Abram in a land full of cursed pagans. Eventually, these pagans were either to be annihilated or to be driven out by Abram's descendants. God uses such difficult circumstances to train His children and develop their faith. Today, believers are blessed with natural abilities, spiritual gifts, and possessions for the work of evangelizing those under the curse of sin, to stand as a bulwark against evil, and to edify the Church. Keeping the right perspective on why we have what we have will promote humility and abundant joy while we serve the Lord.

Abram maintained the proper disposition concerning the land promised him but not yet possessed. He continued to trust God with the "big picture" and the "timetable" of His promise and was willing to be a "stranger and pilgrim" on earth in the interim between the promise and realization of it. Abram wasn't a settler; he was a pilgrim and lived a nomadic lifestyle. Abram passed through the land unto Shechem among the oaks (not the plain) of Moreh. It is here that the God of Glory appeared unto Abram for a second time to reconfirm His covenant with Abram. Appropriately, Shechem means "shoulder," implying "strength," and Moreh means "instruction," and that is just what Abram received from God's visit, strength and instruction. The believer today receives the same provisions from God as we behold Him through Scripture and draw upon Him through prayer.

Historically, Shechem has been a place of decision. It is situated between the mountains of Ebal and Gerizim and at the crossroads of central Palestine. It would be here several centuries later that the Israel-

Seeds of Destiny

ites would assemble to choose between being blessed by God through obedience or cursed by God for disobedience. At this location, Joshua would deliver his final charge to the nation of Israel to follow God (Josh. 24). Shechem would be built up by Jeroboam as a stronghold to divide Solomon's kingdom (1 Kings 12:25).

Abram didn't build an altar in Ur when God met with him or in Haran when God spoke to him, but now Abram was on God's holy ground and in God's holy presence. Abram had arrived at the earthly site set aside for His people to worship Him. The altar he erected was as a flag declaring the land he stood upon was God's land, a place of worship. William Kelly writes concerning God's appearance and Abram's response to worship:

> Here we find for the first time the principle so dear to our hearts – the worship of God founded on a distinct appearing of Himself (it always must be so). Man cannot reason out that which is a ground of worship. It flows from, and is presented to us as flowing from, the appearing of Jehovah. It is not merely the call now, but Jehovah "appeared" unto him. True worship must spring from the Lord, known in that which at any rate is a figure of personal knowledge of Himself. It is not only thus a blessing conferred, but in Himself known. Of course no one means to deny the fact that until He was known in the revelation of His own Son by the power of the Holy Ghost, there could not be that which we understand now as "worship in spirit and in truth;" but at least this set forth the principle.[1]

There are two objects in Abram's life which repeatedly symbolize his walk of separation from the world, the "tent" and the "altar." Abram built altars and pitched tents – there is no record of him erecting a house for himself. As Abram moved about the countryside as a pilgrim, he left no relics of his own prominent stature behind. A lone erected altar unto his God was the only evidence of his presence in the land. The "tent" represents the life of a pilgrim in the world and the "altar" a life of dependency on and worship of God. Hamilton Smith connects the pilgrim life of the believer with his worship:

> After the Lord appeared to Abraham, we immediately read, *"There builded he an altar."* This surely speaks of worship. In the Epistle to the Hebrews those who "go forth" to Christ outside the camp not

only take up their pilgrim character as having no continuing city, but they become worshippers *who "offer the sacrifice of praise to God continually"* (Heb. 13:13-15).[2]

If we want to render acceptable worship to God, we must first have a walk of separation from the world – we must be a pilgrim among pagans. Note the order in Genesis 12:7-8: Abram builds the altar then pitches his tent. Likewise the believer should never contemplate moving anywhere without knowing where he or she is going to worship the Lord (a local church). Dear believer, beware of the danger of mobility. In *"...the time of the end many shall be run to and fro..."* (Dan. 12:4). Many believers have forsaken the protection and accountability of a local church for some high paying job or envisioned career only to shipwreck their lives. Know where you can worship God and have fellowship with His people before you contemplate leaving God's present provision for you. *"...seek ye first the kingdom of God, and His righteousness, and all these things* [food, clothing, and shelter] *shall be added unto you"* (Matt. 6:33).

The Church of Jesus Christ finds itself in the same pilgrim scenario as Abram according to Paul, *"For our [citizenship] is in heaven from, which also we look for the Savior, the Lord Jesus Christ"* (Phil. 3:20). The writer of Hebrews identifies Abram and Sarah as *"strangers and pilgrims on the earth"* (Heb. 11:13). A stranger does not belong where he is at, and a pilgrim belongs where he is going. For Abram, Ur was in the distant past; the possession of the promised land yet future. In the meantime, he lived between these two worlds without possessing either. This summarizes the Christian's experience, for a believer is an ambassador of Christ representing the kingdom of God while on earth (2 Cor. 5:20). Those answering the call of God have no ownership in the present perverse world nor have they yet inherited the eternal one to come. Though temporarily living between these two worlds, each ambassador of Christ is called to maintain the blessed hope (Tit. 2:13), which is the promise of Christ's return (Jn. 14:1-4) as an imminent prospect (2 Tim. 4:8). Every activity of all believers could be suddenly concluded at any moment! Faith that does not keep this coming glory in view will certainly fall prey to the present evil world, as Lot will demonstrate in Genesis 14. Let us follow Abram's pilgrim example of living life. He didn't settle in or get comfortable but clung onto hope by

Seeds of Destiny

faith. In doing so, a believer will be found faithful at the Savior's coming and not feel ashamed while standing in the Lord's glorious presence (1 Jn. 2:28).

Where did Abram pitch his tent? Between Bethel and Hai. Though we are not directly faulting Abram for this decision, there is a note of application for the believer in the dwelling place Abram chose (Gen. 12:8). Bethel means "the house of God," and Hai means "a pile of rubble, a ruin." Abram chose not to pitch his tent at Bethel, the house of God, but went to the east of Bethel. Too many Christians have pitched their tents between the dwelling place of God and the worthless things of the world. They have one hand in the "cookie jar" of indulgence and one hand on their Bibles, only to discover that their fellowship with God is dry and unsatisfying. If we are dwelling with God, God will be seen in our lives.

Perhaps the following story will illustrate the thought. A little girl was perplexed after hearing a sermon, "Mom, I am confused. The preacher said that God was bigger than we are. Is that true?" "Yes, that is true," her mother responded. "He also said that God lives in us. Is that true, too?" "Yes," her mother again replied. "Well," said the little girl, "if God is bigger than us and He lives in us, wouldn't He show through?" God shows through our lives if we are in communion with Him. If we are prone to test boundaries, rebel, and let our flesh have control, the works of the flesh will be seen by others rather than the fruit of the Spirit, which shines forth Christ to others.

> Take time to be holy, the world rushes on;
> Spend much time in secret with Jesus alone,
> By looking to Jesus, like Him thou shalt be;
> Thy friends in thy conduct His likeness shall see.
>
> William Longstaff

A Trial for Abram
Genesis 12:10-20

We have been greatly encouraged by Abram's faith thus far. Initially, it was Terah leading Abram in the journey to Haran (Gen. 11:31), but from Haran to Canaan, Abram's faith led the way (Gen. 12:5). We have also learned three important principles from his life to avoid: first, partial obedience is still **disobedience in part**. Secondly, **delayed** obedience is also disobedience and prevents us from obtaining God's best blessing for our lives, and thirdly, we must **dwell** with God to remain vibrant and faithful as an ambassador for Christ. A fourth mistake of Abram is revealed to us in Genesis 12:10. A famine came to the land. Faith cannot be trusted if it is not tested. So Abram's faith was once more placed in the "refiner's fire" to bring into open view the dross of his life which needed purging. Would he remain in the land divinely conferred to him for a possession or abandon it? Would he tarry and seek God's assistance through the trial, or would he seize personal control of the matter and search for help elsewhere? Abram chose to **divert** into the Egypt to alleviate his problem. Egypt is a symbol of the world throughout Scripture. Ridout comments, "Alas, Abram did as we are all prone to do, he sought relief from all his difficulties, rather than profit by the trial."[1] Beloved, "don't waste a good trial," but count it pure joy for the Lord is building patience in your faith (Jas. 1:2-3).

Scripture speaks of Abram going *"down"* to Egypt (Gen. 12:10), and when he forsook Egypt, Scripture speaks of him *"going up out of"* Egypt (Gen. 13:1). When pilgrims of God venture "down" into Egypt, a selfish desire to explore the world system for aid and comfort is represented, while "coming out" of Egypt pictures their dependent reliance on God's faithfulness for the same. Abram wasted years in Haran and now was set to squander more time in Egypt. Abram, apparently, did not consult God, and God chose not to intervene in this matter until the

Seeds of Destiny

covenant plan was in jeopardy. Sometimes the best teacher in life is practical experience – understanding is gained by failing. Abram's trip *down* to Egypt would be a costly lesson. From the whole of Scripture, one learns that the granaries of the earth and manna from heaven are two vastly different spiritual diets – worlds apart!

First, his marriage was affected by the journey. Perhaps Abram noticed the lingering stares and admiring glances directed towards his beautiful wife as they journeyed through the promiscuous and pagan population. He had not anticipated this horrible situation and found himself confronted with a decision for which he was unprepared. Often Satan strikes a pernicious blow to God's unguarded servant through forcing quick decisions in the midst of ungodly company. Abram feared that these immoral descendants of Ham would murder him just to have his wife. To save his own neck, Abram was willing to compromise his wife. He simply informed Pharaoh that Sarai was his sister, implying that she was not his wife. Technically, this was true, but only half-true, hence a blatant lie nonetheless. It has been well stated: "When the devil encourages a half-truth, he wants people to believe the wrong half."

How important and secure do you think Sarai felt? Her husband was supposed to provide for her and protect her, but instead he allowed her to be inducted into Pharaoh's house? Apparently, instead of defiling her, Pharaoh was considering marrying her. God alone would be the guardian of her purity and honor now.

Secondly, the pagan culture had an influence on his family and Lot. After their trip to Egypt, Lot was not satisfied with the simple life any more. His mind had become compromised with worldliness, and in Genesis 14, we learn that his indulgent pursuit of worldliness led to his fall.

Thirdly, Abram came out of Egypt with a lot of "stuff" (Gen. 12:16, 13:2). The more stuff the believer has, the more opportunities Satan is allowed to entangle and strangle us with things. The Lord strictly taught that His disciples must forsake all to follow Him (Lk. 14:33). This was something that the disciples understood was necessary in order to serve Christ effectively, and they sacrificially obeyed (Matt. 4:22; Lk. 5:11). Apparently, Abram came out of Egypt with more servants to help him manage all his stuff. There can be little doubt these individuals brought their own gods with them. The Lord has called us to a good and simple life concerning evil (Rom. 16:19) and to be content with the necessities of life (food, clothing, shelter, etc. – 1 Tim. 6:6-10).

Lastly, Abram likely brought a servant girl named Hagar back with him from Egypt to be his wife's maid. It sounded like a good idea at the time; a young girl around the house could be a big help to Sarai. Yet, if Abram had not ventured into Egypt, there would have been no Hagar to tempt him in the matters of bearing the needed son. This seemingly unpretentious matter led to the unfolding of two nations (Jew and Arab) which have been venomously hostile towards each other from the beginning.

It also seems from the order of the narrative in Genesis 13-16 that the famine and Abram's departure from the Promised Land occurred shortly after his arrival to Canaan. God affirmed a covenant with Abram when he was 75 years old (Gen. 12:4). About ten years later, Sarai opted for the legal custom of bequeathing Hagar to Abram as a concubine (a wife of secondary status) to bear her a son that would then be adopted by Abram with full rights of inheritance (Gen. 16:3). Likely, Hagar had been Sarai's maid for several years before she would consent to share Hagar with her husband in this manner. Abram had a great victory in faith in arriving at Canaan, but as is often the case, while the taste of victory is still sweet in our mouths, a different trial arrives to test and stretch us in new ways. Satan never sends a postcard to warn the believer of the next assault, and he usually attacks where our defenses are the weakest and our confidence is the most or when we voluntarily let our guard down.

What should Abram have done before going to Egypt? He should have sought God's counsel on the subject. If God gave him the land, certainly God would sustain him in it. C. H. Mackintosh writes, "It is better to starve in Canaan, if it should be so, than live in luxury in Egypt; it is better to suffer in God's path than be at ease in Satan's; it is better to be poor in Christ, than rich without Him."[2]

Fortunately for Abram, God intervened and plagued Pharaoh because of his possession of Sarai. Abram had feared being murdered by the Egyptians because of Sarai, but instead, because of her, the Egyptians lavished him with presents. God plagued Pharaoh's house, and in time, Abram's deceit was found out and Pharaoh returned Sarai and then commanded him to leave Egypt at once. Alas, the world discards God's people, not because of their holy testimony, but because of their own shameful conduct. Abram chose to venture into the world, but it was the world that disposed of him. Unbelief renders its own fate. Often the consequence of doubting God's Word leads individuals into the very evil they sought to avoid. J. N. Darby explains: "The sons of men would build a tower lest they should be scattered abroad, and the Lord scattered them because they built it. Abram fearing lest Pharaoh should take his wife, says she is his sister (as if God would not preserve him), and therefore Pharaoh takes her into his house."[3]

Although Abram had feared and compromised, God was with him. Despite his failure God brought blessing to him, returned his wife to him and graciously forced him out of Egypt (the world). Since God has called the believer to be His representatives in the world, certainly He will sustain us in this role if we trust in Him alone and do not divert into the world for secular wisdom and strength. We cannot have close association with the world without being affected. This requires the Christian to test everything and to keep short accounts with God in confessing sin (1 Jn. 1:9). The Christian life is an existence of separation that still allows evangelistic connections in the world. The plight of the pilgrim ensnared by the clutches of the world is well summarized by Herbert Taylor:

> What Egypt was to Abram, the world and worldly-mindedness are to us. How many Christians have wept over similar folly! In turning from the heavenly manna, we say with Israel, *"Our souls loatheth this light bread"* (Num. 21:5), and, in heart at least, return to the flesh-pots of Egypt. When we fail to enjoy the rich provision of spiritual pleasures prepared by our heavenly Father, our souls crave for something. Instead of at once flying to Him, and saying, *"My soul, wait thou **only** upon God,"* we run to the world, and seek in its empty show to find some satisfying portion. If we seek Christ alone, we shall find that He not only saves, but satisfies; but when we try to enjoy the world and Christ together, our hearts will still be craving. Christ will not share our hearts with another. Oh, who is so miserable as a cold, backsliding Christian? He can really enjoy neither the world nor Christ.[4]

The tragic experience in Egypt concluded with Abram returning to Canaan and being restored with God. There had been no altars in Egypt! How sweet restoration with our Creator is after we have failed. Nothing can satisfy God more than seeing the wanderer and backslider, whom He has created, redeemed, converted, taught and provided for be restored unto Himself! Abram was not restored to a lower position after his failure, for, in fact, his position as a child of God was unchanged. He returned to Bethel, where he had pitched his tent in the beginning, and called upon the name of the Lord in renewed worship. He enjoyed the same sweet fellowship with God as he had before. How marvelous is God's forgiveness and how sweet His restoration, which beholds no diminished relationship, but bestows full communion to the repentant child.

>Do you ever feel down hearted or discouraged?
>Do you ever think your work is all in vain?
>Do the burdens thrust upon you make you cheerless,
>And you fear that you shall never the victory gain?
>Have faith in God, the sun will shine,
>Though dark the cloud may be today,
>His heart hath planned your path and mine:
>Have faith in God, have faith alway.
>
>May Agnew Stephens

Too Much Stuff
Genesis 13:1-9

Abram returned from the trial of Egypt to face another difficulty, for in time sin will reap a due harvest of consequences. Though he had been restored to his God, the result of his failure could now be witnessed in others. The failure of one saint pulls others into evil also. Lot had been adversely affected by the trip to Egypt and now lacked the wherewithal to walk by faith and pursue personal integrity. Besides this spiritual deficiency, scripture twice states that Abram and Lot could no longer dwell together – they were rich in cattle, silver and gold (Gen. 13:2), and they had an abundance of stuff (Gen. 13:6). This is the first mention of "riches" in the Bible. Certainly, the principle of first mention in Scripture has a lasting application concerning "hoarding" riches. What effect does wealth and too many possessions have on God's people? The result is strife among the brethren (Gen. 13:7). When brethren strive together, they cease to be a testimony for God.

How are brethren to consider their possessions? The early church held the proper view of "equality" and thus maintained and enjoyed unity. *"And the multitude of those that believed were of one heart and of one soul; neither said any of them that any of the things which he possessed was his own; but they had all things common"* (Acts 4:32). The Apostle Paul teaches that there should be equality among the brethren (2 Cor. 8:13-14): *"For I mean not that other men be eased, and ye burdened, but by an equality, that now at this time your abundance may be a supply for their want, that their abundance also may be a supply for your want, that there may be equality."* If a brother is in need and another brother is able to meet that need, he should readily do so. Equality is not communism. Holding all things in equality is not the same as everyone having equal portions. When God's people value God, the things of God, and His people, there is unity, but if their focus is shifted unto temporal things, envy, dissatisfaction, and coveting occur. Consequently, Abram and Lot had to separate.

Lot and Abram were dwelling among the Canaanites and Perizzites (Gen. 13:7), and Abram could not endure the thought of there being discord among the brethren in the presence of their enemies. Perhaps, this is the very reason Paul forbids a believer to take another Christian to civil court to resolve a quarrel (1 Cor. 6:1-8). The minute matters we bicker about are nothing compared to hindering the spread of the gospel message or publicly defaming our Lord's name. It is better to suffer loss of that which is temporal than impact the eternal aspects which yield God glory.

So Abram, the one who had been promised the land and was the more spiritual of the two men, gave Lot his choice of the land. It was the quickest way to resolve the conflict between the herdsmen. Although it was His land, Abram waived his rights for the sake of achieving peace and allowed Lot to select his home. The Lord Jesus waived His rights to heaven, and the glory thereof, to become the Man of Sorrows, that we might have peace with God and *all spiritual blessings in heavenly places* (Eph. 1:3).

What did Lot do after he was given the choice? *"Lot lifted up his eyes, and beheld all the plain of Jordan, that it was well watered every where,"* (Gen. 13:10). Lot's carnal appetite for worldliness was enslaved by the tantalizing savor of Egypt still in his mouth. Given a choice between the "big city life" or a wilderness experience with God, Lot chose the plain of Jordan. This choice put Lot's declining spiritual life into a spiraling nose-dive, for what he chose by sight he found to be corrupted and wicked (Gen. 13:13) and quickly lost in Genesis 14. F. W. Grant writes, "The names unmistakably reveal what is before us here. Jordan ("descending") is the river of death, flowing in rapid course ever down to the sea of judgment [the Dead Sea], from which there is no outlet – no escape."[1]

Hamilton Smith provides an insightful overview of the spiritual makeup of the three men who departed from Ur in response to Abram's divine call.

> In Terah we have seen the man of nature who can make a fair profession, but cannot take the path of faith that leads outside the world. In Abraham, we have seen the man of faith who, acting according to the

word of the Lord, takes the outside place, not in faith in God but under the influence of man. Already we have read that when Abraham departed from Haran, *"Lot went with him"* (Gen. 12:4). Again, when Abraham went up out of Egypt, we read, *"Lot with him"* (Gen. 13:1). Now, for the third time Lot is described as the man *"which went with Abram"*(Gen. 13:5). Lot represents a large class who take up a right position outside the world, but do so under the influence of a friend or relative rather than from personal exercise and faith in God. From the beginning of his path, Lot was characterized by walking in the light of another. Alas, in different ways and measures, how often we may, like Lot, act with those who have faith without having it ourselves, only to find that we shall not stand when tried by temptation.[2]

Perhaps the reader can contempt their spiritual wherewithal and identify with one of these three men: (1) a faker, or (2) a follower, or (3) the faithful. The ***faker*** has not spiritual life and, thus, will never dwell in heaven. The ***follower*** has a shallow spiritual existence and, thus, will not experience the heavenly life while on earth. Only the ***faithful*** will enjoy his pilgrimage presently and the inheritance yet to come. In the "Faith Hall of Fame" of Hebrews 11, we learn that Abraham believed though not knowing *where* he was going (Heb. 11:8), he believed without understanding *how* God's promise would be accomplished (Heb. 11:11-12), and he believed though not knowing *why* he was being severely tested (Heb. 11:17-18). This, dear believer, is the faith of a true pilgrim and stranger striving heavenward (Heb. 11:13).

> Once far from God and dead in sin, no light my heart could see;
> But in God's Word the light I found, now Christ liveth in me.
> With longing all my heart is filled, that like Him I may be,
> As on the wondrous tho't I dwell that Christ liveth in me.
>
> Daniel W. Whittle

A Separation Brings Blessing
Genesis 13:10-18

Unlike Lot, who had placed his trust in a secular scene, Abram, at the prompting of God, lifted up his eyes to view the land God had given him (Gen. 13:14). Scripture records three times that Abram *"lifted up his eyes,"* and all three were in response to the visage or the voice of the Lord. We have this occurrence in which Abram was willing to give Lot a portion of his inheritance – the land, but God was re-affirming to Abram that it would be his. The second occurrence is found in Genesis 18:2 when Abram lifted up his eyes to see the Lord coming to visit him, then thirdly, in Genesis 22:13, Abram lifted up his eyes in obedience to the Lord to find a ram to offer in the place of Isaac. In response to Abram's faith shown in separating from Lot, God tells him for the first time in verse 17, *"Arise, walk through the land in the length of it, and in the breadth of it."* Putting both verses 14 and 17 together the Lord told Abram "look up and walk." What a great example to follow – let us keep our eyes "lifted up" and fixed on the Lord and His promises, lest our eyes become unsatisfied with seeing (Eccl. 1:8), and we wander into a realm of ungodliness. Our sight gives direction to our walk!

Lot based his decision on the outward appearance and not on the intrinsic character or the future destiny of Sodom, which was to be judged. He would take up residence in the corrupt and sinful city of Sodom (Gen. 13:12-13). Note Lot's steps of compromise: he lusted after the plain of Jordan after seeing it in verse 10, journeyed towards the plain in verse 11, dwelled in the cities of the plain and pitched his tent towards Sodom in verse 12. We learn that Lot eventually dwelled in Sodom (Gen. 14:12) and became an authority figure in the city (Gen. 19:1 – It was common practice for leaders to sit at the city gate to make decisions for the people.). Finally, Lot became so settled in the world

Seeds of Destiny

that he gave his daughters to the Sodomite men in marriage (Gen. 19:14). The word "Lot" means "covering," and Lot is always found under a cover of disguise. With righteous Abraham, he must outwardly cover his carnal heart; and as a saint of God, he must cover his faith to comfortably live with the Sodomites. So Lot deserted the fellowship of a righteous man for a compromised life. Abram's tent stands in sharp contrast to Lot's house. Thus, when conflict arrived, carnal Lot was unprepared for battle and easily defeated, while spiritual Abram was well armed and fought victoriously.

What a valuable lesson for the believer! The writer of Hebrews exhorts Christians to not forsake the assembling of ourselves together (Heb. 10:25). Why? Because we need each other to encourage, exhort, bear up, pray for, and serve. One of the first signs of a believer approaching the slide of compromise is disassociation with God's people. It makes them uncomfortable to be with others who are a voice of what is right to their conscience. Very few believers just fall into sin. Christians, like Lot, make several wrong decisions called steps of **compromise**, which promotes **complacency** to what is right, and finally leads to **carnality** – worldliness.

The half brother of the Lord, James, expresses bluntly how God feels about worldliness in the believer's life in James 4:4. He likens worldliness to spiritual adultery, which God hates; it is enmity with Him. So much so that James states, *"whosoever therefore will be a friend of the world is an enemy of God."* A worldly Christian in effect declares by his or her life, "God, I hate you." The Christian has been paid for by the blood of Christ and has been baptized into the resurrected life of Christ through the Holy Spirit. The Christian has died to himself and is alive in Christ. He or she has no legal right to choose to live his or her life the way he or she desires. Christ gave His life for us so that we might live eternally with Him. He demands that we live now on earth the life He gave up for us. He was born to die, but we have died in Him to live through a rebirth!

Abram rightly separated himself from Lot, for Lot's carnal longings would eventually lead him into sin. Those who have been wholly consecrated cannot fellowship with those of unholy practice. This is why the Apostle Paul could direct the church at Corinth to cast out (excommunicate) the man who was boldly engaging in immorality (1 Cor. 5:1-

5). The assembly did put him out because they understood that a little leaven (a little tolerated sin) leavens the whole lump (affects the whole assembly). Churches today must take the matter of holy living seriously. If there is sin in the camp, they must exhort, reprove, and if it persists, sweep it out of the assembly. The children of Israel went into the desert "a mixed company" (Ex. 12:38), and it was the mixed company that vexed their souls and brought God's judgment and wrath upon them again and again (Num. 11:4-6). Abram was to be much better off after the "blessed reduction" from his family congregation. In effect, Abram had now obeyed God's original instructions to "leave his kindred" in Ur. His kindred had delayed his obedience in Haran and now sought to trouble him in Canaan.

Did Lot find happiness in Sodom? Definitely not. 2 Peter 2:6-9 informs us that *"his righteous soul [was vexed] from day to day with their unlawful deeds."* Lot's conscience told him that he should separate from evil, but he chose to dwell with the wicked. Perhaps, he thought he could influence the people of Sodom. Yet, it was obvious from Genesis 19 that he had no control over the people's lawless behavior and that he had completely lost his testimony with his own family. Only his two virgin daughters and his wife heeded the warning of God's imminent wrath upon their city. So many of God's people have fallen into the same snare as Lot, thinking that they could adapt worldly techniques in ministry or evangelism or that they were invincible to temptation only to fall prey to the seductive forces of the world and become a casualty in spiritual warfare.

Do you think we will see Lot in heaven? Scripture calls Lot "just" and a "righteous soul" (2 Pet. 2:7-8). He trusted God's words to Abram and departed Ur for an unknown destination. He traveled nearly 1000 miles based only on what his Uncle Abram had told him about the God of glory. Abram saw the glory of God, but Lot trusted without seeing, and God accounts to him a righteous standing based on his faith. Salvation is a gift of God, which He does not take away. But how much we enjoy our salvation is dependent upon our separation from the world and our consecration unto God. Pain and suffering are "inevitable," but misery is "optional." If we sanctify ourselves from filth, He promises to use us as a vessel of honor for His glory (2 Tim. 2:20-21).

Seeds of Destiny

This chapter closes with God reaffirming His covenant again with Abram *"after that Lot was separated from him"* (Gen. 13:14). Abram responds by building his third altar to worship God. Abram was a citizen of heaven and a pilgrim in the land. He seems to have always maintained this perspective – for he lived in tents. He built altars but never a house for himself. *"For our citizenship is in heaven from which also we look for the Savior, the Lord Jesus Christ"* (Phil. 3:20). Abram, in a strange land, was not afraid of going on with the Lord. Let us follow his example of brave consecration!

>Anywhere with Jesus I can safely go,
>Anywhere He leads me in this world below;
>Tho' His hand may lead me over dreary ways,
>Anywhere with Jesus I am not afraid.
>
>Jessie H. Brown

Abram the Hebrew
Genesis 14:1-18

In Genesis 14 a number of key words are mentioned for the first time: battle, war, king(s), thirteen (13th), tithe, peace (Salem), and priest. In fact, the word king occurs twenty-two times in reference to ten kings. It was the tenth king, Melchizedek, who represented God and brought peace to Salem, which is the first mention of Jerusalem in the Bible.

The cities of the Jordan plain, where Lot lived, had been in servitude to an Eastern king named Chedorlaomer for twelve years. The cultural situation rightly captures the hierarchy of evil present in the world today – the heathenism of Sodom never yields except to the spiritual paganism of Babylon. They rebelled in the 13th year, and in the 14th year, the king came with three other kings from the east (Tidal, Amraphel, and Arioch) to recompense the Jordanians for their insurrection. It was not uncommon in ancient days for powerful nations to form a coalition to plunder other adjoining nations and place them in servitude. Such is the case in this chapter as four Eastern kings converged with their armies upon five Jordanian kings and their armies for battle. The Jordanian kings were soundly defeated; their cities were looted, and some citizens were captured, Lot being among the captives.

This battle did not affect Abram at all because he was living a quiet and simple life of faith apart from the wickedness of the Jordan plain. He was a heavenly citizen sojourning on earth – he sought to avoid secular affairs. Lot, however, had desired a name, a place, and a portion on earth; therefore, he was drastically affected by this social upheaval. Abraham sought the Lord's portion and was content. The believer who had refused the world and walked by faith was victorious, and the one who walked by sight had fallen under its power. Herbert Taylor comments:

Seeds of Destiny

Lot's riches evidently made him an attractive object of spoil to king Chedorlaomer. How he must have wished, when he found himself a poor, humbled captive, that he had never settled on the plains of Sodom! But he had to learn this lesson, that the security of the possession is assured by the Giver of it. When God gives He also secures. Lot gave to himself the well-watered plains of Jordan, and, having no power to retain them, in one day lost all the accumulated wealth of years. Abram, on the other hand, had learnt practically –

Why should I ever careful be, since such a God is mine?
He watches over me night and day, and tells me 'Mine is thine.'[1]

Shortly after Lot's capture, *"There came one that had escaped, and told Abram the Hebrew."* The wonder of Abram's power is revealed in one word first appearing here in the Bible; the word is *Hebrew*. The meaning of the Hebrew, "the passenger," beautifully encapsulates the pilgrimage of Abram and his strangership in a world estranged to God.

When Abram learned of what had happened, he quickly assembled his 318 hired soldiers, no doubt well trained, to pursue the enemy. We learn from Genesis 14:13 that Abram was dwelling in peace with the Amorites via a treaty. It seems that this treaty favored Abram in that some of the Amorites came with General Abram and his armed forces into battle also (Gen. 14:24). Abram divided his men against the enemy, pursued them some 140 miles north, then engaged them in battle another 100 miles north until he had recovered all the people and goods taken from the Jordanian cities. Then he returned with what he had recovered to the valley of Shaveh, which is likely the Kidron Valley near Jerusalem.

Two kings rushed to meet victorious Abram. The King of Sodom, an evil man, is mentioned first and perhaps, therefore, reached Abram first, but before this wicked king could converse personally with Abram, the King of Salem (Jerusalem) intervened. His name was Melchizedek, and besides being a king, he was also a priest. He met with Abram, and set bread and wine before Abram to call his mind into remembrance of his God. Lastly, he blessed Abram. Melchizedek means "king of righteousness," and he was also the king of Salem, which means "peace." The writer of Hebrews (Heb. 5:5-6, 7:1-22) likens Melchizedek to the Lord Jesus, *"made like unto the Son of God"* (Heb. 7:3). Melchizedek is a legitimate type of the Lord Jesus. The Lord Jesus *"made peace through the blood of His cross"* (Col. 1:20) and, therefore, is the Prince of Peace (Isa. 9:6). In a coming day, the Lord Jesus shall rule the world with justice and with righteousness forever (Isa. 9:7); thus, Melchizedek foreshadows the Lord's millennial glory on Earth.

Melchizedek had *"no record of days,"* that is, no recorded birth or death, though certainly he experienced birth and death. Some have taught that Melchizedek was a theophany (a preincarnate visit of Christ to the earth), but the writer of Hebrews disproves this notion for Melchizedek was *"made like unto the Son of God."* Melchizedek was not personally the Son of God, but a *type* to speak of the eternality of Christ as our High Priest in heaven, who is the eternal Son of God. The writer of Hebrews also tells us that, like Christ, God appointed Melchizedek to his priestly office (He had no human ordination.). B. H. Carroll highlights the awe and brevity of Melchizedek's appearance in the narrative:

> As he approaches Salem, afterwards Jerusalem, a personage mightier than Abram steps out of the shadows to bless him and then recedes into the shadows and is swallowed up forever. The episode is the most unique, startling, dramatic and mysterious in all history. We hold our breath in surprise, as the brief incident seems to step out of the skies and step back again. The author tells the story with the simplicity and brevity of a child, without one word of explanation to satisfy the curious. A silence falls on the scene and its incident is unbroken for nearly 900 years. It is then broken by the Psalmist king of Israel, whose prophetic spirit foresees the ascended Messianic king on the throne in heaven and exclaims "Jehovah hath sworn, and will not repent: Thou art a priest forever after the order of Melchizedek" (Ps. 110:4).[2]

In hope that sends a shining ray far down the future's broadening way,
In peace that only Thou canst give, with Thee, O Master, let me live.

W. Gladden

A Priest Intervenes
Genesis 14:19-24

What effect did Melchizedek's sudden appearance have on Abram? Abram had been brought back to reality and to remembrance of his Lord – he would only exalt God for the victory. Naturally, he would have been tempted to keep all the plunder of the conquest, but God knew that possessing these things and the people of a pagan culture would only serve to pull Abram away from Himself. But just at the right time, before the temptation was too great, a priest intervened on Abram's behalf. In return, Abram was moved to give Melchizedek a tenth of the spoil as an offering to God.

What a picture of the priesthood of Christ! The believer is invited to come boldly to the throne of grace in heaven to obtain help in a time of need from our Great High Priest, the Lord Jesus (Heb. 4:15-16). This is a provision available 24 hours each and every day. The Lord wants us to rely on His grace, so we are not given over to temptation and sin. Paul declares, *"there hath no temptation taken you but such as is common to man; but God is faithful, who will not suffer* [permit] *you to be tempted above that ye are able, but wil, with the temptation, also make a way to escape, that ye may be able to bear it"* (1 Cor. 10:13).

The second provision for the believer not to be given over to sin is to bring the Lord Jesus into remembrance. It is hard to lust after an individual, covet another's possessions, or be given to substance abuse if our minds are stayed upon the Lord. Isaiah 26:3 reads, *"Thou wilt keep him in perfect peace, whose mind is stayed on Thee, because he trusteth in Thee."* Perhaps this is why Jehovah instituted so many special days and feasts for the Jews to keep; He wanted their minds to be continually occupied with Him. This would make it more difficult for the Jews to forget their God. Likewise, the Lord gave the Church a remembrance feast called the Lord's Supper the night before He died to aid our retention and appreciation of His work at Calvary and His moral beauty. He said to "do it often." Certainly, the early Church thought it important as they met weekly on Sunday in obedience to the Lord's dying request (Acts 20:7).

God had been brought to Abram's remembrance by the intervention of a godly priest named Melchizedek. Abram was now ready to receive instruction from the Lord, which would strengthen him against the evil proposition ahead. It is evident that Abram intently listened to the instruction of Melchizedek, for Abram repeated back to Melchizedek his very words, *"the Most High God, the possessor of heaven and earth"* (Gen. 14:22).

The King of Sodom then met with Abram and requested that he return only the people and keep the spoil for himself. However, Abram declared that his Most High God is the possessor and controller of all things. Abram gave God the glory for the victory; therefore, he was not obliged to keep the spoil. Only what was given to Melchizedek as a gift to God, what the men ate during their conquest, and what the Ammorites wanted for their efforts was taken, and the rest was returned to the Jordanians.

The King of Sodom represents Satan in this narrative, just as the King of Tyre personifies Satan in Isaiah 14. The King of Sodom was a defeated king – Satan was defeated at Calvary (Jn. 12:31). The King of Sodom ruled over wickedness – Satan, the prince of this world, rules over wickedness presently (Eph. 2:2). The desire of the King of Sodom was, *"give me the persons* (souls)" – Satan's desire is to keep souls from turning to Christ that they might be saved (Jn. 8:44; 1 Tim. 5:15; 2 Thess. 2:9-10). The proposition offered to Abram by the King of Sodom was nothing less than a powerful solicitation to sin. It is when we think we are strong that we are most prone to forget the warning, *"Let him that thinketh he standeth take heed lest he fall"* (1 Cor. 10:12). If not heeded, how ready we are to be flattered by Satan and to fall into his grip.

What would have happened if the "king of righteousness" had not called Abram unto remembrance of his God just at the right time? Perhaps Abram would have been self-promoted in his own mind and kept what he had fought for. Let God's people rely on Christ's intercession to sustain them from evil, and let them often call to remembrance and

Seeds of Destiny

savor the splendors of the Savior. Tasting the glorious Christ will cure any appetite for the world that we may have.

It is worthy to note that on this occasion of tender communion between Melchizedek and Abram in Jerusalem that Abram pitches no tent and builds no altar. William Kelly remarks:

> And as there was no altar, so the course of pilgrimage is run. Separateness from the world and heavenly worship are no longer found. A tent and altar would be as unsuitable, reared by Abram at this juncture, as before they were exactly to the purpose. It is the millennial scene when God alone is exalted, His enemies confounded, His people saved and blessed.[1]

> Onward, Christian soldiers, marching as to war,
> With the cross of Jesus going on before;
> Christ the royal Master leads against the foe;
> Forward into battle, see, His banner go.
> Crowns and thrones may perish, kingdoms rise and wane,
> But the Church of Jesus constant will remain;
> Gates of hell can never, against that Church prevail;
> We have Christ's own promise, and that cannot fail.
>
> Sabine Baring Gould

Faith that is Counted
Genesis 15:1-6

It is evident at this juncture that the narrative passes from a more public and outer view of Abram's path of faith to an inner exposure of his life and experiences. It is important for the believer to realize that we are not merely called to be a witness of divine truth, but to testify of how truth has affected our own lives. The Psalmist highlights the effect of this reality upon rearing our children. *"Let thy work appear unto thy servants, and thy glory to their children"* (Ps. 90:16). Our children must be exposed, not just to divine truth, but also to the glorious things the Lord is doing in our lives, the assembly, and our witness to the lost. This will truly affect our children for eternity. Abram had chosen to be a witness for God over being a citizen of the world and had decided to praise God in his accomplishment in lieu of boasting of personal effort. The Lord encouraged Abram in his faith by visiting him in a vision. *"After these things the word of the Lord came unto Abram in a vision, saying, Fear not, Abram: I am thy shield, and thy exceeding great reward"* (Gen. 15:1). *"After these things,"* refers to Abram's refusal of the world's gifts and honors in Genesis 14. Until this point in Scripture, we have read that "Jehovah called," "Jehovah appeared," and "Jehovah said." In Genesis 15, we read for the first time of "the word of Jehovah" coming to mankind. Jehovah would now inscribe a distinct and new significance into the life of Abram with the profound and fresh declaration.

Genesis 15:1 alone introduces the first mention of *"word," "vision," "shield,"* and *"reward"* and the exhortative phrase *"Fear not"* in the Bible. Also in this verse is the first of many *"I am"* affirmations of God. God is revealing Himself in a more personal way to Abram. Jesus informed the Jewish leaders that *"Your father Abraham rejoiced to see My day: and he saw it, and was glad"* (Jn.

Seeds of Destiny

8:56). Then to soundly declare His deity He spoke, *"Verily, verily, I say unto you, Before Abraham was, I am"* (Jn. 8:58). The Lord Jesus asserts divine "I am" disclosures to reveal Himself more fully to His disciples as their God. John's writings, clearly uphold the deity of the Lord Jesus in this manner. *"I am the light of the world." "I am the door." "I am the way, truth, and life." "I am the Good Shepherd." "I am the resurrection." "I am the Alpha and Omega."* God speaking to Moses said, *"I am that I am"* (Ex. 3:14). The Lord Jesus is the Great I Am! Concerning this fundamental truth, the Lord bluntly warned His hearers of the consequences of not acknowledging Him as the Great I Am: *"...if ye believe not that **I am [ ]**, ye shall die in your sins."* The "He" in this verse (after *"I am"*) is not in the original text.

How fitting that God would reveal Himself as a *shield* for Abram. Abram was chosen alone, but he was not alone. Though he had aroused the world's enmity, he need not fear the world in which he had already gotten the victory, for God was with him. Knowing "I Am" personally conveys rest and peace to the one's soul. God was Abram's protector. Likewise, the believer today has the *"shield of faith"* (Eph. 6:16) and the rest of the armour of God for protection. By putting on this spiritual provision we can *"be strong in the Lord, and in the power of His might"* (Eph. 6:10). Abram did not need the plunder of heathen cultures as a recompense for his courage and holy living – his reward was God Himself. It is in this vision that God first discloses His Divine title of "Adonai Jehovah" – the Lord God (Gen. 15:2).

Perhaps Abram was starting to doubt God's word as he and Sarai continued to age and yet had no children. This would be natural tendency of any man, for a decade had passed since God had met with him at the oaks of Moreh and promised him children. And only one other time since then had God spoken to him about the matter (after Lot separated from him). So while God had Abram's undivided attention, He instructed Abram to *"Look now toward heaven."* Faith would require Abram to look away from Sarai, his natural abilities and in fact everything earthly. When Abram had the proper "up look," God reaffirmed it would be *"his seed"* that would be innumerable.

The fact that Abram attempted to help God accomplish His promise by offering Him Eliezer his servant as an heir, indicates some doubt in Abram's mind concerning what God had previously told him. Eliezer represents man's practical solution to the problem. It was the civil custom to pass your inheritance on to your chief servant if you had no children. But God had a different plan, one that would show His creativity and ability and would not leave any room for man to boast. The longer Sarai was barren and went beyond childbearing years the greater the miracle would be.

It is a reminder that God's way is rarely man's way. Why? Because God's way is perfect (Ps. 18:30), and His ways are past finding out (Rom. 11:33). Moses declared, *"The secret things belong unto the Lord our God; but those things which are revealed belong unto us and to our children forever, that we may do all the words of this law"* (Deut. 29:29). Mankind has a limited understanding of himself and his world. He only knows what God has told him through Scripture, his conscience, or what he has determined as truth through observing creation. Beyond this, man is oblivious to truth, nor could he comprehend it in his present fallen state. But man's limited understanding of God and creation also becomes in itself the very medium by which faith in God is to be exercised.

Faith is the ability of the soul to reach beyond what can be verified by the human senses and trust what he cannot confirm by his own understanding. Hebrews 11:3 reminds us that it is only by faith that we know that the visible things we see did not happen by chance from visible realms, but from the hand of the invisible Creator. This is why one must have faith to please God, *"for without faith it is impossible to please Him"* (Heb. 11:6).

God performed no signs and wonders for Abram. He simply reconfirmed His word to Abram. That was good enough for him – he simply trusted God and believed. God responded by accrediting a standing of righteousness to Abram's account. This accrediting, or accounting, of divine righteousness to a sinner exercising faith is seen throughout the Bible and is thoroughly explained by the Apostle Paul in Romans 4 and 5. Obviously, God wanted no confusion on this matter for the words "believe," "counted," and "righteousness" occur all for the first time in the Bible in one verse (Gen. 15:6) and in one Divine declaration just after the first reference of "the word of the Lord" in the Bible (Gen. 15:1). Genesis 15:6 again appears three times in the New Testament: Romans 4:3, Galatians 3:6, and James 2:23. In Abraham's

Seeds of Destiny

case what preceded imputed righteousness? His faith. In Noah's case what preceded imputed righteousness? God's grace. Combining these two important truths we have *"For by grace are ye saved through faith; and that not of yourselves, it is the gift of God"* (Eph. 2:8). Both God's means of salvation through grace and man's responsibility to lay hold of this gift by personal faith are clearly presented in Genesis, as throughout the Bible.

Hearing the word of the Lord fortified Abram's faith. Each exposure to God's promises was making his faith stronger. Like Abram, all believers must be continually exposed to God's Word to keep our faith strong and renewed. We tend to be forgetful and spiritually lazy. As we neglect meditating on Scripture, our minds cease to be refreshed, and our faith grows cold. Our spiritual sight diminishes to the point that we only see natural solutions. True faith sees God-size solutions!

> May we read these Scriptures, and their truths believe,
> Own our need as sinners, and God's Son receive;
> In assurance resting, His commands obey,
> And in His grace growing, live for Him each day,
>
> A. P. Gibbs

Faith that Obeys
Genesis 15:7-21

Abram's faith responded in obedience to God's instructions for preparing animal and bird sacrifices. True faith produces good deeds, including obedience. A soul that has been declared righteous by God should seek to live righteously. Those who have a position in Christ should practice Christ. The New Testament epistles provide further details about how justification is accomplished. Paul informs us that a believer is justified by God's grace (Rom. 3:24), by Christ's blood (Rom. 5:9), and by faith (Rom. 5:1). James declares one more astounding fact pertaining to justification: *"Ye see, then, how that by works a man is justified, and not by faith only"* (Jas. 2:24). Humanly speaking, this all seems confusing. How can justification be so complicated if God simply accredited Abram a righteous standing based on his faith?

Using your God-given imagination for a moment, in your mind's eye envision a huge reservoir in the upper elevations of a mountain range. Melting snow from an even higher elevation gently streams down into bubbling brooks, which, in turn, fill this reservoir to full capacity. An enormous dam holds back the vast resource except for what water is rushing out from its base into a deep channel. This channel conveys the water a great distance to a collection pool in the flat plains below. As individual head gates about this collection pool are opened, the vital blessing of the reservoir is applied to parched fields already sown with seed. Thus, the immense reservoir so far above in the mountains is responsible and necessary for an abundant harvest to follow. Justification is, from a biblical sense, pictured in this imaginary scene. The reservoir pictures God's vast grace waiting to be bestowed from heavenly realms above. The channel represents the means in which God's grace is conveyed to mankind – through the

Seeds of Destiny

blood of Jesus Christ. The act of opening the head gates symbolizes an individual trusting in the gospel message and, thus, receiving God's manifold grace through the blood of Christ. The harvest of good works that follows is the practical demonstration of a justified soul. It is the proof of a changed life or as James concludes, *"Even so faith, if it hath not works, is dead, being alone"* (Jas. 2:17). Thus a believer is justified by grace, through Christ's blood, by personal faith and is evidenced by good works.

So Abram, being justified, did exactly what God said. God, however, responded with silence until the end of the day. Perhaps this was to demonstrate to Abram that His covenant would take time to complete and that he and his seed would have to be patient. In the meantime, Abram had to drive the unclean birds from devouring the prepared sacrifices. In the Matthew 13 Kingdom Parables, birds are used to symbolize Satan's evil influence and operations to oppose the Kingdom of God. Certainly, Satan would be in opposition to God's covenant with Abram and the forthcoming Messiah who would bless all families of the earth. In application, seeing that all spiritual blessings for the believer find their origin in the one sacrifice of Christ, the enemy will always seek to belittle His all-sufficient work and cast doubt on the integrity of His person.

It was the ancient eastern custom for two men making a binding agreement to kill an animal and split it in half. Instead of shaking hands or signing a contract, the two men would walk through the animal parts. They were publicly proclaiming that, if they did not maintain the agreement they were making, the other party had the right to do to them as they had just done to the animal. How many marriages would be preserved today if men and women took their marriage covenants with God this seriously?

Would God ask Abram to walk through the animal pieces with Him to make a covenant? No. God would walk between the animal pieces alone. God caused a deep sleep to come over Abram, and God made a binding covenant with Himself to bless Abram. If Abram had walked with God through the midst of those animal pieces, the covenant would have been broken as soon as Abram failed God, and Abram would have had to die. Since all men fail God (excluding the Lord Jesus), God made a unilateral covenant with Himself. *"For when God made promise to Abraham, because He could swear by no greater, He swore by Himself"* (Heb. 6:13). Now God had invoked His immutable word and His oath to bless Abram (Heb. 6:17-18). There is nothing mankind or all the spiritual principalities of the universe can do to prevent this covenant from realization. Appendix B provides a detailed explanation of the 400-year prophecy presented in Genesis 15:13.

So God walked through the midst of the animal pieces – *"a smoking furnace and a burning lamp that passed between those pieces"* (Gen. 15:17). Why such descriptions of God's presence in this affair? The then future story of Israel can be summed up in these two figures – the "smoking furnace" and the "burning lamp." The smoking furnace represents those dark periods of time when Israel was being refined through suffering and fiery trials. The "lamp" pictures those bright spots in Israel's history when Jehovah directly intervened on earth to bring salvation and deliverance from aggression, captivity and evil. The thicker and darker the smoke, the brighter the lamp would seem. Certainly this would characterize the Israelites' experience in Egypt and their awesome deliverance.

In application for the present day, we might think upon Paul's attitude concerning his sufferings for Christ's sake. *"For our light affliction, which is but for a moment, worketh for us a far more exceeding and eternal weight of glory; While **we look not at the things which are seen, but at the things which are not seen**: for the things which are seen are temporal; but the things which are not seen are eternal"* (2 Cor. 4:17-18). Herbert Taylor clarifies the principle of thought life:

> If we as Christians look at the things which are seen we shall be in all manner of trouble and gloom; instead of a *smoking* furnace we shall speak of it as a *burning* furnace, and instead of a *burning* lamp we shall see a *smoking* lamp. It will be just reversed from God's beautiful and divine order; the trial will be felt cruelly sharp, and the promise of God will be dim and obscure. When we take things as God would have us take them, we have "songs in the night."[1]

Let this be encouragement to the believer – the darker the cloud upon us, the brighter the future will seem. From our vantage point,

Seeds of Destiny

there may be a dark thunderhead looming over us, but from heaven, a brighter reflection of the Son's glory is enjoyed. Let us hope in that!

Though the land was not fully possessed by Abram, the peoples of the land listed in Genesis 15:19-21 had an opportunity of blessing through him. They could both know and be reconciled to God through the covenant promise of God to Abram, *"in thee shall all families of the earth be blessed."* This covenant has its ultimate fulfillment in the redemptive work of Christ. Certainly, Uriah the Hittite, Caleb the Kenizzite, and Tamar and Rahab of the Canaanites are some of the inhabitants that received divine blessing by trusting Abram's God. *"For the grace of God that bringeth salvation hath appeared to all men"* (Titus 2:11).

> Put thou thy trust in God, In duty's path go on;
> Walk in His strength with faith and hope, So shall thy work be done.
>
> Paul Gerhardt

Devotions in Genesis

God Needs Help Again?
Genesis 16:1-6

The three laws of the harvest are: (1) you reap what you sow, (2) you reap more than what you sow, and (3) you reap later than you sow. Paul explains, *"For he that soweth to his flesh shall of the flesh reap corruption; but he that soweth to the Spirit shall of the Spirit reap life everlasting."* (Gal. 6:8). The full legitimate harvest from Abram's expensive trip into Egypt had not been fully realized yet. A young maiden name Hagar likely came out of Egypt when Abram's entourage returned to Canaan. She had no doubt been a beneficial servant to Sarai. Yet, she was too available and too close to the situation not to be a temptation for this older couple who had no children.

Something of the world had been introduced into Abram's house and by its very availability ensured chaos the moment Abram walked in the flesh and not by faith. Too often a believer introduces some secular thing into their home unaware that in due season what was thought to be dormant and harmless solicits the flesh to manifest itself. These worldly influences are like spiritual land mines. One false step of faith and the child of God becomes a casualty of carnal appetite. Just as the Jews symbolized spiritual sanctification by sweeping all the leaven from their homes during the feast of unleavened bread, the believer should take great care to remove all secular provisions of enticement from their homes. If it is not there to start with, it will never pull you under its power.

It was not an unusual social custom for a man to take a second wife if his first wife could bear him no children. This practice was to ensure that there was an heir that could manage the family affairs when mom and dad were aged or departed. This is likely why Elkanah married Peninnah (1 Sam. 1:1-5). She was a second wife to bear him children because Hannah, his first wife, could not conceive and bear children. In

Seeds of Destiny

Genesis 15, Abram volunteered to help God keep His promise by allowing his servant Eliezer be his heir. However, the matter of "heirship," and "sonship" were already settled in God's mind. In Genesis 16, it was Abram's wife, Sarai, that devised a scheme to help God keep His word.

What contrasting accounts of Abram's faith are set upon the holy page in adjoining fashion – the pinnacle of simple trust in Genesis 15 and the utter crime of disbelief in Genesis 16. Abram's present and past instances of disbelief can be traced to three sources: family ties, difficult living conditions, and perceived threatenings. His faith had weathered the pagan culture, vast materialism and family strife like a bulwark, but now his own wife would cast doubt on God's word.

She approached Abram and invited him to take Hagar (who was Sarai's personal property) as a concubine (a wife with secondary status) and raise up children for her through this union. Her words, *"Behold now, the Lord hath restrained me from bearing,"* are seasoned with a bit of malice. What she was really saying was "Behold the Lord has failed me, and we need to take matters into our own hands." Would Abram lapse in his faith – have a moment of disbelief? Unfortunately yes, he joined with her the same way believers today embrace the law on the principle of fruitfulness, all the while affronting "justification." Waiting is hard work for faith! We want difficult situations resolved fast, forgetting that God is orchestrating the details of billions of other lives to bring about the greatest blessing to all concerned. We want "to learn to swim without water" so to speak; we want the fruit of the trial without the struggle. We want our new "marching orders" now, but we forget that our character development may not be sufficient for the task ahead. The Christian life is certainly one of "working" and "waiting," while all the time "worshipping" the God who knows all and controls all – we best wait for His timing and not rush ahead of His perfect plan. Matthew Henry describes this travesty of Abram's doubt and the lesson for us to learn:

> This was done without asking counsel of the Lord. Unbelief worked, God's almighty power was forgotten. It was a bad example, and a source of manifold uneasiness. In every relation and situation in life there is some cross for us to bear: much of the exercise of faith consists in patiently submitting, in waiting the Lord's time, and using

only those means which He appoints for the removal of the cross. Foul temptations may have very fair pretences, and be coloured with that which is very plausible. Fleshly wisdom puts us out of God's way. This would not be the case, if we would ask counsel of God by his word and by prayer, before we attempt that which is doubtful.[1]

Sarai told Abram, *"I pray thee, go in unto my maid; it may be that I may obtain children by her"* (Gen. 16:2). The Hebrew word for "obtain" is *banah*, which means "to build" or "to make." Sarai wanted to build up a household through Hagar. There is a principle introduced here that is repeated in Scripture. In the Jewish culture, the groom was responsible for building a "house near to" or "an additional room adjoining" his father's house before he could obtain his bride. Although the groom built the house for his bride, the wife was the builder of the household. God's plan was for the husband to be the head of and the provider for his family and for the wife to bear the children, nurture them, and keep and maintain the home. In Ruth 4:11, both Leah and Rachel are acknowledged as the ones who *"did build (banah) the house of Israel."* Proverbs 14:1 reads, *"Every wise woman **buildeth** (Banah) her house, but the foolish plucketh it down with her hands."* The wise mother builds her family up and keeps the home (Titus 2:5; 1 Tim. 5:14).

Sarai's plan seemed to work: *"Abram hearkened to the voice of Sarai."* (Gen. 16:2), and Hagar quickly conceived. However, in every human device there is ample opportunity for pride, and such was the case in this family – for Hagar was carrying Abram's child, a child that Sarai apparently could never give her husband. Hagar became proud and despised her mistress. Polygamy was not God's best plan for marriage, and the Bible never upholds it as a happy and blissful situation. He told Adam that one man and one woman shall become one flesh. Polygamy, as seen in Abram's household, promoted jealousy and envy.

Who did Sarai blame for this bad situation? Was it herself? After all, it was her proposal. No, she blamed her husband: *"my wrong be upon thee,"* she told him. Abram refused to accept the blame of her own conniving and instructed her to resolve the problem as she saw fit. So Sarai dealt harshly with Hagar, so much so that she fled from her mistress' presence into the wilderness. God was not about to let this be

Seeds of Destiny

the solution to the matter, however. His chosen covenant family had distrusted Him and made bad choices, but they were destined to learn to live with the consequences of those choices. What was God's method to resolve a situation like this? When we have done wrong, we must humble ourselves, confess the ill, and graciously accept judicial and natural recompense. Sarai tried to alleviate the matter by venting anger at the "bondwoman" and raising a high hand.

God's justice and righteousness are not reflected in this type of behavior. He did not approve of Sarai's actions. This unjust behavior had to be reproved, or else an ill sense of godliness might develop within His covenant family's understanding of Himself. God is a just God and expects His children to behave in the same righteous manner.

Abram and Sarai were not content to allow the Lord to bless in His timing. Their lapse of faith would be felt for many generations, and the Arab-Israeli conflict wages on even unto this day.

> Lord, let me give and sing and sow and do my best, though I
> In years to come may never know what soul was helped thereby.
> Content to feel that Thou canst bless all things however small
> To someone's lasting happiness so, Lord, accept my all.
>
> Prudence Tasker Olsen

A Well for Hagar
Genesis 16:7-16

The day came when Hagar could bear the mistreatment no longer. Her only recourse was to run away with her unborn child and trek back to Egypt. God was watching over Hagar; He knew the journey through the wilderness would be too much for her. Her departure was sweetened by a personal visit from "the Angel of Lord." It is the Lord's first appearance in Scripture by that title. He had come to comfort and to encourage a distraught woman. We understand "the Angel of the Lord" to be a "theophany." A theophany is a pre-incarnate visit of Christ to the earth as His Father's messenger. Normally, His appearance is that of a man, but He may also be in the midst of a pillar cloud or a burning bush. He is called "the Angel of the Lord," not to be confused with "an angel of the Lord," which could be any one of millions of the ordinary holy angels.

In the New Testament, the Son of God is called the Word (Jn. 1:1; 1 Jn. 1:1). The English word "angel" means "messenger" in both Hebrew and Greek. The role of the Son in the Trinity is to do the Father's will; therefore, part of this activity would be to communicate the Father's will to humanity. When the Son did this in the Old Testament, He is referred to as "the Messenger (Angel) of the Lord." In the New Testament, the Son became a man to bring the ultimate message of God to humanity. The Lord Jesus was a living message – He was both the message and the messenger of God. Other than the title of "the Angel of the Lord" identifying this individual as the second person of the Godhead, He can also be identified by the context of the passage. The Angel of the Lord is worshipped as God by others (Josh. 5:14; Judg. 6:18-20), makes covenants and promises that only God can keep (Gen. 16:10, 22:16-17), and in most occurrences, clearly identifies Himself as God (Gen. 31:11-13; Ex. 3:2-6). These temporary theophanies are not

Seeds of Destiny

possible or needed now to do the Father's will. The Son of God became flesh (Jn. 1:14) over 2000 years ago and completed the Father's will on earth until the moment comes when He will bodily return to judge wickedness and to rule and reign in righteousness forever. He lives today and forever as glorified humanity. C. H. Waller comments on the scene before us:

> Whenever God showed His face to men it was His Son they saw [Jn. 1:18]. In the first place in the Old Testament where the Angel of Jehovah is named, we find Him seeking a lost sheep of the house of Abraham. That lost sheep was Hagar, the mother (in-law she may be called) of all that are cast out and lost."[1]

The Lord met Hagar in the wilderness by a fountain of water (Gen. 16:7) – a well (Gen. 16:14). This is the first mention of a well in Scripture. How fitting for the all-sustaining Lord to meet a distressed woman fleeing for her life at a well in a desert place. Interestingly, the first occurrence of a "well" in the New Testament is when the Lord meets a Samaritan women with a devastated life at Jacob's well (Jn. 4:6). He offers her "living water" (Himself) to satisfy her spiritually parched life. Like Hagar, she believed and obeyed the Lord and received a great blessing from him. The Prophet Isaiah writes, *"With joy shall ye draw water out of the wells of salvation"* (Isa. 12:3). There is a fountain of lasting joy that springs up from the believer's spirit when Christ dwells within. For Hagar, this refreshment to her spirit was not found in Egypt (the world), it was received on the way to Shur (Gen. 16:7). The Lord would not allow Hagar to get into Egypt but intervened on her behalf to protect her from Egypt. How often the Lord has protected His children from entangling circumstances leading to despair through direct communion with Himself on the way to Shur!

Peter mentions a "well," for the final time in Scripture, when he warns against false teachers. *"These are wells without water, clouds that are carried with a tempest, to whom the mist of darkness is reserved for ever"* (2 Pet. 2:17). False teachers offer falsehoods, which culminate in false hopes. The Lord Jesus is God's messenger of truth, who offers an abundant life of joy despite circumstances (Jn. 10:10).

156

Devotions in Genesis

The "lie" is more than happy to escort those parched souls willing to follow it to the closest open grave. No bubbling fountain of refreshment is there; only a dry hole awaiting its condemned occupant. However, when one embraces the Savior, a jubilant fountain of refreshing spiritual drink is enjoyed, and blessing is obtained. The abundant life is found, and like Israel in the midst of the wilderness, we, too, can sing to the well, *"Spring up, O well"* (Num. 21:17). Drink, yea, drink abundantly! For from out of the well the sheep are watered (Gen. 29:2), and through Christ, God refreshes His sheep.

The Lord told Hagar that she would bear a son; his name would be "Ishmael," and his descendants would become a great nation. Ishmael's name was given for the occasion. Ishmael means "God shall hear," and God heard her affliction and came to help her in a time of need. His name would be a constant reminder that her Egyptian gods failed her, but the one true God heard her crying and assisted her. What affliction might you be bearing today? Perhaps death of a loved one – *"Precious in the sight of the Lord is the death of his saints"* (Ps. 116:15). Perhaps deep heartache over a rebellious child or an unfair circumstance – *"They that sow in tears shall reap in joy"* (Ps. 126:5). Or perhaps some personal sin you cannot seem overcome has you discouraged – *"Have mercy upon me, O God, according to thy lovingkindness; according unto the multitude of thy tender mercies blot out my transgressions"* (Ps. 51:1). Whatever your "ill" is, know that God is watching and that He knows all about it. God met Hagar at a well and gave her a new hope; there is a Well waiting for you, too – His name is Jesus Christ! He gives hope and direction for the future.

Not only did the Lord tell Hagar what to name her unborn son, but He also informed her of his character. Ishmael would be a *"wild man"* and would be in constant conflict with the surrounding inhabitants. Ishmael was a son of flesh and what issues from the flesh behaves itself as flesh and in opposition to that which is spiritual. *"That which is born of the flesh is flesh, and that which is born of the Spirit is spirit"* (Jn. 3:6). Nature can only produce the same nature.

Since he would *"dwell in the presence of all his brethren,"* we understand that Ishmael, including his descendants, would have an adversarial relationship with Isaac, the spiritual son of promise, and his descendants, the Jewish nation.

Seeds of Destiny

    The Lord also told Hagar to go back and be in submission to her mistress, and this she did. A few months later, just as God said, Abram's family was blessed with a baby boy – they named him "Ishmael." Abram was 86 years old.

    Though Abram has demonstrated incredible faith in his God, there were brief periods of doubt, each having its own end and consequence. From these situations and trials we must endeavor to glean lessons for ourselves. Thus far, four valuable principles have been derived from Abram's self-inflicted adversity: (1) Partial obedience is still **disobedience in part**. (2) **Delayed** obedience is also disobedience. (3) **Dwelling** apart from God brings a dry and unsatisfying existence. (4) **Diverting** into the world when trouble comes will not solve your problems. In this chapter, we learn that **deviation** from God's will has painful consequences. Nothing is said of Abram for 13 years after his lapse of faith in taking Hagar as a concubine to bear a son. This mistake is much different than the error of "delay." "Delay" yields to the truth eventually, but "deviation" causes the soul to seek another approach than the way God has revealed – it is placing "the flesh" over "promise." If Abram had not "diverted" into Egypt during tough times, Sarai would not have suggested Hagar as a solution – there would have been no Hagar. Concerning obedience to God's revealed will, these are five behaviors to be avoided, or the harvest of consequences will be much more than one could have ever imagined. Abram is about to learn all about the laws of the harvest.

    Understanding can wait, but obedience cannot.

                                     Geoffrey Grogan

    Faith and obedience are bound up in the same bundle. He that obeys God, trusts God; and he that trusts God, obeys God.

                                     Charles Haddon Spurgeon

New Names
Genesis 17:1-8

After thirteen years of silence, God again appeared unto Abram. Why thirteen years and not five, or seven or twelve? Because in the Bible, the number thirteen is associated with rebellion, disobedience, or some other form of depravity. The first occurrence of thirteen is in Genesis 14:4: *"Twelve years they served Chedorlaomer, and in the thirteenth year they **rebelled**."* The principle of "first mention" is clearly associated with rebellion. Thirteen relates to Abram's disbelief in Genesis 17:25 and to Haman's decree to kill the Jews, God's chosen people, on the thirteenth day of 12th month (Est. 3:8-13). Solomon built a magnificent temple for God in seven years, but it took thirteen years to finish building his own palace (1 Kings 6:38-7:1). Thirteen judges are recorded ruling over Israel during a time when everyone did what was right in their own eyes. The Israelites marched around rebellious Jericho thirteen times before God destroyed them. God lists twenty-three grievances in Romans 1:29-31 against fallen humanity, and the thirteenth is "haters of God." Of course, the greatest "hater of God" would be Satan himself; thus, he is referred to thirteen times in the book of Revelation as the "Dragon." The first man to instigate mass rebellion against God on earth was a man named Nimrod, who was the father of pagan Babylonian religion. Nimrod was the thirteenth in the cursed line of Ham (Noah's youngest son). Lastly, the Lord used a total of thirteen evil characteristics in Mark 7:21-22 to describe a depraved and rebellious heart. God waited thirteen years to meet with Abram because he had rebelled against God's word, as symbolically represented in the number thirteen.

It is, therefore, significant that God chose to utter the word "covenant" thirteen times in this chapter. Perhaps God was addressing Abram's past lapse of faith through the meaning of the number thirteen,

Seeds of Destiny

in the same way that the Lord Jesus reproved Peter in John 21. Peter had denied the Lord three times, and the Lord also inquired of Peter three times concerning his love for Him (Jn. 21).

How does God convey the significance of His covenant with Abram? Nine times God speaks of it as *"My covenant;"* three times He calls it *"an everlasting covenant,"* and once God directly states *"the covenant between Me and you."*

In Genesis 15, Abram's *justification* was witnessed, but in Genesis 17, it is his *sanctification* unto God that is paramount. God was calling Abram to separate from the flesh's desires and ways to be nigh to Him. God appeared and spoke to Abram, *"I am the Almighty God; walk before Me, and be thou perfect."* These words should deeply penetrate the heart of everyone professing to know God. Spiritual life would be incomplete if we had salvation without Christ dwelling richly in our hearts by faith (Eph. 3:17). God's command *"Be ye holy for I am holy"* is applied both to those in the Old Testament and in the New (Lev. 11:44, 1 Pet. 1:16). Understanding who God is should cause His children to walk in a way that reflects the holy family resemblance. A child's nose, eyes, body build, etc. are normally patterned after his/her parents' related features. Likewise, the child of God should resemble family holiness – for our Father is holy.

In God's statement to Abram, He reveals Himself by the new name *El Shaddai*, meaning "Almighty God." Although God had already made a covenant with Abram, He now was going to back it up with all His omnipotent power. Abram listened to the Lord and was moved to fall upon his face in utter reverence for His God. In the presence of Almighty God, Abram recognized his frail existence. In Genesis 15, Abram had been thinking of himself while in God's presence, but now his thoughts were brought to a higher plain. Only God and His bidding were paramount – he would now walk by faith and doubt no more.

Abram, who doubted and stumbled in his faith in Genesis 16, was now exhorted to *walk before God* perfectly in Genesis 17; this can only be accomplished by walking in faith. The children of Israel were exhorted to *walk after God* (Deut. 13:4), and both Enoch and Noah *walked with God*. Colossians 2:6 admonishes those who have received Christ *to walk in Him*. Arthur Pink provides the following observation:

To walk *before* is suggestive of a child running ahead and playing in the presence of his father, conscious of his perfect *security* because he is just behind. To walk *after* becomes a servant following his master. To walk *with* indicates fellowship and friendship. To walk *in* denotes union. We might summarize these varied aspects of the believer's walk as intimated by the four different prepositions thus: we walk 'before' God as *children*; we walk 'after' Him as *servants*; we walk 'with' Him as His *friends*; we walk 'in' Him as *members of His body*.[1]

Abram needed a complete walk of faith! God aided Abram in his walk by changing his name – it would serve as a reminder of who he was in God's sight. His original name meant "exalted father," yet he had lived 86 years without children and, even now, only had one son. His new name, "Abraham," meant "father of multitudes." Abraham's new name must have seemed humorous to the inhabitants of the land: "We are supposed to call you what? A father of nations? Excuse me, Abram, have you been out in the sun too long? Are you feeling well? Perhaps we should remind you that you only have one son?" Perhaps they were laughing then, but no one is laughing now. Ishmael, Abraham's son, had twelve princes; Jacob, Abraham's grandson through Isaac, had twelve sons, and Esau, Abraham's other grandson through Isaac, had five sons. Besides this, Abraham married Keturah after Sarah's death and had six more sons that also became nations in themselves. Ishmael became the father of the Arab world, and Jacob the father of the Jewish nation.

Seven times in this chapter, God said, "I will" in making promises to Abraham. God used the perfect number of seven to proclaim His perfect promise and plan to Abraham. God kept His word to Abraham – He was the father of many nations. Yet, the repercussions of his lapse of faith with Hagar can plainly be seen in the world today as a scene of continual violence is staged in the Middle East. Today, these descendants of Father Abraham, 120 million Arabs, surround about 6 million Jews in the land of Israel.

Sarai also got a new name, Sarah, meaning "princess," for she would be the mother of kings and nations. The added Hebrew suffix in both Abram's and Sarai's new names has the "hawm" or "raw" sounds, respectively. The only way to properly make the "aw" sound is to

Seeds of Destiny

exhale a large volume of air through one's open mouth. God would have had to breathe out upon His pilgrim family to say their new names. Scripture records a few instances of God breathing upon someone, then that person(s) received a new life. When God breathed upon Adam, he became a living being, and when the Lord breathed upon the disciples, they received a new life in the Holy Spirit (Jn. 20:22). When the Holy Spirit came upon the disciples to form the Church and to fill and equip them for ministry, there was the sound of rushing air in the room. When God changed Abram and Sarai's names, He was giving them new identities – a new life in Him.

> Breathe on me, breath of God, fill me with life anew,
> That I may love what Thou dost love, and do what Thou wouldst do.
> Breathe on me, breath of God, until my heart is pure,
> Until with Thee I will one will, to do and to endure.
> Breathe on me, breath of God, till I am wholly Thine,
> Until this earthly part of me glows with Thy fire divine.
> Breathe on me, breath of God, so shall I never die,
> But live with Thee the perfect life of thine eternity.
>
> Edwin Hatch

A Token
Genesis 17:9-27

Besides a new name and a new walk, Abraham would also receive a token of the covenant God had made with him. No doubt Abraham was excited to learn that God was going to give him a sign concerning the covenant. However, the sign was not a wonder in the sky or a miracle of healing, it was circumcision. Imagine for a moment if we were Abraham, how we might reply to the Lord: "Lord, my hearing is not what it used to be, could you please repeat that bit about the sign You're going to give me – I thought you said something about circumcision." Then the reply: "You heard right, Abraham – circumcision shall be My sign to you of My covenant with you." So Abraham, a 99-year-old man, and all the males of his house were circumcised the very day God had commanded it (Gen. 17:26-27). Then, his descendants for thousands of years would continue this symbolic ritual to honor God and to acknowledge His covenant with them. Paul tells us in Romans 4:11 that circumcision was *"a seal of the righteousness of the faith which he had yet being uncircumcised."* Circumcision was a "token" of Abraham's righteous standing gained by faith in God's promise.

Why circumcision as a sign? What is the organ of the body that best identifies an individual as a man? Right – that's it. So, by stripping away a piece of foreskin from this organ, God was symbolizing the stripping away of an old identity and the reliance on God for a new one. The act of circumcision in Genesis 17 complements beautifully the name changes given Abram and Sarai. God was about to enact His covenant with them by giving them a son. It was only fitting that they realize their new identities as God's chosen people and as human instruments to bless the entire world. Abraham was already declared justified by God before circumcision was instituted (Rom. 4:11). The "circumcised life" was something Abraham was living before God.

It is the same for the believer today. When individuals humble themselves as sinners before God and confess their need for a Savior, God responds by cleansing and regenerating them (Tit. 3:5), sealing them with the Holy Spirit (Eph. 1:13), and declaring them righteous (imputing divine righteousness to their account – Rom. 4:4-5; 2 Cor. 5:21). *"If any man be in Christ, he is a new creature (creation); old things are passed away; behold, all things are become new"* (2 Cor. 5:17). However, our new identity in Christ demands that we live the "circumcised life," which is the "cutting off" or "putting to death" of the desires and the will of our flesh. Paul summarizes in Romans 2:29 that it is the circumcision of the heart God wants in a believer's life, not just an outward show.

In one sense, the act of *circumcision* for the Old Testament Jew is similar to the act of a New Testament Christian who follows in *believer's baptism* – water baptism. A circumcised life is one that acknowledges being dead to self and alive in Christ. In this sense physical circumcision and water baptism are alike. Yet, the similitude breaks down when comparing the fuller dispensational truth of Scripture. Under the Law, parents circumcised their baby boys without their consent; whereas, believer's baptism in the Church Age was *always* after Gentiles believed the gospel message (Acts 10:47, 16:31-34).

While the Lord is speaking to Abraham, He foretells of a miracle birth in Abraham's family. In a year's time Sarah would bear him a son, and his name would be Isaac. Abraham responded to this news with a laugh of amazement, not doubt: *"Shall a child be born unto him that is an hundred years old?"* God concludes His visit with Abraham by promising to bless Ishmael. Why? Because he was Abraham's son and because Abraham His friend requested it.

> Consecration is the narrow, lonely way to overflowing love. We are not called upon to live long on this planet, but we are called upon to be holy at any and every cost. If obedience costs you your life, then pay it.
>
> Oswald Chambers

Communion with God
Genesis 18:1-8

In Genesis 17, God revealed Himself to Abraham as the Almighty God – the only One who can make and complete promises despite every difficulty. This revelation consequently required Abraham to be perfect in his confidence in God and be perfect (mature) in his walk before God. He was to have no confidence in his own flesh. In Genesis 18, we are permitted to witness the blessed privilege of communion for those who walk by faith with Almighty God.

The Lord appeared again unto Abraham near the oaks of Mamre. It was the heat of the day, so Abraham was sitting within the door of the tent and out of the direct sun. What was Abraham's response when he saw the Lord (a theophany) and two men with Him (whom we later learn were angels)? The 99-year-old man ran to meet the Lord (Gen. 18:2). Because Abraham was a man of faith, he had spiritual discernment to distinguish the Lord from the other two men (angels). *"Lord, if now I have found favor in Thy sight, pass not away, I pray Thee, from Thy servant."* Those who draw nigh to God are the first to sense the Lord's presence and His working in their lives.

Abraham did his part to "refresh" the Lord; *"Let a little water, I pray you, be fetched, and wash your feet, and rest yourselves under the tree."* This is the first occurrence of foot washing in the Bible – man is refreshing God by washing His feet. The last biblical reference of foot washing is when the Lord Jesus (God incarnate) washed the feet of His disciples (Jn. 13). God, in the world, once bore man's filth to avail a provision for man to be cleansed of the world's filth (1 Jn. 1:9).

Abraham hastened into the tent of Sarah to arouse her to prepare a meal for their unexpected guests. Abraham then ran to the herd to get a tender calf for dinner (Gen. 18:7). It was hurried work to prepare a meal for their guests, but definitely not "fast food." How often do you see a 100-year-old man running in the heat of the day? Rarely. But Abraham delighted in the Lord and enjoyed His fellowship. The Lord delighted in Abraham also. So much so that Scripture records that God considered him a friend (Isa. 41:8, 2 Chron. 20:7).

It is worthy to note that Abraham "bowed" himself towards the ground in front of his visitors. The Hebrew word for "bow" is *shachah*, which is the usual word for "worship" in the Old Testament. Somehow Abraham knew that these men were special visitors, perhaps coming to convey more news of God's covenant promise. As this is the first occurrence of *shachah* in Scripture, it seems only fitting that the "first mention" standard of man bowing down and worshipping his Creator be established as appropriate throughout the remainder of the Bible.

Abraham and Sarah graciously set a table for the Lord and His two angels under the shade of an oak tree, and Abraham stood by like a waiter while his guests ate. What is the purpose of the Lord's Supper that Jesus Himself instituted the night before He died? Paul writes the purpose of this feast it is to proclaim the Lord's death and to remember Him (1 Cor. 11:24-26). When His saints set the table with bread and wine and sing of the Lord's matchless grace, infinite mercies, and loving-kindness with pure hearts, the Lord is "refreshed." Although our focus is to refresh the Lord, we ourselves are also refreshed. It delighted Abraham to refresh the Lord by washing his feet and setting a table before Him, but he was also refreshed by the Lord's presence while resting under the same shadow of a tree. The words of the Shulamite bride in the presence of her lover describe the experience well: *"I sat down under his shadow with great delight"* (SOS 2:3). How wonderful to set a feast of bread and wine before the Lord each week and to refresh Him with worship and praise, while the whole time resting under the shadow of His cross!

> In the secret of His presence how my soul delights to hide!
> Oh, how precious are the lessons which I learn at Jesus' side!
> Earthly cares can never vex me, neither trials lay me low;
> For when Satan comes to tempt me, to the secret place I go.
> When my soul is faint and thirsty, 'neath the shadow of His wing,
> There is cool and pleasant shelter, and a fresh and crystal spring.

> Ellen Gorch

I Will Certainly Return
Genesis 18:9-22

After dinner, the Lord spoke to Abraham, *"I will certainly return unto thee according to the time of life; and lo, Sarah, thy wife, shall have a son."* Sarah overheard this conversation and laughed within herself. It was a cynical and internal snicker of disbelief. Though there was no audible noise, the Lord asked why she laughed. Now she knew that this was the Lord for how could anyone else know her thoughts. She denied laughing within herself. The Lord responded with a staggering question to assert one of the greatest expressions of truth in the Bible, *"Is anything too hard for the Lord?"* Perhaps we should not be too hard on Sarah for Hebrews 11:11 reads *"Through faith also Sarah herself received strength to conceive seed, and was delivered of a child when she was past age, because she judged Him faithful who had promised."*

Twice in this portion of Scripture the Lord declares, *"I will return unto thee."* These words have encouraged God's people through the ages not to lose heart. The night before the Lord Jesus was crucified He comforted His disciples with the same promise, *"I will come again, and received you unto Myself"* (Jn. 14:3). The final Holy Page declares three times, *"I come quickly."* For anyone else but the Lord of Glory to make such a promise would be presumptuous. Dear believer, don't lose heart, He is really coming back for you!

For ye have need of patience, that, after ye have done the will of God, ye might receive the promise. For yet a little while, and He that shall come **will come**, *and* **will not tarry**. *Now the just shall live by faith: but if any man draw back, my soul shall have no pleasure in him* (Heb. 10:36-38).

Seeds of Destiny

When dinner was over, Abraham walked with his three guests towards Sodom. Genesis 18:17 should be an encouragement to all of us who talk to ourselves on occasion, for God talks to Himself in an audible voice. The two angels went on ahead to view the wickedness of Sodom first hand. Did God not know that Sodom was evil without sending angels to inspect the city visibly? Certainly, the Lord told Abraham that the cry of wickedness was great (Gen. 18:20). Then, why did God personally come to earth, and why did He send two angels to Sodom to personally witness the wickedness?

Not only is God righteous and just, but He will be seen to be righteous and just by all. No one will be able to accuse God of not being fair. Two angels would personally visit Sodom and, therefore, be witnesses to the wicked condition and the deserving judgment of Sodom. Yet, God in His mercy also used these angelic messengers to deliver the righteous souls (Lot and his family) from judgment.

Every circumstance in Genesis 18 speaks of a righteous man's open communion with God. The Lord and the two angels drew near Abraham in human form. They readily accepted Abraham's service, speech, and friendship. In the realm of divine fellowship, Genesis 18 is in striking contrast to God's disposition towards Lot in Genesis 19. In Chapter 19, God does not personally visit carnal Lot, nor do the angels appear as men any longer, but as "angels." Even the angels are standoffish and initially refuse Lot's company and provisions. God is not mocked – our carnality necessitates distance and reduced familiarity with Him.

> Nearer, still nearer, while life shall last,
> Till safe in glory my anchor is cast;
> Through endless ages, ever to be,
> Nearer, my Savior, still nearer to Thee.
>
> Lelia Morris

Abraham the Intercessor
Genesis 18:22-33

In the remainder of Genesis 18, we observe Abraham as God's intercessor. One of the present ministries of Christ in heaven is to be our legal representative or "advocate" before the Father (1 Jn. 2:1). This is a special comfort to every believer, especially knowing that Satan slanders us before God's throne day and night (Rev. 12:10). Though the English term "advocate" is only translated once from the original Greek in the New Testament, this Greek word is more frequently translated "comforter," as in the four references to the Holy Spirit in John's Gospel account. The role of the "Advocate" or "Comforter" is to legally plead one's case or to speak on the behalf of another in a court of law – a legal intercessor. Thayer's Greek definition describes the meaning as "Christ's pleading for pardon of our sins before the Father." When does Christ plead our case? When we acknowledge and confess our sins? 1 John 2:1 states that Christ **is** our advocate when we sin, not when we confess our sins, though we should. Concerning the continuing ministry of advocacy by the Lord Jesus, S. Emery writes:

> His valid ministry, therefore, on our behalf, is not on the basis of an effective, verbal and persuasive pleading before the Father, but on the basis of a perfect satisfaction for all our sins ever before the Father's face. He is our propitiation of undiminishing value. ... His very presence before the Father is the plea. Continuance in the family of God is never in question, but forgiveness of our sins, and cleansing from all unrighteousness, is experienced only when we make confession (1 Jn. 1:9).[1]

James Gunn writes in his book *Christ the Fullness of the Godhead*:

Christ is not a mere suppliant petitioner. He pleads for us on the grounds of justice, of righteousness, of obedience to the law, and endurance of its full penalty for us, on which He grounds His claim for our acquittal. The sense therefore is, "in that He is righteous."[2]

When a believer sins, Satan may abruptly call God's attention to the despicable deed, but Christ is at the right hand of God the Father. He also acknowledges the unrighteous behavior of the believer but then states that the penalty for this lawless deed has already been paid by Himself at Calvary. In this way, all heavenly hosts, powers and principalities will see that God is righteous and that He has accounted justly for every wrong the believer has done. God hates sin, but because He judged Christ for sin, He can extend the repentant sinner a full pardon and family status as His adopted child (Rom. 8:15). Though we never need to fear the judicial penalty of our sins being laid upon us, we will long to live in holiness before our Father so as to stay in fellowship with Him and to not provoke His chastening hand. Our souls have been liberated through the work of Christ to serve God out of love and not out of fear of judgment, for judgment is past and true love does not fear (1 Jn. 4:18).

Understanding the continual scene in heaven should cause the child of God to keep "short accounts" with God. As soon as one is conscious of sin, the sin should be confessed. The great preacher, C. H. Spurgeon, was once walking across a busy and dangerous street with another Christian man. Spurgeon stopped in the middle of the street, bowed his head, then momentarily lifted up again and proceeded to walk across the street without saying a word. The man reproved him for stopping, "What were you doing back there, it looked like you were praying?" Spurgeon replied, "Indeed I was, a cloud came between me and my Savior, and I wanted to remove it even before I got across the street." God desires His children not to sin (1 Jn. 2:1). But when we do sin – *"If we confess our sins, He is faithful and just to forgive us our sins, and to cleanse us from all unrighteousness"* (1 Jn. 1:9). Let the child of God stay in active fellowship with his Father by holy living and confessing the moment we stumble.

God was conducting an investigation personally into the great cry and sin of Sodom and Gomorrah (Gen. 18:20). The visible presence of God's angels in the judgment of Sodom serves as a reminder that the

Devotions in Genesis

righteous must not live among the wicked. One can only imagine how the distressing moans of wickedness from our liberal culture wrenches the forbearing heart of God. We will see in Genesis 19 that living in wickedness cost Lot everything. True, he salvaged two of his daughters, but he lost their hearts to a polluted, immoral culture. When faced with the dilemma of being childless, they resorted to the tactics of sexual perversion they were accustomed to seeing and laid with their own father.

Lastly, God had come to earth to seek an intercessor. He found one in Abraham who stood in the gap for Sodom. He was successful in interceding for the wicked city – God finally agreed to spare the city if there were ten righteous souls there. However, the angels found only four souls willing to heed the warning of judgment, and the city was destroyed after Lot, his wife, and two daughters escaped. How thankful Abraham must have felt in the success of his earnest efforts for the deliverance of Sodom. But how much sorrow the next morning to view the smoldering eastern plain. Abraham witnessed the sure, just, and awesome wrath of God upon wickedness that day. All his efforts had only saved a few, while the entire city had been judged. How fully ripe the grapes of earth are today. In stillness the Lord's sharp sickle hangs over the world. One swift thrash and the grapes of the earth will be gathered for *the great winepress of the wrath of God* (Rev. 14:19). Yet the church slumbers while the masses slide into eternal damnation! Let us make intercession for the lost while it is yet day, for night is near and God's judgment is sure.

Moses, likewise, stood in the gap for sinful Israel in Exodus 32:7-14. They were dancing naked around an idol, and God was ready to destroy them and make a nation out of Moses. But Moses interceded, and the KJV reads *"The Lord repented of the evil which He thought to do unto His people"* (Ex. 32:14). Did God really change His mind? Whose "will" was done that day? God's, of course. God really did not change His mind, but from man's perspective, it seemed as though He did. God is long suffering and slow to judgment, but He desires to have someone plead the case of the guilty that He may show mercy upon them. Isaiah 59:16 reads *"And He (God) saw that there was no man, and wondered that there was no intercessor; therefore, His arm brought salvation unto Him, and His righteousness it sustained him."*

Seeds of Destiny

When it came to ultimately finding someone to stand in the gap for all mankind, there was no one who could righteously plead man's case. Therefore, God sent His own Arm (His Son) to be the intercessor for us. The intercessor had to be God Himself to be the perfect sacrifice and to sustain the judgment of a Holy God for all man's sin.

In Genesis 17, Abraham was exhorted to walk purely before the Lord. His walk with the Lord in Genesis 18 is clearly intimate and faithful. In this chapter, Abraham enjoyed four distinct privileges of this walk: (1) the providing of refreshment **for the Lord**, (2) full communion **with the Lord**, (3) the opportunity for intercession **before the Lord**, and (4) the receiving of revelation **from the Lord**. The New Testament Church and every local church today can enjoy these same four qualities of walking with Christ. In Acts 2:42, we read that the early Christians *"continued steadfastly in the apostles' doctrine* (teaching God's Word), *and fellowship* (sharing with God's people), *and in breaking of bread* (the Lord's supper – worshipping God), *and in prayers* (speaking to God)." Are you walking properly with the Intercessor of your soul?

> I hear the accuser roar of ills that I have done;
> I know them well, and thousands more Jehovah findeth none.
> Though the restless foe accuses – sins recounting like a flood;
> Every charge our God refuses; Christ has answered with His blood.
>
> unknown

Immersed in the World
Genesis 19:1-3

Lot met the two angels at the city gate of Sodom. In Genesis 18, the Lord and two angels appeared to faithful Abraham in the light of day, but in Genesis 19 it is only the two angels who come to visit carnal Lot at evening. The lack of divine revelation and personal communion between the Lord and Lot is thus portrayed. Though the angels had been sent to administer judgment upon Sodom, their twofold ministry is evident for they also *"minister for them who shall be heirs of salvation"* (Heb. 1:14). Yes, God will judge the world, but He also knows how to deliver the righteous, no matter how carnal, out of it! Peter, speaking of Lot, writes, *"The Lord knoweth how to deliver the godly out of temptations, and to reserve the unjust unto the day of judgment to be punished"* (2 Pet. 2:9).

Lot was concerned with the visitor's safety and offered to provide them lodging for the night at his home. Initially, they refused. What a rebuke to Lot – the angels preferred to abide in the streets of a perverse city than spending an evening with a righteous man living an indulgent life. The angels certainly had no problem sharing Abraham's hospitality earlier in the day. Abraham's tent stands in sharp contrast to Lot's house.

The word "street" occurs for the first time in the Bible in Genesis 19:2. The street of Sodom is in drastic variance to the last street mentioned in the Bible, a street of gold in the New Jerusalem (Rev. 21:21) – God's eternal dwelling place with His saints. The first street was shadowed in the darkness of night and the wickedness of man, but the last street is illuminated by God's glory and speaks of purity and holiness. Truly the street of Sodom led to destruction, while the street of gold leads to God and eternal life. There is a wide road leading to hell and a narrow way that leads to eternal life with Christ Jesus (Matt. 7:13-14).

Lot finally convinced the two angels to abide in his home for the night. The fact that Lot prepared them a feast of "unleavened bread" may sug-

Seeds of Destiny

gest that his wife was not willing to receive their guests. Leaven, first mentioned here in the Bible speaks of sin, corruption, or evil doctrine throughout Scripture. The unleavened bread stood in sharp contrast to Lot's "leavened life." The next occurrence of unleavened bread in Scripture is found in the institution of the Passover Feast (Ex. 12). Though the Israelites were immersed in a pagan Egyptian culture God instructed them to eat unleavened bread and in fact remove all leaven from their homes (Ex. 12:15). Though in the world they were not to be of the world. So dear Christian, if you have secret stashes of leaven lurking about in some dark secluded corner of your home, "get it out of your house!" Henry Morris writes, "Leaven, of course, being involved with the fermentation process, is a perfect symbol of decay and corruption, and it is important that spiritual fellowship not be contaminated with it."[1]

In previous chapters we have witnessed Lot descending step by step through a sequence of compromises, which now have settled him in spiritual carnality. How did he feel about his spiritual condition and the evil situation that was now his? 2 Peter 2:8 informs us that *Lot "dwelling among them, in seeing and hearing, vexed his righteous soul from day to day with their unlawful deeds."* He was miserable and seemingly under constant rebuke from his own conscience. Or, as Warren Wiersbe describes the situation, "impression, without expression, leads to depression," which is what happens when we know what we should do and do not do it. Even though spiritually contaminated and emotionally grieving, Lot apparently held a position of authority within the civil structure of Sodom. Because of accessibility to the people coming and going from the city, the city gate was often the location where governing officials met to consult the people and make judgments.

Perhaps Lot thought he could make a difference in the city, maybe bring spiritual revival. Maybe he thought his children could be a testimony to their friends. Possibly Lot was congratulating himself on achieving the best of both worlds – the eternal spiritual blessings of knowing God and the temporal benefits that worldly influence and earthly possessions confer to the flesh. Whatever his thinking was, it was flawed. God's message has always been the same to His people concerning the world and ungodliness: *"[I will] bring them up out of land"* (Ex. 3:8), *"come unto Me"* (Ex. 32:26), and *"separate yourselves"* (Num. 16:21). The Lord said to His disciples, *"I have chosen you out of the world, therefore the world hateth you"* (Jn. 15:19). The world hates godliness, and God hates worldliness in the believer's life (Jas. 4:4).

The believer must counterbalance the call to holy separation with the call of the Great Commission – *"Go ye, therefore, and teach all nations..."* (Matt. 28:19). Where is the symmetry between the Lord's commands to "separate" yourselves and to "go out"? It is being in the world, but not of the world. A ship is designed to operate in water, but when water floods into the ship, it ceases to behave as intended – it sinks. It is the same with the believer's vessel. It is designed to be in the world as a testimony for God, but when the world gets into the Christian's life – you're sunk. The children of darkness are then quite eager to make an open spectacle of the fallen comrade and, thus, a "castaway" in Christian service (1 Cor. 9:27). Though failures are not final with God, the consequences to a Christian's testimony can be so devastating that recovery to full ministry is nearly impossible.

Scripture, likewise, speaks of two contrasting means that call the believer's heart out of the world. The first is to set one's mind on things above, and the second is by constant exposure of the temporary and shakable things on earth. The writer of Hebrews summarizes the latter aspect of the world: *"... removing of those things that are shaken, as of things that are made, that those things which cannot be shaken may remain. Wherefore, we receiving a kingdom which cannot be moved, let us have grace, whereby we may serve God acceptably with reverence and godly fear; for our God is a consuming fire"* (Heb. 12:27-29). The world is nasty and temporal, but heaven is wonderful and eternal.

What activities in the world may Christians engage in without damaging their testimony or bringing reproach upon the name of Christ? Instead of deriving a list of "dos" and "don'ts," let us look at the following principles, guidelines and warnings from Scripture. The Old Testament is full of "dos" and "don'ts" to show man that he could not keep such a list, which reflected God's holiness. These standards and regulations were to prove to man that he was a sinner (Rom. 3:20), then to point him to the solution – the Savior (Gal. 3:24). However, the New Testament imposes very few "dos" and "don'ts" upon the Christian. It is not that God's standard of holiness has changed, but the motive for service has changed. Instead of fear, it is love; instead of God's judg-

Seeds of Destiny

ment looming overhead, it is His grace that falls as dew from heaven upon parched hearts (Hos. 14:5). So, God now lets us work out (not work for) our own salvation in reverence for who He is (Phil. 2:12) and allows love to be the motive for our service (2 Cor. 5:14).

If Scripture clearly approves or disapproves of a specific matter, the response is simply to obey the command. If the behavior is not addressed in the Bible, one must determine what is wise behavior and what is foolish conduct by studying the principles, warnings, guidelines, and promises contained in God's Word. On questionable matters: study, pray, ask for godly counsel, listen to your conscience and the prompting of God's Spirit. Some, like Lot, ignore their conscience and to practice filthy living to the point that their conscience becomes seared and dull. By studying God's Word, we "sharpen" our conscience and become more sensitive to it. Dear believer, if after indulging in some activity, you feel guilt, repent of it, and refrain from that activity in the future. The Christian has an anointing of the Holy Spirit that will bless him or her with discernment as to what is true and false – right and wrong (1 Jn. 2:20, 27).

I must go home by the way of the cross; there's no other way but this.
I shall never get sight of the gates of light if the way of the cross I miss.
Then I bid farewell to the way of the world, to walk in it never more;
For my Lord says, "Come," and I see my home where He waits at the open door.

Jessie Pounds

A Man Without Respect
Genesis 19:4-14

The news of Lot's guests lodging in Sodom for the night spread through the streets like wildfire. Young and old alike scurried from every quarter of the city to besiege Lot's home. These Sodomites were so vile that they shouted their perverse intentions from the streets for all to hear. They had no shame or remorse for their homosexual lifestyle. God's abhorrence for the modern day "Gay Liberation" movement is evident from this passage, Leviticus 18:22, 20:13 and from Paul's flaming commentary on the subject in Romans 1. Paul concludes that those who reject God's revelation are given over to their own vile affections (Rom. 1:20-24). Without God the worst of man's depraved flesh becomes evident in homosexuality (Rom. 1:25-28), and thus, their own consciences prove to them that they deserve the judgment of God for their perverse lifestyle (Rom. 1:32).

Did the inhabitants of Sodom respect Lot? No, not really. Lot had dwelled long enough in Sodom that he was thinking like the Sodomites. He had so closely mingled with them in daily life that he now calls them *brethren* (Gen. 19:7). His solution to protect his newly acquainted guests from harm was to hand over his two virgin daughters to satisfy the Sodomites lustful appetites. Delitzsch summarizes Lot's behavior as being an attempt to avoid sin by sin.[1] He was willing to relinquish protection of his own daughters and give them over to be abused by a mob of evil men. Though we strongly disapprove of Lot's solution to this desperate situation, the fact that he had guarded his daughters' chastity in such an immoral atmosphere is one of the few praiseworthy notes of Lot's life.

These wicked men surrounded Lot's house and would have forced their way in, except that the angels smote them all with blindness. This type of disorienting blindness was the same inflicted by God upon an

Seeds of Destiny

invading Syrian army in 2 Kings 6 that had besieged His prophet Elisha. This blindness was not connected directly with sight, but a condition that left the victim disoriented; for even a blind man can find a nearby door. The Sodomites fumbled about as dizzy children do when they have been quickly spun around and then left to walk unaided.

The angels granted Lot an opportunity to warn all his family of the imminent judgment of the city pending their departure. As the angels did not force Lot to depart until just before dawn, he had several hours to accomplish this task. Lot warned his married daughters and sons-in-law living in the city but didn't bother to sound the alarm to his own sons. Perhaps he knew they were so controlled by reprobate thinking that they would not heed his warning. What respect did Lot have among his extended family? None, they mocked their father and chose to remain in Sodom and face the wrath of God. When a man begins to associate himself with the world, he will eventually do so thoroughly.

Lot was a miserable man who had completely lost his testimony. He was not respected or valued by anyone, except the Lord. His own daughters showed they had no respect for their father in that they later commited fornication with him to have children. No matter how much Lot might have tried to protect his family and raise them up properly, they had been too deeply immersed in the world and, thus, had perverted minds and base thinking. F. W. Grant applies Lot's situation to the believer's thought life:

> How is it possible to say to the world, "I will walk with you," and stretch out the other hand to God, saying, "Walk with me?" But if this be so, communion with God must be how rare a thing! How many things must be substituted for it, and, with the terrible self-deception which we can practice on ourselves, to be taken to be this even! With most, indeed, how little is Christ abidingly the occupation and enjoyment of the soul! And when we would be with Him, in our seasons of habitual or special devotion, how often do we perhaps all realize the intrusion of other thoughts, unwelcome as, to Lot, were the men of Sodom. We are apt, at least, to console ourselves that they are unwelcome, perhaps to silence, or seek to silence, conscience with the thought, as if this relieved us from responsibility about them. Yet who could assert that Lot was not responsible for the intrusion of the men of Sodom? If their being unwelcome settled the whole matter, there is no

doubt that they were unwelcome. But why had Abraham no such intruders?

The thoughts that throng upon us when we would gladly be free – at the Lord's table, at the prayer-meeting, or elsewhere, – have we indeed no responsibility as to these? The effort necessary to obtain what when obtained we can so little retain while other things flock in with no effort, does it not reveal the fact of where we are permitting our hearts to settle down?[2]

> Jesus the very thought of Thee, with sweetness fills my breast;
> But better far Thy face to see, and in Thy presence rest.
> Savior, our only joy be Thou, as Thou our crown shalt be;
> Be Thou, O Lord, our glory now, and through eternity.
>
> Bernard of Clairvaux

Remember Lot's Wife
Genesis 19:15-38

The fact that Lot and his family are intoxicated with worldliness is plainly evident throughout Genesis 19. Firstly, Lot was so attached to his existence at Sodom that the angels had to lay hold of him and pry him from Sodom (Gen. 19:16).

Secondly, even after Lot understood that righteous souls must be separated from ungodly living, he still longed to have a bit of the world in his life. The angel told him to separate and to flee to the mountains for safety, but Lot begged him to allow him to dwell in a "little" city (Zoar) that he die not. This was the very problem: Lot was not willing to die to self and live for God. It is a marvelous testimony of God's grace that the selfish request of carnal Lot saved the inhabitants of Zoar from God's wrath! In the end, Lot, a ruined man, found out that the world offered nothing substantial. Lot felt alone and threatened. Though he had a just position, he was estranged from God, and worse yet, he had been deserted by the world. The world had exacted its price and proven its hatred for all that have been declared righteous. At this realization, Lot is driven by his own fears into further isolation.

Lot learned the hard way what Paul would pen later, *"bad company corrupts good character"* (1 Cor. 15:33 NIV). Satan will never entice the believer with pleasure, glamour, and sensuality without a hook in the bait. **There is always a hook!** Gobbling up the bait ensures double jeopardy to the child of God – a crushing weight of consequences and a throbbing conscience that haunts the believer day and night. Satan will not leave the child of God alone until he has used every effort to force a believer out of communion with God and into the most terrible extremes of evil.

Thirdly, the angels had commanded that they not look back towards Sodom – they were to make a "clean break" from the world. But, the heart of Lot's wife was still in Sodom, and as God rained down fire and brimstone upon the city, she either stole a glance at her old life or was lagging far enough behind that she instantly experienced the judgment of

God. She either instantaneously became a pillar of salt or perhaps was buried by tons of salt when the catastrophic upheaval destroyed all the cities of the plain. The Hebrew word translated "looked back" is *nabat* which means "to look intently" or "to regard with pleasure." Christian discipleship requires forsaking the pleasures of the world and following Christ unhindered. The Lord said, *"No man, having put his hand to the plough, and looking back, is fit for the kingdom of God"* (Lk. 9:62).

If Lot had been a good family protector, he would have had his family in front of him to ensure that they did not look back or linger behind. But his wife, being behind him, was not protected. She thought she could still embrace what grieved the Lord and was, thus, forbidden. In the end, she got the desire of her heart, but it cost her very life. *"For the wages of sin is death, but the gift of God is eternal life through Jesus Christ our Lord"* (Rom. 6:23). Though Lot was ensnared by the world, he had previously obtained a righteous position before God through exercising faith in Abraham's call. His wife, however, was a mere professor, who, though departed from Sodom, left her heart there. H. C. Leupold memorializes her demise: "She appreciated but little what the delivering angels had done for her. Almost escaped, she allowed her vigilance to relax. So she became a warning example to all who do not make a clear-cut break with the life of wickedness."[1]

The angels did not find ten righteous souls in Sodom, so why was Lot spared from judgment? Because of faithful Abraham's intercession to God and his right relationship with God (Gen. 19:29). What miraculous grace is presently being bestowed to your friends and family because of your intercession for them before the Throne of the Universe? What mercy is God presently imparting to beloved believers in distress because of your intimate relationship with Him? Without Abraham's faith, righteous Lot would have perished with all the unrighteous souls in Sodom. We really do affect blessing to others by living consecrated and holy lives and by soliciting our Lord for help on their behalf. *"The effectual fervent prayer of a righteous man availeth much"* (Jas. 5:16).

Although Lot's wife became the salt of the earth, it was not what the Lord had in mind when He told His disciples, *"ye are the salt of the earth"* (Matt. 5:13). Lot's wife was used as an example by the Lord in Luke 17:32 to warn those listening not to think lightly about His offer of salvation. During His entire ministry the Lord told His listeners to

Seeds of Destiny

remember only two people – Himself and Lot's wife. The choice He gave to His listeners was Himself or the world; the consequences of this choice would be life or death, blessing or judgment. We were created for God's good pleasure (Rev. 4:11), and God will get glory from us one way or another – through willful submission or through the judgment of disobedience. *"Every knee should bow ... every tongue should confess that Jesus Christ is Lord"* (Phil. 2:10-11).

The fierce wrath of God fell upon Sodom and Gomorrah as the sun was rising on the earth (Gen. 19:23). In a coming day, the bright and morning star which instills hope to God's saints that the night is nearly past (Rev. 22:16) will give way to the most spectacular dawning this world has ever witnessed. The Son of Man shall rise in full fury to execute vengeance upon the wicked, and His glory shall shine throughout all the earth (Rev. 1:13-18, 19:11-21).

And what of Lot? Driven by the fear of man, instead of faith in divine revelation, he ventures unto the mountain to which he was originally commanded to go. There he defiled his two daughters and passed from the pages of history with no record of his end. But the seed sown to his flesh would produce a lingering harvest, a posterity that would become the enemy of God's people for centuries. In retrospect, Lot's life counted for naught, for he lived for the moment and flirted with the god of this age. In contrast, Abraham, though not a perfect man, drew near to God and became the father of all spiritual seed (Rom. 9:7-8).

> Nearer, still nearer, Lord to be Thine,
> Sin, with its follies I gladly resign;
> All of it's pleasures, pomp and its pride,
> Give me but Jesus, my Lord crucified.
>
> Lelia N. Morris

The Same Mistake Again?
Genesis 20:1-16

We are not told why Abraham went to dwell in Gerar. Isaac later went there as a result of a famine (Gen. 26). Genesis provides the historical account of three different famines that directly affected Abraham, Isaac, and Jacob on an individual basis. It is not likely that a famine brought Abraham to dwell in Gerar at this particular time, or the Holy Spirit would have recorded it. As Sarah obviously did not appear pregnant in Gerar, Abraham's relocating there occurred directly after the destruction of the Jordanian cities. Perhaps there were others who distanced themselves from the location where the wrath of God had been visibly poured out upon the wicked.

Abraham repeated the same mistake in Gerar that he had made in Egypt; he portrayed his wife as his sister. Interestingly, the Philistines are Egyptians, though living in Canaan – the land promised to Abraham. The scene is not too different today for the world invades the church and encroaches upon the eternal covenant of God in Christ.

Abraham had a weakness in character in this area, and the last matter had never been fully been brought to confession and repentance. New circumstances would now test the patriarch. Just as faith cannot be trusted unless it has been tested, character cannot be validated until circumstances verify it. How else do we really know what is in our heart? Abraham felt he must lie concerning Sarah's relationship to him to protect himself from the men of the land who might want his wife and kill him for her. He surmised that *"the fear of God is not in this place"* (Gen. 20:11). Yet, Abraham forgot that, though God may not be present with the Philistines, God had promised to be with him and a shield before him (Gen. 15:1). From this unfortunate episode, we learn that the flesh in God's people never changes. Abraham was promised

Seeds of Destiny

grace to be delivered from trial, but his flesh had not changed. It still maintained the same desire to rely on its own wisdom.

Why would Abimelech want a 90-year-old woman as a wife? The situation is quite different than that of Genesis 12 when she was swept into Pharaoh's house. In Genesis 12, we read that Sarah was very fair to look upon. The life span of the patriarchs at this time was nearly double that of our present age. Thus, Sarah as a 65-year-old would have been a beautiful woman in her late thirties or early forties today. Pharaoh wanted her for sensual reasons, but the circumstance in Genesis 20 is quite different. Sarah, now a woman of ninety, is no longer spoken of as beautiful, but her wealth was vast. By today's standards, Sarah would be like a woman in her mid-fifties. Naturally speaking, she was well past the childbearing years, but Abimelech saw an opportunity to make a financial gain and a political alliance with Abraham by inducting her into his household. She was not likely pregnant yet with Isaac, or Abimelech would have known that she was indeed married. The Bible clearly reveals the vanity of marrying another for sensual reasons, for financial gain, or for political ambitions! Marriage is to be a covenant of companionship between one man and one woman, not a medium for temporal agendas.

Once more God intervened on Abraham's behalf. He visited Abimelech in a dream and warned him that Sarah was the wife of Abraham and that, if he committed adultery with her, he was a dead man. Abimelech pleaded ignorance in this matter for he was told that she was not married. Abimelech understood his immediate duty and, thus, returned Sarah to Abraham, severely rebuking both of them for lying to him. Grievous is the sin of adultery to God! He was willing to punish a whole nation because of one act of adultery. Abraham's bent was more severely reproved by Abimelech than by Pharaoh nearly 25 years earlier. Pharaoh asked questions about Abraham's behavior, but Abimelech directly reproved both Abraham and Sarah for lying about the matter. In fact, Abimelech's three questions and one statement in Genesis 20:9-10 affirm that Abraham had only thought about himself and not about the repercussions of his sin upon his wife or Abimelech. Our sin, even if of a simplistic nature, rarely, if ever, affects only ourselves. Let us not be like Achan whose secret sin of stealing a wedge of gold and a Babylonian garment from Jericho cost the lives of

36 of his countrymen. Sin in the camp tears and injures the body of Christ, no matter how secret. Abraham experienced God's grace and deliverance in the wake of personal failure to such an extent that he never repeated this sin again.

What is fascinating about this historical record is that even the pagan inhabitants of the land understood the importance of the marriage relationship and sexual sanctity, which the marriage covenant secures. Abimelech knew that he had wronged God's man, so he gave him sheep, oxen and servant, and paid him a thousand pieces of silver to make amends for the wrong done, and invited Abraham to remain in the land as his guest.

True repentance should be accompanied by an effort to make restitution for the wrong done (Ex. 22:1). Not only does sin offend God and its victims, but it also causes damage, which should be repaired as much as possible through ample restitution. Abimelech not only repented of the wrong, but he sought to right the wrong through gifts to Abraham. However, let us not miss the just and stinging reproof administered by Abimelech to Abraham for doing a thing "that ought not to be done." Not only had Abraham sunk beneath his calling, he had also lowered himself below the conduct of any moral man of the world. Similarly, every believer today invites the rebuke of the world when he or she is acting under the toxic power of disbelief. Abraham had become a reproach among men and deserved to be reprimanded for his deed.

Abraham's failure in the world relates exactly to what the Lord taught His disciples their final evening together before His death (Jn. 15). When a believer does not abide in Christ, his testimony withers away, then the men of the world gather the fruitless branches up to be burned (Jn. 15:6). It is not the Lord that burns the believer up, for this would speak of eternal judgment, but it is the world that burns up his testimony and makes him utterly useless as a witness for Christ. The Lord has done His part to encourage these fruitless branches to bear fruit, for He has cleaned them and *"lifted them up,"* according to John 15:2, into the light of truth. The English phrase in John 15:2 *"taketh away"* is more often translated as an act of "lifting up" or "raising" (Acts 4:24; Luke 9:17, 17:13; Rev. 10:5; Matt. 9:6), and this the Lord does because He wants fruit from the unfruitful branches. From fruitful

Seeds of Destiny

branches (believers), He desires increasing fruit production – *"more fruit"* (Jn. 15:2) and then *"much fruit"* (Jn. 15:5). Thus, the believer's testimony and ability to please God directly increases as he or she is washed by the Word and chooses to abide in Christ instead of his or her own flesh.

> He all my grief has taken, and all my sorrows borne;
> In temptation He's my strong and mighty tower;
> He has all my sins forgiven, and Him I do adore
> From my heart, and now He keeps me by His power.
> He will never, never leave me, nor yet forsake me here,
> While I live by faith and seek His blessed will;
> A wall of fire about me, I've nothing now to fear,
> With His manna He my hungry soul shall fill.
>
> Charles Fry

Love Thy Enemies
Genesis 20:17-18

In response to Abimelech's actions to take Sarah into his harem, God had completely stopped all conception of Abimelech's people. However, God told Abimelech that Abraham was His prophet and that Abraham would pray for his people to be healed. Despite what Abimelech thought about Abraham in this matter, God still thought fondly of His servant and friend Abraham. How the Lord loves His children even when they are in the deep mire of sin. How can the child of God ever be depressed knowing what kind thoughts He has for us? Forget what others think; it is only what God is thinking that really matters, and He loves you.

Abraham prayed to God for Abimelech's healing, and God answered Abraham's prayer – He removed the Gerarites inability to have children. An amazing thing transpired as Abraham prayed for those who had mistreated him – he experienced healing also. When God opened the wombs of Abimelech's women, he also opened the womb of Sarah. This is the same wondrous discovery Job experienced according to Job 42:10: *"And the Lord turned the captivity of Job, when he prayed for his friends; also the Lord gave Job twice as much as he had before."* Do you want emotional healing in your life? Pray for those who persecute you, forgive them of their wrongs against you; and you will set a prisoner free only to realize that you were the one taken captive by your own hardened heart.

The Lord taught, *"If ye forgive men their trespasses, your heavenly Father will also forgive you; but if ye forgive not men their trespasses, neither will your Father forgive your trespasses"* (Matt. 6:14-15). In light of the debt of sin we have been forgiven by God, how can we not extend to others our forgiveness for lesser offenses? (See the parable of the Unforgiving Servant in Matthew 18:23-35.). To forgive liberates

Seeds of Destiny

the heart for free expression of love through service again. Those who hold grudges must realize that the root of bitterness that is festering in their own heart will affect every relationship they have, including their fellowship with the Lord.

The Lord again taught, *"Love your enemies, bless them that curse you, do good to them that hate you, and pray for them which despitefully use you, and persecute you"* (Matt. 5:44). Have you ever tried to pray to God while you are angry? It doesn't work. As we pour our hearts out to the infinite Creator, our hearts become humbled and softened. Prayer is transforming! We may start by asking the Lord to "stomp'em," but as we continue to pray, we are overtaken by the hurt and pain that the offending party is inflicting on themselves, their family, the Church, and Christ. Suddenly, our pain does not seem so great when looking at the big picture. Next time you are offended by someone, try praying for them – prayer really softens the unforgiving heart. Then, as in the day of your salvation, the healing that comes with forgiveness will be yours afresh.

> As we practice the work of forgiveness we discover more and more that forgiveness and healing are one.
>
> Agnes Sanford

> Doing an injury puts you below your enemy; revenging one makes you even with him; forgiving it sets you above him.
>
> Unknown

Who's Laughing Now?
Genesis 21:1-8

Back in Genesis 17, God promised Abraham that in a year Sarah would bear him a son, and God, as always, kept His promise. It had been 25 years since God had originally promised Abraham a nation from his own seed. Though man may fret and fume, God is in no hurry in affecting His plans. Sarah bore Abraham a son in her old age and in accordance with God's ultimate plan. The birth of Abraham's son of promise is a splendid picture of the incarnation of the Son of God. *"When the fulness of the time was come, God sent forth His Son"* (Gal. 4:4). Though Isaac would be the heir of Abraham, it would be through the One Isaac represented, Christ, that all divine promises to Abraham were made secure. The years of anticipation were finally concluded, but the fruit of the wilderness journey, namely patience and matured faith abided still. How the words of the Lord years earlier must have resounded again in Abraham's mind, *"Is anything too hard for the Lord"* (Gen. 18:14).

The Lord told Abraham to name his son Isaac, which means, "he laughs." Isaac's name was appropriate seeing that Abraham had laughed in celebrated amazement at God's promise of a natural son (Gen. 17:17) and that Sarah had laughed within herself in disbelief (Gen. 18:12). Perhaps even the inhabitants of the land were laughing at Abraham's name – "the father of multitudes"? But God had the last laugh – He brought into the world a son from the dead womb of an old woman (Rom. 4:19). How did Sarah respond? *"God hath made me to laugh, so that all that hear will laugh with me"* (Gen. 21:6). In Genesis 16, she spoke as though God had failed her, but in Genesis 21, she acknowledges God's grandeur and integrity. It would seem that the inhabitants thought this event so unusual that Abimelech was compelled to enact a peace treaty with Abraham and his new son – something he did not do when Ishmael was born.

Ishmael represents the "frailty of the flesh," while Isaac portrays the "strength of the Spirit." Paul confirms this analogy in Gal. 4:29: *"But as then he that was born after the flesh (Ishmael) persecuted him that was born after the Spirit (Isaac), even so it is now."* God's miracle solution to a barren couple's problem was not "Ishmael changed;" it was "Isaac born." God demonstrates the same activity in the regeneration of the believer (Tit. 3:5) – God's miracle solution to a barren life is eternal life through rebirth, not a "make over" of the old nature, which is putrid to God. Ishmael was the son of a bondwoman (a slave) – illustrating that, naturally, we are slaves to sin with no hope of deliverance. Regeneration, however, implants life – the very divine nature of God – within those earthen vessels who accept His offer of salvation through Christ (Jn. 1:12-13). No spiritual rebirth – no spiritual life, no spiritual fruit to God, no heaven to enjoy (Jn. 3:3). The birth of Isaac did not improve Ishmael, but it did bring out the hidden opposition to the child of promise begotten by God. Just as salvation by the law is in opposition to grace, the flesh nature is in opposition to the spirit nature, which is begotten of God (Rom. 7:21-23). The two natures within the believer war with each other. Thus, God's begotten children must live by faith according to the new nature and not according to the flesh, for there is absolutely nothing in the flesh that pleases God (Rom. 7:18).

Although Abraham had fathered a son previously (Ishmael), the Lord God spoke of Isaac as being Abraham's only begotten son (Gen. 22:2, 12; Heb. 11:17). What is meant by this term "only begotten?" Genesis 22:12 clarifies the phrase, in that Isaac was "the only son" given Abraham by God. In the mind of God, Ishmael was a result of Abraham's disbelief; thus, he was not in His covenant plan to bring forth the Messiah. Isaac was the son of promise given to Abraham by God through a miraculous birth. The term "begotten," used in context of fulfilling a promise of God, means "special" or "unique."

The term "begotten" is applied to the Son of God from three "unique" vantage points in Scripture. He is the only begotten of the Father (Jn. 1:14, 18; 3:16, 18), which speaks of the Son's unique position and relationship as the eternal Son of God, the One who was with the

Father in glory from the beginning (Jn. 1:1, 17:5). In Hebrews 1:6, the term "begotten" is applied to the Son's incarnation, as well as to His resurrection and ascent back to glory in Hebrews 1:5. The Son is "unique" in all three of these facets. The birth of the Lord Jesus was a miracle, "unique" because God opened a virgin's womb for the first time to give birth. The birth of Isaac, a type of Christ, was a miracle also, in that He opened a dead womb for the first time. Perhaps then, even in the birth of Isaac, we see the resurrection of Jesus Christ – coming forth from what was dead unto glorification. Though the virgin birth would never be repeated, for the Lord Jesus needed to suffer only once for sin, the opening of the dead womb of a woman occurred again when John the Baptist was born of Elizabeth. This provides hope to everyone that dies in Christ that they, too, will experience resurrection unto glorification (1 Thess. 4:13-18; 1 Jn. 3:2-3; Titus 2:13).

What are miracles? Everything mankind has observed in creation he has sought to characterize by rules of order. Conservation of energy and motion, laws of gravity and thermodynamics and the like represent our knowledge of creation based on observation. Therefore, God has to cause some non-regularities in our ordered world in order to call our attention to the fact that there is an outside influence to be reckoned with – the Creator. Such were the births of Isaac, John the Baptist, and Jesus Christ. Before each miracle (an irregularity in an ordered system) occurred, Scripture records that the people understood the natural order that was in place. These were not ignorant people. They knew how babies were made and when procreation could no longer happen. If they had not known these things, no miracle would have been recognized, and God would have gotten no glory in doing it. In the case of Sarah and Elizabeth, they both were past menopause and physically incapable of bearing children (Gen. 18:11; Lk. 1:18,36). In the case of Mary, the mother of Jesus, she was a virgin (Lk. 1:34). So, it is really thanks to science that we have the wherewithal to actually recognize the hand of God in our lives! Without the understanding of order, we would not be able to recognize a miracle when one occurs.

Abraham knew that Isaac was a miracle child and that God was bringing about the covenant He had made. The token of the covenant was imposed on Isaac when he was eight days old – he was circumcised. This practice would propagate down through the generations of Abraham until

Seeds of Destiny

the reality of what it symbolized would be completed – the spiritual circumcision of Israel. Circumcision represents both physically and spiritually "the separation of the flesh." A knife accomplishes the former, and nails the latter. Judicially speaking, we have been positionally circumcised through Christ (Col. 2:10-13). Practically speaking, we are called to circumcise the flesh nature daily (Rom. 2:29; 1 Cor. 7:19) – we are to continually die to what God has already declared dead in Christ. By dying, we live Christ!

> If I gained the world, but lost the Saviour,
> Were my life worth living for a day?
> Could my yearning heart find rest and comfort
> In the things that soon must pass away?
> If I gained the world, but had no Saviour,
> Would my gain be worth the life-long strife?
> Are all earthly pleasures worth comparing,
> For a moment with a Christ-filled life?
>
> Anna Olander

Devotions in Genesis

Isaac is Heir
Genesis 21:9-34

Isaac grew and was weaned, which means Sarah nursed him. Like Isaac, a child of God must have *"the sincere milk of the Word"* to grow (1 Pet. 2:2). No milk – no growth. Milk provides calcium for strong bones that provide the structure for the body. Many want to grow in the Lord and be strong for Christ, but they are unwilling to suckle the rudiments of the Word in order to develop a strong faith.

Isaac was nursed as a baby, but there came a time when he had grown enough to be weaned. Likewise, the writer of Hebrews exhorts believers, *"seeing ye are dull of hearing. For when for the time ye ought to be teachers, ye have need that one teach you again the first principles of the oracles of God, and are become such as have need of milk, and not of [solid food]"* (Heb. 5:11-12). The other problem, which stunts the spiritual growth of many, is continuing to nurse when they should be eating solid food (learning the more difficult things of God). There should be a natural progression of growth of a new convert from being taught and discipled to being a teacher and a discipler. There is a time for milk, but it should give way to steak and potatoes eventually!

Abraham made a great feast on the day that Isaac was weaned. Isaac was probably two or three years old. Ishmael was approximately 16 years old. It was Isaac's special day, and Ishmael, Abraham's son by a lapse of faith, made the mistake of mocking young Isaac. Family tension had likely been high since Isaac's birth, but now a crescendo of envy put the home into turmoil. Perhaps Sarah saw Hagar and Ishmael as a threat to Isaac's full inheritance, or she became weary of the constant family reminder of her own deceitful conniving. Sarah pleaded with her husband that they be banished from the family. The request grieved Abraham, but God permitted the expulsion. God informed Abraham that his seed would

Seeds of Destiny

be in Isaac called, but He would bless and increase Ishmael's descendants also.

According to God's instruction Abraham put them out. But why did Abraham send Hagar and his son, Ishmael, into the wilderness with only a meager ration? Because Hagar and Ishmael represented the frailty of Abraham's flesh and the child of God is to make no provision for the flesh; in fact the flesh is to be **put to death**. *"But put ye on the Lord Jesus Christ, and make not provision for the flesh, to fulfill its lusts"* (Rom. 13:14). *"Always bearing about in the body the dying of the Lord Jesus, that the life also of Jesus might be made manifest in our body"* (2 Cor 4:10). *"And they that are Christ's have crucified the flesh with the affections and lusts"* (Gal. 5:24). Perhaps this is why "death" is first rendered in this chapter, the desires and power of Abraham's flesh must be put to death. Circumcising the flesh is painful, and it hurt Abraham deeply to put away his son Ishmael, but, in doing so, he would be living solely in God's provision and promise found in Isaac. There would be no back up plan – it was Isaac or no one.

So Hagar and Ishmael were sent into the wilderness with a ration of bread and a skin of water. It was not long before their water was exhausted and their parched souls tottered on brink of death. Interestingly, the Hebrew word *maveth*, translated "death," first appears in Scripture in Genesis 21:16. Previously, Scripture recorded violent acts of murder and the timing in which prominent individuals died, but this is the first reference to the act of dying. Hagar and Ishmael were dying. Though death seemed to be nigh, the Lord was nearer to them than death.

When the Lord spoke, Hagar was too weak to answer Him. But, the Lord encouraged her by reaffirming His promise to enlarge Ishmael into a nation, then He opened her eyes to behold a well. This scene is especially encouraging to all of us who, at some time or another, have been too emotionally spent, too physically fatigued to verbalize our supplications before the throne of grace. It is during these silent intervals within the vale of shadows that Romans 8:25-27 bolsters our courage and props up our faith:

> *But if we hope for that we see not, then do we with patience wait for it. Likewise the Spirit also helpeth our infirmities: for we know not what we should pray for as we ought: but the Spirit itself maketh intercession for us with groanings which cannot be uttered. And He that searcheth*

the hearts knoweth what is the mind of the Spirit, because He maketh intercession for the saints according to the will of God.

Hagar had a second "well experience" with the Lord that day – an experience that gave her and Ishmael life. The Lord had promised Hagar in Genesis 16 and Abraham in Genesis 17 and 21 that Ishmael would be the father of a great nation. The Lord did this because Abraham requested it and for the simple fact that Ishmael was Abraham's son (Gen. 21:13). The Lord keeps His promises!

It is interesting to note that Ishmael's name is never referenced in this chapter, although he is spoken of fifteen times. He is called the "son of Hagar," the "son of the bondwoman," "her son," "the lad," "the child" or referenced by the pronoun "him" or "he." In a chapter where God had brought forth the "only begotten son" of Abraham, picturing the only begotten Son of God, there would be no competition – the chosen son was to get all the glory. *"I am the Lord: that is My name; and My glory will I not give to another"* (Isa. 42:8).

Genesis 21 closes with the man of the world affirming that God was with the man of faith. Earlier, when the man of faith slipped from the path of righteousness, Abimelech reproved Abraham, but now his consistent walk of separation is admired, and God's personal blessings acknowledged. The world, generally speaking, respects the child of God who walks worthy of their calling!

> Everlasting glory unto Jesus be!
> Sing aloud the story of His victory!
> How He left the splendor of His home on high,
> Came, in love so tender, on the cross to die.
> Yes! He came from heaven, suffered in our stead;
> Praise to Him be given, "first born from the dead!"
> Jesus, meek and lowly, came the lost to save;
> He the victim holy, triumphed o'er the grave.
>
> Hannah K. Burlingham

Seeds of Destiny

After These Things
Genesis 22:1-2

The phrase *"after these things"* in the first verse of Genesis 15 and Genesis 22 provide the boundaries for three distinct phases of God's working in Abraham's life. In Genesis 12–14, Abraham's public testimony is presented as a man walking by faith and separate from the world. In Genesis 15–21, his personal relationship with God while exercising faith is witnessed. In the final chapter of his life, Genesis 22–25, God foreshadows through typology His great plan of redemption and consequent blessing to mankind through Abraham and his son Isaac. The glory of Christ at Calvary, the wooing of His bride and His exaltation are distinctly portrayed in the narrative.

Genesis 22:1 marks the seventh, and the last time on earth, that God met with and spoke to Abraham personally. In Genesis 12:1-2, God called Abraham to separation. After arriving in the Canaan, God provided a witness of Himself to Abraham. In Genesis 13:14, God acknowledges Abraham's godly character after he separated himself from carnal Lot. God identified Himself as Abraham's shield and reward in Genesis 15:1 – God would be Abraham's endurance and protection. After Abraham's lapse of faith, which produced Ishmael, God called Abraham to renewed faithfulness (Gen. 17:1). In their sixth, meeting God and Abraham enjoyed sweet fellowship together, and Abraham exercised his privilege of intercession (Gen. 18:1). Then, lastly, in Genesis 22, the obedience and love of Abraham for his God are witnessed.

The exact timing of the events in Genesis 22 are unknown as the chronology affords us a 35-year gap between Genesis 21, the weaning of Isaac, and Genesis 23, the death of Sarah occurring when Isaac was 37 years old. Since Genesis 21:34 records that *"Abraham sojourned in the Philistines' land many days"* and Genesis 22:1 acknowledges that the events of Genesis 22 occurred *"after these things,"* it can be conjectured that Isaac was a young man of perhaps twenty to thirty years of age.

The Hebrew word for "lad" in Genesis 22:5 and 12 is *naar*, which is flexible in meaning and may be applied to refer to any male from a small boy to a young man. It is used to speak of the young men who accompanied Abraham to Moriah. Since Isaac is an outstanding type of Jesus Christ, perhaps Isaac was in his early thirties when he was to be offered up as a sacrifice, as was the Lord Jesus. F. W. Grant comments concerning the submission of Isaac:

> Isaac's own submission is perfect and beautiful. He was not the child that he is often pictured, but, as it would appear, in the vigor of early manhood. He nevertheless submits himself absolutely. How fitting a type of Him who stops the resistance of His impulsive follower with the words, *"Put up again thy sword into its sheath: the cup which My Father hath given Me, shall I not drink it?"*[1]

It is interesting that only a single narrative concerning the life of Isaac is inserted between his birth and his "would be" sacrifice (i.e. the feast at his weaning). Consequently, only one excerpt of information is provided between the Lord's infant years and the initiation of His three-plus-year ministry when He was 30 years of age (His three days at the temple when He was 12 years old).

The first mention of significant words in the Bible establishes the "tone" by which that word will resonate throughout Scripture. Such is the case in this chapter with the first mention of the words *"love," "worship,"* and *"lamb."* How fitting for these three words, which are so intimately tied in meaning, to be rendered in a chapter where the father is asked to offer his only begotten son and is willing to do it. August Van Ryn reverently summarizes, "There is no worship without love and there is no love without lamb."

Genesis 22 shadows the events of Calvary when God *"spared not His own Son"* (Rom. 8:32). This is clearly seen by the first occurrence of "love" in the New Testament, *"And, lo, a voice from heaven, saying, This is My beloved Son, in whom I am well pleased"* (Matt. 3:17). Likewise, this same expression of the Father's love for the Son is found in the first mention of the word "love" in Mark and Luke's Gospel accounts also (Mk. 1:11; Lk. 3:22). However, it is the first occurrence of the word "love" in John's account that fittingly describes God's love for us. *"For God so loved the world, that he gave his only begotten Son, that whosoever believeth in him should not perish, but have everlasting life"* (Jn. 3:16). Three times God declares His infinite love for His Son, but then He tells of His awesome love for us. It is a love so great that He will judge His only beloved Son on our behalf that we might be declared holy and be restored into a joyful relationship with Him.

It is apparent that God knew Abraham was now ready for the ultimate test. The phrase *"And it came to pass after these things,"* in Genesis 22:1 refers to Abraham's 25 years of moral grooming and spiritual schooling to prepare him for the greatest test of his life. God told Abraham to go to a specific mountain in the land of Moriah (near Jerusalem) and to offer his *"only son"* whom he loved as a burnt sacrifice. No reason was given, and Abraham asked no questions. It is worthy of noting that the narrative emphasizes three times that Isaac was his *"only son."* God completely understood the gravity of the sacrifice and consequential agony to Abraham's soul. Abraham was in such intimate communion with God that God allowed Abraham to feel, at least in a measure, the anguish God would feel in giving His own Son for the suffering of death for mankind.

A millennium forward in time from this event, David would offer a burnt sacrifice to God on a mount of Moriah to stay a judgment of pestilence against Israel (1 Chron. 21). Pride had lured David to number the men of Israel, and God responded with a disciplinary plague. A generation later, Solomon would build a spectacular temple on Mount Moriah, the same location that the Lord had appeared unto David when he offered the sacrifice to avert the plague (2 Chron. 3:1). Another millennium later, the Lord Jesus Christ would be tried and crucified on or near Mt. Moriah. In a future millennium, the Lord Jesus will reign from this location, which will then be honored as the religious capital of the world (Zech. 14:16-17). Through the events in this chapter, Mt. Moriah (Jerusalem) is initiated as the focal point for worship on earth for as long as the earth is present, with the only exception being during the Church Age. During the Church Age, all believer-priests (Christians) become the temples of God and lift up worship and living sacrifices heavenward unto God wherever and whenever they desire (1 Pet. 2:5, 2:9; Rev. 1:6; Rom. 12:1). In Genesis 22, the redemptive plan of God is again presented in seed form: The Father giving His only Son for the sin sacrifice of humanity. On this side of Calvary, that is "after these things," the believer enjoys complete restoration and union with God. As believer-priests we have the opportunity to worship God continually and to offer ourselves frequently as a living sacrifice.

>Though our nature's fall in Adam shut us wholly out from God,
>Thine eternal counsel brought us nearer still, through Jesus' blood.
>For in Him we found redemption, grace and glory in Thy Son;
>Oh, the height and depth of mercy! Christ and His redeemed are one.
>
>>Robert Hawker

The Father Offers His Son
Genesis 22:3-8

In this chapter, Abraham demonstrates true worship to God in three astonishing ways. The first means of worship is seen in verse 3 – **obedience** to God's revealed word. Interestingly, the first mention of "obedience" in the Bible is found in this chapter (Gen. 22:18). A. P. Gibbs writes in his book *Worship – The Believers Highest Occupation*: "The believer's authority to worship is not the traditions of men, nor reasonings of human wisdom, but the clear revelation of God's Word."[1]

How did Abraham respond to the revealed Word of God? By faith. *"By faith Abraham, when he was tried, offered up Isaac"* (Heb. 11:17). *"Was not Abraham our father justified by works when he had offered Isaac his son upon the altar?"* (Jas. 2:21). C. H. Mackintosh writes, "faith never stops to look at circumstances, or ponder results; it only looks at God."[2] If faith were not involved, Abraham appeared on Mt. Moriah as a lunatic and a murderer. But Abraham had counted the full cost and had made a deliberate decision based on faith to offer Isaac. Because it was faith that had constrained him to act, Abraham proved that Jehovah was indeed his God, his reward, his shield and his true friend.

Abraham began by preparing for worship – it was going to require much physical and emotional exertion on Abraham's part to accomplish God's command. He rose up from his bed early, cut firewood for the trip, gathered Isaac and two men as helpers, saddled his ass, and departed on a 40 to 50-mile journey to Moriah. He wasted no time in accomplishing what God had commanded. Personally, I do not think Abraham told Sarah what God had asked him to do. By getting an early start, he may have prevented any discussion of the matter with Sarah, thus preventing any hindrance or delay for him in performing God's will. If Sarah had been aware that Isaac was going to die and that she

Devotions in Genesis

would never see him again, she would have certainly been weeping at their departure. Sarah's traumatic remorse would have provided Isaac with clues if not complete information about the purpose of their trip. Genesis 22:7 indicates Isaac's ignorance about the intended sacrifice even up to the juncture of offering. Sarah's silence in Genesis 22 succeeds her laughter at Isaac's birth in Genesis 21 and precedes her death in Genesis 23.

It took Abraham three days to reach Moriah, the appointed sacrificial site. Why did the journey require three days and not two or four? Because in Abraham's mind, God's will and command could not be thwarted; thus, Isaac was as good as dead for those three days. After the Lord's crucifixion on Friday, His marred body, stiffened by the chill of death, was laid in a lonely tomb. His body lay lifeless in that dismal place until Sunday when He awoke from the slumber of death and was raised up in a glorified body just before dawn. The divinely inspired page arouses our affections and appreciation for the Lord and His redeeming work through various topological details in this chapter, including Isaac's three-day journey, but even more so as the narrative slows in Genesis 22:7-14 to fill every captivating moment with our reverence and awe.

The second aspect of worship demonstrated by Abraham is in Genesis 22:5. He instructed the two young men to wait at a distance from Mt. Moriah while he and Isaac offered a sacrifice then he and Isaac would return to them. How did Abraham know that Isaac would return with him? We get a clue from Hebrews 11:17-19. Abraham by faith knew that Isaac was the promised seed and that God could not breach His word – so if he struck Isaac down, God would have to raise him back to life. This took an extraordinary amount of faith considering this was his only son and that there had never been a resurrection from the dead before. This facet of worship **acknowledges who God is** – His character and attributes. Abraham believed that God could not lie and that He had the power to awaken Isaac from the dead. Abraham made a deliberate decision to leave the young men at the base of the mount so that nothing or no one would obstruct his obedience to God's command. No distractions or hindrances would be tolerated.

The third manner in which worship is demonstrated is in **sacrifice**. Sacrifice requires self-denial. It requires the soul to lose something it

Seeds of Destiny

values. King David demonstrated this principle on the same mount a thousand years later. Even as God was judging the nation for David's sin of numbering the people, David ascended Mt. Moriah quickly to offer sacrifices unto God. He chose the threshing floor of Ornan for the location to build an altar (1 Chron. 21:18-30; 2 Chron. 3:1). Ornan offered to give David the ground needed to build an altar, the animals for sacrifice, the grain for a meal offering and the wood to burn, but David would not receive anything from Ornan without paying full price. He told Ornan, *"I will not...offer burnt offerings without cost"* (1 Chron. 21:24). David understood that a sacrifice is not a sacrifice unless you have sacrificed something. It must cost you something in order to have value. In Abraham's situation, he was committed to sacrificing the most precious part of his life – his son. This principle of worship is simple – self is denied, and God is magnified.

The Church is not called to offer animal sacrifices today. The Levitical system served a purpose but was retired when what it foreshadowed replaced it – the Lord's own sacrifice (Heb. 9:13-14). Today, we are to offer our bodies as living sacrifices by living holy and pure lives (Rom. 12:1-2). Every time we deny the impure desires of the flesh and make a conscious decision to be holy in thought and conduct, we have offered a living sacrifice unto God. The natural yearnings of the flesh were put to death again – that is the sacrifice to God. Think of it – every moment of every day can be a worship experience with God. What kinds of sacrifices may Christians offer the Lord? Doing good, sharing what we have with others in need, and praising God with our lips (Heb. 13:15-16). Showing others the sacrificial love of Christ (Eph. 5:2). Sharing financial resources with Christian workers (Phil. 4:18). There are many ways to sacrifice self unto God. When one does so with a humble heart and pure motive, a sweet-smelling fragrance ascends into the nostrils of God for His gratification.

> O head, once filled with bruises, oppressed with pain and scorn,
> Overwhelmed with sore abuses, mocked with a crown of thorn!
> O Head, to death once wounded in shame upon the tree,
> In glory now surrounded with brightest majesty!
>
> Paul Gerhardt

Devotions in Genesis

God Will Provide a Lamb
Genesis 22:9-14

So, Abraham and Isaac ascended the mount together but not hand in hand. One cannot survey this somber scene without a reverent interlude to contemplate the pattern that it so clearly represents – Calvary. The two young men assisted Abraham and Isaac in their journey to the mount, but they were not permitted to ascend it – this was a private matter between the father and the son. A few months before Christ's crucifixion, Moses and Elijah journeyed to earth to converse with the Lord. This interchange likely occurred on a mountain north and east of Galilee. Perhaps they were strengthening the Lord Jesus through encouragement to continue bringing glory to His Father by fulfilling His will. This event occurred near in place to Calvary but just as the two young men could not invade Abraham's moment of sacrifice, Moses and Elijah were prohibited from the mysterious transaction of redemption exacted by the Father on His Son at Golgotha, the place of the skull. Trespassing upon holy ground would not be tolerated. To ensure no intrusions, the Father shrouded His suffering Son in a veil of darkness.

Abraham carried the fire and the knife up the mount, both symbols of judgment. Isaac, a strapping young man, bore the wood for the fire. Prior to being judged by the Father at Calvary, the Lord had shouldered His crossbeam until physically unable. Then, after arriving at the place of public executions, He was nailed to His cross and lifted up for all to mock and jeer. *"He was despised and rejected of men, a man of sorrows, and acquainted with grief..."* (Isa. 53:3). And there, while in synaptic shock, profusely bleeding, and struggling to breathe, He awaited alone the forthcoming cup of God's wrath to be poured out upon Him. Human sin must be punished! Isaac inquired about a missing animal for sacrifice. Abraham responded that *"God will provide*

Seeds of Destiny

Himself a lamb," and He did some 2000 years later in the Lord Jesus. John the Baptist heralded the Lord Jesus as *"the Lamb of God which taketh away the sin of the world"* (Jn. 1:29). During the night before His death, the Lord inquired, *"Father, if Thou be willing, remove this cup from Me; nevertheless, not My will, but Thine, be done"* (Lk. 22:42). The Lord knew that there was no other way and drank it to the last drop.

Abraham erected his fifth altar recorded in Scripture. He had built altars previously at Shechem, at Bethel, at Hebron, and at Beersheba, but none of these existing monuments of devotion would suffice on this day. For this sacrifice must be at Moriah, and the offering must be Isaac, his beloved son. Isaac freely let himself be bound by his aged father, and the Lord freely allowed Himself to be bound, abused, and crucified by mankind. John 10:17-18 reads, *"Therefore doth My Father love Me, because I lay down My life, that I might take it again. No man taketh it from Me, but I lay it down of Myself. I have power to lay it down, and I have power to take it again. This commandment have I received of My Father."* Hamilton Smith remarks, "It is significant that in all the offerings, the victim was first killed and then laid on the altar. Here the offering becomes a more striking type of Christ in that he was first bound to the altar before the knife was taken to slay him."[1] Likewise, Christ was first affixed to a tree and then shed His blood. Abraham *"laid the wood in order."* Perhaps, the cruel Roman apparatus that brutally tortured thousands unto death is pictured here – a cross.

Abraham drew the knife to slay his son, but *"the Angel of the Lord"* called out to him to not harm his son, then showed him a ram God had prepared for sacrifice. Abraham had passed the supreme test of loyalty. God justified (declared him righteous) Abraham in Genesis 15 when he simply believed God's word, but now Abraham's justification was proven in his obedience no matter what the cost. Both the saved and the lost are given an opportunity to obey God. For the saved, obedience shows love for God (Jn. 14:15). For the lost, the step of obedience demonstrates a newfound reverence for God and a trust in the gospel message for salvation. *"He that believeth on the Son hath everlasting life; and he that believeth not the Son shall not see life, but the wrath of God abideth on him"* (Jn 3:36). The Greek words translated "believeth" in this verse are different. The first word translated "believeth" or "believes" in John 3:36 is *pisteuo* meaning "believe in" or "to trust in," but the second occurrence of "believes" is derived from the word *apeitheo*, which implies the act of "disobedience." There were Jews in John 8 who believed "on Jesus," but not "in Jesus" The demons believe on Jesus, but they are not offered salvation through Him (Jas. 2:19). The Lord will return to judge the wicked, *"In flaming fire taking vengeance on them that know not God, and that **obey not the gospel of our Lord Jesus Christ**"* (2 Thess. 1:8). Unfortunately, today many claim to believe "on Jesus," but they have not yet obeyed the gospel – they have not believed "in Him."

Abraham uttered two prophetic statements while upon the mount that day. First, *"God will provide Himself a Lamb for a burnt offering"* (Gen. 22:8). Secondly, *"In the mount of the Lord it shall be seen [provided]"* (Gen. 22:14). Both speak of the future sacrifice of Christ, which the Lord Himself declares to the Pharisees, *"Abraham rejoiced to see My day: and he saw it, and was glad"* (Jn. 8:56).

Abraham did rejoice that day. God had provided Himself a substitute sacrifice instead of Isaac and, thus, delivered Abraham from the greatest trial of his life. In general there are two ways in which God deals with those who trust Him during times of trial. Herbert Taylor explains:

> Sometimes He allows them to pass through the trial, without deliverance, and in such cases His presence is an unfailing support. Of this, the furnace and the lion's den in Babylon afford illustrations; so also the martyrdom of Stephen and the lonely exile of the aged John. Not unfrequently, however, the Lord brings His people right up to the trial, abreast with it as it were, and suddenly and unexpectedly, in answer to their unquestioning faith, cuts off the waters of the Red Sea, or delivers Peter out of prison just before his appointed execution. Thus here with Abraham, God held back his hand that was uplifted to slay his son.[2]

Isaac's death would have served no purpose. In the end, God had provided an offering for sacrifice – a ram caught by its horns. An animal uses its horns to protect itself or to substantiate its territory in the wild either through rubbings or fighting. Thus, throughout Scripture, the "horn" is used to symbolize power and strength. With the provision of the ram, the "type" of the Lord Jesus is transferred from Isaac to the ram for the suffering of death. Correspondingly, the Lord laid aside His glory and position in heaven to become a man in order to be a humble substitute for us at Calvary (Phil. 2:6-8). Meekness is "power in control" and is represented by the restrained ram – an innocent animal substitute caught by its horns. Perhaps another reason it was caught by its horns was to preserve it from being damaged (from being cut or torn by the thicket), thus being an unblemished sacrifice. The Lord Jesus lived His entire life without sin – He was without blemish. For the ram, it was a quick end, but for Christ it was immense suffering for hours as He bore our sin and the wrath of a righteous God. Calvary was a brief moment in human history but timeless in God's eternity.

> Lord, e'en to death Thy love could go, a death of shame and loss,
> To vanquish for us every foe, and break the strong man's force.
> O what a load was thine to bear, alone in that dark hour,
> Our sins in all their terror there, God's wrath and Satan's power.
> The storm that bowed Thy blessed head is hushed for ever now,
> And rest divine is ours instead, whilst glory crowns Thy brow.
>
> H. L. Rossier

Devotions in Genesis

The Father Departs the Mount
Genesis 22:15-24

"And Abraham called the name of that place "Jehovah-jireh" [God provides], as it is said to this day, In the mount of the Lord it shall be seen." The pattern of God's plan for human redemption was thus impressed upon the holy pages of Genesis. A human saga so traumatic yet so awe-inspiring that our finite minds are captivated to pondering Calvary from a heavenly perspective of divine anguish. God would judge His innocent and only begotten Son on Mount Calvary near Jerusalem for our sin. Only by embracing the Savior's cross at Jerusalem would man find forgiveness and a solace to comfort his grieving soul. To the Jew, God declares, *"O Zion, that bringest good tidings, get thee up into the high mountain; O Jerusalem, that bringest good tidings, lift up thy voice with strength; lift it up, be not afraid; say unto the cities of Judah, Behold your God"* (Isa 40:9)! Concerning the Gentiles, it was the Lord's will for evangelism to begin at Jerusalem then spread to the uttermost parts of the world (Matt. 28:19-20; Acts 1:8). During the Millennium Kingdom, the message to the world shall be *"And it shall come to pass, that every one that is left of all the nations which came against Jerusalem shall even go up from year to year to worship the King, the Lord of hosts, and to keep the feast of tabernacles"* (Zech. 14:16). The Lord ascended into heaven from Jerusalem, and He will return to Jerusalem to establish His earthly kingdom (Acts 1; Zech. 14).

God responded to Abraham's faith and worship by blessing him and Isaac. True worship brings blessing to the worshipper and those who are near. Mary worshipped the Lord in Simon the Leper's house just six days before the Lord's death (Mk. 14:3). She anointed the Lord's feet with costly perfume, then wiped off the excess with her own hair. 1 Corinthians 11:15 tells us that a woman's long hair is her glory, so in this voluntary act, she was laying her glory and a costly sacrifice at the feet of the Savior. On an earlier occasion, a repentant immoral woman initiated a similar act of worship in Simon the Pharisee's home (Lk. 7:36-37). What was the result of Mary's worship? Not only was the Lord refreshed, but Mary also carried a continuous reminder of her devotion and love for the Lord in the sweet aroma of her own hair. Besides this, we are told that the whole house was filled with the odor of the ointment (Jn. 12:3). Everyone with a heart for the Savior appreciated her sacrifice.

Scripture records that *"Abraham returned"* from the Mount. Where was Isaac? I am sure that he was with his father, but the inspired word omits Isaac's descent. It would seem that the purpose of this omission was to bring the typology one detail closer to the future events of Calvary. Both the Father and the Son were initially at Calvary. The Father to judge sin, and the Son to be the sin sacrifice, but afterwards the Lord Jesus went to a grave and was then raised up on the third day.

The Genesis account is also silent concerning the life of Isaac from the events of Genesis 22 until he meets his bride in Genesis 24. Likewise, Christ's ministry was not public after the events of Calvary, for He was raised up and ascended into heaven. In a coming day, He will personally and physically return in the clouds to retrieve His bride from the earth into heaven's glory (Jn. 14:1-4; 1 Thess. 4:13-18; Acts 1:11). From that juncture of time forward, the Lord Jesus Christ shall be known by all!

Scripture upholds Isaac as a wonderful "seed" of the destiny of Christ but also as a practical example of the essence of the believer's life now. F. W. Grant explains this practical aspect of the Christian life found in Isaac in the same way Paul approaches the subject in Romans 12:1-2:

> Isaac, given up to death, does not really die. In will and intent he does; in fact, it is his substitute. So Israel, at an after-time, coming to pass through Jordan to the land of their inheritance, find Jordan all dried up, and a broad way made over its former bed. There is no need to interpret. Death is the reality of it we do not know: we do not die, but are dead, with Him who is "resurrection and life" to us. The sorrow, the bitterness, the sting, of death was His who is now, as the consequence of it, in the glory of God for us; but by virtue of it, our position is changed; our place is no more in the world; we belong to

Him and to heaven, where He has gone for us. On the one side of it, this is in fact our salvation, our perfect blessing, our highest privilege; but it involves, on the other, the living sacrifice of our bodies, of that which links us with the world out of which we have passed. Alas! That we should have to speak of this as trial, but this is surely what all sacrifice implies, and "sacrifice" the apostle calls it. But it is a living sacrifice – a sacrifice, not in death, but life, – a surrender to Him, in which we prove what is His good and acceptable and perfect will.[1]

What has Abraham taught us about worship? Worship to God is offered **through obedience to God's Word, acknowledgement of who God is, and by sacrifice that costs the offerer something**. In application, we understand the following principles concerning worship of our God:

(1) Our worship of God grows with greater spiritual understanding of His person as revealed specifically through His Word.

(2) We cannot stop with our soul's salvation; God desires for us to increasingly know Him, which will naturally translate into increased love and adoration of Him.

(3) True spiritual service can only be rooted in a heart of worship for God.

(4) We must submit to God's order in worship to please Him and, consequently, refresh ourselves in His presence. Disorder honors the prince of darkness, but submitting to divine order glorifies the Father of light.

Abraham passed the ultimate test! His life, like ours, was characterized by a series of tests. He learned from his failures and, by God's grace, endured the consequences of those errors in judgment. More striking than his failures are the rich episodes of faith, which surmounted logic and reason to trust in God alone. This trust has been shown in Abraham's willingness to separate from his native land and kindred, from Lot, from Ishmael and all his plans for him, and even from his beloved son Isaac at the Lord's bidding. He had proven to God that he loved Him more than anyone else.

The Lord Jesus does not ask us today to prove such love by physically sacrificing loved ones on a pile of wood. He does, however, demand that He have the first place in our hearts: *"He that loveth father*

Seeds of Destiny

or mother more than Me, is not worthy of Me; and he that loveth son or daughter more than Me, is not worthy of Me" (Matt. 10:37, also see Luke 14:26). The church at Ephesus was solemnly warned by the Lord Himself concerning their diminishing love for Him – He was no longer their first love (Rev. 2:4). Examine your heart today. Is the Lord Jesus your first love?

> More love to Thee, O Christ, more love to Thee!
> Hear Thou the prayer I make on bended knee;
> This is my earnest plea: More love, O Christ, to Thee.
> Once earthly joy I craved, sought peace and rest;
> Now Thee alone I seek, give what is best;
> This all my prayer shall be: More love, O Christ, to Thee.
>
> Elizabeth Prentiss

Burial of a Stranger
Genesis 23:1-11

It is quite significant that Sarah is the only woman in all of Scripture whose age at the time of her death is recorded, 127 years. Though Sarah was not perfect, she was a woman of outstanding faith (Heb. 11:11; 1 Pet. 3:5-6). Perhaps this is the very reason her span of years is recorded – she finished well. Practically speaking, Sarah's age at death allows us to determine Isaac's corresponding age when this tragic event took place; he was 37 years old.

Abraham was a stranger in the land (Gen. 23:4); he held no legal title to the land upon which he dwelled to lawfully bury his wife. Therefore, he asked the children of Heth for a piece of property to bury his wife's body, namely the cave of Machpelah near Hebron (Gen. 23:19). The price of the property was agreed to, and Abraham purchased it and buried his deceased wife. She was the first of the patriarchal family to die in the Promised Land. Her burial in Canaan and not their homeland would serve as a declaration to the inhabitants of Canaan and to their descendants that the land upon which they lived and died was truly their home forever.

Such was the mentality of the Patriarchs concerning their burial location. Though strangers now, they wanted to be in the land of everlasting possession when the day of resurrection arrived. Then they would be no longer strangers and sojourners – the land would be their possession. Later, Isaac was buried in Canaan (Gen. 35:27-29). After Jacob died in Egypt, he was brought back and buried in Canaan (Gen. 50:13). Before Joseph died in Egypt, he took an oath from the children of Israel that they should carry his bones from Egypt to Canaan (Gen. 50:25-26; Ex. 13:19).

The testimony of Abraham is established in two ways. First, Abraham audibly confessed to the sons of Heth, *"I am a stranger and a*

Seeds of Destiny

sojourner with you." Abraham acknowledged his walk of separation from the world. The sons of Heth replied, *"Thou art a prince of God among us."* It is one thing to talk about your walk with the Lord and living a consecrated life apart from the world. It is quite another thing for the world to acknowledge your faithful walk with God and your portion in Him. Abraham walked the talk. His humility before God and man is apparent for twice we read that Abraham *"bowed himself to the people of the land"* (Gen. 23:7, 12).

If you have not noticed yet, the narrative through Genesis, as with the next three books of the Bible, is continuous – observe each chapter begins with a "connecting" word (a conjunction or a conjunctive adverb) such as "and," "then," "now," "thus," etc. Genesis 21 through 25 are strongly linked together in "type" fulfillment between the First and Second Advent of Christ's comings to the earth. These chapters in Genesis, then, also parallel the Kingdom parables of Matthew 13. These seven parables bridge the gap between the First Advent of the Lord to earth to become a man to suffer for sin and His Second Advent in which His kingdom will be established and all that is evil and wicked will be removed. The "kingdom of God" was foretold in the Old Testament, announced by John the Baptist and Jesus, and rejected by the Jews. The kingdom was then spiritually offered to the Gentiles in the interim before it will be physically established on earth and, in the finale, become the eternal state of the new heaven and new earth. All this is shown in chronological order in Genesis 21 through 25.

In Genesis 21, we have the birth of the promised son – the only begotten son of Abraham (Heb. 11:17), which pictures Christ's birth. In Genesis 22, the offering of the son by the father is observed, which foreshadows Calvary. Genesis 23 records the death and burial of Sarah. These events speak of the rejection of Jesus the Messiah by the Jews, their subsequent disciplinary "blindness" (Rom. 11:7), and that, as a nation, they are a treasure reburied in the purchased field (Matt. 13:44). In Genesis 24, the Holy Spirit is introduced to us in type as the servant of Abraham who traveled out of the land of Israel to woo a bride for the father's son. The Holy Spirit is presently wooing a Gentile bride for the Lord Jesus. Genesis 24 concludes with the bride and the groom meeting for the first time (picturing the rapture of the church), and both returning to his father's home (heaven) where the bride is loved and cherished forever. Genesis 25 records that Abraham took another wife (Keturah). In seed form, Abraham's marriage to Keturah typifies the future restoration of the adulterous and divorced wife of Jehovah – Israel (Jer. 3:8; Ezek. 16; Hosea 2:14-23). The climax of Abraham's life is in Genesis 25:5 when the son, with his new bride, inherits all things. This, of course, pictures the Lord Jesus establishing His kingdom on earth with His bride, the Church, who will rule and reign with Him (2 Tim. 2:12; Rev. 4:4; Matt. 20:20-28).

Let us refocus now on the content of Genesis 23. Through the "Kingdom Parables," the Lord Jesus was foretelling that the Jews, who had already been scattered and lost among the nations for 600 years for committing spiritual adultery (Ezek. 36:16-25), would be nationally found for the purpose of offering Himself as their King. They would reject Him and, thus, continue to be lost among the nations until their repentance during the last days of the Tribulation Period. In order to be able to retrieve them from the nations later and to restore them as His people, the Lord first had to pay the debt of their sin at Calvary. In the fifth of the Kingdom Parables, Christ alludes to this: *"The kingdom of heaven is like unto treasure hid in a field, the which when a man hath found, he hideth, and for joy thereof goeth and selleth all that he hath, and buyeth that field"* (Matt. 13:44). Just as Abraham bought the field for a price and would hide Sarah in it, God the Father would purchase Israel through the blood of His own Son and leave them hidden in the world until their restoration.

> I'm a pilgrim and a stranger, rough and thorny is the road,
> Often in the midst of danger, but it leads to God.
> Clouds and darkness oft distress me, great and many are my foes;
> Anxious cares and thoughts oppress me: but my Father knows.
> O how sweet is this assurance midst the conflict and the strife!
> Although sorrows past endurance follow me through life.
> Home in prospect still can cheer me; yes, and give me sweet repose.
> While I feel His presence near me: for my Father knows.
>
> Mary S. B. Dana

Seeds of Destiny

Buried Again
Genesis 23:12-20

There is a brief hint of Israel's physical and spiritual resurrection in the narrative in Genesis 23:3: *"Abraham stood up from before his dead."* Ezekiel describes this national wonder in chapter 37 of his book. In a vision, he describes a valley of dry bones before him that pictures the nation of Israel dead in the world. God instructs Ezekiel to prophesy upon these dry bones. As he does, the bones begin to assemble themselves into full human skeletal structures. After 2600 years of Gentile rule, Israel became a political reality in May 1948, even though the nation still remains dead in a spiritual sense. As Ezekiel preached, the skeletons took on flesh – this great army had the appearance of life, but in fact there was no life within them.

This event coincides with the fig tree (Israel) shooting forth her fig leaves before summer (before the Tribulation Period) in Matthew 24. There are leaves upon the tree, depicting a religious reality, but there is no fruit. Spiritual fruit can only come through spiritual rebirth. The nation of Israel will not experience spiritual rebirth until the end of the Tribulation Period. During the Tribulation Period, the Jews will be offering sacrifices again under the Levitical system. Before the Anti-Christ can stop these sacrifices during the middle of the Tribulation Period, they must begin again (Matt. 24:15, 2 Thess. 2:4-6). Finally, at the end of the Tribulation Period, the Jews will receive the Holy Spirit and obtain spiritual life in Christ. This is illustrated in the vision when Ezekiel prophesies to the wind (speaking of the Holy Spirit in type) to come and give life and breath upon the great army. There is a yet future resurrection of the hidden treasure – the nation of Israel unto spiritual and eternal life.

Sarah, who pictures Israel (e.g. Israel is the woman who bore the only begotten son in Rev. 12:1-2), was buried in the cave of Machpelah near Hebron. The Hebrew root word for "Hebron" comes from *cheber*, which means "a society or a fellowship." The Hebrew root word for "Machpelah" is derived from *kaphal*, which means "to fold together," or by implication, "to repeat" or "to double." Exodus 19:5 and Psalm 135:4 inform us that God considers Israel "a treasure" unto Himself. It seems, then, that what is pictured here in Sarah's death is the spiritual death of the nation of Israel (They were cut off from God.), which occurred after the offering of the Son, but before the wooing of a Gentile bride for the Son. A "society" and a "treasure" were, thus, hidden again in the world, a second time or a "double" time. However, at the Lord's Second Coming, He will be accepted by the Jewish nation (Zech. 12:10), and they will then receive the Holy Spirit and be restored unto God as His people. The events surrounding Sarah's death, the fact that she was buried in a cave, that the cave was called Machpelah and was near Hebron convey a prophetic portrait of God's future dealing with the nation of Israel.

When Sarah died, the marriage covenant with Abraham was severed (Rom. 7:1-6); this event was followed by a marriage covenant instituted in Genesis 24 between Isaac and Rebekah, thus portraying the New Covenant in Christ's blood, which put away the Old Covenant. The death of Sarah allows Abraham to receive a new wife in Genesis 25 (Keturah) after Isaac is joined to Rebekah. The marriage with Keturah, who bears Abraham six sons, depicts the future restoration of a refined and fruitful Israel with Jehovah. This event occurs after the church is in heaven with Christ (for Isaac and Rebekah were joined together in Genesis 24). The Old Covenant had its strength in the law, which could not be kept and, thus, brought death, but the New Covenant is empowered by God's grace through Christ's blood. As a result, the New Covenant brought salvation to both Jew and Gentile (Lk. 22:20; Eph. 3:6-7).

The Lord God has etched all these symbols, names, and personal experiences into Scripture to acutely disclose His Son and His ultimate plan of redemption to us! Even Stephen, while preaching to the Sanhedrin in Acts 7, declared that prophetic patterns in the lives of the Patriarchs were given as examples for the nation of Israel to witness. He told them that neither Joseph nor Moses had been accepted when they had been first presented to their brethren as king and deliverer,

Seeds of Destiny

respectively. But the second time, Joseph's brethren acknowledged their brother as king and their wrong in selling him into slavery. Also, Moses, on his second presentation, was accepted as the deliverer after the "bricks without straw" setback. Both Joseph and Moses married Gentile women. When Stephen drew the analogy of rejection to its climax, the Jewish leaders could not tolerate the truth any longer and murdered him.

> Not all the blood of beasts, on Jewish altars slain,
> Could give the guilty conscience peace, or wash away its stain.
> But Christ, the heavenly Lamb, took all our sins away,
> A sacrifice of nobler name and richer blood than they.
> We now look back to see the burden Thou didst bear,
> When hanging on the accursed tree, for all our guilt was there.
> Believing, we rejoice to see the curse remove;
> We bless the Lamb with cheerful voice, and sing redeeming love.
>
> Isaac Watts

A Bride Sought for Isaac
Genesis 24:1-33

In Genesis 24, the character types of the previous three chapters continue in prophetic role-play. Abraham continues to represent God the Father, as Isaac does the Lord Jesus. Sarah has died picturing the rejection of Christ by Israel and their subsequent spiritual blindness and separation from God. In this chapter, two new characters emerge in a divinely arranged pattern of things to come. Abraham's "unnamed servant" epitomizes the Holy Spirit, and Rebekah depicts a virgin Gentile bride called the Church.

Isaac and Sarah must have had a special mother-son relationship for he was still grieving some three years after her death (Gen. 24:67). Abraham was in the autumn years of his life (140 years old) and knew it was time for Isaac to have a lifetime companion and helper – a wife. Isaac's grief is a figurative "seed" for the three years the Lord Jesus grieved during His earthly ministry over the spiritual deadness of Israel (Lk. 13:7, 34). It was after Calvary that His Father sent the Holy Spirit to seek and woo a Gentile bride for Him (Jn. 14:16, 26, 16:8-11). This bride would be the Church.

Abraham might have increased his political vitality in the region by arranging a marriage between Isaac and a damsel of local nobility, but, simply put, the inhabitants were pagan; they knew not the Lord God and as Canaanites were cursed. The righteous should never seek an unrighteous spouse (2 Cor. 6:14). A believer is born of the Spirit, and, thus a child of God. A believer, then, has no portion with an unbeliever, who is not born again. Unbelievers are referred to as children of wrath (Eph. 2:3), children of disobedience (Eph. 2:2), children of darkness (Eph. 5:8), and as children of the devil (1 John 3:8-10, i.e. unbelievers who imitate the devil's behavior, not because they are begotten of him). Such marital unions are guaranteed to have deep spiritual problems.

Seeds of Destiny

Throughout Scripture God's charge has always been to marry only within God's people (Deut. 7:3-4; 1 Kings 11:4; Ezra 9; 1 Cor. 7:39). Among Abraham's kin in Mesopotamia there would certainly be a maiden acquainted with the God of Glory whom he had before given testimony of. Abraham was too old to journey to Mesopotamia, so he commissioned his servant, probably Eliezer from Damascus (Gen. 15:2, 24:10), with the matter of obtaining a bride for Isaac from his extended family (Gen. 24:4). Before his servant left, Abraham bound him to vow by oath that he would return with a wife for Isaac – if the young woman would come. If she would not journey with Eliezer, he promised not to allow Isaac to depart from the land to seek her. Isaac, the child of promise and the chosen seed of Abraham, must remain in the Promised Land. If God did not provide a wife for Isaac, the servant would be released from his vow. The oath was acknowledged by the placing of his hand under Abraham's thigh and was pledged in *"the name of Jehovah, the God of heaven, and the God of the earth."* Abraham had an intimate understanding of his God.

Though Abraham initiates the venture, Abraham and Isaac are both referred to as masters in Genesis 24. Perhaps in *type*, the equality of the Father and Son are in view. The Lord Jesus said, *"I and my Father are one"* (Jn. 10:30). The Lord's majestic station in glory had been relinquished at His first advent, then fully restored after His resurrection and return to heaven (Jn. 17:1-5). The Lord has always inherently been equal with God, for He is God, but His sovereign position over all creation was laid aside from the time of His incarnation through the event of His resurrection. The Lord Jesus has not come into His kingdom yet, but even now, as His Father seeks a Gentile bride through the wooing of the Holy Spirit, all appropriate honor and glory has been reinstated to Him. This is seen in seed form in that both Abraham and Isaac bear the title of "master."

The servant of Abraham discerned the proper location to seek a bride for Isaac, then sought divine providence through the prayer to bless his labor. Matthew Henry comments on our need to follow the servant's example of both applying wisdom to life's challenges and beckoning the throne of grace for assistance and blessing.

> We have leave to be particular in recommending our affairs to the care of Divine providence. He [the servant] proposes a sign, not that

he intended to proceed no further, if not gratified in it; but it is a prayer that God would provide a good wife for his young master; and that was a good prayer. She should be simple, industrious, humble, cheerful, serviceable, and hospitable. Whatever may be the fashion, common sense, as well as piety, tells us, these are the proper qualifications for a wife and mother; for one who is to be a companion to her husband, the manager of domestic concerns, and trusted to form the minds of children. When the steward came to seek a wife for his master, he did not go to places of amusement and sinful pleasure, and pray that he might meet one there, but to the well of water, expecting to find one there employed aright. He prayed that God would be pleased to make His way in this matter plain and clear before him. Our times are in God's hand; not only events themselves, but the times of them. We must take heed of being over-bold in urging what God should do, lest the event should weaken our faith, rather than strengthen it.[1]

The servant wisely went to a location of feminine labor, then prayed for help. The Lord honored that prayer by presenting just the right damsel at the proper moment to do exactly what had been requested for her. Her difficult laboring to water the camels proved her physical tenacity and cheerful selfless character; both would be needed for the strenuous journey homeward. The watering of all those camels by the only suitable young maiden in the city to be Isaac's bride was an answer to prayer and a miracle. The Church began on the day of Pentecost in the same way. Christ's disciples were praying in one accord (Acts 1:14), then a great miracle happened in Acts 2 – the Holy Spirit came and baptized believers into the body of Christ, thus, forming the Church.

Notice that the servant's name was never given and that his only objective was to accomplish the will of Abraham. This required the servant to testify of the highly favored Isaac to the prospective bride, to negotiate and render a virgin's dowry to the bride's family, then to deliver her back to Isaac safe and sound. The servant's speech to the family focused on Isaac, the man willing to marry their daughter and to share his great inheritance with her. Likewise, the Lord told his disciples that the Holy Spirit would be sent of His Father after He was ascended into heaven (Jn. 16:7, 14:16-19; Acts 1:4-5). The Lord also told His disciples that the Holy Spirit would not speak of Himself (i.e. He

Seeds of Destiny

would not speak of Himself on His own initiative), but of the Lord Jesus (Jn. 16:13). The Holy Spirit seeks to glorify the Lord Jesus (Jn. 16:14). He speaks of Christ's glory, His beauty and His lovely character.

One of the works of the Holy Spirit upon the conversion of a repentant sinner is to bestow him/her a spiritual gift(s) for the purpose of edifying the Church (1 Cor. 12:4, 11; 1 Pet. 4:10). It is, then, no surprise to see that the servant not only paid the price of the dowry (which pictures the price of the Church's redemption – the blood of Christ) but also gave Rebekah gifts on behalf of Isaac.

The attitude of Abraham's servant is worthy to note. Success inflates the pride of flesh, but humbles the spiritual man. Abraham's servant recognized that the hand of God had delivered to him success, a miracle, and an answer to his prayer. He reverently bows down and worships the Lord (Gen. 24:26) and then praises Him for hearing and answering his prayer (Gen. 24:27). Before the chapter is over, he will again bow down and worship the Lord for his goodness and mercy (Gen. 24:52). While on the tiresome journey of life may we all heed the example of Abraham's servant: By faith let us petition the Lord for our essential needs and bow our hearts low unto Him who is worthy of all our worship and praise!

> I heard the voice of Jesus say, "Come unto Me and rest;
> Lay down, thou weary one, lay down thy head upon My breast."
> I came to Jesus as I was, weary, and worn, and sad;
> I found in Him a resting place, and He has made me glad.
>
> Horatius Bonar

A Bride Bought for Isaac
Genesis 24:34-56

The ancient marriage custom before us is depicted by B. H Carroll:

> The custom was for the betrothal to take place at the house of the bride's father, and Eliezer comes in the name of this master and the betrothal is undertaken. The marriage is consummated whenever the bride is taken to the bridegroom's house, and he meets and takes her in. As soon as the betrothal is completed, Eliezer, according to custom, takes the lady to his camel and hands out the presents sent by the bridegroom.[1]

Rebekah's family agreed to the marriage, and with Rebekah's eager words of commitment, *"I will go,"* the servant departed to begin the trek home with Isaac's espoused bride. Rebekah was being drawn down an unknown road, in the companionship of a stranger, to marry a far-off man. By faith, she was pursuing a distant object of glory, knowing full well that she also would be blessed by laying hold of it – Isaac.

In the historical Jewish betrothal custom, a man would approach a virgin's father to ask for her hand in marriage. If the father was agreeable to this, they would then negotiate the bride's price (virgin's dowry), often with the assistance of a third party. Once this had been finalized, the virgin's parents would have the prospective groom over for dinner. At this meal he would pour a glass of wine and offer it to the virgin daughter – the prospective bride. If she accepted the glass from the suitor's hand – it meant yes, I will marry you. If she did not accept the glass, his offer was rejected. If the marriage offer was accepted, the couple was then considered betrothed – they were bound by a marriage covenant. This began an interval called a "time of purity" in which the groom built a house near his father's house or added on a room to his father's house for him and his bride.

Seeds of Destiny

During this time of purity the bride was not idle either, for she was preparing her wedding gown and had to be ready to be called away by her husband when he came for her. Once the groom's father was satisfied that the new home was completely finished and furnished, he would instruct his son to go get his bride. When arriving at the bride's home, he would shout for her to come; she would quickly join him, and they would return together to the new home. After this, they enjoyed personal intimacy together and a marriage feast to celebrate their marriage and new home with their friends and relatives.

The parallels between Christ's relationship with the Church and that of the groom to the bride in the Jewish betrothal custom are impressive. When an individual accepts the gospel invitation, the dowry is applied (the blood Christ shed at Calvary). The night before He died, the Lord poured a glass of diluted red wine and gave it to his disciples to drink. He told them: *"This cup is the new testament in my blood, which is shed for you"* (Lk. 22:20). They received it and drank it, and a new covenant was acknowledged. Each time a believer drinks of the cup at the Lord's Supper, he is reaffirming "I do" to the Lord Jesus. The Lord promised His disciples later that evening that, though He was leaving to prepare a place for them, He would return for them. When will the Lord come? While still on earth, the Lord admitted that only the Father knew (Matt. 24:36). So, the Son is busy preparing a home for His bride.

The bride (the Church) should not be idle either in light of her betrothal. She is to maintain pure conduct. Paul states, *"I am jealous over you with godly jealousy; for I have espoused you to one husband, that I may present you as a chaste virgin to Christ"* (2 Cor. 11:2). The Church must not commit spiritual adultery with the world (Jas. 4:4). As the bride worked on her wedding gown, so the Church is to be adorning herself with righteous acts, which reflect the character of her Groom (Rev. 19:8). This is why the Lord Jesus implores the Church at Laodicea to buy from Him white raiment, that they would be clothed *"and that the shame of thy nakedness do not appear"* (Rev. 3:18).

> Safe in the arms of Jesus, Safe on His gentle breast,
> There, by His love overshadowed, Sweetly my soul shall rest.
>
> Fanny Crosby

A Bride Brought to Isaac
Genesis 24:57-67

What do you think occupied Rebekah's thoughts during the journey across the prolonged stretch of barren land? The blistering sun and wind, or frigid temperatures at night – not likely. She was learning all she could about Isaac from Abraham's unnamed servant, picturing the Holy Spirit. Similarly, the Holy Spirit is the "Comforter," literally "the One called alongside of" to speak of Christ and accompany the Church along the perilous journey homeward. Just as Rebekah was contemplating marriage and her initial face-to-face encounter with her husband, the church anticipates being ushered into the presence of the Lord. Those expectations alone created within her a web of excitement and exhilaration to finish the journey despite the hardship. Before her, a day was dawning that would reveal the son of Abraham, and in a twinkling of an eye, all her passions and affections would culminate in one blessed crescendo! This was her hope to face the future with confidence and great expectation. Where did this rendezvous occur, and what affections characterized the advent of their marriage?

And Isaac went out to meditate in the field at the eventide: and he lifted up his eyes, and saw and, behold, the camels were coming. And Rebekah lifted up her eyes, and when she saw Isaac, she lighted off the camel. For she had said unto the servant, "What man is this that walketh in the field to meet us?" And the servant had said, "It is my master": therefore she took a veil, and covered herself. And the servant told Isaac all things that he had done. And Isaac brought her into his mother Sarah's tent, and took Rebekah, and she became his wife; and he loved her: and Isaac was comforted after his mother's death (Gen. 24:63-67).

Seeds of Destiny

Rebekah's "blessed hope" became a reality, not at Nahor, her home, nor at Isaac's home, but in a field between their two localities. This is beautiful typology of Christ returning for His bride the Church in the clouds above the earth. This is the "blessed hope" for every believer, as Paul states in Titus 2:13. The Lord is preparing a place for His Bride. In the interim, the Church is exhorted to be, and ultimately will be, that pure virgin bride of Christ (2 Cor. 11:2; Eph. 5:27). The Church, like Rebekah, is venturing ever closer towards her beloved, enduring hardship and longing for that first meeting in the clouds between heaven (God's home) and earth (our pilgrim place). Let the Church keep saying "I do," for in a moment, in a twinkling of an eye, we will be ushered into the presence of our beloved Groom and Lord (1 Cor. 15:51-52).

It is worthy to note the specific activity of Abraham's servant in accomplishing his mission of obtaining a wife for Isaac. Hamilton Smith summarizes:

> The servant was sent to Mesopotamia with this single object in view. Having found the bride and brought her to Isaac, his mission would be accomplished. It was not part of the servant's work to interfere with the political or social interests of Mesopotamia. The Holy Spirit is not here to improve or reform the world, or bring peace to the nations, or even convert the world. He is not here to right the wrongs of the poor, remove oppression, or relieve man from disease, want, and misery. There is One that in due time will indeed bring peace and blessing to the world. One who has been here and proved that He had the power and grace to relieve man of every pressure. Alas! We nailed Him to a cross, and He is gone, so the misery of the world remains. Nevertheless, He is coming again to bring in the blessing. But in the meantime Jesus is in heaven and the Holy Spirit is down here to obtain a bride for Christ.[1]

Each of the Patriarchs was unique in character and engaged in activities consistent with their character. Abraham built altars to worship; Isaac dug wells to maintain peace, and Jacob lived in tents as a quiet man. Though Isaac would dig many wells in the future, we find him now dwelling by the well of Lahairoi before and after he received his bride (Gen. 24:62, 25:11). Lahairoi means "Him that liveth and seeth me." It expresses communion with the eternal and omniscient God. So when Isaac received his bride, he brought her into the presence of God also.

Note Isaac and Rebakah's behavior at the consummation of their marriage. Rebekah dropped from her camel and covered herself with a veil as an act of *reverence* for Isaac and his authority, while Isaac is said to have *loved* Rebekah. This is exactly what Paul declares in Ephesians 5:33 to be the basic blueprint for a good marriage: *"Nevertheless, let every one of you in particular so love his wife* (sacrificially give to her) *even as himself; and the wife see that she reverence her husband"* (i.e. that she respects his authority over her). Truly, this was a match made in heaven. Some Patriarchs took more than one wife, usually for the wrong reasons, but Isaac only had eyes for Rebekah and never took any other woman as his wife. What a splendid picture of the love the Lord possesses for the Church for all eternity.

> Oh! I am my Beloved's, and my Beloved's mine!
> He brings a poor vile sinner into His house of wine!
> I stand upon His merit; I know no other stand,
> Not e'en where glory dwelleth, in Immanuel's land.
> The bride eyes not her garment, but her dear Bride-groom's face;
> I will not gaze at glory, but on my King of grace –
> Not at the crown He giveth, but on His pierced hand:
> The Lamb is all the glory of Immanuel's land.
>
> Anne Ross Cousin

Seeds of Destiny

The Son Inherits All the Father Has
Genesis 25:1-18

The typology sequence we have been studying, which initiated in Genesis 21, reaches its climax in the first six verses of Genesis 25. Abraham had a wife restored to him again after the death of Sarah. Her name was Keturah, and she bore him six sons. Truly, Abraham was the father of many nations. Abraham's marriage to Keturah foreshadows the restoration of Israel to Jehovah and the resultant blessing to the Gentile nations during the Kingdom Age following Israel's restoration. Israel had played the harlot by embracing other gods, so the one true God wrote the nation of Israel a *"bill of divorce"* (Jer. 2:26-29, 3:8; Isa. 50:1). Yet, the prophets foretold that the repentant wife (Israel) would be restored unto her husband (God) in a future day (Hos. 2:14, 19-20, Ezek. 16). This restoration will occur during the latter part of the Great Tribulation (Zech. 12:10, Zech. 14). Note the prophetic sequence: the church is retrieved to heaven to be with the Lord (Gen. 24:61-67), the Jews are restored during the conclusion of the tribulation period (Gen. 25:1), and then the Lord Jesus returns to establish His rightful kingdom on earth (Gen. 25:5).

In Genesis 25:5, Isaac inherits all that his father has. What a wonderful pre-announcement of Christ's reign on earth, when He will rule and reign over all that His Father has. Presently, the Lord Jesus has been exalted by His Father and has a name above every name (Phil. 2:9). However, He has not yet received His kingdom. Presently, He sits at His Father's right hand (Heb. 1:3) and upon His Father's throne in heaven, while He waits to receive His throne on earth (Rev. 3:21). The inheritance of Isaac and the remarriage of Abraham symbolize the two climactic events that will occur at the end of the Tribulation Period: the restoration of Israel to God and the Son inheriting His rightful position as King of kings and Lord of lords on earth. He will rule and reign in righteousness and peace, and all the inhabitants will worship Him.

The typological focus of Isaac representing Christ concludes in Genesis 25:5. And so here a summary will be designated, not of the "seed" (Isaac) but to the seed's future manifestation (Christ). Christ was promised long before His coming (Lk. 1:70), appeared at the appointed time (Gal. 4:4), was conceived by a miracle (Lk. 1:35), was assigned a birth name by God (Matt. 1:21), bore the wood associated with His sacrifice (Jn. 19:17), was willing to be offered (Jn. 10:17-18), was offered as a sacrifice by His Father (Jn. 3:16, Isa. 53:10), was obedient unto death (Phil. 2:8), was raised up from the dead (Eph. 1:19-22), and now waits to personally meet His Gentile bride who He purchased with His own blood (1 Thess. 4:13-18) and to rule and reign with her in His kingdom (2 Tim. 2:12). Thus, "the seeds" of Genesis 21 through 25 declare in testimony the destiny of Christ.

Before leaving the great Patriarch of faith, let us briefly review what made Abraham a great man and friend of God: (1) He was a mighty man of faith and by covenant became the father of the faithful. (2) He was a perpetual worshipper erecting altars where he journeyed, except for the occasion of venturing into Egypt for a short season. (3) He had a great capacity for friendship. Not only was he the friend of God, but he was able to bridge friendships with the Amorites, the Canaanites, and Abimelech without compromising his testimony. (4) He sought peace when strife arose. Whether the conflict was with the herdsmen of Lot or Abimelech, Abraham humbly trod the low road of self-sacrifice to gain peace. (5) He had courage to act when required. He forsook Ur for a land he had never seen and forsook his gods for the one true God he did not know. When Lot was taken captive, he struck quickly and powerfully against overwhelming odds, naturally speaking. (6) He was hospitable to visitors, as seen in Genesis 18. (7) He ruled his family for God and ensured God's commandments were obeyed in his household. (8) He was obedient to God's commands – even to the offering of his only son. Abraham was not a perfect man, but his pilgrimage Godward and the quality of his faith have been an example to God's people for four millennia. His testimony has withstood time.

> Father Abraham, had many sons, Many sons had Father Abraham,
> I am one of them and so are you, So let's just praise the Lord!

Seeds of Destiny

The Second Born is Chosen
Genesis 25:19-26

Genesis 25 especially demonstrates the faithfulness of God. God always honors His word and promises. He promised Abraham a prolonged life on earth (Gen. 15:15). The old Patriarch, Abraham, died at the good old age of 175. He was buried with his wife, Sarah, in the cave of Machpelah. God promised Abraham that Ishmael would be the father of a great nation because he was Abraham's son (Gen. 17:20, 21:13). God promised to make Isaac the seed of promise, and God blessed Isaac with children, but not initially.

The Lord did not bless Isaac and Rebekah with children in the early years of their marriage. Their home was subdued with silence. No crying babies, no bustle of children at play, or scurrying little feet to embrace papa returning home from the field; no joy of parenthood. The matter grieved Rebekah. Just as the Lord makes intercession for the church to be fruitful, Isaac besought the Lord through prayer on Rebekah's behalf. It is interesting that this is the only prayer offered by Isaac, as recorded in Scripture; perhaps this point highlights the importance of the continued intercession of the Lord Jesus in heaven on behalf of His church.

The Lord heard Isaac's prayers and opened Rebekah's womb. During Rebekah's pregnancy, she became aware that a prenatal war had erupted in her, womb, so she asked the Lord about the matter. The Lord told her *"Two nations are in thy womb, and two manner of people shall be [born of thee], and the one people shall be stronger than the other people and the elder shall serve the younger."* She was carrying twins and not just twins but boys and not just boys but the heads of two future nations. The latter portion of the prophecy *"the elder shall serve the younger"* evidently refers to the boys' descendants rather than to them personally. What first time mother wouldn't be excited to hear such news from the Lord about her pregnancy? Knowing that Rebekah had obtained this divine information will aid our understanding of later circumstances that beset this family. In time, Rebekah would bear Isaac two boys, both in one birth. They would be her only children.

The time of Rebekah's birth pangs and travail came, and just as God had informed her, twins were born unto her and Isaac. The older son was hairy and red; thus, he was named Esau, meaning "hairy." He became a man of the field and a hunter. Incidentally, there are only two individuals given the term of "hunter" in Scripture; they are Nimrod and Esau – both were rebels. Immediately after birth the younger son grabbed the heel of his older brother and, was, thus named Jacob, which means the "heel-catcher" (and in extension, "a supplanter" or "schemer").

How long did Isaac pray for Rebekah to conceive and bear children? A long time because Isaac was 60 years old before he became a father. The Lord said, *"For every one that asketh receiveth; and he that seeketh findeth; and to him that knocketh it shall be opened"* (Matt. 7:8). Isaac asked the Lord, did his part to conceive children, then kept asking. Sometimes Christians petition the Lord for direction, but then they do not move their feet so God can direct their path. Or, when the first closed door bumps their nose, they get offended or hurt and cease from asking for guidance. Dear Christian, keep asking and keep seeking until you find the open door of opportunity that God has provided.

>Behold the throne of grace!
>The promise calls us near,
>To seek our God and Father's face,
>Who loves to answer prayer.
>
>Beyond our utmost wants
>His love and power can bless;
>To praying souls He always grants
>More than they can express.
>
>John Newton

Seeds of Destiny

Birthright for Bean Soup
Genesis 25:27-34

Though Jacob was a schemer, Scripture describes him as a *"plain man."* Apparently, he preferred to remain at home and indoors and live a quiet life. The Hebrew word for "plain" is *"tam,"* which means "gentle or undefiled." Jacob, in contrast to his brother Esau, was a man preferring "brains rather than brawn" in accomplishing life's tasks.

Apparently, one of Jacob's "homebody" hobbies was cooking. One particular day Jacob prepared a pot of bean soup. Esau returned from the field and was famished. Esau declared that he would die soon if he did not get something to eat. He asked Jacob for a bowl of that good smelling soup before he passed out from low blood sugar. Jacob was not obliged to offer any soup to Esau but was willing to negotiate a trade with him. Union talks concluded quickly with an agreement; Jacob swapped Esau one bowl of soup for Esau's birthright.

It was customary for the oldest son to get a family blessing from his father before he died and to acquire a double portion of the inheritance. Esau agreed and made a vow to trade his birthright, so Jacob relinquished the savory soup and a morsel of bread to Esau. Esau ate and was satisfied. Although the deal was not fostered in deception, there is a scant flavor of "scheming" in Jacob's stew. He presumptuously snatched at the promised blessing before it was ripe and in doing so demonstrated contempt for God's purpose in time. Besides this, Jacob's response to famished Esau, his twin brother, was deplorable. Surely, any desperate stranger wandering out of the desert would have received better hospitality at Jacob's tent. But Esau is treated more like a traveling salesman with bad merchandise than a brother. Jacob fully lived up to his name, "a trickster" or "schemer."

Men normally have felt that the first-born son should receive the greater honor and inheritance than other siblings to follow. Scripture states that Esau despised his birthright, which represented his "spiritual heritage." The writer of Hebrews declares him to be a "profane" person (Heb. 12:16-17) because he did not value spiritual matters (the blessing) over temporal desires (food). Esau pictures the natural man's propensity to be lured by his own lusts and worldliness – to value things seen and not the promises of God. He is not interested in spiritual matters, but the thrill of the day and what he can indulge in now. He is not mindful of the future, but when the future arrives, he is remorseful concerning the consequences of past actions, yet not repentant. The "Esaus" of the world are sorry they get caught, sorry they did not think ahead, sorry they did not get what they wanted, but are not repentant before God. Because they do not know God, they cannot walk by faith; therefore, they are blind concerning spiritual and eternal matters. Our world is full of people like Esau. It is no wonder that God declared, *"Jacob have I loved, but Esau have I hated"* (Rom. 9:13). We understand this statement to be in the "comparative" sense and not an "absolute" declaration, for God loves all men, but hates their behavior (Matt. 10:37; Lk. 14:26; 2 Pet. 3:9). Even though Esau's behavior was grievous, God promised to bless him (Gen. 27:38-40).

It is true that God had pre-selected Jacob for His eternal purpose in time (Rom. 9:12), but He did not force Esau to be faithless and rebellious in character. Nor did He seduce Jacob to value the birthright. The application to the Christian is clear. God has a sovereign plan for our lives; let us be in the center of it! In everything we do or say, we must have the eternal perspective in view as much as is possible. What "counts for eternity?" What is the "fluff of life?" Then, when we stand before the Lord (Rom. 14:10-12; 1 Pet. 1:17), we will not have a reason to be "whiners" like Esau; we will be "winners" of the reward and the prize bestowed by Christ Himself.

> Character is what you are in the dark.
>
> Dwight L. Moody

> The measure of a man's real character is what he would do if he knew he would never be found out.
>
> Thomas Macaulay

Like Father, Like Son
Genesis 26:1-5

Another famine viciously assaulted the land of Canaan. It was the second famine to burden the inhabitants since the time Abraham first arrived from Haran. Abraham had paid a high price in consequences for venturing out of the Promised Land into Egypt after the previous famine. God ensured Isaac would not do the same by solemnly warning him not to abandon his inheritance – He would supply his needs and protect him from injury.

Isaac had been tempted to leave Canaan but heeded the divine warning and terminated his journey westward at Gerar. Gerar was as close to Egypt as one can venture without deserting Canaan. In fact, Isaac, unlike Abraham his father and Jacob his son, never left Canaan. Isaac never ventured more than about 50 miles from his birthplace. He at no time traveled north of the city of Jerusalem, west of the Mediterranean Sea, south of Beersheba, nor east of Jordan River. He was a Patriarch of the "heavenly land" – an inheritance that could not be disposed.

Unlike Abraham and Jacob, Isaac only wed one woman. Dispensation typology is clearly displayed in these realities. In Genesis 24, Isaac lays eyes for the first time upon his virgin bride, the only wife he will ever have. After the gathering of the church to the air, Christ will forever be with His church in a heavenly land. Wherever Christ resides, that will be paradise for the church. The dispensation of the Church is also witnessed in the names employed by God to personally address the patriarchs. To Abraham and Jacob, God identifies Himself as Almighty God (*El-Shaddai*) to declare His authority and position, but to Isaac, He is *Elohim* (Gen. 26:24) to express His majesty or *Jehovah* (Gen. 26:2, 24) to convey relationship and self-existence. God the Father meant for us to ponder the immense appreciation He holds for His resurrected and exalted Son, as seen through His relationship with Isaac.

Abimelech, a title meaning "father of the king" and not a proper name, was ruling over Gerar. Given seventy to ninety years had passed since Abraham's visit in Gerar, it is extremely unlikely that this was the same Abimelech who had reproved Abraham. Often certain family behavioral bents are passed from one generation to the next or, as commonly stated, "the apple doesn't fall far from the tree" and "like father like son." This patriarchal family was no different. Though Isaac did not abandon Canaan, he did commit the same sin of his father in fear of his own personal safety. He lied to the inhabitants concerning his relationship to his wife. Certainly, the influence of Gerar was not profitable for either Abraham or Isaac, as both their testimonies were marred there.

Should Isaac have remained in Gerar? No, he was pushing the boundaries and flirting with Egypt. To face the world requires one to turn away from the Lord. What the world chases after, the church should flee from. Might we remain in the place where we enjoyed communion with God. If Isaac was not in communion with God, why then did God bless him? It is true that as a descendant of Abraham he would receive God's general blessing in sovereign purpose. But personal blessing requires personal obedience. God was compelled to bless Isaac because He promised to if Isaac did not go down to Egypt (Gen. 26:3). God's promise of blessing preceded Isaac's cowardice and deceptive act. Isaac chose to remain in Canaan, and God blessed him (Gen. 26:12). Yet, there is a notable difference between obtaining God's blessing without His fellowship and enjoying both. We must not allow the "end to justify the means" if the means is clearly in opposition to God's Word.

Isaac journeyed to Gerar to escape a perilous trial only to be confronted by another of his own doing. He departed from home without consulting the Lord. But God intervened and offered deliverance, that is, if Isaac would exercise faith in Him. After encountering Jehovah, Isaac should have returned from where he came, but instead he took up residence in a wicked place for *"a long time"* (Gen. 26:8). He did not venture into Egypt, but he did not journey home either. One cannot successfully clutch the world and embrace the Lord at the same time.

Seeds of Destiny

Isaac stayed too long on the border of concession and unfortunately compromised his testimony and marriage. We should never judge an individual's spiritual condition as right because he/she is enjoying prosperous circumstances. There are unforeseen consequences of pushing the boundaries with God, and time will indelibly bear these out. The believer should endeavor to remain in the center of God's will.

> Mine eyes are unto Thee, my God, My soul on Thee doth wait,
> My hope is in Thy faithful word, and in Thy love so great.

F. J. M.

She is My Sister
Genesis 26:6-16

    Ladies, how would you feel if you were in Rebekah's shoes? Let's say that your husband of twenty years finally agreed to take you on the second honeymoon you have always wanted. He coordinates the whole trip to some secluded romantic getaway on a remote island in the south Pacific. However, after your arrival you learn why the airline tickets were so cheap. The social economy is backwards, and not at all like the travel brochure indicated. The natives are eyeing you over a little too closely for comfort and like what they see. Your husband's anxiety overcomes him, and he decides to ask you to lie about your relationship, so they won't kill him to get you. He says, "Just tell them you are my sister." You're dumbfounded but being the submissive wife that you are – you agree. This unfortunately removes his protection from you, and before you can gain composure, you are led as a captive by a group of native men to be abused and assaulted as they please. Ladies, what loving and kind thoughts would you have towards your husbands? Somewhere between "hang 'em high" and "lock and load?" How would you feel about yourself? The same way Rebekah did – unimportant, insecure, and unprotected. Rebekah, like her beautiful mother-in-law years earlier, was sequestered as part of Abimelech's harem (Gen. 20:2).

    Abimelech was keeping a close watch on Isaac and Rebekah. Perhaps he knew of the trouble Isaac's father, Abraham, had caused their nation a generation earlier when he posed Sarah, his wife, as his sister. His prudence paid off, for from his window he observed Isaac and Rebekah caressing and concluded that they were husband and wife, not brother and sister. Abimelech summoned Isaac, and Isaac confessed to lying about the whole matter, then explained why he had deceived Abimelech. It should be noted that even this pagan king understood that there was an appropriate manner for a husband, and wife to touch each other which was not appropriate for an unmarried man and woman. He also understood the importance of not committing adultery and destroying the family unit. He seemed to understand that the strength of a society is only as strong as the families that compose it. If the marriage of a man and woman is degraded, the family will suffer, and when the family cell is eroded away, the society and church composed of those broken families also suffers. In this case, the erosion began with Isaac ignoring his responsibility to love his wife.

Paul uses the marriage relationship of a husband and a wife as a prop to try to explain the mysterious spiritual relationship of Christ with the Church but does so in a way that also exhorts husbands and wives in proper behavior (Eph. 5:22-33). In what fashion should a man demonstrate love for his wife? In the same manner that the Lord Jesus confirmed His love to His bride the Church. From this passage, we conclude that the Lord's love for His Church is "stable," "sacrificial," "sanctifying," "satisfying," and "secure." Husbands should likewise strive to apply these qualities of love in their marriages.

Biblical love is initiated by "giving." John 3:16 reads, *"For God so loved the world, that He gave His only begotten Son, that whosoever believeth in Him should not perish, but have everlasting life."* God initiated the cycle of giving! John wrote, *"We love Him, because He first loved us"* (1 Jn. 4:19). As God touches our heart through expressed acts of love, we swell up with unconstrained affections towards Him, and we, as enabled by His Spirit, want to love Him in return. God demonstrated by the giving of His Son that true love must be willing to suffer. It is in this way that our love is matured and perfected.

This circle of expressed love ought to transpire in marriage also. Five times the Bible commands husbands to love their wives. Yet, we find no imperative command for wives to love their husbands. In fact, Paul states that younger wives need to learn how to properly love (meaning, "be kind and affectionate to") their husbands and children. Thus, men are tasked with "initiating" the cycle of love in the home. As a man unselfishly loves his wife, just as God unselfishly loved us, his actions of love will naturally result in tender reciprocation by his wife. Most wives have no difficulty submitting to their husband's leadership when unselfish love is being enjoyed. In summary, husbands love, cherish, and nurture your wives (Eph. 5:25-29), and wives submit and respect your husbands (Eph. 5:22, 31). God often asks the most important and difficult of us in order to test our love for Him!

Isaac did not show sacrificial love for his wife. I think before marrying a wife every man should vow that he will give his own life in order to protect and secure his wife's – that is what Christ did for us. *"But God commendeth his love toward us in that, while we were yet sinners, Christ died for us"* (Rom. 5:8). While we (the future bride) were far away, the groom initiated to resolve our problem – sin. Husbands are to be the "initiators" in family matters. If there is a problem, they are accountable and responsible to resolve the matter regardless of the cost to themselves.

God constantly demonstrates an initiating type of love but in no greater way than in the giving of His Son. There was a chasm between God and man, but God's initiating love motivated the resolution and brought restoration. Did it cost Him something? Magnitudes beyond human comprehension! His inexhaustible compassion for us was displayed in one exploit. Where? It was upon a Roman cross when His Son willingly suffered and died on our behalf.

Isaac was restored to his wife, but it seems that Rebekah's respect and love for Isaac never recovered from this incident. She did not have a forgiving spirit and, instead, became controlling – a manipulator. It is true that she "lived with" Isaac after this act of cowardice, but she seemingly ceased to "live for" him. In the next chapter, Rebekah blatantly usurped Isaac's authority twice. God blesses marriages that abide by His Word. Husbands love your wives with an obligational mindset of serving, and wives submit to your husband's authority, and you will experience liberation of responsibility and the wonder of marriage that Isaac and Rebekah did until selfish ambition shattered and split up their family.

We like someone *because*. We love someone *although*.

Henri De Montherlant

Isaac the Well Digger
Genesis 26:17-35

God greatly prospered Isaac while he was living in Gerar – to the extent that he could not dwell there any more. Consequently, Abimelech invited him to leave. This is a real testimony to God's faithfulness. God had warned him not to go down to Egypt to find a solution for hard times but to endure in the land, and He would bless him. That is just what God did. He exceedingly increased his possessions and did so while in the midst of a famine.

The Philistines envied Isaac so much that they filled with dirt the wells his father, Abraham, had dug. This created a hardship on Isaac, who had numerous animals to water, and generated an atmosphere of animosity between Abimelech and Isaac. The narrative indicates that Isaac sought to make peace by redigging two wells of his father's at Beersheba (Gen. 16:14, 21:25-33) before giving over these wells and moving to the valley of Gerar to dig two new wells. The new wells "Esek," meaning "contention" or "dispute," and "Sitnah," meaning "hatred" or "opposition," were also relinquished to the Gerarites to keep peace. Isaac returned to Beersheba and dug a third new well, which was uncontested, and so finally peace was achieved. What a testimony – *"blessed are the peacemakers for they shall be called the children of God"* (Matt. 5:9). Isaac differs from both his father Abraham and his son Jacob in his passiveness. He possessed no spirit of aggression and in fact was never in battle.

It was when Isaac moved back towards Beersheba that his circumstances improved. Beersheba means "the well of the oath." The Lord responded to his arrival by meeting with Isaac in open communion and reaffirming the Abrahamic covenant with him. A refreshed Isaac responded first by building an altar to worship God. He may have built other altars, but this is the only one mentioned in Scripture. Then he pitched his tent at the very location where the Lord had met with him. Isaac was not budging – he had learned the hard way the consequences of straying from God's fellowship for any period of time. It was at this location that Isaac found both blessing and the peace of God. Isaac took God's promise of blessing so seriously that he decided to dig a well there also to see if God would bless him – which He did.

It is here that the life of the believer is "well" pictured. The Christian is dwelling with the Lord in fellowship (pictured in Isaac's pitched tent), sacrificing his first fruits in worship, then relying on His further blessing to continue through life and quench the attack of the enemy. The Holy Spirit is enabling the will of the Father to be accomplished in our lives and is pictured in the water of the well. Consequently, on the very day Abimelech confirmed a peace treaty with Isaac, Isaac's servants struck water while digging a fourth new well. The blessing of peace was a testimony to the presence of the Spirit of God in the matter. Paul exhorts the Ephesian believers to *"[endeavor] to keep the unity of the Spirit in the bond of peace"* (Eph. 4:3). Only the effectual working of the Holy Spirit can create a bond of peace among believers (literally "making us one in thought and action"). We cannot make peace, but we should endeavor to keep what God has created – it is truly sweet! We destroy unity and peace when we lose the mind of Christ and begin to think individually, as though we were not part of the body of Christ.

The Apostle Paul instructs the Christian: *"If it be possible, as much as lieth in you, live peaceably with all men"* (Rom. 12:18). His exhortation in the next verse is not to avenge ourselves but to let the Lord repay evil. This is what Isaac did. There are times in life when it is just not possible to live peacefully with people, no matter how hard you try. But keep undertaking it. There are times in which a believer can invoke his civil rights, like Paul did in the book of Acts, but there are times when it is better not to. If invoking our legal entitlements would hinder the spread of the gospel or bring reproach upon the name of Christ, the Christian should gladly sacrifice those rights. If it is a matter of disagreement between believers, let the elders of their assembly decide, but do not take a brother or sister to civil court to settle grievances (1 Cor. 6:5-8). If it is a matter of sin and the individual is a believer, he or she should then be rebuked (Matt. 18:15). If repentance is obtained,

Seeds of Destiny

forgiveness with restoration should naturally follow (Lk. 17:3). If there is no repentance, there should be a releasing attitude by the offending parting (Eph. 4:32) and a willingness to forgive the matter later, when repentance is achieved. This response to offenses will prevent a root of bitterness from growing in one's heart. It is noted that biblical repentance and restoration is not possible without acknowledging sin and repenting of it!

There will be incidents in this age when bad things happen to good people. We live in a world under the curse of God. When such events occur, the Christian will find it comforting to meditate on 1 Peter 2:19-20. Peter explains to us that, when we suffer wrongfully and take it patiently, this is "well" pleasing to God. Why? Because, it reminds God of the time His Son suffered for sins not His own. Christ's example of suffering innocently should encourage us to do the same knowing that it is a sweet smelling sacrifice of self unto God.

Though Abraham and Isaac were not perfect men, the faith of Abraham and the meekness of Isaac are wonderful character testimonies of godly men.

> All men's miseries derive from not being able to sit quietly in a room alone.
>
> Blaise Pascal

> Have courage for the great sorrows of life and patience for the small ones; and when you have laboriously accomplished your daily task, go to sleep in peace. God is awake.
>
> Victor Hugo

Obey My Voice!
Genesis 27:1-33

It was customary to recognize important events and solemn occasions by a feast. The passing on of the family birthright constituted such an occasion, so Isaac charged Esau to prepare a feast and then proceeded to dictate the menu – savory venison, his favorite food. This is a sad commentary on Isaac – he allowed his own appetite to delay the important spiritual matter at hand. This same propensity for self-indulgence has crippled many families in our present culture. Fathers are occupied with satisfying their own base appetites with temporal things rather than the important spiritual matters of raising godly seed. Mothers are laboring outside the home only to find their mobility exposes their minds to secular propaganda, undue stress, and disquieted children who feel undervalued. The mighty dollar has no value in heaven unless it is spiritually transformed here and now for the glory of God and the furtherance of His kingdom (Lk. 16:9). Let us not squander what has spiritual significance for that which is for fleeting gain with no eternal value.

The Lord told Rebekah before her sons were born that her younger son, Jacob, would rule over her older son, Esau (Gen. 25:23). From her point of view, God needed some assistance in restraining Isaac from conferring the birthright blessing to Esau. After all, this was God's will – right? She knew that the blessing did not belong to Esau, so she was determined that he did not receive it, despite undermining her husband's authority in the family. There is a pattern of events and resulting consequences in the marriage of Isaac and Rebekah that is all too prevalent in Christian marriages today.

This downward spiral of family harmony begins when the husband does not love his wife sacrificially and does not implement good spiri-

Seeds of Destiny

tual leadership in the family. Then, the wife, who would normally demonstrate that she is submitted to her husband's authority, develops techniques of manipulation to control him. She does this almost unconsciously to provoke him to do what he should be doing in the family. With years of experience, these techniques of control become refined and so inherent within the marriage relationship that they are accepted as the norm. The consequence – healthy intimate communication is lost in the relationship. Disclosure and intimacy will never be fostered in a relationship as long as one spouse is trying to control the other.

This is exactly what had happened to Isaac and Rebekah's marriage. Isaac lost Rebekah's heart in Genesis 26, when he passed her off as his sister, and in this chapter, Rebekah did not see Isaac doing God's will – not doing what she knew of God's will. So, she took matters into her own hands, directing Jacob to lie and deceive his father. Notice her commands recorded in verses 8, 13, 43, 45: *"obey my voice"* and *"I will send and fetch thee."* God's order in the family had broken down, and now the family would reap chaos. Another factor in this tragedy for the family was that the parents had favorites among the children. Esau was Isaac's favorite son, and Jacob was Rebekah's (Gen. 25:28, 27:5-6). All children are a gift from God and should be loved and treated accordingly; parents should be good stewards of such blessings (Ps. 127).

It is a natural propensity of our nature to impose our will on others, to try to control or manipulate each other. Whether directed at friends, our spouse, family members, or church brethren, these tendencies will lead to broken communication and hard feelings. The following is a list of "Dirty Fighting Strategies for Getting Your Own Way" from David Augsburger's book *When Caring is Not Enough*.[1] Review these selfish bents, and if the Lord speaks to your conscience, repent and forsake the behavior.

1. **Timing** – Catch them off guard rather than choose a good time.
2. **Turf** – Pick your best turf rather than choose a neutral place.
3. **Anxiety** – Step up anxiety rather than set a caring atmosphere.
4. **Fogging** – Filibuster, fog, and fume instead of communicating equally.
5. **Mystifying** – Ramble, chain react, confuse rather than be clear and honest.
6. **Generalizing** – Universalize and exaggerate instead of simplify and focus.
7. **Analyze** – Intellectualize, theorize, advise instead of admitting pain.
8. **Gunnysacking** – Save up grievances rather than deal with here and now.
9. **Neutrality** – Be silent, superior, detached rather than open and present.

10. **Temper** – Hide anger then ventilate rage rather than clean anger.
11. **Blaming** – Find who is at fault rather than practice no-fault fights.
12. **Righteousness** – Find who is right instead of find what's right.
13. **Exit** – Walk out, clam up, shut off instead of working through.
14. **Questioning** – Use clever or concealed questions instead of statements.
15. **Triangling** – Pit people against people instead of dealing firsthand.
16. **Put-downs** – Use sarcasm, jibes, digs rather than share humor.
17. **Undermining** – Undermine self-esteem rather than enrich self-respect.
18. **Guilt** – Play either judge or martyr to hook guilt not responsibility.
19. **Mind-reading** – Read or rape the other's mind rather than listen, wait, learn.
20. **Delaying** – Ignore, forget, postpone rather than honor commitments.

Rebekah's manipulation would result in a major family ruckus. Jacob listened to his conniving mother's direction, and together they conned old and nearly blind Isaac out of issuing Esau the birthright blessing. Apparently, Isaac's near blindness was indicative of his diminished spiritual foresight at this time in his life. The words *"feel"* and *"felt"* first appear in the Bible in Genesis 27. Did Isaac know that Jacob was impersonating Esau? It would appear so. He logically surmised that not enough time had transpired to hunt game and prepare it (Gen. 27:20), and Isaac clearly recognized Jacob's voice (Gen. 27:22). But Isaac followed his "feelings," which allowed his mind to manufacture an Esau after feeling a hairy arm, which in fact was nothing more than goat skin affixed to Jacob's arm. Reasoning the facts, logically evaluating truth, and praying for guidance will always provide a better solution than following our ever-changing feelings. After Esau returned with the savory dish, Isaac learned just how easily one can be deceived by their own feelings.

Rebekah usurped Isaac's authority and blatantly deceived her husband. For the scheme to work, Jacob was compelled to repeatedly lie. Only by lying and deception would his father be bamboozled. Note Jacob's lies: He told his father he was Esau; he told him that he had prepared the venison as he had requested; he told him he had been able to serve him quickly because God had provided the game, and again he declared to Isaac that he was Esau. Does God condone such behavior? Certainly not! He is Holy, and God's people are to put away all lying (Eph. 4:25). But there are rare occurrences in Scripture when God seems to be tolerant of the ill and judges this sin to a lesser degree, if the motive of the individual was honorable.

Seeds of Destiny

For example, Rahab the harlot is never rebuked for hiding the Jewish spies and lying to the local authorities about the matter. Besides saving the lives of the spies, she was offered salvation for her kindness (Josh. 2:2-3, 6:25). The Hebrew midwives were to kill the Jewish baby boys at birth. But they lied to Pharaoh as to why they were not able to accomplish his command, but *"God dealt well with the midwives"* (Ex. 1:20). Hushai was David's spy in rebel Absalom's court. Absalom received him as a counselor because Absalom believed his lies. Hushai defeated the counsel of Ahithophel and saved King David's life. God does not condone lying; He is able to work His will without the aid of human deception, but He is also able to maneuver the moral failures of man to accomplish His before determined purposes. Yet sin, no matter how minor in our own eyes, has consequences before a Holy God. We should never justify lying by an "end justifies the means" mentality. The above examples were unique circumstances that flowed within the mainstream of messianic current. Perhaps this understanding will help resolve the disparity in the reader's mind as to how God could bless such a prolific liar as Jacob and still be righteous. Henry Morris has this additional comment on the subject:

> It would seem that the only way of understanding this situation is to conclude that, whatever may have been wrong with the stratagem and deception of Jacob and Rebekah, the sin of Esau and Isaac was infinitely more grievous. God does not approve of lying, and Jacob and Rebekah well knew this. They were sensitive and spiritual people; but they had decided that, as bad as deception might be in God's sight, it had become necessary in this case in order to prevent a much worse sin, that of blasphemously presuming to convey the most holy of God's promises to a man who neither wanted it nor would honor it, and to do so directly in the face of God's commandment against it. Such an eventuality surely would have incurred God's most severe judgment on both Isaac and Esau, and this they felt they must prevent at all costs.[2]

The bottom line of the matter – Jacob was God's man. There would be consequences of Jacob's lies, but the predestined counsel of God would not be subverted by Jacob or any man's failures (Rom. 3:3-4, 9:11). As Paul puts it, *"It is not of him that willeth."* Isaac willed to give the blessing to Esau. *"It is not…of him that runneth"* (Rom. 9:16).

Esau went to the field and quickly prepared the venison (Gen. 27:5, 30). The matter was not determined by Jacob and his mother's efforts, but of election – God's purpose in time. In fact, God's foreknowledge ensures that He will effect the foremost blessing to mankind by employing man's failures as channels of His grace that man might know salvation is of God alone.

> The mother's heart is the child's schoolroom.
>
> Henry Ward Beecher

> Let parents bequeath to their children not riches, but the spirit of reverence.
>
> Plato

Seeds of Destiny

A Family Split Apart
Genesis 27:34-46

Isaac, now awakened to the frailty of his flesh and the irrevocable purposes of God, reaffirms the promises of God to Abraham in the blessing to Jacob. Before, Isaac had bluntly defied God's direct revelation on this matter. God had clearly stated that *"the elder shall serve the younger"* (Gen. 25:23). Isaac meant to bless Esau – *"Be lord over thy brethren, and let thy mother's sons bow down to thee."* In any case, Isaac pronounced the blessing upon Jacob and did so with the inspiration of God, although personally he thought he was blessing Esau and, thus, undermining God's will.

What did this birthright blessing confer to its recipient? In the general sense, it delegated rule in the family, clan and later tribe. The recipient secured a double portion of the inheritance (Deut. 21:17). The blessing also acknowledged who represented the family before God in worship – who would act as the priest for the family. Besides the unfolding of sovereign purpose in Jacob's life, the personal implications of this blessing to Jacob were immense.

Esau's awareness of the deceitful plot was accompanied by rage and fierce intentions of vengeance. "If there was no Jacob" he thought, then "I will obtain the blessing by default." Like Cain, who also opposed the declared will of God, Esau sought to gratify his own rebellious anger by shedding the blood of his brother, a man, like Abel, that was approved of God. Rebekah feared for Jacob's life and instructed him to flee some 400 miles northeast to Haran, to find refuge with her relatives, namely Uncle Laban. She commanded Jacob without consulting Isaac, then conspired to get her husband's approval of that which she had already devised and executed. She pleaded with Isaac to send Jacob to Paddan-aram to find a woman to marry from her extended family, thus preventing him from marrying a Canaanite woman.

Throughout this chapter, Isaac's carnality was met with Rebekah's carnality – flesh against flesh. Was there any question what the result of this matter would be?

One sin leads to another if not confessed, and the personal consequences in this family piled up rapidly. *"Be sure your sin shall find you out"* (Num. 32:23). Others may not detect our sin, but it will always find us out. It may expose itself through a plagued conscience, emotional disorders, physical pain, etc., but unconfessed sin will find us out – it is a promise. This was the lesson Rebekah was learning. Isaac agreed with Rebekah's concern and sent Jacob away to Haran. Rebekah's strategy was simple; after Esau calmed down, she planned to send for Jacob and fetch him from Paddan-aram (Gen. 28:2). But her deceitfulness and manipulation would have a high price – she would never lay eyes on her beloved Jacob again. This family would be adversely changed forever.

What do you think Rebekah would have done if she could have relived that day? I think, knowing the full cost of her actions, she would have submitted to her husband's rule over her and trusted God to work out the details in His timing. Even when the situation doesn't make any sense, leave the matter with the Lord. Ladies, if you have a husband who is spiritually lethargic, surrender him unto God, but **do not** try to control him by imposing your will upon him through manipulation. Everyone is under some human authority, and Paul explains to us that when we oppose that authority we are opposing God (Rom. 13:1-2). This is, of course, unless it opposes God's authority, in which case we should be willing to passively reject such authority and to suffer the consequences patiently (Acts 5:29-41; 1 Pet. 2:19-20). God has imposed human authority over us for the purpose of teaching us to submit to the One who placed it there.

Although Isaac was on the eve of dispensing blessing in opposition to the counsel of God, we must note the utter humility of his faith by which he blessed Jacob. Isaac spoke as one who had at his disposal the treasuries of heaven (Gen. 26:28) and the armies of heaven (Gen. 26:29). Later, when Isaac was speaking to a grieving Esau over the matter of the birthright blessing, he declared, *"I have blessed him; yea, and he shall be blessed."* Isaac rose above his own pretensions about

Seeds of Destiny

the matter to acknowledge that God was sovereign over all matters, including his own family.

> Good family life is never an accident but always an achievement by those who share it.
>
> James H. S. Bossard

Jacob Leaves Home
Genesis 28:11-22

    Isaac fell prey to his wife's manipulation and consented to dispatch Jacob to the region of Paddan-aram to obtain a wife, a daughter of Laban, Rebekah's brother. But before Jacob departs, Isaac acknowledges that it is Jacob who was chosen of God, and He invokes the blessing of Abraham upon Jacob in a personal way (Gen. 28:3-4), very similar to the blessing he himself had received from God through Abraham years earlier (Gen. 26:3-5). Rebekah did not know that her scheming would deprive her of the company of Jacob for the balance of her life. As a side note, Scripture does not record the event of Rebekah's dying, although Scripture later documents her burial place. Perhaps, in this way, Rebekah is a continuing portrait of the Church, which the Lord Himself promised would live and reign with Him forever (Jn. 10:28). *"Whosoever liveth and believeth in Me shall never die"* (Jn.11:26).

    How old do you think Jacob was when he fled to Paddan-aram to find a wife? Perhaps thirty or forty years old, as Hollywood would suggest. There is enough information in Scripture to determine his age. First, we must ascertain how old Jacob was when Joseph, his son, was born. We know that Joseph was thirty years old when he started ruling over Egypt (Gen. 41:46). He ruled during the seven years of plenty and the first two years of famine conditions (Gen. 45:6) before his father Jacob came to live in Egypt. Thus, Joseph was 39 years old when Jacob came to Egypt. According to Gen. 47:28, Jacob was 130 years old when he came to Egypt. Therefore, Jacob was 91 years old when Joseph was born.

    Rachel gave birth to Joseph just prior to Jacob completing his 14-year labor commitment to Laban – the bridal dowry of Leah and Rachel

Seeds of Destiny

(Gen. 30:25). Thus, Jacob would have been approximately 77 (91-14) years of age when he went to Haran. He was an eighty-four year old man when he married Leah and Rachel seven years later. Matthew Henry also places Jacob's age at marriage at 84. The nation of Israel finds its beginning and expansion in Jacob's family. Among his four wives, there would be a minimum of eleven pregnancies in a seven-year period (with the possibility of more than eleven pregnancies for other daughters born during this time).

Esau married of the daughters of Heth at the much younger age of forty (Gen. 26:34), but Jacob was content to live a single life more than forty years after his twin brother had married. Those who look to get married usually do, but often out of the will of the Lord. To wait upon the Lord for His favor in this area takes patience, but *"whoso findeth a wife findeth a good thing, and obtaineth favor from the Lord"* (Prov. 18:22). It is not scouting out Mr. Right or Miss Right that is appropriate but waiting upon the Lord to provide the right person for you to "find." Then, the task of "becoming" Mr. Right and Mrs. Right becomes a lifelong process. Biblical betrothal means "loving the one you marry" in lieu of "marrying the one you love." Marital commitment becomes the foundation to build lasting love upon.

Jacob lived to be 147 years old according to Genesis 47:28. Thus, he had lived over half his life before going to Haran to acquire a wife. He was not the young man he is so often thought to have been. He also had lived over half of his life without a personal conversion experience. He yet did not know the God of Abraham and the God of Isaac – he still referred to the Lord as his father's God (Gen. 31:5). But now, God was going to directly intervene in the life of Jacob.

How different was Jacob's leaving for Paddan-aram from Eliezer's a century earlier. Eliezer went openly with patriarchal blessing, a train of camels bearing presents and servants for company. Jacob, exiled and on foot, slips away without money or a traveling companion. Jacob was apprehensive about his future, so through a dream, the Lord graciously and dramatically unfolds time to show Jacob his destiny.

Generally, the Lord reveals to His children only the marching orders for the day, on that day. In this way, we learn to trust Him in the same way the Israelites did for their daily provision while in the desert. *"Then said the Lord unto Moses, 'Behold, I will rain bread from heaven for you; and the people shall go out and gather a certain [amount] every day,* **that I may [test] them, whether they will walk in my law,** *or not'"*(Ex. 16:4). On rare occasions, as with Jacob now, the Lord may illuminate a portion of our future path, but normally He provides just enough light to show the next step of faith in the journey. This is how a believer walks with the Lord, and perhaps why the Lord Jesus often sought communion with His Father in the wee hours of the morning. We can do no better than to follow His example.

> Sweet are the seasons when we wait
> To hear what God our Lord will say,
> For they who watch at Wisdom's gate
> Are never empty sent away.
>
> Edward Denny

A Ladder and a Pillar in God's House
Genesis 28:11-22

As Bethel is some 60 miles north of Beersheba, the first two or three days of Jacob's trip pass over in silence. Jacob, nearing to the closure of another day, set up camp for the night. In the wilderness, the accommodations are a bit scant, so Jacob made use of what was available: he rolled his pillow (a stone) to the head of his extra firm mattress (the ground) and retired for the day. Sleep was not exactly what God had in mind for Jacob at this moment; He sought to rattle his soul through a vision of His glory. While dreaming, Jacob observed holy angels ascending and descending on a broad and extensive ladder reaching from the earth to the canopy of heaven with God Himself positioned at the top. This was no ordinary ladder; in fact the Hebrew word *sullam*, translated "ladder," is only used here in the Bible. Thus, the form of the ladder cannot be compared with any other ladder mentioned in Scripture – it was unique. Perhaps the ladder was a stairway to heaven or perhaps the image of an old rugged cross connecting earth with heaven.

In the dream, God spoke to Jacob and reconfirmed the covenant He had made with Abraham and Isaac. Mark again the consistency of God's Word in verse 14. Jacob was promised seed that would be as the dust of the earth. Isaac was promised descendants as numerous as the stars of heaven (Gen. 26:4). Abraham, in whom the covenant was established, was promised both (Gen. 22:17). Why the difference? Because Isaac represents the resurrected Christ who has inherited a heavenly land, and Jacob represents the expansion of the nation of Israel, which will inherit an earthly land during the Millennium.

The Lord told Jacob, now a homeless wanderer, that He was with him. God promised to return him to the land that He had promised as an inheritance to his descendants. What a comfort to know that God is with the believer during the difficult times of life. Jeremiah had some reservations when the Lord commissioned him as His spokesman to the people. Jeremiah told the Lord he was too young to do what He had asked him to do. God encouraged Jeremiah with these words, *"be not afraid of their faces; for I am with thee to deliver thee"* (Jer. 1:8). The writer of Hebrews also acknowledges the continued presence of the Lord with us: *"I will never leave thee nor forsake thee"* (Heb. 13:5).

Though Jacob had heard about the Lord all his life, he was ignorant of the Lord's presence – something he acknowledged (Gen. 28:16). There is a tremendous difference between knowing facts about someone and appreciating him or her on a personal basis. Many people rationalize that because they have acquired facts about Jesus that they are assured of heaven. One need only review the information that demons divulged in the presence of Christ to discover that information doesn't confer salvation. In Luke 8:28, the demons knew Jesus by name, that He was the Son of God, and that He had the power to torment them. Demons declared to Jesus, *"Thou art Christ, the Son of God"* (Lk. 4:41), and that Jesus was from Nazareth, had power to destroy them and was the Holy One of God (Lk. 4:34). Their very knowledge of Jesus Christ constrained them to a dreadful existence that anticipated the horrors of hell awaiting them in a future day (Matt. 25:41).

It is a saving faith "in" Jesus Christ (Jn. 3:16-18) and not knowing mere facts about Him that affects God's grace and, thus, grants salvation. After salvation is received, a believer then seeks to remain in fellowship with the Lord. This is done by continually seeking the Lord's presence through prayer and mediation (Heb. 4:15) and practicing His presence in daily conduct. He has promised *"I will never leave thee, nor forsake thee"* (Heb. 13:5). Comprehending that the Lord is eternally with you is not only a comfort in troubling times, it is the ultimate accountability to live a pure and holy life.

Yes, Jacob knew facts, but he didn't know the Lord in a personal way yet. Notice, the angels ascended the ladder before they descended on it (Gen. 28:12). That means that the angels were already there with Jacob – carrying out God's will when the vision began. Afterwards, Jacob realized that God was with him and took his stone pillow, stood it up on end and anointed it with oil. He now called the place "Bethel,"

Seeds of Destiny

which means "the house of God." However, Jacob would soon learn that there was a vast difference between acknowledging the presence of God and sacrificing your life to Him by faith. Though Jacob was a "supplanter" and ignorant of God's presence, the Lord never speaks harshly to Jacob or of Jacob in all of Scripture. Every time God addresses Jacob personally, it is a message of blessing and promise, never one of rebuke or discipline. God had made a sovereign selection to accomplish His will – Jacob was God's man, and God loved him despite his frailties and spiritual dullness (Rom. 9:11-13). *"Was not Esau Jacob's brother? saith the Lord: yet I loved Jacob and I hated Esau"* (Mal. 1:2-3). Of course the verse reaches far beyond these two brothers to God's dealings with their descendants, but God's sovereign choice is illustrated none the less. From our perspective, the matter may seem quite unfair, but we must remember that God had to choose somebody from the seed of Isaac to bring forth the nation of Israel and the coming Messiah – He chose Jacob. *"For My thoughts are not your thoughts, neither are your ways My ways, saith the Lord"* (Isa. 55:8).

Clearly, Jacob was still not converted at this instant. Note his conditional pledge to God in Genesis 28:20-21: *"If God will ... then shall the Lord be my God."* Some see the "if" as meaning "since," which is often the case in the New Testament. But the context of the passage, given the conditional "then" statement, seems to speak more accurately of Jacob's lack of trust, rather than a declaration of faith. If God would be with him, he would then believe on Him, trust Him, and give Him a tenth of what he had. Some words just do not belong in the same sentence when talking to God: *"if...then," "never...Lord"* (Jn. 13:8), *"me first"* (Lk. 9:59) or *"Lord this shall not be"* (Matt. 16:22). The Christian should submit to the Lord because He is the Creator of all and the Lord over all. Obedience is not optional. We should be looking for signs from the Lord to be more faithful, or the sign furnished may be a painful one. *"For whom the Lord loveth he chasteneth, and scourgeth every son whom he receiveth"* (Heb. 12:6). The Lord said it is a perverse generation that looks for signs to believe (Matt. 12:39).

What did the vision symbolize? Apparently, 2000 years later, a devout Israelite named Nathanael was reclining beneath a fig tree and meditating on this same passage of Scripture when his brother Philip found him and declared to him that Israel's long anticipated Messiah had arrived; He was Jesus of Nazareth. Though reluctant to believe that Jesus was the Christ, Nathanael followed his brother to investigate. Upon Nathanael's arrival, the Lord Jesus told Nathanael where he had been and about his character to which a stunned and elated Nathanael responded *"Thou art the Son of God; thou art the King of Israel"* (Jn. 1:49). Jesus replied *"...Thou shalt see greater things than these ... Hereafter ye shall see heaven open, and the angels of God ascending and descending upon the Son of man"* (Jn. 1:50-51). Jesus identified Himself as the ladder of Jacob's vision. He would be the link, the mediator between earth and heaven by which God could righteously commune with repentant sinners. *"For there is one God, and one mediator between God and men, the man, Christ Jesus"* (1 Tim. 2:5).

God's "grace and glory" are portrayed in the ladder. The ladder foreshadowed the cross of Christ, the only way by which man can safely walk beyond the flames of hell and into the awaiting arms of a compassionate Creator. The Lord Himself said, *"I am the way, the truth, and the life; no man cometh unto the Father, but by Me"* (Jn. 14:6). But, concealed still deeper in the vision of the ladder is the visible and glorious kingdom of Christ on earth. The New Jerusalem will hover above it, the redeemed and the angels will go to and fro freely in the presence of God (Rev. 21), and the glory of God will fill the earth!

> Savior, come, Thy saints are waiting, Waiting for the advent day,
> Thence their promised glory dating; Come, and bear They saints away.
> Come, Lord Jesus, come Lord Jesus, Thus Thy waiting people pray.
> Till it comes, O keep us steady! Keep us walking in Thy ways;
> At Thy call may we be ready, On Thee, Lord, with joy to gaze;
> And in heaven, and in heaven Sing Thine everlasting praise.
>
> Thomas Kelly

Seeds of Destiny

The Trickster is Tricked
Genesis 29:1-25

Jacob arrived in the land of Paddan-aram and inquired of his Uncle Laban from shepherds who were gathered at a well to water their flocks. Not only did these men know of Laban, they likely worked for him because it was from Laban's well that they watered all the sheep. They diverted Jacob's attention to one of Laban's daughters approaching the well to water the sheep in her care. Her name was Rachel, whose name means "a sheep." Jacob, understanding that the woman was the daughter of his mother's brother and that it was such a woman whom his parents had instructed him to marry (Gen. 28:2), attempted to get a private meeting with Rachel by suggesting that the shepherds attend the cattle and leave the sheep. The shepherds had a legitimate reason for not departing from the well (The sheep must all be gathered before the rock covering the well was removed – all were watered together.) and, therefore, did not leave.

Jacob removed the stone covering the well for Rachel and watered her sheep. Then the gravity of the whole matter overwhelmed him – his emotional composure plummeted. He wept in front of her and kissed her (an appropriate greeting for kinfolk as in Genesis 29:13). Notice that the narrative records the phrase "mother's brother" three times (Gen. 29:10). Jacob had just completed his first major trip from home, and certainly, his beloved mother, his closest friend, was being missed. Perhaps Jacob was overwhelmed by the gracious means by which the Lord had guided him to Laban's well and to Rachel. The "well" continues to be a symbol of God's blessing. The Lord refreshed and blessed a distraught Hagar near a well on the way to Shur 150 years earlier, and then Abraham's servant located Isaac's bride, Rebekah, at a well a hundred years prior to the events of this chapter.

Rachel left Jacob, perhaps so he could attend to her sheep and ran ahead to inform her father of the special visitor. Jacob was welcomed by Uncle Laban and, in the course of a month, secured a place of refuge and employment with him. Why was everything working out so delightfully for Jacob? Jacob had received the birthright in lieu of Esau and, thus, obtained the family blessing. He had successfully and safely trekked across 400 miles of dismal terrain. He had miraculously located his kinfolk and a potential wife within moments of his arrival. Over the next twenty years, he would beat Laban at his own game of deceit. But the harvest of Jacob's deceit and trickery had not fully ripened yet, it was still future. God must righteously judge all sin. There is a judicial penalty and consequential retribution for every sin. Thankfully, the Lord Jesus bore the judicial penalty for all sin at Calvary, yet the practical outworking and damage of sin is still present today. Jacob was God's man, but God had yet to apply His righteous judgment in retribution for Jacob's past behavior.

In just one month, one of Laban's two daughters captured Jacob's heart. It was Rachel, the younger and more beautiful daughter of Laban. Rachel may have been as young as ten to twelve years old, as it was customary for pre-adolescent girls to attend the sheep in this ancient culture. Jacob had nothing to offer Laban for his daughter's hand in marriage, except himself. So his love for Rachel leaped into action, and he sold himself into servitude. Rachel's dowry would be seven years of manual labor for Uncle Laban. Laban might have been pondering Jacob's vast inheritance yet in Canaan and perceived a future windfall. Genesis 29:20 portrays Jacob as a lovesick man: *"[These years] seemed unto him but a few days, for the love he had for her."* Jacob had an "initiating love," which intermingled both action and sacrifice in one just cause!

Finally, the impending wedding day came, and Uncle Laban hosted a lush feast to celebrate. Rachel is perhaps twenty years old now. One must wonder if the fruit of the vine, not love, blinded Jacob's eyes that night, as he did not realize until morning that he had been with the wrong girl. Laban tricked Jacob and gave him Leah, Rachel's older sister, for a wife. In this instance, God's justice is ironic; the trickster was conned at his own game of illusion. Jacob drank from his own cup of deceit and received a fair retribution for deceiving his father in the mat-

Seeds of Destiny

ter of the birthright blessing. Now, the Creator was working in the life of Jacob. These would be hard school days for Jacob, but God loves His children too much to leave them un-Christlike.

A penetrating blow had softened the clay of Jacob's heart. With paramount purpose, Jacob was placed on the Potter's wheel. Each circumstance in his life would supply the wheel with the motion and energy to assist the Master's hand in molding Jacob's heart to the pattern of Christ. The forming process on the Potter's wheel is a lifelong venture. Sometimes the wheel seems to be spinning so fast we may fear flying apart. What a delightful promise is expressed to the Christian in 1 Corinthians 10:13: *"God is faithful, who will not permit you to be tempted (tested) above that ye are able, but will, with the temptation (testing) also make a way to escape, that ye may be able to bear it."*

When tumult strikes and our peace is jeopardized, the Potter's hand carefully constrains the clay from flying apart. As Paul's emphasizes in Romans 8:28, *"All things work together for good to them that love God."* Molding takes time and trials, but behold behind the Potter, motionless on the shelves of centuries past, are countless vessels gleaming with sovereign purpose and embellished with glorious righteousness. With the marriages to Leah, then to Rachel, Jacob's spiritual journey shifts into high gear. The route would be filled with grueling exercises, inspiring instruction and much heartache, but let us observe and learn as he lunges ever forward to destiny, and ever Godward in spirit.

> Have Thine own way, Lord! Have Thine own way!
> Thou art the Potter; I am the clay.
> Mold me and make me after Thy will,
> While I am waiting, yielded and still.
>
> Adelaide Pollard

Fulfill Her Week
Genesis 29:26-35

Whether true or not, Laban posed the custom of marrying the older daughters before the younger as the reason for the deception. No doubt he was concerned about finding a husband for his "weak–eyed" daughter who was advancing in years. Laban wastes no time in offering love-sick Jacob another proposition, "If you fulfill Leah's bridal week and agree to work for me another seven years you can have Rachel as a wife also." Jacob was agreeing to take both Laban's daughters as wives. It was later forbidden to marry two sisters in each other's lifetime (Lev. 18:18). The turmoil in Jacob's life resulting from marrying two sisters serves as a good example why. We believe that Jacob received Rachel as his wife immediately after a week-long marriage celebration with Leah had concluded (compare with Judges 14:17). He then worked off a further seven-year debt again. Scripture supports this interpretation as Rachel bore Joseph (her first son) at the end of the 14-year dowry period (Gen. 30:25) but was miserably barren while Leah bore children the seven previous years (Gen. 29:31). Husbands, though Jacob was tricked into doing so, there is a wonderful principle illustrated here for us to follow: Jacob labored just as hard after receiving his wife, as he did to obtain his wife. Husbands, do you esteem your wife now as much as you did before you were married? Do you still convey on paper those little explanations of love you once did? Do you still phone your wife just because you long to hear her voice? Do you still leave messages on steamed over bathroom mirrors for her to discover during her next shower? Are you courting her affections by investing personal time with her?

Women have a deep need for expression and connection. Many wives long just for some intimate communication with the one they vowed to love until "death do us part." Men, marriage is work from start to finish. Jacob toiled for Rachel before he married her, then continued to labor for her endearment after he married her! So, the activities and affections shown during courting one's future wife should continue through one's married life! The heartstrings tied before you say "I do" should be double knotted through marital commitment.

Ironically, it is not Rachel, but Leah, that God blessed with children. Genesis 29:31 explains that God opened Leah's womb because she was unloved by Jacob ("hated" is a comparative term equivalent with "unloved" – Deut. 21:15). The younger and more attractive Rachel had a monopoly on Jacob's love and endearment. So God had pity upon Leah and revived her soul through the gift of child bearing – not just children, but sons – while at the same time restricting Rachel's womb! Leah gave her sons names that followed her plight within the awkward family situation. Yet, in meaning, these names seem to highlight key steps in salvation: Reuben means "a son," Simeon "hearing," Levi "joined to," and Judah "praise." When an individual is presented with Christ (the **Son** of God), and **hears** and believes the gospel message, he is then spiritually **bonded** with Christ and, consequently, has a swelling heart that bursts forth **praise**!

Jacob entered this chapter with no wives and departed with two – one he loved and one that bore him children. Jacob did not labor for Leah; he toiled fourteen years for Rachel, seven before obtaining her and seven afterwards. Likewise, the Savior labored for His bride at Calvary and continues to work on her behalf in heaven now. How is He laboring for us at this present moment? He is the Great Shepherd who attends to us (1 Pet. 2:25; Jn. 10:11-16). He is the Great High Priest who gives us grace to be overcomers and not undergoers (Heb. 4:14-16). He is our Advocate who declares to our accusing enemy that our sins have been judicially paid for (1 Jn. 2:1; Rev. 12:10). He is our Offering Priest who perfects our worship before the throne (Heb. 13:10-15). He is our Forerunner and Anchor who encourages us to run well and with hope, and to follow His perfect example (Heb. 6:19-20). He is our Lord – the Church's Head and Groom (Eph. 1:22-23). He is faithfully leading, guiding, cleansing us so that we will be ready for the impending wedding day to be presented to Himself as a glorious bride.

He saw me ruined by the fall,
Yet loved me not-with-standing all,
He saved me from my lost estate,
His loving-kindness, oh, how great!

        Samuel Medley

Seeds of Destiny

Blessings Despite Feminine Strife
Genesis 30:1-13

God's plan for marriage is for one man and one woman to become one person until death itself parts them (Gen. 2:24, Matt. 19:5-6). The repercussions of two women (even worse, two sisters) united in marriage to one man soon became obvious. The works of the flesh, namely envy, strife, pride, and wrath, were amply stirred up. What a troublesome family predicament for bewildered Jacob. Leah was rejected by her husband, at least at the first, and forlorn Rachel was void of maternal blessing, at least for the moment. The birth of Leah's children was clearly miraculous for, though she had limited physical unions with her husband, God blessed with frequent conception. Leah was a godly woman, who credited the Lord for enabling her to bear children. Perhaps Leah's fruitfulness caused Jacob, who would be eager to establish a family, to spend more time with her in those early years, though Rachel indeed was his first love. God is sovereign over the womb! Naturally speaking, Rachel had the advantage, but God, for His glory, enjoys blessing the underdog. In this manner, He acquires all the glory, *"But God hath chosen the foolish things of the world to confound the wise; and God hath chosen the weak things of the world to confound the things which are mighty"* (1 Cor. 1:27).

Childless Rachel, exasperated with the situation, demands from Jacob, *"Give me children, or else I die."* Note, she would not be satisfied with just one baby; she demanded several. What else did she expect poor Jacob to do more than what he had already been doing? Keep in mind that he is approximately 90 years old now. The basis of Rachel and Leah's happiness and self-importance was their ability to bear Jacob children. Is this the true measure of happiness for a married woman? It is acknowledged that children are a blessing from God in Psalm 127:3 – *"children...the fruit of the womb is His (God's) reward,"* but children are not an end in themselves. Children of believing couples are to be godly seed (Mal. 2:15) and are to be a blessing unto others and God. If reared properly, children will be a delight to parents as well. Proverbs 29:17 reads, *"Correct thy son, and he shall give thee rest; yea, he shall give delight unto thy soul."* Well-mannered, self-giving children endow joy; however, selfish, disobedient and disorderly children torment everyone! The true measure of good parents is not in being able to bear children, for that is God's department, but in how successful they are in raising them up for God. These sisters were seeking joy in the wrong place.

When will a woman experience fulfillment and joy in the depths of her being? Joy is composed of **J**esus, **O**thers, and **Y**ou. When a married woman seeks strength and communion with the Lord to serve others before herself, she experiences joy. God's blueprint of service for her is to be a faithful companion and helper to her husband (Gen. 2:18), to be a selfless nurturer to her children (Tit. 2:4; 1 Tim. 2:15), and to be a virtuous homemaker (Tit. 2:5; 1 Tim. 5:14). Those women who are unmarried will discover their source of joy in the Lord also and then seek to demonstrate it by serving others.

Jacob's family was expanding. Rachel and Leah's ambition to bear children and the sharp competition between the two women forced Jacob to embrace their handmaids as wives also (as concubines – wives of a secondary degree). The expression Rachel employs, *"upon my knees,"* is also used in Genesis 50:23 to imply a meaning of "children counted as my own." Rachel would count any children born from Bilhah, her handmaiden, as her own. So the baby race commenced, and a "baby boom" resulted. Those quiet and peaceful days Jacob had enjoyed in his own tent in Beersheba were over. In just ten years, He found himself the husband of four wives and the father of 11 sons and at least one daughter. Genesis 37:35 records the fact that Jacob later had more than one daughter. Dinah may be Jacob's only daughter at this time, and her name is only mentioned due to her experience with Shechem in Genesis 34.

It is at this time that God intervened in the business arrangements of Laban and Jacob in such a way to prosper Jacob. Genesis 30:43 records, *"And the man [Jacob] increased exceedingly, and had much cattle, and maidservants, and menservants, and camels, and asses."*

Seeds of Destiny

However, as God blessed Jacob and enhanced his wealth, Uncle Laban's countenance towards Jacob increasingly soured. The moment of Jacob's departure from Laban was nearing – it was almost time for Jacob to return home.

In Genesis 29, we traced the names of Jacob's first four sons and discovered how the meanings of their names pattern the steps leading to salvation. In Genesis 30, the names of his following sons represent the process of sanctification in the believer's life. The sons born to Jacob in Genesis 30 are seven total. Dan was born of Rachel's handmaiden Bilhah; his name means "judging." Naphtali, also born to Bilhah, means "wrestling." Gad was born of Leah's handmaiden Zilpah; his name means "good fortune" (implied from the blessing of a defending army or "troop of children"). Asher was also born to Zilpah, and his name means "happy." Then, Leah bore Jacob two more sons, Issachar, meaning "hire" and Zebulun, whose name means "dwelling." After Zebulun was born she proclaimed, *"God hath endued me with a good dowry; now will my husband dwell with me."* Jacob had not betrothed Leah; therefore, she had not been endowed with a dowry when he married her. But Leah never sent Jacob a bill; she acknowledged that many children were a good dowry. *"Lo, children are an heritage from the Lord; and the fruit of the womb is His reward. As arrows are in the hand of a mighty man, so are children of one's youth. Happy is the man who hath his quiver full of them; they shall not be ashamed, but they shall speak with the enemies in the gate"* (Ps.127:3-5).

In ancient days, older children, especially young men, would defend the family against attacking enemies. Leah had a small troop of children – what a reward and protection for the family. But children, which are likened unto arrows, do not fly straight naturally.

One day, my oldest son yelled at me, "Dad, watch this crazy arrow," as he released an arrow from his bow. The arrow sprang forward and arced into the ground some 20 feet short of the target. After examining this arrow, it was found to have a bent shaft. The Psalmist reminds us that children are gifts from God, but they are born with bent shafts. As children are sharpened by Scripture and sinful bents are corrected and straightened by discipline, they become an awesome weapon in the father's bow. These arrows fly true when released. They inflict a penetrating wound into the heart of a dark world for Christ's sake. Parents, do not release "crazy arrows;" this will do more harm than good. May we delight in our children enough to train them up for God and know the "good fortune" of a godly troop of children!

> What gift has Providence bestowed on man that is so dear to him as his children.
>
> Cicero

> The great man is he who does not lose his child's heart.
>
> Mencius

Seeds of Destiny

A Special Son is Born
Genesis 30:14-43

Reuben, Leah's oldest son, perhaps five or six years of age at this juncture, was out playing in a field during the wheat harvest when he stumbled upon some mandrakes. The lad picked and delivered the fruit to his mother. Rachel heard of the matter and demanded that Leah give her some of this esteemed fruit. Apparently, Rachel had a monopoly on Jacob's husbandry duties, and Leah was bitter about it. So the women negotiated a deal. When Jacob ventured from the field that evening, he would remain in Leah's tent for the night, and in return for this favor, Rachel would obtain the mandrakes. One can only imagine how Jacob felt about the whole matter. Was he flattered that his wives were bargaining over his manly services, or was he distraught because of the constant turmoil among his wives in which he was now a mere pawn.

Why so much fuss about a few mandrakes anyway? Henry Morris explains:

> The mandrake is a small orange-colored berrylike fruit, much esteemed in ancient times as an aphrodisiac and inducer of fertility. It has been called the "love-apple" and, in Western countries, the "May-apple." It has also been used as a narcotic and emetic, especially its large roots. It was no doubt because of its supposed value in promoting fertility that both Leah and Rachel desired it.[1]

It would seem that Leah won Jacob's affection again for a time, for she bore him two more sons and at least one daughter. But God had not forgotten Rachel, and he hearkened to her prayers and opened her womb. Finally, after twelve to thirteen years of marriage, Rachel had a son of her own. His name was Joseph, which means "adding." Joseph's name was prophetic in nature because the Lord did add to Rachel one more son – Benjamin – before she died in Genesis 35. Benjamin's name means "Son of my right hand!"

Joseph's name was also prophetic in that he is one of the strongest "types" of the Lord Jesus in Scripture. The Lord Jesus was called the "second man" or "last Adam" (Rom. 5:12-21; 1 Cor. 15:45-47). The first Adam was a "subtractor" (Humanity suffered loss through him.), but the last Adam (pictured in Joseph) would be a great "Adder" (He would freely restore what was lost.).

Salvation itself is a three-part reality consisting of a process of God sandwiched between two acts of God. Salvation begins when an individual believes the Gospel of Jesus Christ and is, consequently, regenerated by the Holy Spirit (Jn. 1:12-13; Rom. 1:16; Titus 3:5). After this act of God, the long process of "sanctification" begins – sometimes referred to as "progressive sanctification." Peter exhorts believers to labor in this process, *"Like newborn babies, crave pure spiritual milk, so that by it you **may grow up in your salvation**,"* (1 Pet. 2:2, NIV).

Through sanctification, the believer is separated and carved out of the world to be like the Lord Jesus, to be used by Him, and to glorify God. The Holy Spirit, thus, saves the believer from being ruled by his or her inherent depraved nature and from the clutches of the corrupt world system. Although God uses a host of ways to conform the believer to the likeness of His Son, two general means are employed. First, an individual must invest time in God's Word to know Him and His will (Jn. 15:3, 17:17). Secondly, God will manage trials, tests, suffering, persecution, and circumstances to fashion holy character and to acquaint us more fully with Himself. Not only does the Bible express God's will, but it also exhorts us to understand it and submit to it (Eph. 5:17; 1 Thess. 4:3, 5:18; 1 Pet. 2:15). The Bible expresses God's will in terms of proper conduct and holy living which is required of all Christians. God's will for the believer's life has already been declared, what we need now from the Lord is day by day guidance! *"Trust in the Lord with all thine heart, and lean not unto thine own understanding. In all thy ways acknowledge Him, and He shall direct thy paths"* (Prov. 3:5-6). If you are toiling in Scripture to know God's will and then submitting to what you understand, you need not be anxious about the daily specifics of your life; His faithful hand will guide you. Furthermore,

Seeds of Destiny

because you are an available and consecrated vessel, He will use you for His glory!

> Take time to be holy, let Him be thy Guide,
> And run not before Him, whatever betide;
> In joy or in sorrow, still follow thy Lord,
> And looking to Jesus, still trust in His Word.
>
> William Longstaff

Salvation in the Names
Genesis 30:14-43

The final aspect and conclusion of our salvation is identified by Paul in Romans 13:11: *"our salvation [is] nearer than when we (first) believed."* Salvation abruptly concludes as it began, through a one-time act of God. The grand finale is called "glorification." It occurs when the redeemed shall be caught up into the clouds with the Lord of glory after receiving a Christ-like (eternal and incorruptible) body (Phil. 3:21; 1 Cor. 15:51-52; 1 Thess. 4:13-17). Thus, a believer can claim "I am saved," "I am being saved," and "I will be saved." Or as commonly taught, the Lord has saves us from the "penalty" of sin (past), the "power" of sin (present), and "presence" of sin (future).

There seems to be a pattern represented in the names and order of Jacob's sons in this chapter which give brief glimpses of God's plan of salvation for mankind. Through the process of sanctification, the believer is to *Dan* "judge himself" (1 Cor. 11:28; Phil. 2:12) as he *Naphtali* "wrestles" between what is right and wrong in a dark world. As he submits to God's Word and his conscience, the believer experiences victory and God's blessing – *Gad* "good fortune" and *Asher* "happiness." Then, the last four sons represent the blessings of being translated into God's presence – the saving of the body. The child of God is rewarded or *Issachar* "paid his hire" for the service he has done with godly motivation. Where does this occur? At the judgment seat of Christ in heaven, thus, the believer will *Zebulun* "dwell" with God forevermore. Finally, blessing upon blessing is *Joseph* "added" to the child of God as he learns for eternity the riches of God's grace (Eph. 2:7) and worships *Benjamin* "the Son sitting at the right hand" of God. Our salvation begins and ends with the Son of God, who has no ending. This reality is portrayed in Jacob's children, starting with Reuben, "a son," and finishing with Benjamin, "the son of my right hand." Both

Seeds of Destiny

advents of Christ and the Lord's ongoing work between the two advents are represented in the names of Jacob's sons.

What is also interesting about the order of Jacob's children is that a defiled woman (Dinah) is presented between Zebulun and Joseph. The first four sons of Jacob represent the salvation of the soul, the next four picture sanctification – being saved from influences of the world – and the last four, the saving of the body – being snatched away to heaven. Thus, the defiled woman is presented in the last set of sons. Revelation 17 tells us that, while the Church is in heaven, a defiled woman representing the culmination of all anti-God religions will be on earth and in league with the beast (the anti-Christ) during the Tribulation Period. The names of Jacob's sons both "shadow" our salvation and future prophetic events.

Jacob, the "supplanter" had lived up to his name. Jacob had relied on his own cunning and craftiness to deceive his father into blessing him and enticing Esau to relinquish his birthright. In the next chapter, he *"stole away unawares to Laban."* The concluding verses of Genesis 30 again expose Jacob's self-reliant character. Jacob had accumulated much experience in the breeding of livestock. He knew from observation that if he continued the selective breeding of animals with recessive traits (such as brown color in sheep) with animals having either dominant or recessive traits that statistically more animals with recessive traits would be apparent over time.

In accordance with his business arrangement with Laban, this outcome would increase his flocks and herds. Yet, he could not trust God with this matter and set about to manipulate the breeding and birthing process of the livestock with some mystical self-concocted contraption (Gen. 30:37-39), a testimony to the folly of his own mind. He had to do something to help God (or so he thought). Even Jacob was surprised at the proportion of striped, speckled and spotted offspring. But God revealed to Jacob in a dream that He was the One responsible for the livestock irregularities (Gen. 31:10). God was compensating Jacob for Laban's deceit. Oh that we might permit matters of injustice to be judged by the Lord. God had been with Jacob the entire time, but Jacob declined to fully acknowledge God's control and plan for his life.

Search me, O God, and know my heart today;
Try me, O Saviour, know my thoughts, I pray.
See if there be some wicked way in me;
Cleanse me from every sin and set me free.
Lord, take my life and make it wholly Thine;
Fill my poor heart with Thy great love divine.
Take all my will, my passions, self and pride;
I now surrender, Lord in me abide.

                J. Edwin Orr

The Shepherd is Blessed
Genesis 31:1-13

What vocation does God use as an archetype for spiritual leadership in the Bible? Might it be those in agricultural occupations such as farming, attending vineyards, or fig picking? Or perhaps construction trades such as tent making, hewing stones, or carpentry? Better yet, those holding authority: a captain of soldiers, a ruler of the people, or the monarch presiding over the land. These are all admirable callings and trades, but God's role model for spiritual leadership is the meek and lowly shepherd. Although viewed as a modest vocation in Bible times, these men were a special blend of tough guy and tender foot, a necessity for tending sheep.

To develop this leadership analogy to maturity, a few examples of shepherdry are necessary. The Lord, the spiritual leader and head of the Church, is called the Good Shepherd (Jn. 10:14), *"the Shepherd and Bishop of your souls"* (1 Pet. 2:25), and the *"Chief Shepherd"* (1 Pet. 5:4). The writer of Hebrews acknowledges *"Lord Jesus, that Great Shepherd of the sheep"* (Heb. 13:20). Even King David, in his classic 23rd Psalm, proclaims, *"The Lord is my Shepherd, I shall not want."*

Peter and Paul employ shepherd imagery in describing the spiritual duties and affections of those in local church leadership. Peter exhorts other elders to *"feed the flock of God which is among you, taking the oversight of it"* (1 Pet. 5:1-4). Peter, no doubt, recalled the direct instruction from the Lord, as recorded in John 21, to feed the Lord's sheep and wisely passes this exhortation on to others shepherding God's sheep. Later, Paul instructs the Ephesian elders to *"Take heed, therefore, unto yourselves, and to all the flock, over which the Holy Spirit hath made you overseers"* (Acts 20:28).

God sharply rebuked the spiritual leaders of Israel by the prophet Ezekiel: *"Woe be to the shepherds of Israel that do feed themselves!*

Should not the shepherds feed the flocks?" (Ezek. 34:2). However, the prophet ends the chapter by acknowledging the future blessings to Israel through the Lord Jesus, the Great Shepherd, during the Kingdom Age.

God demonstrated the benefit of having a shepherd leading the nation of Israel when He hand-picked a shepherd boy named David to rule. Although David was not perfect, he had a heart for God and a love for God's people, and his reign set the standard of comparison for all other Biblical monarchies. No doubt, the courage drawn upon by David to protect wee lambs from ravenous lions and bears was again utilized in battling Israel's adversaries through his 40 years of service.

Spiritual leaders throughout the course of Biblical history are likened to shepherds, and those in their care are likened to sheep. But what about the family fold? Does the Bible use the shepherd analogy for family leadership? Yes, Job likens a man's children to a flock of sheep (Job 21:11), and the Biblical duties and affections of a father towards his family closely align with the instructions given to shepherds. Whether it be Christ shepherding the Church (Jn. 10), church leaders pastoring local churches (1 Pet. 5:1-5, Acts 20:28-31, Eph. 4:12), or men caring for their families, the functional responsibilities are basically identical. Shepherds are to lead, protect, feed, attend, and watch over the sheep, while being a good example and a humble servant. A good shepherd will give his life for the sheep.

The conclusion: husbands and fathers are to be good shepherds of their families, for no authority and responsibility conferred by God is without direct accountability to Him also. Although Jacob had been a tent dweller in Canaan, he had now gained twenty years of shepherding experience in Haran, which would be helpful in guiding his growing family. In the next several chapters, we will glean from Jacob's shepherding experience and learn from his mistakes as he leads his family on a spiritual pilgrimage.

After completing his 14 years of service to Laban, Jacob sought to part company. However, Laban knew that his prosperity had acutely increased as a result of Jacob's presence with him. To keep Jacob, and more importantly God's blessings, he agreed to allow Jacob to name his wages. Jacob did and an agreement was made – Jacob would receive all the striped, spotted, and speckled cattle and goats and the

Seeds of Destiny

brown sheep from Laban's herds and flocks as wage for caring for Laban's livestock. What seemed like a prosperous business agreement at first was clearly a bad deal for Laban in time. His herds and flocks were diminishing, both in quality and quantity, something that certainly alarmed his sons, who were anxiously watching their inheritance dwindle right before their eyes. Tensions were mounting. Though Jacob was shrewd, he was a man of honor and, therefore, was constrained to fulfill his agreement with Laban to care for his animals. It was time again for the Lord to intervene in Jacob's life. After twenty years of verbal silence, the Lord spoke to Jacob, *"Return unto the land of thy fathers, and to thy kindred; and I will be with thee"* (Gen. 31:3). Andrew Fuller comments:

> If Jacob had removed from mere personal resentment, or as stimulated only by a sense of injury, he might have sinned against God, though not against Laban. But when it was said to him 'Return unto the land of thy fathers and to thy kindred, and I will be with thee,' his way was plain before him. In all our removals, it becomes us to act as that we may hope for the Divine presence and blessing to attend us else, though we may flee from one trouble, we shall fall into many, and be less able to endure them.[1]

It is so easy to run from trouble during difficult times unless we understand that God has His way in these matters and that, if we flee prematurely, we are actually withdrawing from God's presence. John Darby puts it simply this way, "Although God in His faithfulness be with us, we are not always with Him."[2] After feeding the five thousand men (plus women and children), the Lord sought solitude to pray unto His Father. He sent His disciples to the other side of the Sea of Galilee by boat. Those twelve men, obedient to their Lord, launched out into a sea that soon met them with life threatening force. They toiled all night in a raging storm but prevailed not. They believed death crouched within each battering wave that broke upon their battered vessel. The sea lunged ever upward for a grip that might drag them into the murky horrors below. Yet, they were safer being in that boat than being any other place on earth. Why? Because they were being obedient to the Lord's command – His revealed will. The very thing that they feared, the raging sea, was the very means in which the Lord Jesus was brought closer to them (He walked upon the sea to save them from the storm.). Most often, it is God's presence in overcoming what we fear most that results in greatest appreciation for His faithfulness and spurs our faith onward to embrace the next challenge with confidence.

> O God, our Help in ages past, our Hope for years to come,
> Be Thou our Guide while life shall last, and our eternal Home.
>
> Isaac Watts

Seeds of Destiny

The Shepherd Leads
Genesis 31:14-55

Jacob reviewed his message from God with Rachel and Leah and acknowledged the specific destination of their journey – Bethel. *"I am the God of Bethel, where thou anointedst the pillar, and where thou vowed a vow unto Me; now arise, get thee out from this land, and return unto the land of thy kindred"* (Gen. 31:13). God was calling Jacob home! But where exactly was home? Home is wherever man and God dwell together in fellowship. Jacob was summoned back to Bethel where he had first experienced God's presence.

As the spiritual leader, Jacob had a huge responsibility in overseeing his family's demeanor towards God. Progression and continuance towards Bethel symbolized increasing family devotedness towards God and brought the finale of intimate fellowship with Almighty God increasingly nearer! It is the same for each Christian family. Men are to consistently advance their families towards a holy loving God. It is this spiritual fellowship that God yearns for and that our parched souls desperately require for survival! Fathers must make every effort to encourage their children to come into a relationship with God by believing the gospel of Jesus Christ and by experiencing a spiritual birth. Then, fathers should encourage their children's continued pursuit of God and maintaining of eager communion with Him, which is the incredible privilege of every child of God.

Notice that, before Jacob's family's journey began, Jacob explained the word of the Lord to Rachel and Leah (Gen. 31:4-13). Husbands must prioritize their schedules so that teaching their wives and children the Word of God is first place. Often today, parents assume the easy way out by teaching a list of "dos and don'ts" or "the whats," but seldom invest the time to teach "the whys" of Scripture. Then, when their children are grown, parents wonder why their children drifted away

Devotions in Genesis

from the Lord. If parents want the "whats" to remain in their children, they must be faithful to teach the "whys." This should not be done through the proclamation of traditions or the enforcing of personal preferences, but through family exploration of God's Word and mutual discovery of His precepts. Thus, children learn to consult the Book to answer every question or to obtain guidance for life's dilemmas. Fathers must be men of the Book! The family will readily follow the father's leading if they understand that the direction is really God's. This is what Jacob did. If a man is a good husband, he never needs to fear that his wife will not stand by him in difficult times. Jacob's wives stood with Jacob.

Jacob gathered his family and all his goods and departed without telling Uncle Laban he was leaving. The tension between Laban and Jacob had been escalating since the agreement concerning who would retain what livestock based on color and spots. God had significantly increased and invigorated Jacob's livestock over the past six years through controlling the breeding and birthing process of the animals (Gen. 31:12). Jacob was afraid of Laban's retaliation if he knew Jacob was leaving with what Laban might consider his property, so he secretly slipped away with his family and his livestock. Jacob had already maneuvered his flocks and herds to graze three days journey away (We assume to the southwest.) without raising suspicion (Gen. 30:36). This would afford him the most expedient escape and put the maximum distance possible between him and Laban.

Laban learned of Jacob's departure after three days. It is possible that Laban immediately pursued after Jacob upon hearing the news. However, Laban may have delayed a few more days as it was the appropriate time to shear the sheep, and wool collection was lucrative business. Jacob could not travel fast with his young family and hordes of animals (Gen. 33:13) – at best twenty miles per day. However, Laban drove hard after Jacob and trekked nearly 300 miles to the range of Gilead in only seven days (an average of forty miles a day). On the seventh day, Laban and his brethren overtook Jacob. In the mountains of Gilead, there was no escape for Jacob, so Laban set up camp and sought a good night's sleep before the next day's confrontation. The next day Laban hotly protested Jacob's sneaky departure. Laban would have probably done Jacob harm, but the Lord had interceded on Jacob's behalf the night before. God injected a dream in Laban's mind that severely warned him not to violate Jacob in any way – Jacob was under His protection and direction.

Unknown to Jacob, Rachel had stolen "images" from her father's house. Jacob invited Laban to search his camp and punish by death the one with whom the idols were found. Rachel hid them under her attire and asked to be pardoned from rising during the search of her tent because of menstrual woes. So Laban did not find his longed for images. Twenty years of suppressed hard feelings and bitterness could no longer be restrained – Jacob verbally lashed out at Laban. Jacob substantiates his integrity and faithfulness to Laban over the years despite his bents of lying and cheating. Jacob highlighted the fact that he had personally covered the costs of wounded livestock under his care, which was not the customary practice. Normally, if a shepherd brought to his master a lamb that had been injured by a wild beast, or even part of a lamb that had been killed (Amos 3:12), it was proof that the shepherd had performed his duty bravely – he was not financially accountable for the loss under such circumstances.

Instead of pleading guilty to his obvious crimes, self-seeking Laban diverted Jacob's attention to the fact that everything he had came from him and he should be grateful. Laban knew God was with Jacob and he could do nothing against him, so he proposed a non-aggression pact with Jacob. Jacob agreed. Laban and his sons erected a pillar supported by a heap of stones to commemorate the occasion. Laban named the monument "Mizpah" meaning "watchtower;" the pillar would be a sentry of sort to guard the boundary between Jacob and Laban. Jacob offered sacrifices to God, and in the morning, Laban withdrew in peace without his images, daughters, grandchildren and livestock, and with a long 300-mile journey ahead of him. God had delivered another miracle in the life of Jacob.

Laban and his sons are not mentioned again in Scripture, perhaps this is the mercy of God. Laban represents the natural man of this world who has personally witnessed the truth of God, observed God radically change lives, and profited directly from God's blessings but chooses to close his eyes and ignore this revelation. These unfortunate souls, darkened in their minds by a deliberate act are, thus, prone to walk in the darkness of corruption, idolatry, covetousness, greed, lying, etc. while the whole time the glaring truth of God's light is shining upon them.

Until this chapter, the word "image" has been exclusively used to describe humanity's unique "God likeness" in certain aspects (having a spirit, emotions, intellect, a moral nature, communicative ability, etc.). Therefore, it is possible to be created "God like" without being "like God" in behavior or character. The Hebrew word, "teraphim," which means "healer," is employed in Genesis 31:19 to describe the "images" that Rachel stole. Arthur Pink explains:

> Scholars tell us that the word "teraphim" may be traced to a Syrian root which means 'to inquire'. This explains the reason why Rachel took with her their family 'gods' when her husband stole away surreptitiously from her home – it was to prevent her father from 'inquiring' of these idol 'oracles' and thus discovering the direction in which they had gone.[1]

There are other Scripture references that affirm that "teraphims" were used for consultation (Judges 17:5, 18:6; Ezek. 21:21; Zech. 10:2). Whether Rachel took the idols to protect Jacob from being found, or whether she, like King Saul's daughter, Michal, wanted her own personal tool of communicating with familiar spirits, we cannot say. It should be noted that Rachel could have buried the images to accomplish the same result of stealing them if safety had been her objective. But with certainty, we can say God was offended that these idols dwelt in Jacob's house, for He commanded Jacob to purge them out in Genesis 35. Might we heed the warning and remove from our homes that which would rob our affection from the Savior or squander precious time and resources designated for the kingdom.

O Thou great all-gracious Shepherd, shedding for us Thy life's blood,
Unto shame and death delivered all to bring us nigh to God!
Now our willing hearts adore Thee, now we taste Thy dying love,
While by faith we come before Thee – faith which lifts our souls above.

C. A. Wellesley

All Alone
Genesis 32:1-23

Jacob's anxiety had been escalating for several days because he perceived that he was sandwiched between two threatening militant foes – Esau to the west and Laban to the east. God graciously intervened to rescue Jacob from Laban, but now brother Esau was approaching. If Jacob had recognized God's handiwork in buckling Laban's infuriated heart, he would have retained an enormous peace offering of 580 animals with which he meant to bribe Esau and escape his revenge.

God sent an angelic escort (likely well armed) to accompany Jacob on his journey. These servants from heavenly realms did more than just momentarily appear to Jacob – they met with him! Certainly, this unique encounter must have urged Jacob forward in his journey to Bethel. Jacob sent out messengers to find Esau and announce his arrival. The messengers were able to return with a report much sooner than expected, because Esau was already advancing towards them with 400 men. The news of Esau's approach was unnerving, and Jacob became *"greatly afraid and distressed"* (Gen. 32:7). So what did Jacob do? Did he pray or cry out to God for help? No, not at first; rather, Jacob chose to meet imminent danger by his own devices instead of resting in the Lord – he sought to manage the situation in his own strength and according to his own intellect. As a precautionary measure to reduce his losses if attacked, he divided his people and livestock into two groups. It was only after Jacob finished all his "busy work" to protect himself that he prayed to God for deliverance. This is Jacob's first recorded prayer, and though a wonderful prayer, it was just a bit late to demonstrate a complete trust in his Creator.

Jacob humbly asked for God's deliverance based on His covenant promises. If this supplication had been uttered earlier in Jacob's "doings," we may have complimented him, but it is "natural man's" tendency to either rely on himself solely, or to add a short prayer to his own arrangements hoping to gain a little divine assistance in the matter. That is what Jacob did, and it is what we all are prone to do. The cycles of Jacob's praying and planning are praiseworthy: he plans (Gen. 32:7-8), he prays (Gen. 32:9-12), he plans (Gen. 32:13-23), he prays (Gen. 32:24-32) and he plans (Gen. 33:1-3). Yet, let the cycle begin with prayer and not planning; in this matter is the heart's trusted resource revealed – our wit or God's grit.

After righteous King Jehoshaphat had confirmed a military alliance with wicked King Ahab to war against Syria, he said to Ahab, *"Inquire, I pray thee, at the word of the Lord today"* (2 Chron. 18:4). It is utter mockery of God to solicit His counsel and assistance when one has already determined the matter through human reasoning. C. H. Mackintosh writes:

> *We must be really brought to the end of everything with which self has aught to do; for until then God cannot show Himself. But we can never get to the end of our plans until we have been brought to the end of ourselves.*[1]

God had resolved the quarrel with Laban – why could Jacob not trust Him to work in Esau's heart also? Unknown to Jacob, that was exactly what God was doing.

On the eve of confronting Esau, Jacob isolated himself from his family in order to fret over his dilemma. This was a critical point in Jacob's life for he was completely alone with God. To be secluded with God is the only true agency of realizing our frail devices and, more importantly, our depraved hearts. The Lord, incognito, visited Jacob. It is worthy of note that the Lord began the wrestling match for the Scripture states, *"there wrestled a man with him (Jacob)"* (Gen. 32:24). But verse 25 also states, *"he (Jacob) wrestled with Him (the Lord)."* Both the Lord and Jacob desired something from the other. Jacob, nearly 100 years old, wanted a blessing from the Ancient of Days. The Lord wanted Jacob broken and yielded before Him. If the Lord has ever wrestled with the reader, it is for the same purpose – to obtain "broken-

Seeds of Destiny

ness." We understand this unnamed man to be a theophany (As explained earlier, this is a pre-incarnate visit of Christ to the earth as the Father's messenger.).

Let us remember John's solemn words concerning the enemy that lurks about and threatens to devour, *"greater is He that is in you, than he that is in the world"* (1 Jn. 4:4). The Lord with anyone is a majority. Actually, the Lord alone is a majority! Elisha's servant discovered this truth when God opened his eyes to see the horses and chariots of fire that filled the surrounding mountains (2 Kings 6:17). He intensely feared the Syrian army that had surrounded them at Dothan for the sole purpose of killing Elijah. Why? Because God was providing Elijah with tactical information about the enemy which he, in turn, gave to the king of Israel to spoil the Syrian invasion. Elijah did not fear the enemy; he was just concerned about performing the will of God. And there is the lesson; do His will, and don't be anxious about the rest.

Jacob was agonizing about the enemy when he should have been concentrating on obeying God's instructions. But despite Jacob's misplaced focus, in the end, the Lord drew out Jacob's faith at Peniel by first withholding what He intended to impart, and then by bestowing it only after Jacob declared, *"I will not let Thee go, except Thou bless me."*

> Come, O thou traveler unknown, whom still I hold but cannot see,
> My company before is gone, and I am left alone with thee.
> With thee all night I mean to stay and wrestle till the break of day.
> My prayer hath power with God, the grace unspeakable I now receive
> Through faith I see Thee face to face, I see Thee face to face, and live.
> In vain I have not wept and strove; Thy nature and Thy name is love.
>
> Charles Wesley

A New Name and a New Walk
Genesis 32:24-32

The unnamed wrestler graciously blessed Jacob (Gen. 32:29) and was realized to be the Lord by Jacob himself (also see Hosea 12:3). Further evidence is given in Genesis 35:9 that it indeed was the Lord who tangled with Jacob: *"God appeared unto Jacob again"* after he arrived in Bethel. Since this is the only other occurrence of a divine messenger personally appearing to Jacob, we must conclude, as Jacob did, that he had scuffled that night with the Lord Himself.

The Lord could have "pinned" Jacob at any time but did not choose to do so. The Lord was longsuffering with Jacob and was willing to wrestle the whole night with him. What was the Lord's purpose in this activity? Certainly not to defeat or destroy Jacob, but to teach him to be yielded and broken before Him. Jacob had used his resources to outwit Esau, con his father Isaac, and escape from Laban, but Jacob was about to learn he was no match for the Lord. By divine skill, Jacob was crippled, making wrestling very difficult and painful. In Genesis 32:32, we read that the *"hollow of Jacob's thigh...shrank."* How well the harmonizing words of John the Baptist blends with this event: *"He (Christ) must increase, but I must decrease"* (Jn. 3:30).

Jacob, being disabled, resorted to the only tactic left, holding on to the Lord with all his might. In the end, the Lord was victorious because Jacob's "will" had been broken and his only recourse was to cling to God. It is at this moment of "self-brokenness" and reliance on the Lord that Jacob received a blessing. The lesson for the Christian is simply this: it is when we yield ourselves and cling only to the Lord that we receive and comprehend God's blessings for us and become a blessing to others. *"The sacrifices of God are a broken spirit; a broken and a contrite heart O God, Thou wilt not despise"* (Ps. 51:17).

Seeds of Destiny

We read in Luke's Gospel account of a colt that found his purpose and fulfillment in life in being what the Creator wanted him to be. The colt of an ass, which had never been saddled before, became instantly broken in the presence of the Lord Jesus on Palm Sunday. It was only in submitting to the Master that this little colt learned purpose in life. He was to carry his Master, the lowly and just Messiah, down the Mount of Olives before a cheering crowd. The young colt was born to serve the Master and to fulfill a 600-year-old prophecy (Zech. 9:9). It is when we are broken before God that we will be able to learn of Him and then, like the colt, be what He wants and find the true meaning of life. Being with the Creator and seeking to please Him results in sustained joy!

Jacob had sent his family over the brook Jabbok (modern Zerqa) while he remained on the other side alone. Ironically, Jabbok means "he will empty." Once Jacob's "will" had been broken and his self-dependence emptied, he then became a fit vessel for God's use.

What "application" is there for us in the *"sinew which shrank?"* First, all God's people will fail from time to time. Like Jacob, we wrestle with God, go our own ways, and just simply fail to do what is right. We are all prone to wander. The Jews religiously pulled the sciatic nerve, or thigh vein, from slaughtered animals before they prepared the meat for consumption. It was a continual reminder of how God dealt with Jacob when He wrestled with him. Likewise, God is dealing with all of us according to His wisdom and love, perhaps we should follow this Jewish example and not feast upon the failures of others.

None of us does what is right all the time; therefore, none of us should "rejoice in the iniquity" of others. This is simply an activity of pride our mind enjoys engaging in to substantiate self: "I don't sin like he does; therefore, I am better than he is." Paul clarifies our natural propensity to sin: *"There is none that doeth good, no, not one"* (Rom. 3:12). The best advice: do not compare yourself with others – it will lead to depression or pride, and do not focus on the failures of others – it will lead to their pain or your vanity.

The "sinew shrank," but it was not removed from Jacob, nor is the "flesh" eradicated from the believer's life upon conversion. Yieldedness to the Lord shrinks self-dependence that we might walk by faith and in the strength of God's Spirit. Thus, the hand that touched and withered Jacob's natural strength also imparted a more excellent vitality from above. This is God's way.

Jacob received a new name that day – Israel, which means "he who strives with God," or perhaps "God's rule" or "a prince of God." In a real sense, all are true – Jacob strove with God long enough to learn God ruled his life. Jacob also got a new walk. For the rest of his life, he would limp upon his disabled leg. The pain and the loss of mobility would be a constant reminder that he had wrestled with God and that God had won! Let the believer walk by faith in the light of revealed truth and not wrestle with God. God will never harm us, but He may hurt us to make us more faithful. Before we close, ponder Jacob's words to the Lord one more time, *"I will not let thee go."* Jacob sought to be alone in misery, but after embracing the Lord, his soul clung to His presence.

> Not I, but Christ, be honored, loved, exalted;
> Not I, but Christ, be seen, be known, be heard;
> Not I, but Christ, in every look and action;
> Not I, but Christ, in every thought and word.
> Not I, but Christ, in lowly, silent labor;
> Not I, but Christ, in humble, earnest toil;
> Christ, only Christ! No show, no ostentation!
> Christ, none but Christ, the gatherer of the spoil.
> Christ, only Christ, ere long will fill my vision,
> Glory excelling, soon, full soon, I'll see –
> Christ, only Christ, my every wish fulfilling –
> Christ, only Christ, my all in all to be.
>
> Mrs. A. A. Whiddington

Time to Meet Big Brother
Genesis 33:1-11

The dreaded day lingered before Jacob like an impending vaccination before a five-year-old. The moment had arrived when Jacob would recognize just how useless his plans were and just how unjustified his fears were. The day before Jacob had arranged for a gift, actually five separate droves of animals, to be presented to Esau. A total of 580 animals, comprising goats, sheep, cattle, camels, and asses were to be presented to Esau as a gesture of good will prior to Jacob's coming.

Jacob spent the final moments before encountering Esau staging his wives and children at various intervals in front of him. We fault Jacob here because the shepherd selfishly used his sheep to buffer himself from potential jeopardy. The Lord declared that the good shepherd will risk all, even his own life, to deliver his sheep from harm (Jn. 10:10-13).

Many fathers today are descending into the same abhorrent behavior! Instead of training children regarding what is appropriate behavior, many parents are bowing to the pressures of society and government-operated education to train their children in the way of Cain! Humanism, New Age propaganda, perverse media, and the deterioration of parental authority are main beachheads by which the Adversary is eroding God-ordained family order and values. God forbid that humanism should be the foundation for our children's reasoning when God has preserved sixty-six divinely inspired books through centuries of time. An immutable moral standard must be embedded early in a child's life. As they mature, scriptural precepts and guidelines should be taught to help them discern between what is wise conduct and what is foolish. With these moral tools, a child can honorably navigate his or her behavior in the vast ocean of humanity and through the raging storms of relativism and, by God's grace, avoid a shipwrecked life.

Parents should be active in teaching and exhorting their children from Scripture. How to respectfully speak to adults, how to discern appropriate attire, how to choose music with integrity, how to establish a healthy diet, and how to maintain purity and overcome lustful temptations are just some of the territories parents and children need to explore together. Children are not mutton (meat) for the world system to devour, but precious eternal souls, which need molding. Children are the only eternal assets God has entrusted parents with. Everything else that we have will rot, rust, evaporate, be consumed or get stolen. Jacob feared Esau, and, consequently, he neglected the stewardship of his family and behaved like a "hireling!"

Being a good shepherd is hard work! It may mean withstanding peer pressure exerted on the child, the government's education system, and the badgering of other parents, but fathers must stand firm. So exhibit courage, raise the crook when needed, fling the sling if threatened and fend off devouring foes; your children's future prosperity is at stake.

Within moments of meeting Esau, Jacob's apprehensions were transformed to jubilee. Instead of a hotheaded brother seeking his "double portion," a warmhearted Esau embraced him. Esau must have been stunned to see how much Jacob had increased in posterity and prosperity in only twenty years. The gift from Jacob to Esau was enormous. But Esau didn't want it – he had "enough" already (Gen. 33:9). But Jacob insisted that he receive it *"because God hath dealt graciously with me, and because I have enough"* (Gen. 33:11). Esau begrudgingly received the gift. Buried in the original language is a matter worth noting. The Hebrew word for "enough" in Genesis 33:9 is *rab*, which means "abundant." *Rab* is also translated "much" or "suffice" in other passages of Scripture. However, the Hebrew word used to speak of Jacob's "enough" is *kol*, which means "all" or "every" or "the whole" and, by implication, "everything." Esau had much, but in Jacob's own mind, he had everything; he had Almighty God for his resource. Yes, Jacob had a bent to rely on his own "doings," but now he understood that, despite himself, God was the One who was really in control of his life and the resource of every good thing. *"Oh, how great is Thy goodness, which Thou hast laid up for them that fear Thee,*

Seeds of Destiny

which Thou hast wrought for them that trust in Thee before the sons of men!" (Ps. 31:19).

>Immortal, invisible, God only wise,
>In light inaccessible hid from our eyes,
>Most blessed, most gracious, the Ancient of Days,
>Almighty, victorious, Thy great name we praise.
>
>Walter Smith

The Shepherd Leads Softly
Genesis 33:12-20

Esau offered to escort Jacob and his family on their spiritual journey. Now years of shepherding experience come into play! Jacob responded to Esau's offer in Genesis 33:13-15:

And he said unto him, "My lord knoweth that the children are tender, and the flocks and herds with young are with me: and if men should overdrive them one day, all the flock will die. Let my lord, I pray thee, pass over before his servant; and I will lead on softly, according as the cattle that goeth before me and the children be able to endure, until I come unto my lord unto Seir."

Here Jacob displays a spectacular barrage of shepherding wisdom:
(1) He "knows" his family's needs, limitations, and what they can endure.
(2) He will "lead softly" according to that knowledge.
(3) He will not "overdrive" them for even one day so that harm may not result.
(4) He will not "allow others to interfere" with his task of guiding his family.

Leading the family's spiritual journey is the father's responsibility, not the mother's, not the government's, not the school's, not friend's and not even the Church's (although any of these may assist). Jacob understood this and did not delegate his responsibility even under pressure to do so! Too many men today are shirking their God-given occupation for complacency! Fathers must know their families' needs and

Seeds of Destiny

limitations, then lead them softly by a pure example, not overdriving them by authority or scattering them by delegating it.

Just how threatening was Esau when he finally encountered Jacob after twenty years? *"Esau ran to meet him, and embraced him, and fell on his neck, and kissed him: and they wept."* How silly Jacob must have felt to have fretted so much. We do find fault with Jacob in his conversation with Esau – He lied to his brother. He told Esau to proceed to Edom and that he would meet him at Mt. Seir (Gen. 33:14). Yet, after Esau and his men departed, Jacob went the direction Esau faced away from – west to Succoth. Paul states that we should *"lie not one to another"* (Col. 3:9). There is no reason for a Christian to lie. If the situation is so distasteful that the results of the truth are deplorable, just do not say anything and willingly receive the consequences. Jacob was still partially relying on his own intellect and clever resources instead of solely depending on the Lord. It is hard for the flesh to surrender, but it must! Jacob may not have trusted Esau, and Edom was definitely not in their travel agenda – it was not the heavenly land, but there was no reason for Jacob to deceive his brother. Through God's intervention, Esau had attained a forgiving heart.

God had delivered Jacob victories over both Esau and Laban without any bloodshed! How did Jacob respond? He built an altar and led his family in worship. Jacob named the altar "El-elohe-Israel, meaning *"God, the God of Israel."* For the first time, Jacob acknowledged the Lord as his God. It had been the events of this chapter that had led to Jacob's conversion. However, like so many of God's people today, he lingered in the comfort of a victory celebration so long that he became complacent in doing God's will. In this case, Jacob built a house in Succoth (Gen. 33:17), which was on the east side of the Jordan River, and then bought a field in Shechem (Gen. 33:19) instead of traveling another 15 miles further south to Bethel – his God-given destination. He was settling instead of sojourning. This is the depressing existence so many Christians find themselves in today. It is a vicious circle of comfort, complacency, carnality, chastening, conquest and celebration. Let us be continuing the Lord's bidding and rejoicing in Him as we labor to redeem the time (Col. 4:5).

Our God is at home with the rolling spheres, and at home with broken hearts.

> M. P. Ferguson

We cannot win the war against injustice until we win the war against apathy!

> unknown

Seeds of Destiny

Jacob – Where is Your Daughter?
Genesis 34

Although we commend Jacob for leading his family in worship in Genesis 33:17-20, he committed a serious mistake which would have devastating family consequences in Genesis 34. Jacob first halted his family's journey at Succoth and then again at Shechem, where he pitched his tent only 15 miles from destination Bethel! He lingered there long enough for a local fellow named Shechem to become romantically interested in his daughter Dinah. Dinah, who was six or seven years old when her family departed Haran, was still quite young, not more than fifteen, perhaps sixteen years old and socially naïve. She had ventured from home *"to see the daughters of the land,"* but in fact, it was the "sons of the land" that noticed her. Genesis 34:2 states the offense plainly, *"Shechem ... saw her, he took her, and lay with her, and defiled her."* Although Shechem's crime may have been a common practice among the Canaanites, the matter incited outrage in Jacob's family and ushered in an era of trouble for Jacob. The Lord again reminded Jacob of his destination (Gen. 35:1-2), but only after staggering transgressions against God had been committed by his family (Namely, murder, theft, coveting, possibly fornication, bearing false witness, and embracing foreign gods.).

Fathers must continue leading their families in the will of the Lord. Slackness in the family pilgrimage Godward provides opportunities for the flesh nature within family members to be stimulated while spiritual fruitfulness declines. Stopping short of the destination of "Christlikeness" or pausing from *"pressing toward...the high calling of God in Christ Jesus"* is unacceptable (Phil. 3:14). All family activities must be weighed and decisions rendered according to this infallible standard. If Jacob had not paused at Shechem, Dinah would not have been defiled!

It is noted that a sexual relationship between a man and woman does not constitute a marriage covenant, although it consummates it. Even in ancient days, an agreement was made between the families, and usually, a dowry was paid to the bride's father, or if parental authority had been removed, a monarch oversaw the matter of arranging marriages. The Lord Jesus acknowledged that the man and the woman living together in John 4 were not married. In 1 Corinthians 6:16, Paul states that a man becomes one flesh with a harlot through a sexual relationship, but they are not married, for the reproof is to repent of this behavior – not to marry the harlot. Exodus 22:16-17, Deuteronomy 22:13-21, and Genesis 34:4 all reference the fact that an unmarried virgin woman was not considered married after having been with a man. The marriage covenant sanctifies and protects the sexual union of a man and a woman, but this union outside marriage is just plain sin. Let us call it what it is.

We see that Shechem loved Dinah and desired her for his wife as shown by his actions – he wanted to do the right thing. This response was later prescribed by the law, unless the daughter's father prohibited the marriage (Ex. 22:16-17; Deut. 22:13-21). He and his father Hamor visited Jacob's family, not to apologize but to discuss the matter of marriage. Both the bride's and the groom's families were involved in determining such matters – children did not just run off and get married. Other than Esau marrying the daughters of Heth against his parents wishes, and perhaps the Shulamite bride in the Song of Solomon, there is no Biblical examples of children marrying when and whom they wanted to – they were "given in marriage" (Lk. 17:27, 20:34-35; Matt. 24:38, 22:30; Mark 12:25).

The phrase "given in marriage" is normally applied to daughters, but we understand that the parental authority of parents is over their sons also (Matt. 22:2; Gen. 24). Although sons "leave" to establish new family heads, daughters are "given" in marriage (Ps. 78:63; 1 Cor. 7:38). A son will leave his parents and cleave to a wife. In this way, she experiences a transfer of authority (her father's to her husband's). This transition of authority is clearly stated in Numbers 30:3-16 in that a father could nullify a vow to God made by his daughter (living under his authority), or a husband could nullify a vow to God made by his wife.

Seeds of Destiny

    This transfer of authority may explain why, when Paul explains divine order in 1 Corinthians 11:3, the wife is nestled between Christ and the man. It is apparent from Scripture that daughters lived at home and under parental authority until they were wed. If the daughter must leave the protection of the home for schooling or for work, she still remains under her father's authority.

    Examples of virgins that remained under parental authority though they were removed from the father's house would be: (1) Jephtath's daughter went into the mountains (out of his home) to bewail her virginity for two months, but then returned to live in her father's house (Judges 11:34-40). (2) Although Esther was taken to the women's court for one year of beauty treatments, her adopted father, Mordecai (Est. 2:7), walked every day to the court of the women's house to encourage her and to check on her (Est. 2:11). This ceased once she was married. It is noted that widows did not need parental permission to remarry, but were to marry in the Lord if they remarried (1 Sam. 25; 1 Cor. 7:39). It is noted that these are only biblical principles to consider in marriage and not commands. The parents should guide the courting process, but ultimately the bride and groom are the ones who determine whether to marry or not.

    Although Jacob seemed to control his anger after learning of Dinah's defilement, he blundered in addressing Hamor – he allowed his sons to speak for him. They had no intentions of allowing an infidel to marry their sister. Jacob's sons had only one thing on their mind – vengeance. Shechem had defiled their sister, and he was going to pay. An ingenious plan was developed to execute their wrath. If all the men of Shechem could be persuaded to circumcise themselves, they then would have diminished capability to defend themselves when attacked. It was an evil plan and was implemented to a disgusting conclusion – Simeon and Levi, two brothers of Dinah murdered all the men of Shechem and spoiled the city three days after all the men had been circumcised. Jacob may have come to Shechem in peace (Shalem means peace – Gen. 33:18), but he departed in different manner. The men of Shechem graciously offered Jacob peace, to intermarry with their children and citizenship, which would convey full rights to the land. Jacob's sons reciprocated deceit, wrath, and murder resulting in all the surrounding inhabitants viewing Jacob as odious. His testimony was ruined!

What should a father do in such stressful family situations? Not what Jacob did. He delegated his responsibility, although God still held him accountable as the family leader. Often, intense family situations are colored with anger and hostility and present the opportunity for others under the father's authority to seize control and speak for their father. The wise father will defuse such situations to prevent the "flesh" from ruling the circumstance. He will seek the Lord's guidance and strength to bring a peaceful closure to the matter, while keeping his family from sinning. A discerning father is observant. He will know what his children are engaged in and ward off inappropriate behavior. If Jacob would have been more protective of Dinah, the whole situation could have been avoided.

The Bible clearly teaches that the sexually purity of the daughter should be protected and guaranteed by her father. He is her permanent chaperon, assigned to that office by God until the daughter experiences a transfer of authority from her father to her husband. Thus, a new family is created. Both sons and daughters are to remain virgins until marriage (1 Cor. 6:9, 5:11; 2 Tim. 2:20-22), but since God created women as "responders" and not "initiators" as He did men, God gives daughters the added protection of fathers to maintain purity. The error of Jacob in this chapter was in not protecting Dinah. She went out into the world and fell prey to a seductive man.

Jacob's response to his sons' poor behavior in Genesis 34:30 shows the worst of "self." The words "me," "I," and "my" occur nine times in one verse. Jacob was completely preoccupied with the "consequences" of his sons' behavior for himself rather than with how his children had grieved God. How Satan enjoys getting Christians wrapped up with sin's consequences rather than with obeying divine ordinances. Obedience relieves the chastening repercussions of one's sin. However, the impediments of a cursed world, which resulted from man's first rebellious act, still afflict every child of God. God is grieved over sin (lawless acts against Him). Yet, the consequences of sin are just! Dads, let us not think selfishly of how our children's bad behavior will reflect on us; let us reprove, instruct, and correct with the grief of God's heart being the motive.

Seeds of Destiny

> My life, my love I give to Thee,
> Thou Lamb of God who died for me;
> Oh, may I ever faithful be,
> My Saviour and my God!
>
> Ralph E. Hudson

Devotions in Genesis

Trading Idols for God
Genesis 35:1-6

Jacob had lived near Shechem for approximately ten years. It was now time for him to ascend from the low moral ground of Shechem to the dwelling place of the Most High God. So, God again called Jacob to return to Bethel (Gen. 35:1-2) and to build an altar there unto Him. Interestingly, God follows the command by recounting the circumstance that drove Jacob to Bethel in the first place – serious distress. Jacob was fleeing Esau when he first arrived at Bethel, and God disclosed Himself to Jacob in a dream. God now overshadowed Jacob's mind with "why" he had erected the last altar twenty years earlier. It is proper for us to remember from where we have been rescued (hell) and from what we have escaped (God's wrath) when we worship God. We acknowledge His goodness in saving our souls from the mire of sin and from the eternal destruction we were destined to suffer if it were not for His grace. Reminding ourselves of our own nothingness causes our hearts to lean upon God.

God's decree, though not directly mentioning idols, sufficed to admonish Jacob for his tolerance of foreign gods in his house. Jacob knew these strange gods were among him, but now his conscience was prodded about the matter. He immediately sought to sanctify his household and to purge these images from his family's presence. Why were there idols in Jacob's house in the first place? Although Jacob had experienced a conversion experience, certain members of his family and some of his servants were still embracing false gods (Remember Rachel stole her father's images before leaving Haran.). We applaud Jacob for abruptly gathering his house together, instructing his family from God's very words, then calling them to sweep the household clean of any false gods. One must wonder if the ills of Genesis 34 could have been avoided if Jacob had purged these evil images from his family at the onset of their spiritual expedition and terminated his journey at Bethel as instructed.

Jacob also directed his family to exchange their coverings for clean ones. Garments throughout Scripture seem to represent the outward expression of the inward condition of man's heart or his spiritual position. As discussed earlier, God exchanged Adam and the woman's garments of fig leaves for that of animal skins in the Garden of Eden. The fig leaves represented man's attempt to fix his condition of nakedness and to ease his conscience. The fig leaves symbolized a bloodless religion and did not reflect God's solution for man's sin through substitutional death. Why were the hides of animals considered righteous attire? Because the future work of His Son was pictured in the skin coverings. His Son, like the innocent animals, had done nothing wrong, but He was put to death as a sacrifice to resolve man's spiritual nakedness before God. Then man could be clothed in divine righteousness.

Of course, the outworking of imputed righteousness should be apparent! As mentioned before, this is why the Lord pleaded with the church at Laodicea: *"buy of me...white raiment, that thou mayest be clothed, and that the shame of thy nakedness do not appear"* (Rev. 3:18). It is also the source of Paul's appeal to the Christians in Rome: *"But put ye on the Lord Jesus Christ, and make not provision for the flesh, to fulfill the lusts thereof"* (Rom. 13:14). Just prior to Christ showing off His new bride, the Church, before the hordes of the wicked, a few surviving Jews, and a handful of faithful Gentiles on earth, Revelation 19:7-8 records the following:

> *Let us be glad and rejoice, and give honor to Him: for the marriage of the Lamb is come, and His wife hath made herself ready. And to her was granted that she should be arrayed in fine linen, clean and white; for the fine linen is the righteousness of [the] saints.*

Thus, the believer, who has a position in Christ, should shine forth the glory of Christ as manifested in good works enabled by the Holy Spirit. These manifestations of God's handy work in our lives are described as clean white garments of practical righteousness. The Christian home ought to be a holy refuge and not pagan playground. Fathers have the responsibility to purge and whisk away defilement that would hinder the spiritual vitality of the home. Only then will it be possible for our families to shine forth the glories of the Lord! *"Give unto the Lord the glory due unto His name; bring an offering, and come before Him, **worship the Lord in the beauty of holiness"*** (1 Chron. 16:29).

Jacob's family readily responded to His instructions, and *"they gave unto Jacob all the strange gods which where in their hand, and all their earrings which were in their ears."* Jacob quickly got rid of this evil paraphernalia and buried it all under an oak tree. The fact that Jacob did not melt them down and try to reuse the metal for other practical or legal uses is admirable. He realized that God's people must *"Abstain from all appearance of evil"* (1 Thess. 5:22). This, in principle, is good counsel for new converts that may be tempted to sell tokens (magazines, music, movies, etc.) of the old life, which ought to be destroyed as not to stumble others.

Why did Jacob's family give him their earrings? Earrings were frequently used in the manufacturing of idols or to support other immoral idolatrous practices (Ex. 32:2-4; Hos. 2:13). Thus, not only was Jacob ridding his family of their idols, but he was also ensuring that they did not have a provision to create new ones. What wisdom! Think how today's family would be transformed for God if all believing fathers purged everything that displaced the Lord from their family's presence, then ensured that no new toy, activity, relationship, or job would diminish their affection for the Savior. Then might Paul's passionate exhortation *"Set your affection [not affections] on things above, not on things on the earth"* (Col. 3:2) be achieved. The believer is not to have affections, but one affection – Christ. On the flip side, there are two dangers in family consecration to guard against. First, that the family itself does not become an idol to be worshipped. Secondly, that the local church meetings are not neglected. An overly strong manifestation of family order may displace proper church order to the extent that the balance that Scripture expresses for these two divine institutions is not upheld.

God created civil order, church order and family order, and none are to be ignored or neglected. Concerning the church, we are not exhorted to support "churchianity," but the "formal meetings" of the local church for prayer, teaching, the breaking of bread and fellowship (Acts 2:42). If your family is not at these meetings, you are casting a vote to close down the assembly! The local church is nothing more than an orderly gathering of God's people together. Meetings and ministries beyond these fundamental gatherings should be evaluated individually for their spiritual merit and impact on the family. Many churches today think that because they have a building it should be used every night. Nonsense! This is too stressful for the family and God's people in general. This vain mentality causes the church to detour from the Great Commission – evangelism and discipleship into busyness and committee life.

Because the Lord intervened on Jacob's behalf and put fear into the inhabitant's hearts, they dared not pursue Jacob to seek revenge for the slaughter at Shechem. Once more, we observe our Sovereign God ensuring the preservation of His chosen people despite all odds against them. He had completely controlled Uncle Laban and his brethren, Esau and his 400 men, and the enraged inhabitants of Canaan. What evil fallout might be threatening you today? Do not fret; the Lord is in control!

The inspired text notes the burial of Deborah, Rebekah's nurse, after the worship experience in Bethel. Jacob had known Deborah since his infancy. The fact that she was with Jacob and not Isaac confirms that Jacob had visited his frail father in Beersheba and that Rebekah his mother had died prior to his returning, thus releasing Deborah from her responsibilities and allowing her to abide with Jacob's family.

Because of God's faithfulness, Jacob succeeded in leading his family to Bethel. Interestingly, God had sent angels to meet Jacob, had personally spoken to him twice, and had wrestled with him once at Peniel, but did not have open fellowship with him until he had arrived at Bethel. It was when Jacob rendered complete obedience in returning to Bethel that God again appeared to Him and blessed communion was realized.

> Happy the home where prayer is heard, and praise is wont to rise;
> Where parents love the sacred Word, and all its wisdom prize,
> Lord, let us in our homes agree this blessed peace to gain;
> Unite our hearts in love to Thee, and love to all will reign.
>
> Henry Ware

The House Where God Lives
Genesis 35:7-29

It was at Bethel, "the house of God," where God had first appeared to Jacob and had given him a preview of the future kingdom of Christ. It was upon Jacob's return to Bethel that God again emerged from heavenly realms to bless Jacob and to reconfirm the Abrahamic covenant to him. Had Jacob's passion for God matured through the years of urgencies and emergencies? Just as wheat ripens to bow its head before the Creator at harvest time, Jacob's adoration and reverence for "who God is" had ripened through personal experience of divine grace. Twenty years on the Potter's wheel had transformed Jacob. Bethel was no longer just Bethel to Jacob. He now called it "El-Bethel," meaning "the God of the house of God" (Gen. 35:7). Jacob no longer had an affinity for just a spot of dirt but for a real God who abode there. What greater heritage can a father leave his children than his personal passion for God?

This phrase, "the house of God," is used rather loosely in today's Christian vernacular. Often Christians ignorantly use it to speak about a building in which the church gathers for meetings. The term "house of God" occurs 90 times in the Bible with 87 of these references describing the Old Testament reality of God dwelling in a tent or temple to commune with the Jews. This was made possible through continual animal sacrifices to provide atoning blood for their sins. The remaining three references of "the house of God" are in the epistles and refer to the Church. *"But if I tarry long, that thou mayest know how thou oughtest to behave thyself in **the house of God, which is the church** of the living God, the pillar and ground of the truth"* (1 Tim. 3:15). God now lives within and among His people, not in buildings. The tabernacle and the temple in the Old Testament represented man's limited access to God, for these structures were designed to keep man at a distance and to sanctify a holy God. But, the aftermath of Calvary brought

Seeds of Destiny

full justice for sin and peace with God. To refer to a church building as "the house of God" is to confuse God's covenants and the dispensational economies in which He is working. It is pulling dead Judaism into living Christianity.

There is a natural pull of the flesh for a visible expression of legalism, though God has called us to a spiritual occupation and heavenly citizenship. Christians often refer to the big room (where the church meeting occurs) as "the sanctuary." Under the Old Covenant, this term applies to the area of the temple or tabernacle in which the priest officiated national worship. Under the New Covenant, it is never applied to a physical room where Christians gather to worship but to where worship is directed (before the throne in heaven).

Some believe a human priesthood or clergy is necessary to officiate worship in Christianity, as under the Old Covenant. Yet, all Christians are believer priests (1 Pet. 2:5, 2:9; Rev. 1:6; Rom. 12:1). Other Christians practice the wearing of priestly ephods – special robes to designate special position in Judaism. Some sects of Christianity practice the lighting of candelabras and/or incense canisters, which pulls the "golden lampstand" and "altar of incense" of the tabernacle into Christianity. Even "fundamental" Christians use terms such as "prayer altar" to describe furniture in the church building where one must pray or a "marriage altar" for a marital ceremony. The only "altar" that the Christian now has is found in Hebrews 13:10. It is Christ Himself. It is only through Him that we offer praise and worship to the Father, not through some "wooden idol" situated in front of the church pews. Let us endeavor to keep the "House of God," the Church, the habitation of God, holy and free of religious idols. These Old Testament articles, in their day, served as relevant patterns of the provisions that would come through Christ to the Church. Therefore, what merely foreshadowed things to come should now be discarded from our church gatherings, lest these distract us from Whom they represented – Christ in our presence!

The advents of Christ are wonderfully depicted in metaphoric form in the narrative (Gen. 35:16-20). Jacob departed Bethel to travel to Ephrath. During this journey, a very pregnant Rachel entered into hard labor to deliver her second son. This son was born at Bethlehem and was named "Benoni" by Rachel just before her death, but Jacob re-

Devotions in Genesis

named him "Benjamin." Jacob then buried Rachel at Bethlehem and set a pillar upon her grave. In this messianic portrait, Jacob represents God the father, Benjamin the Lord Jesus, and Rachel, Benjamin's mother, the nation of Israel. Consequently, the names: Bethel means "house of God," Ephrath means "a place of fruitfulness," Bethlehem means "house of bread," Benoni means "son of my sorrow," and lastly, Benjamin means "the son of my right hand." Now, let us put the prophetic story line together.

The Son left the house of God (heaven), was born in Bethlehem (Lk. 2:15) of a Jewish virgin, and thus, became "the bread of life" offered to mankind for eternal life (Jn. 6:35). His earthly ministry transpired after departing His home in heaven, but before presenting a fruit harvest of souls to God through the work of His cross (Is. 53:10-11). He was born to be the man of sorrows (Is. 53:3), but after Calvary, the Father raised Him up to the seat of honor at His right hand (Heb. 1:3). To reaffirm that God had not forgotten His covenant to restore and bless Israel (Rom. 11:26), a pillar was erected on Rachel's grave. Historically, pillars were erected to visually acknowledge a covenant (Gen. 28:22, 31:45). The Lord Jesus sealed the New Covenant with His own blood. Christ and His work are clearly revealed through the birth of Benjamin.

Shortly after the birth of Benjamin and the subsequent death of Rachel, a very unfortunate sin occurred within Jacob's family. His first born son, Reuben, had a sexual relationship with Bilhah, Jacob's concubine. Genesis 35:22 records that Jacob *"heard it,"* but tragically never reproved the sin. If sin is not reproved, it is condoned in the minds of our children. Suppose you and your children are taking a stroll around the block, and you witness some teenagers smashing bottles on the sidewalk. This is all new to your children, and they await instruction from you to authenticate what is right or to reprove what is wrong. If you say nothing, you have condoned the sin and approved this behavior in their minds. Parent cannot afford to be silent where sin is apparent!

This chapter closes with the death of Isaac. He was 180 years old when he died, meaning that Jacob was 120 years of age and Joseph was 29 to 30 years old. Although not directly mentioned as a "type" of Christ in the New Testament, Joseph, by parallel life circumstances, is

Seeds of Destiny

quite a beautiful portrait of the Lord Jesus. It is, therefore, interesting that the death of Isaac, one of the strongest person "types" of Christ, occurred approximately at the same time that Joseph was exalted in Egypt. Although men come and go, the Father has maintained a steady "resemblance" and "remembrance" of His Son before us in Genesis.

> "Man of Sorrows," what a name For the Son of God who came
> Ruined sinners to reclaim Hallelujah! What a Savior!
> Bearing shame and scoffing rude, In my place condemned He stood;
> Sealed my pardon with His blood; Hallelujah! What a Savior!
> Lifted up was He to die, "It is finished," was His cry;
> Now in heaven exalted high; Hallelujah! What a Savior!
> When He comes, our glorious King, All His ransomed home to bring,
> Then anew this song we'll sing: Hallelujah! What a Savior!
>
> P. P. Bliss

The Beginning of Edom
Genesis 36

It is tempting to say, until you remember that this is the Word of God, that "this is a boring chapter." What benefit can be derived from stumbling through hard to pronounce names with no story line? The descendants of Esau – big deal! Right! In fact, this chapter provides considerable information pertaining to the history of a prominent people in the Bible, a nation that will be prominent again in a future day. The people are the Edomites, and as we learn in Genesis 36, they are the descendants of Esau who settled south and east of the land of Israel.

Notice in Genesis 36:31, *"These are the kings that reigned in the land of Edom, before there reigned any king over the children of Israel."* Then, in the following verses, we have a listing of the kings of Edom. C. I. Scofield makes the following comment concerning this verse:

> It is characteristic of Scripture that the kings of Edom should be named before the kings of Israel. The principle is stated in 1 Cor. 15:46. First things are "natural," man's best, and always fail; second things are "spiritual," God's things, and success. Adam – Christ; Cain – Abel, Cain's posterity – Seth's posterity, Saul – David, etc.[1]

Throughout the Bible, God generally reveals the best natural solution to man's problems or the best logical chance to overcome an adverse situation first. Then, to confound what seems logical, God chooses the least likely means of resolution to bring blessing. And, finally, through this unusual and divine protocol, God bestows a greater blessing to humanity through the most unexpected or unforeseen methods. Thus, a greater blessing is realized than could have ever been accomplished by natural means.

Seeds of Destiny

God created a Jewish nation to represent His name on earth, but through their idolatry and rejection of Christ, God brought the opportunity of salvation promised to Israel to all humanity. What great military leader did God choose to deliver Israel from the Midianites? Gideon – a man hiding from the enemy, who was the least of his brethren, and from the smallest tribe of Israel. Who did God use to topple a giant and to deliver Israel from the hand of the Philistines? A shepherd boy named David, who, by faith, yielded his sling to the Lord. How did God knock down the huge walls of the enemy's fortress? Earthquake? Wind? By having His people walk in silence around the city thirteen times, then all shouting at once. God's ways are not our ways. If God's doings mimicked ours, we would think less of God!

Why did Edom have kings before Israel? Edom represents the world's natural thinking about limiting personal accountability with God by recognizing an in-between level of authority. Why the delay in appointing a king for Israel? God did not want Israel to appoint a king to rule over them because He could oversee them better than any human could. God told the Jews, through the Prophet Samuel, the cost of having a human king rule over them (1 Sam. 8:6-18). But the people would not relent; they wanted to be like the nations and to have a visible ruler over them.

God foreknew this matter, for Moses had instructed the Israelites five centuries earlier concerning the dangers of recognizing a king (Deut. 17). These mandates were given to ensure that future kings (God knew that His people would seek a king instead of Him eventually.) would not stray from the Lord. If the king drifted from the Lord, the people would forsake their God also. In God's grand plan of redemption, He always intended to anoint a righteous king to rule over Israel – David, who typified a descendant of his that would be the King of kings and rule over the whole earth in righteousness. This plan is clearly seen in the promise God made to Abraham and Sarah that some of their descendants would be kings.

The book of Obadiah foretold the doom of Edom, but, in a greater prophetic way, predicted the judgment of all nations in the Day of the Lord. The "Day of the Lord" in Scripture generally speaks of a time of God's judgment but, more specifically, of when Jehovah will intervene in the public affairs beginning with the Tribulation Period. The "Day of

Christ" identifies the moment in time when the Church will be "caught up" into the air unto Christ. The key verse of the book of Obadiah is verse 15: *"For the day of the Lord is near upon all the nations. As thou hast done, it shall be done unto thee; thy reward shall return upon thine own head."* If Edom persecuted Israel, they would be persecuted. If Edom spoiled Jerusalem, they would be spoiled. You reap what you sow! Just as Edom was judged for their crimes against Israel, so shall all nations be judged that have sown evil against the Jews (Matt. 25:31-46; Rev. 19:21). Speaking to the nations concerning Israel, God warns *"for he that toucheth you [Israel] toucheth the apple of His eye"* (Zech. 2:8).

Esau and Jacob did not get along well, and neither did their descendants. So Esau, the oldest son of Isaac, was both rejected and despised by God. His rebellious nature, inclination for worldliness, and opposition to Jacob and his descendants guaranteed divine retribution. Prophetically, Edom pictures the opposition of the nations in relation to Israel. In the end, God will judge and crush all opposition to His restored people. Yet, in God's grace, there will be descendants of Esau that will live through the Tribulation Period and experience the delight of the Lord during the Kingdom Age (Isa. 11:13-14).

> Our Lord is now rejected, And by the world disowned,
> By the many still neglected, And by the few enthroned,
> But soon He'll come in glory, The hour is drawing nigh,
> For the crowning day is coming by and by.
>
> D.W. Whittle

Seeds of Destiny

A Special Son Dies?
Genesis 37:1-19

We resume in the life of Jacob a few years after Rachel's death. Joseph is now introduced as the main character through the end of Genesis. He is, at this juncture in time, seventeen years old. It would seem that Joseph was a bit gullible – he really did not know how bad his brothers were. Apparently, they did not appreciate Joseph being a tattletale (Gen. 37:2), their father's favorite child (Gen. 37:4), or an interpreter of dreams, through which he announced that they would bow down before him (Gen. 37:8). He must have been unusually naïve not to notice their jealousy and envy. Although Jacob was first a bit offended when Joseph told him of his future homage to his son, Jacob pondered the matter and marveled at Joseph's interpretations. Jacob understood that God would somehow bring about His covenant promises through the life of Joseph.

Jacob showed special favor and love to his son Joseph, the first born of Rachel, by giving him a special coat. It was not a "coat of many colors" as commonly taught and as, unfortunately, rendered in the Vulgate (Latin Bible) and Septuagint (the Greek Old Testament). The older Hebrew text speaks of a coat or a robe with long sleeves, which was a mark of special honor. Joseph enjoyed a unique relationship with his father – a relationship that all the other siblings longed for. When can love create problems within a family? When it is not evenly distributed. If family harmony is to be enjoyed, paternal government must be impartial and affection disbursed evenly.

Jacob sent Joseph from the vale of Hebron to Shechem to check on his ten older brothers who were attending Jacob's flocks. Similarly, the Lord Jesus was sent by the Father to attend to the flock of Israel (Jn. 10:14-18). C. Knapp explains in his book *A Fruitful Bough*:

Hebron means fellowship or communion. The vale suggests quiet peacefulness and rest. It was intended, I believe, to point them forward (and point us back) to the fellowship of the Son with the Father in heaven's eternal calm and peace previous to His entrance, at His incarnation, into this scene of sin and toil and sorrows."[1]

Considering past events at Shechem (Gen. 34), it is amazing that Jacob's family would venture near there, let alone send a young man there by himself. After gaining information, Joseph found his brothers at Dothan. They saw him coming from a distance because of his special coat and began plotting to murder him before he even arrived. This was the flesh at its worst – in their envy, they were willing to slay their brother and silence him forever! Dothan and Shechem are not accidental locations for the awful events of this chapter. F. W. Grant explains how these illustrate the movement of Israel from resting with the Lord through submission to wrestling with the legalism in the law:

> Now Shechem we have already had twice before us ... its undoubted uniform sense is "shoulder," which is usually considered to refer to the "position of the place on the 'saddle'".... Figuratively the shoulder finds its place as the burden-bearer, and this with the thought of service and subjection as in the blessing of Issachar afterward: "He bowed his shoulder to bear, and became a servant unto tribute;" but the burden may be one of a very different character, as it is said of the Lord, "The government shall be upon His shoulder:" the place of service and the place of power being here one. How truly so of Him whom this declares!
>
> In the first case in which we have to do with Shechem, I have sought to show that we have the former thought. The oak of Moreh (the "instructor") at the "place of Sichem," Abraham's first resting-place in the land, gives beautifully the fruitfulness of subjection to divine teaching; and here Jehovah Himself appears to him. We need seek no further for the significance of Shechem in the history of Joseph's brethren. From Abraham's place Abraham's seed had but too far wandered when the Lord came as seeking them. Zealous law-keepers they were, and to this Dothan, if I mistake not, very exactly points. It means "laws," in the sense, not of "precepts," (moral – spiritual – guidance, such as the divine law was,) but of imperial "decrees." To

Seeds of Destiny

Israel, away from God and from the path of their father after the flesh, such had the divine word become.[2]

Normally, "types" or "prints" of the Lord Jesus, like "the Rock," "the Good Shepherd," "manna," and "the serpent on the pole" are verified in the New Testament. Joseph as a "type" would be an exception to this principle; however, the analogous content of the person and work of the Messiah is clearly foreshadowed in Joseph in the next 14 chapters of Genesis. Perhaps the only other Old Testament characters that would rival Joseph's personal typology of Christ would be Isaac and Joshua. C. H. Mackintosh writes, "There is not in Scripture a more perfect and beautiful type of Christ than Joseph. Whether we view Christ as the object of the Father's love, the object of the envy of 'His own,' – in His humiliation, sufferings, death, exaltation and glory – in all, we have Him strikingly typified by Joseph."[3] From *Believers Bible Commentary*, William MacDonald writes, "Joseph is one of the most beautiful types (symbols) of the Lord Jesus Christ in the OT, though the Bible never labels him as a type. A.W. Pink lists 101 similarities between Joseph and Jesus, and Ada Habershon lists 121."[4] Pink actually devotes seven chapters of his forty-seven-chapter book *Gleanings in Genesis* to this typology.

Joseph was the beloved son of Jacob's old age. The Lord Jesus was the beloved Son of the "Ancient of Days" (Dan. 7:9; Luke 3:22). The Lord was hated by his Jewish brethren, just as Joseph was envied and despised by his brothers. In a sense, Reuben pictures Pilate's attempts to keep innocent Jesus from being put to death. Neither Joseph nor Jesus had committed any wrong that deserved their cruel treatment. They stripped Joseph of his special coat and tore it. The Roman soldiers also stripped the Lord Jesus of his clothes. Because the Lord wore a special coat without seam, the soldiers cast lots for it, but tore and divided His inner linen garment as foretold in Psalm 22:18.

> We know the love that brought Thee down –
>   Down from that bliss on high,
> To meet our ruined souls in need, On Calvary's cross to die.
> Our Savior – Jesus, Lord Thou art, Eternal is Thy love;
> Eternal, too, our songs of praise When with Thee, Lord, above.

T. P.

Joseph in the Grave
Genesis 37:20-36

His brethren cast Joseph into a hole in the ground – a pit. Jesus was buried in a rich man's tomb. The brothers all agreed to sell Joseph to the Ishmaelites for twenty pieces of silver. Judas, one of the Lord's chosen disciples, betrayed Him for thirty pieces of silver. Silver is a metal that speaks of "redemption" throughout the Bible. This is why the silver trumpets were blown on the Day of Jubilation – the one day every fifty years when all property returned to the original owners (Lev. 25:9). Why are "communion" trays commonly silver in color? Because the cups carried in the tray symbolize the believer's redemption in Christ's blood. Gold is used to symbolize deity, perfection, and holiness, while bronze is used to speak of "judgment."

At this point, Joseph probably wished he could blind the eyes of his enemies, as Elisha would do to the Syrian army encompassed about Dothan more than a millennium later. In a spiritual sense, his brothers were blind to what they were doing and to what the cost of it would be. The hard-hearted and spiritually blind Jews cried out to Pilate, *"His blood be upon us and on our children."* It is also noted that Joseph was sold into the hands of Ishmaelites. Ishmael was the one who had sought the vast inheritance of Abraham, but Isaac, his only begotten son, was the recipient. Satan once aspired to be as God and to acquire the throne of God (Isa. 14). And, for a brief period of time, the Son of God was sold into the hands of Satan and the world he controlled. The Lord Jesus referred to Satan as the *"prince of this world"* three times in John's Gospel account (Jn. 12:31, 14:30, 16:11). But, the Lord foretold that He would be victorious over Satan at the time Satan thought he was the victor (Jn. 12:31-32).

The foreshadowing of the death and burial of the Lord Jesus is strengthened by the presence of balm and myrrh (burial spices). Why

Seeds of Destiny

would the Spirit of God record only two items of cargo that these slave traders were transporting to Egypt if it were not significant? Lastly, Joseph was lifted up out of the pit alive. This is a beautiful illustration of the resurrection of Christ. His brothers would then see Joseph no more until he was reigning over Egypt, and they would be his subjects. Likewise, the last time the Jewish nation saw Christ was at Calvary, and they will see Him no more until the time that He is their King and they are His subjects – yet future (Zech. 12:10).

Joseph's brothers developed a devious and sinister tale to cover their abhorrent behavior. They killed a goat, tore Joseph's coat, and dipped the coat in the animal's blood to give the impression that Joseph had been attacked by some wild beast. These delinquents then presented the coat to their father as a "lost and found" item and asked him if it was Joseph's. Joseph's brothers' evil plot worked. Jacob recognized the coat and surmised that some wild beast had killed his son. Jacob was heartbroken and mourned his son's death for many years. Poor Jacob, he again drank from his own cup. He had deceived his father by killing a kid of goat; now his sons had done the same to him.

Perhaps Jacob's sons, as they beheld their father wail, wondered if their dastardly deed had inflicted too great a cost. If they could have rewound time, perhaps they would have treated Joseph differently. One also wonders if the Jews, after experiencing centuries of heartache, now think crucifying their Messiah was a prudent response to His offer of salvation. Yet, the Jews will continue to suffer desolation and war unto the Messiah comes back to earth the second time (Dan. 9:24-27).

Joseph arrived in Egypt, and Potiphar, an officer of Pharaoh and the captain of the guard, bought Joseph as a servant. God was with Joseph and would protect and bless him while he was in Egypt!

> Low in the grave He lay – Jesus my Saviour!
> Waiting the coming day – Jesus my Lord!
> Up from the grave He arose, With a mighty triumph o'er His foes,
> He arose a victor from the dark domain,
> And He lives forever with His saints to reign.
>
> Robert Lowry

Judah's Sin and Savior
Genesis 38

The Apostle Paul exhorts Christians only to marry in the Lord (1 Cor. 7:39) so that husbands and wives will not be spiritually unequally yoked together (2 Cor. 6:14). Although intermarriage of Jacob's family with a pagan people had been avoided, painfully so, in Genesis 34, Judah compromised and married a Canaanite woman, the daughter of Shua (Gen. 38:12). "Shua" means "riches," and "Canaanite" signifies "the merchant man." Thus, the future relationship between the Jews and the Gentiles is here initially symbolized in this first intermarriage between Judah and a Canaanite woman and their resulting children. The Gentiles would excel in commerce and obtain great riches at the expense of Jewish people. Certainly, the Jewish people have been either slaves or subservient to Gentile powers for most of their national history. Perhaps, the fact that Judah separated himself from his brethren in Genesis 38 is a "seed of destiny" fulfilled when the Jewish nation split after the death of Solomon centuries later. The tribe of Judah generally remained faithful to God, while the isolated ten northern tribes (constituting Israel) fell into idolatry.

Besides "compromise," Judah's second sin is recorded in Genesis 38:1. It is a sin that so often afflicts Christianity today: *"Judah went down from his brethren."* Judah left the fellowship of God's people (his family) and lived in Adullam (about fifteen miles northwest of Hebron) with his Canaanite wife. When God's people isolate themselves from the flock of God, they become the prey of wolves. In effect, they hang a sign around their necks that reads "Satan come and devour me."

The assembling of believers is not just a gathering of Christians, but a group of believers that is to be fitly joining together for the edification of the body in love (Eph. 4:16). In other words, it is not simply

Seeds of Destiny

attendance that is in view, but fellowship (the sharing of ourselves with others). All Christians should be in the safety of a local fellowship. The writer of Hebrews warns that we are not to forsake the assembling of ourselves together (Heb. 10:25). The simple fact of the matter is that we need each other for accountability, exhortation, ministry, prayer support, and, in general, to be built up. "Pastoral care" of the elders, and the edifying ministry of the other saints is a safeguard to the individual believer. A Christian apart from a local assembly is like a burning coal cast from the fire. He soon cools off and ceases to burn brightly for God. Believers on fire for God will ignite and kindle passion in others for the Savior and for serving Him.

Judah lived apart from his brethren for some time, as his wife bore him three sons and two of them had matured to a marrying age. Judah took a wife named Tamar for his oldest son Er. But, because Er (whose name means "enmity") was a wicked man, God slew him. Judah then gave Tamar to his second son, Onan (whose name means "iniquity"), as a wife. In the Jewish economy, it was a common practice for a brother to go unto his brother's widow and father children in the name of the deceased. This protected a family name and inheritance from being lost in the course of time. Moses actually formalized this custom later as part of the Law that Israel would follow (Deut. 25:5-10).

Onan, however, used the custom for physical pleasure instead of fathering children in the name of his brother, so God struck him dead also. It should be noted that "family planning" or "birth control" is not in view here, but the neglecting of a social custom specific to aiding widows. A "text" out of "context" is a "pretext." The point of the text is that Onan was taking advantage of Tamar for sensual reasons instead of fulfilling his legal duty and assisting her in her plight. Having lost two sons in association with Tamar would create a stressful situation in Judah's home if Tamar were to remain. So Judah instructed Tamar to remain unmarried in her father's house with widow attire upon her until Shelah, his third son (whose name means "sprout"), was old enough to marry. Perhaps Judah thought Tamar would forget the whole matter, for in time, Judah proved to be a liar. Indeed Shelah did eventually marry, but it was not to Tamar (Num. 26:20).

What is truth? Truth is that which perfectly conforms to reality. The Lord told the disciples, *"But let your communication be, Yea, yea; Nay,*

nay; for whatsoever is more than these cometh of evil" (Matt. 5:37). As before mentioned, Paul exhorts the believer to put away all lying (Eph. 4:25). The Christian should not try to distort, change, or flavor the truth. That is what Satan does – for He is the father of lies and there is no truth in him (Jn. 8:44). God wants the Christian to state what "exactly conforms to reality" and expound it in love (Eph. 4:15). Judah did not do this; he treated Tamar deceitfully. Consequently, the first two sons of Judah represent the "enmity" and "iniquity" the Jewish people have had towards Christ through the centuries, but yet, there will be at last a "sprout," a remnant, that will be restored to Christ in a future day.

It was God's intention to bring the Messiah through the descendants of Judah (Gen. 49:10). The one who cried out to his brethren to sell Joseph for twenty pieces of silver would later have a descendant – Christ – who would be betrayed for thirty pieces of silver. Since the first prophecy concerning the coming Messiah in Genesis 3, Satan's primary mission has been against the person of Christ. This attack has come in three main fronts:

(1) Attempts to destroy the family line through which the Deliver would come. Examples include: an attempt to pervert the godly line of Seth in Genesis 6, and Athaliah's attempt to kill all the seed royal (her own sons and grandsons) to obtain the throne (2 Chron. 22:10-12). However, one of the king's daughters, Jehoshabeath, protected the only remaining son of Ahaziah – Joash. He was hidden in the house of God for six years until he could take the throne from Athaliah. Joash is in the genealogies of Christ (see Matt. 1).

(2) When this was unsuccessful, direct attempts on the life of the Lord Jesus were made. When He was a child in Bethlehem, Herod attempted to kill Him by murdering all the boys two years old and younger in the area (Matt. 2). Later, attempts would be made on the Lord's life as an adult in Nazareth, when distraught Jews tried to push Him over a cliff (Lk. 4:29) and when the Jewish religious leaders sought to stone Him (Jn. 8:59, 10:31) for His alleged blasphemies.

(3) Having failed to stop Christ's completion of His redemptive work, Satan now concentrates on casting doubt on the Person of Christ, slandering His name, and detouring worshippers into idolatry or heresy.

God had a plan that would not be changed, and Tamar, seeing that she had been lied to, played the harlot to obtain her right and opportunity to bear children in the name of her husband. She had little choice in the matter, for surely superstitious reasoning would prevent any Canaanite man from marrying a woman who had been made a widow twice by mysterious events. In order not to be put to death for committing fornication, she wanted the man who was responsible for her situation to be recognized – it was Judah. Tamar knew that Judah had gone to Timnah to shear sheep and that his own wife had just died. She used this information to selectively lure Judah to lie with her. The Hebrew word to describe "harlot" *cedesha* in Genesis 38:21-22 means "one set apart." It is more likely that Tamar masqueraded as a veiled temple prostitute (in Canaanite goddess attire) rather than posing as a common harlot. Her plot worked. Judah agreed to the price of her services (a kid of goat) and presented her with a pledge that he would pay her the agreed price for her services. His pledge was his seal that hung about his neck on a cord and his staff.

Although we do not approve of Tamar's actions, she was no prostitute for hire. She simply wanted her entitlement. So after their encounter, she returned home without collecting the kid. Judah sent the goat via a friend to where Tamar had been posing as a harlot, but the friend could not find her, and the inhabitants of the area knew of no harlots. Not only was Judah a liar (Gen. 38:11, 14) and immoral (Gen. 38:16), but now he would also be seen as a hypocrite.

Judah was ready to have Tamar burned alive when he found out that she was pregnant three months later. Legally, she was under his authority and engaged to Shelah and, thus, guilty of committing adultery. But his rage soon turned to guilt when he learned that she was the mystery harlot and was carrying his baby (actually babies – twins). Judah confirmed that he had been the dishonest one, and Tamar was acquitted on the matter. Again, the line of the Messiah was hanging on the edge. We read in Matthew 1:3 that Tamar bore Perez, who is in the genealogy of Christ.

Tamar delivered twin boys. During the birthing process, a wee hand poked out through the birth canal, and the midwife tied a scarlet thread on his wrist to identify the first child born. It should be noted that the midwife was skilled in birthing matters, as she knew that there were twins prior to their birth without the benefit of a sonogram. The first son to be born, however, was not Zerah (the one with scarlet thread on his hand), but Perez. Thus, they were named after the birthing experience; Perez means "to breach," and Zerah means "scarlet." How ironic! God gave Tamar, who had only a single opportunity to become pregnant, two sons. Considering all the biological mechanics of ovulation, conception, and two male embryos being formed, the odds of this occurring naturally is extremely slim. All babies are divine miracles, but the dynamics of Tamar's pregnancy speaks of God's spectacular handiwork. A daughter for Tamar would have been wonderful, too, but a little girl baby would not have been able to continue the family name or Messianic line. Now she had two boys! David acknowledges the goodness of God in such matters in Psalms 37:4: *"Delight thyself also in the Lord, and he shall give thee the desires of thine heart."*

God seemingly confirms the same message to Tamar, through the birth of her sons, that was expressed to Rebekah concerning the birth of Esau and Jacob – the older shall serve the younger. This assertion reminds us again that God's ways are not our ways and that it would be a natural thing for the younger to serve the older, but God's system is opposite from human wisdom. There had been attempts to spoil God's design: Isaac planning to give Esau the birthright blessing, and Joseph's brothers selling him into slavery, but the birth of Tamar's twins reaffirmed God's pattern of things to come. Future kings and the Messiah Himself would come from the least likely of backgrounds!

> Behold the throne of grace! The promise calls us near!
> To seek our God and Father's face, Who loves to answer prayer.
> Beyond our utmost wants His love and power can bless:
> To praying souls He always grants more than they can express.
>
> John Newton

Seeds of Destiny

Temptation, Accusation, and Unjust Punishment
Genesis 39

Joseph's character seems to be a culmination of the best aspects of his father, grandfather and great grandfather. He possessed the faith of Abraham, the meekness of Isaac, and the resourcefulness of Jacob. Joseph proved that he was a man of integrity in this chapter. God proved that He was with Joseph and working in his life. God prospered him (Gen. 39:2-3); he was a handsome and well-favored man (Gen. 39:6), and He blessed the work of Joseph, which brought his master, Potiphar, great blessing also. Potiphar, who was the captain of Pharaoh's bodyguard, recognized he had been blessed because of Joseph's presence, so he affirmed Joseph as manager of all his affairs. The agricultural experience Joseph gained here would be of great benefit later when he was overseeing all the farming activities of Egypt.

Joseph managed and cared for everything that was Potiphar's, except his wife. However, Potiphar's wife wanted Joseph to take care of her, too. Joseph recognized that having sex with another man's wife was a great offense against God and his master, so he refused (Gen. 39:9). The Hebrew word for "officer" in Genesis 39:1 is *saris*, which is normally translated "eunuch." It is possible that Potiphar, in order to attain his high status in Pharaoh's court, willingly agreed to become a eunuch. Henry Morris writes:

> It was evidently customary in ancient pagan countries, beginning with Sumeria, to require prominent officers associated closely with the king's court to be castrated, perhaps to ensure full-hearted devotion to the duties required of them and to minimize the possibility of their taking over the kingdom by military coup to establish a dynasty of their own."[1]

This may explain to some extent Potiphar's wife's behavior, but certainly does not justify it. She was relentless with romantic advances – day after day she solicited Joseph. Day after day, Joseph held his ground and would not compromise what he knew was inappropriate and immoral. Her fury increased against Joseph with each denial. Finally, the rage of her flirtations escalated into physically aggression; she grabbed Joseph to try to force him to lay with her. Joseph responded appropriately – he fled. She retained only what she had seized hold of – his garment. Now a woman scorned, Potiphar's wife was out for revenge.

You are what you are when no one is watching. This is when our true character is witnessed. How do you guard yourself on a business trip with a member of the opposite gender or while connected to the Internet? Undisciplined thoughts easily slip into unwise speech and unholy actions. And even if you are innocent of such fantasy, your traveling companion may be the counterpart of Potiphar's wife. Joseph lived in fear of God, and we must realize deep in our hearts that we will one day suffer loss for wicked thoughts and wasted time.

Although our ultimate accountability is to the Lord, we can aid each other to do what is right through daily exhortation (Heb. 3:13), confessing our faults one to another and praying for each other in known areas of weakness (Jas. 5:16), and generally submitting ourselves to one another in the fear of God (Eph. 5:21). Fellow believers are one of the tools Christ uses presently on earth to help His beloved people to stay on the straight and narrow. Accountability is not meddling in each other's lives. It should be mutually desired, upholding the clear teaching of God's Word, and done in forbearing love, in the power of the Spirit, and for the glory of Christ.

> And let us consider one another to provoke unto love and to good works: Not forsaking the assembling of ourselves together, as the manner of some is; but exhorting one another: and so much the more, as ye see the day approaching (Heb. 10:24-25).

It would have been easy for Joseph to enjoy himself with Potiphar's wife while his master was gone. But Joseph was a moral man, who sought to please God above his desires. Rarely do extramarital affairs

Seeds of Destiny

occur as the result of a whim. They result from repetitive compromises that begin with an unchecked look, an unconfessed lustful thought, an intimate conversation, an innocent lunch date, and the slide continues downward to a hotel room or the back seat of a parked car. The cost is enormous – broken marriages and homes. The emotional damage is so immense that the children involved become scarred for life. Children growing up with one biological parent are twice as likely to drop out of school and 2.5 times as likely to become teenage mothers, according to a study by Princeton Sociology Professor Sara McLanahan.[2] These children are also less likely to make the honor roll, finish college or establish stable relationships, and more likely to get in trouble with the law. So the level of commitment a husband and wife exhibit to one another seems to directly affect the commitment children will have in their relationship to God, to their spouses, and to authority in general.

How does one avoid the threat of extramarital affairs? First, do not put yourself in compromising situations. If you must be with a member of the opposite gender for counseling, lunch or business dealings, always ensure others are present for accountability and to keep you from ever being accused of doing wrong. I once had lunch with the chief auditor of a major aerospace corporation. He advised me that 80 percent of his time was spent developing procedures that would keep innocent employees from being accused of wrong doing, and only 20 percent of his time was expended investigating potentially fraudulent people. Likewise, the believer should carefully and thoroughly think through each situation before engaging in it to ensure blamelessness and accountability: "Could I be tempted to sin by being here?" "How will this situation appear to those looking on?"

Secondly, it is possible to be put into a compromising situation that you have no control over. What did Joseph do in such a situation? **He ran.** Men, this is exactly what we should do. Do not flirt with disaster! Do not think that you are stronger than you are! Do not take a chance – just run! Paul instructs the younger Timothy, *"Flee also youthful lusts, but follow righteousness, faith, love, peace, with them that call on the Lord out of a pure heart"* (2 Tim. 2:22).

If Peter had followed these principles, he would not have put himself in a position to deny Christ. We learn in John 18:15-17 that John was known by the high priest, but Peter was not. John entered into the court of the High Priest where Jesus' "mock trial" was convened with no opportunity to deny the Lord – he was already known to be Jesus' disciple. However, Peter, after John got him into the courtyard, was now firmly positioned in a compromising situation. He was unknown to the Jews gathered there. So, when asked if he was a disciple, he had a decision to make. Would he save his own skin and deny Christ, or prove his love and identify with Christ? That courtyard possessed no temptation for John to sin but indeed was a place of stumbling for Peter. Know your weaknesses, and then do not put yourself in a situation to be tempted in an area in which you know you are weak. It is, therefore, possible for some believers to engage in some activities that other believers should keep far away from.

Throughout human history, the unrighteous have pursued two principal agendas against God's people: they have falsely accused the righteous of wrongdoing and tormented them unjustly. Both offenses occurred against Joseph. Potiphar's wife falsely accused Joseph of wrongdoing, and Potiphar judicially punished his loyal servant without a fair trial. Consequently, Joseph was cast into prison. Secondly, she slurred and insulted Joseph's heritage by calling him a "Hebrew." The Egyptians had a racial hatred for the Hebrews (Gen. 43:32), much the way the Jews would later hate the Samaritans. But God was with Joseph in his dark hour. Joseph was shown mercy while in prison and gained favor in the sight of the prison's keeper. Potiphar showed mercy to Joseph by not having him executed for his crime and also by condemning him to the King's prison where he would be well treated. Perhaps Potiphar did this because Joseph's character spoke louder than his wife's accusations. But prison was the only way to satisfy his wife's rage, to quickly alleviate the situation and to "save face" with His servants, family and friends that would certainly learn of the horrid event.

As mentioned previously, Joseph foreshadows the person of Christ and His redemptive work. Like Christ, Joseph suffers, not for sin, but for righteousness, and then attains supremacy over the world and full divine blessing. Although Jesus Christ lived purely before God and mankind, He was falsely accused of wrongdoing, not granted a fair trial, and punished as a criminal unto death. He was slandered by the religious leaders – *"you are born of a fornicator"* (Jn. 8:41), *"you are a Samaritan,"* and *"possessed by a demon"* (Jn. 8:48). But despite the

Seeds of Destiny

insults and His innocence, He willingly *"humbled Himself and became obedient unto death, even the death of the cross"* (Phil. 2:8). It was our death that He died that we might live anew in Him.

> Nailed upon Golgotha's tree – As a victim. Who is He?
> Bearing sin, but not His own, Suffering agony unknown.
> He, the promised sacrifice. For our sins has paid the price.
> Lamb of God, 'tis He, 'tis He, On the cross of Calvary.
>
> Unknown

Joseph Forgotten?
Genesis 40

Joseph seemed to be forgotten in prison, except that an all-knowing God was with him every moment of every day (Gen. 39:21). Joseph could have been bitter, depressed, or anxious, but instead he decided to be a faithful servant in his dire situation. He sought to help others and to serve them. The prison keeper entrusted Joseph with the care of all the prisoners. Why? Because, once again God was blessing Joseph, and because of the prosperity of Joseph, those in authority over him were blessed also.

Why does God bless the believer? Because the Father loves His Son, and we, being "in Christ," will then be the object of God's love and blessing. These blessings in Christ can be identified by scanning Scripture for such phrases as "in Christ," "in Jesus Christ," or "in Christ Jesus." These expressions are not found in the Gospel accounts and only once in the book of Acts. However, the Epistles, which unveil the manifold wisdom and mysteries of God concerning Christ's accomplishments, have over eighty references to these phrases. It is noted that the phrase "with Christ" speaks of positional or identification truths, while the phrase "in Christ" normally speaks of blessing resulting from our spiritual union with the Son of God.

What do we have "in Christ"?
- Rom. 3:24 – Redemption
- Rom. 8:1 – No condemnation
- Rom. 8:2 – Spirit of life (power over sin)
- Rom. 8:39 – The love of God
- Rome 12:5 – Made one in the body of Christ
- 1 Cor. 1:2 – Sanctification

Seeds of Destiny

1 Cor. 15:19	– Hope
1 Cor. 15:22	– Made alive
2 Cor. 2:24	– Triumph, by God's grace
2 Cor. 5:17	– We are a new creation
Gal. 2:4	– Liberty
Gal. 3:26	– Made a child of God
Gal. 3:28	– Equality
Eph. 1:3	– All spiritual blessings in heavenly places
Eph. 2:10	– Created unto good works
2 Tim. 2:10	– Salvation
Jude 1	– Preservation

As the believer maintains a focus on the Lord and all that we have "in Him," life's circumstances will not seem so overwhelming. What we have spiritually in Christ is not even comparable with the temporary trinkets we clutch presently on earth. If the believer determines a character shortfall exists on his part, he can make "a withdrawal" of spiritual blessings from the treasures in heaven (Eph. 1:3). He can lay hold, by faith, of all the love, grace, and peace he desires to exhibit in his own life. *"But my God shall supply all your need according to his riches in glory by Christ Jesus"* (Phil. 4:19). Those united with Christ are blessed because of that union, just as those linked with Joseph were blessed because of their association with Joseph.

Two of Pharoah's officers, his butler and baker, were put into prison and placed under Joseph's care. Given the severity of the baker's punishment later, it is suggested that Pharaoh learned of a plot to murder him – possibly through poison in his food and drink. Pharaoh probably imprisoned anyone and everyone that could possibly be involved with the coup attempt until a thorough investigation of the matter was concluded.

Each of these men had a disturbing dream. Joseph, noticing their fallen countenances, inquired of them. After learning the matter, he informed them that God knew the interpretations of their dreams, so they both confided in Joseph and described to him in detail each of their dreams. It was bad news for the baker. He would be found guilty and be put to death by hanging in three days. But the butler would be found innocent and restored to his position in Pharaoh's court. These events unfolded just as Joseph had said they would. The Lord had given a "three-day" sign from the gloom of a dark dungeon to manifest His glory. 1,500 years later, the Lord would give the Pharisees a similar "three day" sign to acknowledge His victory at Calvary. It was the sign of His resurrection, for after three days He would be raised up from a dark grave unto the right hand of Majesty on high (Matt. 12:38-41).

Joseph had one request of the butler, who would soon be restored unto Pharaoh's presence: *"But think on me when it shall be well with thee, and show kindness, I pray thee, unto me, and make mention of me unto Pharaoh, and bring me out of this house"* (Gen. 40:14). The Lord Jesus said something very similar on the night before He died when he instituted the "Lord's Supper." In essence, the Lord was saying, "When you have been blessed by My death and resurrection, and it is well with you; please call Me into remembrance and show kindness unto Me by lifting up praise and worship heavenward."

Matthew Henry provides the following devotional remarks having one eye upon the butler and the other inspecting our own ungrateful and forgetful hearts:

> The chief butler remembered not Joseph, but forgot him. Joseph had deserved well at his hands, yet he forgot him. We must not think it strange, if in this world we have hatred shown us for our love, and slights for our kindness. See how apt those who are themselves at ease are to forget others in distress. Joseph learned by his disappointment to trust in God only. We cannot expect too little from man, nor too much from God. Let us not forget the sufferings, promises, and love of our Redeemer. We blame the chief butler's ingratitude to Joseph, yet we ourselves act much more ungratefully to the Lord Jesus. Joseph had but foretold the chief butler's enlargement, but Christ wrought out ours; he mediated with the King of kings for us; yet we forget him, though often reminded of him, and though we have promised never to forget him. Thus ill do we requite Him, like foolish people and unwise.[1]

We are creatures that are forgetful. The book of Deuteronomy, which means "second law," was dispensed by God to His people in an attempt to ensure that they would not forget Him or His laws after they were enjoying the blessings of the Promised Land. *"Thou shalt remember"* is a command repeated again and again in Deuteronomy. Dear

Seeds of Destiny

Christian, when you are full (blessed), beware lest you forget the Lord, who brought you forth out of the world and from the bondage of sin (derived from Deut. 6:11-12). It is so easy to be dependent upon God through trials, but so convenient to forget Him when life's pilgrimage is smooth. God uses our difficulties in an attempt to keep us near to Himself.

> I need Thee every hour, Most gracious Lord;
> No tender voice like Thine can peace afford.
> I need Thee every hour, Stay Thou near by;
> Temptations lose their power when Thou art nigh
> I need Thee every hour, In joy or pain;
> Come quickly and abide, or life is vain.
>
> Annie S. Hawks

Joseph Forgets
Genesis 41

Now, it was Pharaoh's turn to dream dreams, and similar to the experience of the butler and baker two years earlier, he was greatly bewildered by two series of mental images. Not only did Pharaoh not know the meaning of his dreams, but none of his wise men could interpret the dreams either. Then, the butler remembered Joseph and how he had told him the correct interpretation of his dream while in prison. After Pharaoh learned of Joseph, he was summoned from prison for the purpose of interpreting Pharaoh's dreams.

After Joseph made himself presentable for Pharaoh's presence, he was brought before him. Joseph spoke boldly to Pharaoh concerning his dream: *"God shall give Pharaoh an answer of peace"* (Gen. 41:16); *"God hath shown Pharaoh what he is about to do"* (Gen. 41:25, 28). In Egypt, Pharaoh was considered a "god;" therefore, to speak of the one true God was inviting death.

Joseph informed Pharaoh of the meaning of his dream. There would be seven years of plenty, then seven years of famine. God doesn't reveal problems without solutions in mind, so Joseph then conveyed to Pharaoh the appropriate course of action to save his empire: Appoint a wise man to oversee all of Egypt's farming and have him store up a fifth of the harvest each year for later use. Pharaoh agreed with the interpretation and plan, and could not think of anyone more wise and prudent for the task of saving Egypt than God's very own messenger.

Although God communicated His word to humanity in various means and manners in past ages, His ultimate message to us came via His Son (Heb. 1:1-2). Interestingly, the prophets of old spoke of the coming of a Redeemer and a Savior, but they did not understand what their utterances meant (1 Pet. 1:10-11). Nor were the heavenly angels

Seeds of Destiny

informed about God's plan of redemption (1 Pet. 1:12). It was even a mystery to Satan, for he would not have sought to crucify Christ, if he had understood God's plan of salvation (1 Cor. 2:7-8). Jesus Christ was God's ultimate message and messenger in one person. Even a pagan king like Pharaoh saw something in Joseph, God's messenger, that caused him to heed the warning.

It is grieving to see so many souls ignore God's warning of impending judgment upon wickedness. Praise God, He did not just inform Pharaoh of the problem, but He also revealed the solution to resolve the problem. What consolation would there be in Romans 6:23 if only the brutal reality of our condemnation was acknowledged without any hope of resolution? *"For the wages of sin is death!"* O beloved of the Lord, be glad the verse does not stop there. *"But the gift of God is eternal life through Jesus Christ, our Lord."* God's spiritual choice to all humanity is the same physical choice offered Pharaoh: "heed the warning now and live later, or ignore the warning now and die later." Which will it be, Pharaoh? Pharaoh chose to live! Those who heed the warning against sin and choose the solution – Christ, will live also.

Joseph was exalted from the prison to the second position of authority over the whole kingdom (Gen. 41:40). He received an exalted name from Pharaoh, "Zaphenath-paneah," which meant "the revealer of secrets." When his chariot passed through the streets of Egypt, a herald passed before his chariot shouting, *"Bow the knee, bow the knee."* In seed form, Joseph's exaltation clearly foreshadows that of Christ. Proportionately to the low extent that the Lord was humbled as a servant unto death, He was exalted in heaven by His Father after His resurrection. In a future day, He will be recognized by all as Lord of lords and King of kings.

> *Wherefore, God also hath highly exalted Him, and given Him a name which is above every name, that at the name of Jesus every knee should bow, of things in heaven and things in earth, and things under the earth, and that every tongue should confess that Jesus Christ is Lord, to the glory of God the Father* (Phil. 2:9-11).

Perhaps Potiphar's wife was doing a bit of shopping one day, and while in the market place, she heard the herald cry out *"bow the knee."* Knowing the consequences of not imparting homage and observing the chariot approaching, she would have quickly bowed the knee to the chariot's occupants. Imagine her horror to gaze up into the face of the innocent man she had falsely accused. She surely feared for her life. Joseph, however, was not out for vengeance; he was about the work of saving Egypt. Egypt is a symbol of the world throughout Scripture. *"For God so loved the world that He gave His only begotten Son, that whosoever believeth in Him should not perish, but have everlasting life. For God sent not His Son into the World to condemn the world; but that the world through Him might be saved"* (Jn. 3:16-17). We understand the "world" to mean the people in the world (that part of creation made in God's likeness). For Christ tasted death for every man (Heb. 2:9) and was the propitiation for all of humanity (1 Jn. 2:2). He did not die for a condemned world system controlled by Satan, as some teach.

We read of "forgetting" twice in this chapter. First, the butler forgot about Joseph for two years after he was released from prison. Then, Joseph, after he was released from prison and exalted in Egypt, was able to forget the thirteen years of being a slave and a prisoner. Joseph was seventeen years old when he was sold into slavery and was thirty years old when he was exalted in Egypt (Gen. 37:2, 41:46). Note that, after the exaltation of Joseph, Pharaoh gave Joseph a wife and a new name. Likewise, the Father will give His Son, the Lord Jesus, a bride in heaven (the Church – Eph. 5:27) and a name above all other names. Joseph did not receive his bride while a servant or a prisoner but in the dignity of royal status.

How do we know that Joseph was able to forget the past? He named his first son "Manasseh," which means "forgetting." He understood God's orchestration of his life and knew that all the evil that had happened to him was for his good and had allowed God to bring a greater blessing upon others. He, therefore, named his second son "Ephraim," which means "fruitfulness." What a testimony of God's forgiving grace.

The word *charizomai* is found twenty-four times in the New Testament. It is translated as various forms of "forgive" fourteen times. Interestingly, only two of these fourteen references are found in the Gospel accounts (Both are contained in one parable in Luke 7.); the remaining occurrences are contained in the Epistles. *Charizomai* means "to bestow a favor unconditionally or to freely give." It expresses the

Seeds of Destiny

type of unconditional *releasing* attitude a Christian should maintain when offended by others. To freely release the matter means that one does not seek revenge, vengeance or become resentful.

The mechanics of forgiveness are mainly addressed in the Gospel accounts and are associated with a different Greek word – *aphiemi*, which means "to send forth, send away." For example, Matthew 18:15-18 informs us how to go about problem resolution with others, while Luke 17:3 instructs us not to *declare* forgiveness until the offending party has repented.

Why did the Holy Spirit mainly use *aphiemi* in the gospel accounts and *charizomai* in the epistles to speak of forgiveness? Apparently, because the Epistles more fully express the motive of forgiveness. *"Forbearing one another, and forgiving one another, if any man have a quarrel against any **even as Christ forgave you**, so also do ye"* (Col. 3:13). *"And be ye kind one to another, tenderhearted, forgiving one another, **even as God for Christ's sake hath forgiven you**"* (Eph. 4:32).

In view of the believer's immense debt of sin that has been forgiven because of Calvary, we must be ready to forgive those who offend us. This will free us from being in bondage to bitterness and enable us to pray for those who despitefully use us. The unresolved matter is, thus, immediately left in the Lord's hands. This liberating activity allows a believer to move the offense into the background of their thinking and not keep it in the foreground. The unresolved issue, though not forgotten, does not rule one's daily life, for it has been turned over to the Lord.

When the offending individual does confess his or her wrongdoing, we have already been well prepared to personally declare the matter forgiven. In light of the huge debt we have been forgiven, we must be willing to forgive the petty offenses, in comparison, of others (Matt. 6:14-15, Matt. 18:22-35). Let us immediately release offenses to the Lord, and then be ready to declare forgiveness when those who have hurt us confess their sin. It is not God-honoring or biblical to declare forgiveness without the offending party confessing their wrong doing and repenting of it.

We close this chapter with Pharaoh directing hungry souls to Joseph for food during the famine. Not only was Egypt to be preserved by Joseph, but all the surrounding countries came to him for food that they might live. The Lord Jesus said, *"I am the way, the truth and the life; no man cometh unto the Father but by Me"* (Jn. 14:6). Many people are crying out to God for help, but they have no spiritual connection with the Father for Him to act on their behalf. It is only through Jesus Christ that salvation is obtained. Peter clearly declared this truth to the Jewish leaders after Christ's ascension into heaven: *"Neither is there salvation in any other: for there is none other name under heaven given among men, whereby we must be saved"* (Acts 4:12).

Joseph did not compromise his integrity, but he lived justly before God despite the evil that was rendered against him. Joseph attended to his own character and allowed God to protect his reputation! What a great example to follow – for it is exactly what the Lord Jesus did!

> The circumstances amid which you live determine your reputation; the truth you believe determines your character.
> Reputation is what you are supposed to be; character is what you are.
> Reputation is the photograph; character is the face.
> Reputation comes over one from without; character grows up from within.
> Reputation is what you have when you come to a new community; character is what you have when you go away.
> Reputation is made in a moment; character is built in a lifetime.
> Reputation makes you rich or makes you poor; character makes you happy or makes you miserable.
> Reputation is what men say about you on your tombstone; character is what angels say about you before the throne of God.
>
> William Hersey Davis

Seeds of Destiny

Joseph Tests His Brothers
Genesis 42

What will happen after the Lord is exalted and united with His Gentile bride? Israel will be tested and refined during the Tribulation Period – a time called "Jacob's Trouble."

Alas! for that day is great, so that none is like it: it is even the time of Jacob's trouble; but he shall be saved out of it. For it shall come to pass in that day, saith the Lord of hosts, that I will break his yoke from off thy neck, and will burst thy bonds, and strangers shall no more serve themselves of him: But they shall serve the Lord their God, and David their king, whom I will raise up unto them (Jer. 30:7-9).

This scenario of events is expressed in Genesis 42. The once rejected Joseph was exalted with his Gentile bride, and he would now test his brethren, who had held him in contempt, to see if their hearts had changed. Yet, the whole time they were being tested, Joseph preserved them through the seven years of famine and even settled them into a place of blessing during the trial. Moreover, Christ will refine, preserve and protect a remnant of the Jews from the Anti-Christ during the seven years of tribulation yet future (Rev. 12:5-6, 12:13-17; Zech. 12:8-10, 14:1-7).

Food was scarce everywhere (Gen. 41:57). The fact that this was a famine of famines is verified by the five specific references to a "severe famine" in Genesis 41 through 47. Abraham had lived through a famine by going to Egypt to live. Isaac had done so by trusting the Lord to take care of him in Gerar – part of the Promised Land. Now Jacob was in a severe seven-year food shortage, and he was faced with the simple reality that his family was in a life or death situation. Realizing that there was grain in Egypt, he sent his ten oldest sons on a 250 mile trip to Egypt to purchase grain so *"that we may live, and not die."*

The Jewish people have gone through immense trials since the Babylonian conquest in 605 BC. They have endured the destruction of Jerusalem in 70 AD by Roman armies and the more recent Holocaust during World War II. The Babylonian invasion and occupation of Israel, which destroyed Solomon's temple, was the result of Jewish idolatry and the ignoring of God's laws (Ezek. 36:17-19, 2 Chron. 36:14-21). The desolation of the Jewish people since the time of Christ's first coming is the result of their rejection of Him as their Messiah (Dan. 9:25-26; Matt. 23:34-39). Yet, the Tribulation Period will be the worst oppression that the Jewish people have faced or will ever face. Zechariah 13:7-9 proclaims that two-thirds of the Jews will be murdered during the Tribulation Period. Matthew 24:21-22 states that it will be the most brutal time mankind will ever know, and if the Lord tarried more than seven years to return to the earth, nobody would be found alive. It is this time period that is symbolized in the narrative of Genesis 42-47.

Joseph's older brothers arrived in Egypt only to learn that they could buy grain through just one man – Joseph (Gen. 41:57). They found their way to Joseph and bowed down before him before voicing their request to buy grain. Thus, Joseph's dream recorded in Genesis 37:7 was fulfilled. Joseph recognized them but did not reveal himself to them. Although he had released his heart from malice, he needed to ascertain whether they had remorseful hearts for their evil done to him some twenty years earlier. Then, he would reveal himself and declare his forgiveness to them.

His brothers told him the truth about their family. However, the test was just beginning, and Joseph accused them of being spies and thrust them in prison. After three days, they were brought before him again. Joseph told his brothers that if they brought the missing youngest son (Benjamin), of whom they had spoken of earlier, back to Egypt, it would prove that they were not spies and were telling the truth. Just to ensure that they would journey to Egypt again with Benjamin, one of them would remain in prison until their return. Not knowing that Joseph could understand every word they were saying, Reuben rebuked his brethren for their evil deed against Joseph and declared that this was retribution for their crime. Joseph chose Simeon to be the hostage, and he was bound before his brothers' eyes. Why was Simeon chosen? Perhaps, in Reuben's absence, he was the next oldest son of Jacob present when Joseph was betrayed. Joseph was, therefore, holding him accountable.

Not only was Joseph testing their hearts for repentance, but he was also going to check their integrity. He ordered his men to return each man's money in the sack of grain they had purchased. In "type," this action was clearly signifying that "the bread of life" could not be bought with money but must be freely received from the Giver of life. The Lord Jesus said, *"I am the bread of life; he that cometh to Me shall never hunger, and he that believeth on Me shall never thirst"* (Jn. 6:35). The money was discovered in their sacks of grain while traveling home. What a perplexing trip this had become. As Jacob's sons informed their father about the sequence of events during their trip to Egypt, poor Jacob was overcome with self-pity. He refused to allow Benjamin, the only son of Rachel still alive (he thought), to return with them to Egypt. Reuben reminded Jacob that they could not return to Egypt without Benjamin. Reuben offered to take Benjamin back to Egypt in his personal protection to get Simeon out of prison and was willing to put the lives of his two sons up for surety that he would return with Benjamin.

Certainly, Joseph longed to reveal himself to his brothers, to embrace them, and to tell them that he forgave them, but the timing was not yet right. More testing and refining was yet required to create the most benefit from the circumstance. What is the application for us? Love, not pity or sentiment, moves God's hand into action. God desires what is best for us, which sometimes means a "tough love" approach when we are willfully disobeying what we know is right. Let us mimic God in our love to others. Our love should always have what is best for the recipient in mind, not what will be best to relieve his or her sorrow and pain.

As an example, the Lord Jesus could have healed Lazarus and kept him from dying, but He chose to arrive at the scene of mourning after Lazarus had been dead four days. The Lord was executing the will of His Father and knew that He would obtain more glory by raising Lazarus from death than by just healing his infirmity. The Lord also knew that, consequently, many Jews would believe on Him because of the miracle. The Lord could have been moved by sentiment for the bereaved or by love for all those who would enjoy the greater blessing by receiving salvation. Sometimes people need to drink from their own cup of consequences to learn a life-changing lesson instead of a believer preempting the hand of God in the situation. Let us be motivated by true love and what is best for the person rather than taking pity on the circumstances.

'Tis mystery all! The Immortal dies; Who can explore His strange design?
In vain the first born seraph tries to sound the depths of love divine.
'Tis mercy all! Let earth adore, Let angel minds inquire no more.
Long my imprisoned spirit lay fast bound in sin and nature's night;
Thine eye diffused a quickening ray, I woke, the dungeon flamed with light;
My chains fell off, my heart was free, I rose, went forth, and followed Thee.

Charles Wesley

"All" Brothers Come for Dinner
Genesis 43

The severe famine continued in the land into the second year. In the course of time, Jacob's family, servants and animals devoured the grain they had secured in Egypt. Finally, the inevitable day that had been tormenting Jacob's soul arrived. He knew his family needed to eat, and Egypt was the only place where grain could be found. Judah reminded his father that they could not return to Egypt without Benjamin – a fact Jacob was painfully aware of. To encourage his father in the matter, Judah pledged his own life as a guarantee that he would return Benjamin to his father once their business in Egypt was completed. Jacob had only one choice – to trust God with the life of his youngest son. So, he sent Benjamin with his other nine sons back to Egypt. He also sent double money for the grain and a gift of nuts, honey, balm and myrrh to soften the heart of the austere Egyptian leader who had dealt so harshly with his family.

The brethren arrived in Egypt and presented themselves before Joseph. After Joseph beheld Benjamin, he instructed the ruler of his house to direct his brothers to his home and to prepare lunch for them, but they were not to dine until he arrived. What did Joseph's brothers think about their luncheon engagement? They believed that the matter was connected with the money found in their sacks after their last trip to Egypt and that they were destined to all become slaves as a result of it. However, the ruler over Joseph's house settled their minds by stating that he had received their money (implying that their account was paid) and that their God had blessed them with the money in their sacks.

When Joseph arrived home for lunch, his brothers again bowed the knee before him and then once more he questioned them about Jacob and Benjamin. Joseph had deeply longed to see Benjamin and to be restored to his brethren. For twenty-two years, he had held back the tears, but now no levee of royal composure could hinder the floodwaters of his melting heart. He was a man of great authority and, therefore, could not be seen as weak; thus, he removed himself to a private chamber to weep. Only after the tears were dried and he had washed his face did he again return to finish his lunch. Yet, being an Egyptian, he could not sit with his brethren to eat – for it was an abomination for an Egyptian to eat with a Hebrew (Gen. 43:32). So Joseph ate with the Egyptians, while his brethren dined at a different table and, to their amazement, were seated around the table in the order of their birth. This arrangement was made even more mysterious when Benjamin received five times as much food as the others had. Yet, there was enough for everyone. All the brothers ate their fill and were merry.

Benjamin was given a place of prominence before his brethren while the ruler, his brother Joseph, sat at another table with Egyptians. It is possible that the foreshadowing of the first king of Israel, Saul, who was a Benjaminite, is in view here.

The tears of Joseph were both a testimony of the sorrow of his rejection and the forgiving love he desired to show in restoration. Likewise, the Lord Jesus was heartbroken over Jewish rejection and wept over them in sorrow knowing the consequence of their rejection – the destruction of Jerusalem (Lk. 19:41). *"O Jerusalem, Jerusalem, thou that killest the prophets, and stonest them which are sent unto thee, how often would I have gathered thy children together, even as a hen gathereth her [chicks] under her wings, and ye would not"* (Matt. 23:37)! However, there is a coming day when Israel will be restored to God. There will be great weeping on that day also, but these will be the tears of restoration and joy (Zech. 12:10; Hos. 2:19-23). The Bible does not say that there will no tears in heaven, as some have taught. What the Bible states is that God will wipe away our tears once we are in His presence (Rev. 7:17, 21:4). What believer could possibly have a dry eye when they behold their Savior face-to-face for the first time!

> Face to face with Christ my Savior, Face to face – what will it be –
> When with rapture I behold Him, Jesus Christ who died for me?
> Only faintly now I see Him, with the darkling veil between;
> But a blessed day is coming, when His glory shall be seen.
>
> Carrie E. Breck

Seeds of Destiny

The Final Test
Genesis 44

It started out as a great day for Joseph's brethren: They had regained Simeon in good health. They had satisfied the Egyptian ruler's doubts concerning their integrity; they had been fed a fabulous meal; they were acquiring an ample supply of grain, and soon they would be returning home to Jacob, with Benjamin. It also was a great day for Joseph as he was reunited with Benjamin. Joseph had witnessed the repentant hearts and true regret in his brothers for their evil deed against him during their first trip to Egypt. His brothers had proven this trip that they were men of integrity in that they returned the money for the grain that they had found in their sacks. Before, they had been willing to trade his life into slavery – a living death – for twenty pieces of silver. Now one final test remained. Would they be willing to sacrifice themselves for the benefit of another?

Joseph delivered to his brothers all the grain they could haul back to Canaan. However, he again commanded the steward of his house to place his brothers' money back into their grain sacks and also his silver cup in Benjamin's sack. The sun was shining brightly upon Joseph's brethren the morning they departed Egypt for home. Yet, they did not travel far before Joseph's steward overtook them and accused them of stealing his master's silver cup. Joseph's brothers were irritated by this accusation and boasted of their past record of honesty to manifest their innocence. They were so certain that they were innocent of the crime that they agreed to become slaves if the cup was found in their possession and that the one found with the cup should be put to death. A search was made, and the cup was found with Benjamin. The brothers were dismayed and were compelled to reload their asses and return to the city to face the wrath of Joseph.

Would Joseph's brothers pass the test? Yes, Judah remembered his pledge and stepped forward to explain to Joseph that Benjamin was a special child to his father and that he feared that his father would die of sorrow if he was not returned. He then offered himself as a substitute for Benjamin. Judah, the very one who was bent on selling Joseph into slavery, was now offering himself as a perpetual slave in exchange for the life of Benjamin. The Lord Jesus said that there is no greater act of love than for a man to give his life for another (Jn. 15:13). Then, He continued by instructing His disciples to love others with this type of love – the same love He demonstrated to them by dying for them (Jn. 15:12-14).

F. W. Grant observes that the entire typology situation before us is centered in Benjamin:

> The key of this typical interpretation is to be in this. Joseph is, as we know, Christ once rejected and suffering, now exalted: this is He whom Israel does not know. A Christ triumphant simply and reigning upon earth is the Benjamin who is found among them, whether in the days of the Lord's rejection or the latter days. The conqueror they were prepared for; the Sufferer – not knowing their own deep need – they have refused. Yet the two are really one: even Benjamin was first Benoni; and for them the Conqueror cannot be till they receive the Sufferer; not the faith of a sufferer merely, but the One who has been this. Power lies with Joseph, not with Benjamin. But Joseph's heart longs after Benjamin: Christ longs to display this character of power for them; but for this they must be brought to repentance, and He uses the ideal, prophetical Messiah to bring their hearts back to Himself the true one.[1]

Judah's heart is stirred and swells with anguish, but his agony for Benjamin is transformed into astonishment by the revelation of Joseph. For now his brethren know him as he truly is – their brother whom they despised and treated so rudely. He is also the king that will preserve their lives during the great famine.

> *And it shall come to pass in that day, that I will seek to destroy all the nations that come against Jerusalem. And I will pour upon the house of David, and upon the inhabitants of Jerusalem, the spirit of grace and of supplications: and they shall look upon Me whom they have pierced, and they shall mourn for Him, as one mourneth for his only*

son, and shall be in bitterness for Him, as one that is in bitterness for his firstborn (Zech 12:9-10).

This moment represents the latter period of the "Tribulation" when Israel will be restored unto God. This event is spoken of many times in Scripture, but nowhere more poetically than Hosea 5:15: *"I [God] will go and return to My place, till they [Israel] acknowledge their offence, and seek My face; in their affliction they will seek Me **early**."* Is it coincidental that it was morning (Gen. 44:3) when Joseph's brothers returned to him and were restored to him?

The Lord Jesus will whisk the Church home without being visibly seen, but when He returns the second time in all His glory to destroy wickedness and reign in righteousness, every eye will see Him (Matt. 24:30; Rev. 1:7). To the Church, He is the bright and morning star (Rev. 22:16) that shines forth the hope of Rapture. But there is a coming day when the "Sun" shall rise in His full fury from the east (Matt. 24:27), and the entire world shall witness His glory. So immense will be the illumination of His presence in the world that even the intensity of the noon day sun will not hold a candle to Him (Rev. 21:23, 22:5).

> How bright that blessed hope! Jesus will come!
> Let us our heads lift up, Jesus will come!
> Morning so bright and clear,
> Mansions of God appear,
> Sin shall not enter there, Jesus will come.
>
> Edward Denny

Come Near to Me
Genesis 45:1-4

Joseph now knew that his brothers had changed. Seeing the pain and sorrow that Jacob had gone through with losing Joseph, they were determined not to let their father suffer that kind of loss again. They had come to Joseph out of dire need and, in the process of having that need met, had shown that they were truly repentant men of integrity and not lovers of themselves. Joseph now discloses to them who he really is and invites them to *"come near to me."* How sweet the close fellowship and communion with Christ is.

The path Joseph's brothers trod mimics the same course a sinner journeys to become a disciple of Christ. We come to Christ's cross because of need and in repentance, then we leave with another cross – one, which requires personal and practical crucifixion of fleshy lusts daily. This means learning Christ and living Christ – this is true discipleship.

The Lord gave a wonderful appeal, as recorded in Luke 14:15-24, for those desiring to join Him in His kingdom. The Lord had prepared a great supper (symbolizing His provision for our essential need) and invited everyone to come and dine with Him (representing the gospel message). The invitations went out; however, some made excuses and rejected the Lord's request. There were some engrossed in materialism, some with careers and business arrangements, while others were preoccupied with personal relationships.

Who was it that desired to be occupied with the Savior and accept His gracious invitation? The poor, the sick, the outcast of society. These received forgiveness of sins and were healed. The Lord boldly proclaimed to the Pharisees, *"They that [are well] need not a physician, but they that are sick. But go ye and learn what that meaneth, I will have mercy, and not sacrifice; for I am not come to call the [self] righteous, but sinners to repentance"* (Matt. 9:12-13). The Lord came to heal the spiritually sick from a disease called sin, but the great Physician will force no one to be healed if they want to reject the cure for the deadly disease of sin.

Many compulsive followers swarmed in behind Christ after this great appeal. However, the enormous following grieved the Lord. Why? Is this not what He wanted – a throng of followers? We read in Luke 14:25-35 that the Lord turned to face the crowds and spoke of "being." The next step after believing and becoming a child of God is to "be" His disciple, not just a follower. John 14:15 records the Lord's plea, *"If ye love Me, keep My commandments."* Is there any greater way to show the Lord you love Him than by doing what He says to do?

Samuel spoke the answer well, *"to obey [God] is better than sacrifice"* (1 Sam. 15:22). Obedience can be forced, but submission is a heart issue, a matter of the will. The Christian experience is not a matter of Christ being in your heart, but of Christ having your heart. "Being" in fellowship with God is dependent on giving Him your will. Submission is the key to "being." Notice the Lord's appeals to "be":

> Luke 14:26 – *"If any man come to Me, and hate not his father, and mother, and wife, and children, and brethren and sisters, yea and his own life also, he cannot **be** My disciple."* From the parallel account in Matthew 10:34-39, we understand that the word "hate" is a comparative term. Our love for the Lord should be so great that any natural affection we might have for another would, comparatively, seem like hate.
>
> Luke 14:27 – *"And whosover doth not bear his cross, and come after Me, cannot **be** My disciple."* The cross was a symbol of shame, reproach, and death. Christ suffered these for us; now He asks the believer to suffer the same for Him.
>
> Luke 14:33 – *"So likewise, whosoever he be of you that forsaketh not all that he hath, he cannot **be** My disciple."*
>
> Matt. 10:25 – *"It is enough for the disciple that he **be** as his [Teacher], and the servant as his Lord."*

Devotions in Genesis

> Matt. 11:28-30 – *"Come unto Me, all ye that labor and are heavy laden, and I will give you rest. Take My yoke upon you, and **learn of Me**; for I am meek and lowly in heart, and ye shall find rest unto your souls. For My yoke is easy, and My burden is light."*

> Summarized in Luke 9:23-24 – *"If any man will come after Me, let him deny himself and take up his cross daily, and follow Me. For whosoever will save his life shall lose it; but whosoever will lose his life for My sake, the same shall save it."*

A disciple is a "learner," which is what the word "disciple" means. The Lord gives the invitation to "learn of Himself" in Matthew 11:28. The disciple is an apprentice that never finishes learning how to be like His Master. "Being" a disciple of Christ is dynamic and active. "Becoming" has the sense of arrival and promotes comfort and complacency. This is why the Lord talked about "being" His disciples instead of "becoming" His disciples. A "disciple" is a title given to those actively pursuing, forsaking, and following principles to become like Christ. In the Christian experience, it is not enough to be a Christ-one (a Christian); one should long to be Christ-like. It is coming to Christ for salvation, then going on with Christ through life afterwards.

The Lord's message on true discipleship dispersed the people. In general, the crowds followed Him no more. Only a few loyalists were willing to make the necessary sacrifices to be His disciples. These disciples *"forsook all, and followed Him"* (Lk. 5:11), including their professions and families (Mk. 1:16-20). **Forsaking** must occur before **following**. Otherwise, there are too many anchors to the old life, which will hinder close exposure to the Savior.

The Lord grew weary of shallow followers; He wanted true disciples. He desired quality in consecration, not a large quantity of half-hearted patriots. Where do you stand in that crowd of followers? Beside the Savior? Perhaps, peeking in behind a few folks to hide your hand in the cookie jar of indulgence? Or perhaps, you are too afraid to stand anywhere near Him knowing that His very meek and gracious presence would bring shame to your shallow allegiance? God had worked in the hearts of Joseph's brothers to bring about change. They had been refined and tested, and their faith was found genuine. Likewise, God's people today, if they have truly embraced the Savior, should be

Seeds of Destiny

changed! Despite refining hardships and trials, they should live for Christ!

While fishing with my sons from the shore of a beautiful Wisconsin lake, we met a mother and son venturing out to do some fishing in a rowboat. Some time later, they began the trip back to shore. However, after significant rowing, the exhausted mother had barely moved the boat from its original spot. As she was resting, I yelled out to her, "pull up your anchor." She laughed at her silly oversight and finally navigated home. The Lord clearly taught "forsaking and following" in discipleship. Everything we seek to hold on to in this life will be an anchor to our spiritual progression homeward. How silly will our oversights seem in eternity?

>Jesus Christ, grow Thou in me,
>And all things else recede;
>My heart be daily nearer Thee,
>From sin be daily freed.
>
>Make this poor self grow less and less,
>Be Thou my life and aim;
>O make me daily, through Thy grace,
>More meet to bear Thy name.
>
>Johann C. Lavater

"But God"
Genesis 45:5-28

After the first brief encounter with his brothers, Joseph had three more dialogues with them. In each of these three meetings, he was moved to tears. On the first two occasions, he removed himself from the room to weep in solitude, but now he commanded the Egyptians to leave the room, and he wept in front of his brothers. Joseph's heart was so full, and his anguish so overwhelming that even the Egyptians heard him sobbing from another room. Joseph identified himself to his brothers, and the first order of business was not to rebuke them for their evil, for he knew they were repentant, but to inquire about his father. This inquiry reminds us of the special relationship that the Lord Jesus has with His Father.

The night before the Lord died, He declared to His disciples: *"But that the world may know that I love the Father, and as the Father gave Me commandment, even so I do."* (Jn. 14:31). He proved His love for the Father at Calvary. He proved by His life on earth that He loved the Father, and twice the Father acknowledged from heaven His love for His Son (at His baptism and transfiguration).

The Lord could only do what He saw the Father do (Jn. 5:19). He did nothing but the Father's will (Jn. 5:30, 6:38). He could only declare the doctrine of the Father (Jn. 7:16). The Lord Jesus did only what the Father had taught Him to do (Jn. 8:28). He sought not His own glory but only the glory of the Father (Jn. 8:50). These facts of Scripture should put to rest the slanderous teaching that Jesus Christ could have sinned. He is God, and God cannot sin. He was externally solicited to sin but not internally in His own members. There was and is nothing in His members that lusts or responds as our fallen flesh does.

Seeds of Destiny

The man Jesus Christ was created "holy" humanity (Lk. 1:35), not the same as Adam, who was made "innocent" humanity (Eccl. 7:29). Adam and everyone fathered by Adam are infected by sin. Sin was an intruder and not part of what God created in humanity. It is sin within our bodies that continually pulls us down into our own pride and lusts (1 Jn. 2:16). Let us not demean Christ by saying, "He knows how I feel" after we have been lusting in our minds about some strange woman or a second piece of cherry cheesecake. The Lord was tempted externally, but was "without sin" (or better translated "sin apart" – Heb. 4:15). The Lord could look upon a woman with His eyes and not lust after her in His heart – the lust of our flesh that resulted from the fall of man was not within Him.

Scripture informs us that Joseph's brothers were terrified at his presence. Joseph encouraged them to come close, to embrace him, and to not be grieved concerning their past sin against him. Genesis 45:5 demonstrates how God mysteriously uses the free will of man for sovereign purpose. Joseph's brethren had sold him into slavery because God had sent him to preserve their lives. God's sovereignty is not an attribute of His character but describes His relationship with His creation. Before creation, God was not sovereign because there was nothing to control. God is completely sovereign over creation and all His creatures. He consistently demonstrates His foreknowledge and sovereignty through invoking His plan of redemption by controlling the failures of men to bring about the fullest blessing to humanity. This aspect is clearly seen in the life of Joseph. Joseph had perfect peace and trust in God's control of his life. *"And we know that all things work together for good to them that love God, to them who are the called according to His purpose"* (Rom. 8:28). This is as true for us as it was for Joseph, even though we may not be compensated until we are fully conformed to the image of God's Son.

God's sovereignty in bringing about His plan for redemption is often seen in the phrase *"but God"* (Gen. 45:8, 50:20). It occurs some forty-three times in the Bible. This is the third time in Genesis. Joseph acknowledged his time in Egypt was not solely through man's power or deceit, "but God" working the matter out to bring a wider blessing to humanity. In what other circumstances in Genesis is God's sovereign activity seen specifically through this phrase? When God intervened after Abimelech took Sarah into his harem (Gen. 20:3). When Laban tried to take advantage of Jacob through business dealings (Gen. 31:7). In the foremost act of divine intervention into humanity's plight: *"**But God** commendeth His love toward us in that, while we were yet sinners, Christ died for us"* (Rom. 5:8). Believer, be very thankful for this little phrase "but God," in Scripture – without it, there would be no hope.

Joseph then commanded his brethren to promptly notify his father that he was alive, *"tell my father of all my glory in Egypt"* (Gen. 45:13), and to come back to Egypt to live in the land of Goshen for there were still five more years of famine. Telling the Father of all the revealed glories of His Son should be the believer's occupation also. Joseph again, while embracing them, wept upon them. Four times he has been moved to tears in their company: twice apart from them in another room, once in front of them, and now upon them. How sweet is the restoration of God's people – now Joseph and his brethren were in open fellowship again (Gen. 45:15). This scene depicts the restoration of Jehovah with a remnant of the house of Israel during the latter portion of the Tribulation Period. Truly, as the Psalmist proclaims, *"They that sow in tears shall reap in joy"* (Ps. 126:5).

Joseph's reunion with his brethren was big news at the palace. Pharaoh instructed Joseph to bring his family to Egypt where they would be sustained during the famine, so Joseph sent his brethren to Canaan with wagons and plenty of grain to secure their journey there and back. Joseph ensured that all the needs of his family would be met. He strictly exhorted them not to argue along the way to Canaan. This was a time of joyful restoration, not of pointing fingers at others for past mistakes. What exhortation for God's people of any dispensation, "do not argue and bicker along the way home." We should be rejoicing in our salvation and in the Lord of Glory, not biting and devouring one another (Gal. 5:15).

Jacob's spirit was revived when he heard that Joseph was alive in Egypt and was the governor over all the land. Jacob regained two sons that day – Benjamin and Joseph. Jacob, ecstatic about the opportunity to travel to Egypt to see Joseph, declared, *"I will go and see him before I die."* Soon Jacob and his sons would be with Joseph, enjoying all the benefits their relationship with him had to offer.

Seeds of Destiny

Jesus! The very thought of Thee with sweetness fills my breast;
But better far Thy face to see, and in Thy presence rest.
But what to those who find? Ah, this no tongue, nor pen can show;
The love of Jesus! What it is none but His loved ones know.
Savior, our only joy be Thou, as Thou our crown shalt be;
Be Thou, O Lord, our glory now, and through eternity.

Bernard of Clairvaux

Jacob Comes to Egypt
Genesis 46

Jacob journeyed to Egypt, but not without stopping at Beer-sheba to offer sacrifices unto God. Long years of discipline in the Lord's school had finally taught Jacob to put the Lord first. Instead of rushing to Egypt to tenderly embrace his lost son, Jacob chose to pause at Beer-sheba to worship His God who had so miraculously worked in safeguarding and honoring his son, Joseph. God also spoke to Jacob in a vision and reaffirmed His presence with him declaring that He would preserve Jacob and his family in Egypt and greatly multiply them unto a great nation. This chapter provides a roster of Jacob's wives, sons, and grandsons that traveled with him to Egypt – in all sixty-six souls. Counting Joseph, his two sons, and Jacob, the total number of souls composing the nation of Israel at this time was seventy. Thus, the number seventy is associated with the nation of Israel in a special way through the remainder of Scripture. There were seventy elders (Num. 11:16), seventy years of Babylonian captivity (2 Chron. 36:21), seventy prophetic weeks determined upon Israel before their restoration (Dan. 9:24-27), and during New Testament times, there were seventy members of the Sanhedrin, and seventy witnesses sent out to Israel by Christ (Lk. 10:1).

God called out *"Jacob, Jacob"* to get Jacob's attention. He responded with "Here am I." This is the second of ten "name duplications" in the Bible. The first was in Genesis 22 when God called out, "Abraham, Abraham," on Mt. Moriah. When God calls a name twice or repeats a command or warning twice, He is emphasizing the seriousness of the matter and the urgency of His message. The Lord often repeated warnings and promises to obtain the same effect. *"Verily, Verily"* (Truly, Truly – Jn. 5:24), or *"Except ye repent, ye shall all likewise*

Seeds of Destiny

perish" (Lk. 13:3, 5), or talking about hell, *"Where their worm dieth not, and the fire is not quenched"* (Mk. 9:44, 46, 48) are examples.

Originally Jacob's family had come to Joseph for food that they might live, and now they were returning to live with Joseph. He would ensure their preservation through the difficulties ahead. It is the same with the believer; we come to Christ as sinners needing salvation. We need eternal life, or we will experience eternal death. Once we come to Christ and humbly confess our need, the Holy Spirit then responds by regenerating that individual and making effective the baptism into the body of Christ. We now live in Him and with Him forever!

Those experiencing regeneration (a rebirth) comprehend the past and finished work of Jesus Christ at Calvary. It was at Calvary that a Holy God, on our behalf, poured out His wrath on our Lord. We know His judgment satisfied the penalty of a violated standard of holiness (the law) by all humanity. We rejoice that, at Calvary, God's anger over human sinfulness was once and for all appeased. But how did God accomplish it all? What was God contemplating about us during Christ's judgment?

Unfortunately, many Christians have not expended the time to peer beyond the cursory to understand these "mysteries of Christ," as Paul calls them. Our consciousness of just what God has achieved in Christ on our behalf or what Christ is continuing to do for us is shallow. If we would bother to absorb more of these truths, it would increase our confidence and peace in Him.

This is why the Christian faith centers in Christ and not in church traditions, church leaders, or church ministries. We find no spiritual "possession" or "position" in such! As discussed in the Genesis 40 devotion, the phrase "in Christ" is used in Scripture to declare the believer's possession in Him. The phrases "with Him" or "with Christ" better relate to the believer's position – what salvation feats have been achieved with Christ. These positional phrases occur approximately forty-five times in the Epistles. Each of these references proclaims our Christian identity and, thus, are called "identification truths."

It is noted that the phrase "with Jesus" (in lieu of "with Christ") occurs only in the Gospel accounts and early in the book of Acts. This observation begs the believer to acknowledge that the Savior is more than just a man named Jesus – He is our Christ and our Lord. The disciples never called Him Jesus after they understood who He truly was! Thus, the New Testament Epistles reveal to us what God chose to veil in the four Gospel accounts!

How does God view the believer positionally "with Christ?" What has been accomplished from God's vantage point with Christ?

We have:
> been **crucified** with Christ (Rom. 6:6; Gal. 2:20)
> **died** with Christ (2 Tim. 2:11; Rom. 6:3)
> been **buried** with Christ (Rom. 6:4; Col. 2:12)
> been **quickened** (made alive) with Christ (Eph. 2:5; Col. 2:13)
> been **risen** with Christ (Eph. 2:6; Col. 2:12)

We are:
> **living** with Christ (Rom. 6:8; 2 Tim. 2:11)
> **seated** with Christ in heavenly places (Eph. 2:6)

We will:
> be **glorified** with Christ (Rom. 8:17-18)
> **reign** with Christ (Rev. 2:26 and 2 Tim. 2:12)
> **inherit** all with Christ (Rom. 8:17, Eph. 1:3)

It is amazing that God can speak of the Christian being glorified with Christ, without glorification of the redeemed having yet occurred. But, as far as God is concerned, the reality is not time dependent – it is a "done deal!" This should give the believer great hope and security to face the future! From God's vantage point, we positionally died with Christ, were buried with Him, raised up with Him, and live in Him forevermore.

The old man – the old self, what we were in Adam before salvation – was **positionally** crucified with Christ, but now the believer is exhorted to **practically** "put off" the old manner of life. The flesh is still present and still wants its way (Eph. 4:22). There is absolutely no way a believer can lose any of these identification realities with Christ, for they are completely based on the perfect work of God on our behalf. God either sees you "in Christ" or "not in Christ" throughout the time continuum. Therefore, our "practice," which we are responsible for, and our "position," which God is responsible for, have no relationship except that understanding our position in Christ is in itself exhortation

Seeds of Destiny

to live holy (Rom. 6:1-6). Israel would find preservation "with Joseph," and the believer finds security "with Christ!"

What a grand day it was when Joseph, the son thought dead for twenty-two years, rode out in his chariot to meet his gray-haired father. They embraced for a long time, and their tears flowed upon each other in that moment of jubilation. Because his father and brethren were shepherds, Joseph obtained Pharaoh's permission to settle them in the premium land of Egypt – Goshen. At Goshen, there would be plenty of grass for their herds and flocks, and they would be separated from the Egyptians who despised them.

> Dying with Jesus, by death reckoned mine;
> Living with Jesus, a new life divine;
> Looking to Jesus till glory doth shine,
> Moment by moment, O Lord I am Thine.
> Never a trial that He is not there,
> Never a burden that He doth not bear,
> Never a sorrow that He doth not share,
> Moment by moment, I'm under His care.
>
> Daniel W. Whittle

A Land, A Blessing and A Promise
Genesis 47

Jacob was 130 years old when he arrived in Egypt. Pharaoh graciously allotted Joseph's family the best of Egypt for a home – the land of Goshen situated in the northeast corner of Egypt and isolated from the majority of the Egyptian population. Why was the land of Goshen esteemed so highly? Apparently, Goshen was bordered by the Nile, for the Hebrews ate fish freely in Egypt (Num. 11:5) and, thereby, provided a resource for agricultural irrigation. Joseph presented his elderly father before Pharaoh, and Jacob blessed Pharaoh. Years earlier, Jacob had suffered an "identity crisis" when he first met his brother Esau after returning from Haran. He had forgotten who he was by covenant and had doubted the One establishing the covenant, which then led him to cringe and bow in fear seven times before his brother Esau. How did Jacob carry himself now, while before the monarch of the most powerful empire? With dignity and composure. Jacob finally understood who he was in God's vast design and even extended Pharaoh a blessing from his God. After Jacob's meeting with Pharaoh, the patriarch returned to the land of Goshen where Joseph nourished his father and brethren throughout the famine period.

The famine was severe and continued in the land year after year. In the course of time, the people had expended all their money buying grain, so they brought Joseph their livestock. After the people had depleted all their livestock to buy grain, they resorted to trading their land for grain. What good is money, cattle, or property if you are not alive to have them? Before the famine was over, Joseph had bought up the whole land of Egypt in Pharaoh's name, except the portion

Seeds of Destiny

belonging to the pagan priests. Joseph relocated the people from the country into the cities to preserve them through the latter years of famine. Finally, the only way the people could survive the famine and obtain grain was to sell themselves into servitude. Advocates of welfare are possibly wondering why Joseph did not just give the grain away instead of selling it. First, by rationing the grain for a fair price, the grain retained value, and a reserve was maintained throughout the famine. Secondly, the typology of the Millennial Kingdom of Christ is best accomplished. Joseph acquired all of Egypt after a terrible seven-year famine, just as Christ will inherit all the earth after the seven-year Tribulation Period.

As stated earlier, this seven-year famine corresponds to and represents the seven-year Tribulation Period that is forthcoming. There will be twenty-one specific judgments by God upon the earth to chasten the Jews and to punish the wicked upon the earth. The Anti-Christ and the powers of darkness will also be rampant upon the earth destroying and killing. In the book of Revelation, this horrific holocaust is enumerated: Chapter 6, one fourth of the world's population will die from pestilence, war, and famine. Chapter 9, one third of mankind will be destroyed by fire, and 200,000,000 soldiers will be annihilated at the battle of Armageddon. In Chapters 7, 13 and 20, we learn that an innumerable host of people from all nations will be martyred by the Beast for not worshipping him and receiving his mark.

Ezekiel 38 and 39 speaks of Iraq, Iran, Egypt, Germany and Turkey coming with Russia to attack Israel during the middle portion of the Tribulation Period – these armies will be annihilated by Christ's intervention through nature. A remnant will be allowed to escape to the north back into Russia (between the Black and Caspian Seas – Joel 2:19-20). Zechariah 13:8-9 confirms that two thirds of the Jews will die during the Tribulation Period. Only a Jewish remnant will survive the refining fire of the Tribulation Period to be restored to God as His chosen people (Rom. 11). There will be numerous other judgments upon the earth that will also cause death and misery. The bottom line – the earth will be no place to reside during the Tribulation Period, as perhaps eighty percent of the world's population will perish.

Throughout this Tribulation Period, God, through His judgments, will be retrieving from man what man has claimed to be his. At the end of the Tribulation Period, man will have nothing. God will have everything and will then use the fullness of a purified earth (Dan. 2:35,44-45, Rom. 8:21) to usher in the Kingdom Age, a thousand years of blessing under Christ's rule. What will the Kingdom Age be like? From Isaiah 2:1-5 and 66:20, we learn that Jerusalem shall be the religious center of the world. Christ will reign from there and from there all the nations will come to praise, worship and learn. There will be no war or violence, only peace. All the earth shall see the glory of the Lord Jesus. Isaiah 4:2-4 informs us that the Jews who live through the Tribulation will gaze upon Christ (the Branch of the Lord) and appreciate His splendor, glory, fruitfulness and beauty. So great will be the glory of the Lord upon the earth that there will be no need for the sun or moon to illuminate it (Isa. 60:18-20).

Strange natural phenomenon will be present through the earth. The wolf and the lamb shall dwell together, as will the kid of goat with the leopard and the calf with the lion (Isa. 11:6-7). Small children shall play by the hole of the asp and an adder's den and not be afraid (Isa. 11:8). The glory of the Lord will be displayed upon the world as *"the waters cover the sea"* (Isa. 11:9). These events should not be confused with the eternal state in which there is a new heaven and earth. The seas and oceans we know today will still be present during the Kingdom Age, but there will be no seas in the new earth (Rev. 21:1). The new heaven and earth are fashioned after the Kingdom Age and Satan's last rebellion on earth (Rev. 20:7-10) and after the old earth we live upon today is destroyed (Rev. 20:11; 2 Pet. 3:10). What a day of blessing it will be when the original curses upon the earth, resulting from man's sin, are lifted. Throw seed on a mountaintop, and a harvest shall be gathered. Weapons will be used as agricultural implements, and a spirit of peace and tranquillity will be upon the whole earth.

Joseph's actions during the famine and afterwards closely resemble those of Christ during the Tribulation Period and the start of the Kingdom Age. Through the judgment of God upon the earth, Joseph literally owned all the people that had come to him for preservation. At the end of the famine, he gave them seed to plant in order to reap an abundant harvest. They would retain eighty percent of their harvest, but twenty percent would be returned unto Pharaoh as wages. This was a good deal for the people considering that the people had no rent to pay and that their only personal expense was a twenty percent annual income tax. The people were glad to be treated so well considering that they had nothing and that the famine had been extremely severe. They acknowledged, *"thou has saved our lives"* (Gen. 47:25). Likewise, those who live through the Tribulation Period and refuse to worship the Beast (the anti-Christ) or receive his mark will be so thankful to be alive during the Kingdom Age that they will gladly come to Jerusalem to worship the Lord yearly (Zech. 14:16-21).

Those, of course, who worship the Anti-Christ will not survive the "Judgment of Nations" at the end of the Tribulation Period (Rev. 19:21; Dan. 12:7-13; Matt. 25:31-46; 2 Thess. 2:10-12). They will be put to death and await their resurrection from Hades (a prison torment for disembodied souls – Lk. 16) unto the "Great White Throne Judgment." At this final judgment, those suffering in Hades will be resurrected to stand under judgment. Each man's works will be shown to be incapable of earning him a righteous standing before God, and, in turn, each person will bow the knee to the Lord Jesus before being cast into an eternal judgment called Hell or the Lake of Fire (Rev. 20:11-15).

Genesis 47 closes with a fitting picture of Israel (Jacob's bones) being returned to the Promised Land during the Kingdom Age. Ezekiel 39:28-29 states that God will not leave one Jew among the nations but will bring them all back to the land of Israel at the end of the Tribulation Period. Joseph pledged to his father that he would bury him with his wife Leah, his parents, and his grandparents in the cave of Machpelah (Gen. 49:30-31). God had promised Jacob when he went to Egypt that He would exceedingly multiply him and that He would guide his descendants as a nation of people back into the Promised Land. Jacob did not want to be buried in a strange land. By faith his earnest desire was to be where he knew his children would someday dwell again.

The death of Rebekah was not recorded in Scripture, but her burial place is made known in Genesis 49:31. Where was she laid to rest? With Abraham, Sarah, Isaac, Leah and later Jacob. Putting together the seed forms previously defined in this book, this wonderfully pictures the reality of the Kingdom Age. God the Father, Christ, the Church, and Israel will dwell together during the righteous reign of Christ on the earth. God the Father is seen in Abraham, the nation of Israel is pictured in Sarah (the unconverted nation) and in Jacob (converted Israel), while the Church is symbolized in Rebekah, and Christ is viewed in Isaac. What a bizarre but incredible time this 1000-year period on earth will be. God will be dwelling on earth again with mankind (i.e. those who live through the Tribulation period and the judgment of nations), restored Israel, Old Testament saints, the Church, and the Tribulation saints. Many of these will have already experienced glorification – the blessing of the first resurrection. Hordes of people will be there, but the Lord Jesus will be the center of attention!

> All for Jesus, all for Jesus! All my being's ransomed powers:
> All my thoughts and words and doings, all my days and all my hours.
> Let my hands perform His bidding, let my feet run in His ways;
> Let my eyes see Jesus only, let my lips speak forth His praise.
> Since my eyes were fixed on Jesus, I've lost sight of all beside;
> So enchained my spirit's vision, looking at the Crucified.
> Oh, what wonder! How Amazing! Jesus, glorious King of kings,
> Deigns to call me His beloved, lets me rest beneath His wings.
>
> Mary D. James

Seeds of Destiny

A Blessing for Joseph's Sons
Genesis 48

It is appropriate that the remaining chapters in the book of Genesis focus on the remembrance of God's promises and blessings to His people. From Genesis 47:27 to the end of Genesis, God poured manifold blessings on Israel, and they promptly multiplied into a great nation. The horrors of the famine were past now; it was time to remember God's past faithfulness and His assurance of future blessing. After Joseph learned that his father was sick and bedridden, he wasted no time in ushering his two sons, Ephraim and Manasseh, into Jacob's presence for a final blessing. Joseph has been married by this time approximately twenty-five years, so his sons could have ranged in age from toddlers to young men.

Jacob recounted how "God Almighty" had appeared to him in the land of Canaan, had blessed him, had promised him that He would make a great nation of him (Gen. 48:4), and had fed him throughout his entire life (Gen. 48:15). What a wonderful testimony of God's faithfulness to His people; certainly, if He attends to the sparrows, He will not be slack to provide His children with their daily needs (Matt. 6:25-34). Jacob declared to Joseph that his two sons also would be a part of a future Hebrew nation and, therefore, desired to bless them. Joseph drew out his young sons from between his knees and carefully placed Manasseh on his left and Ephraim, his younger son, on his right. This positioning was to ensure that Jacob's right hand would be upon Manasseh's head, as to receive the blessing of the first born.

However, Jacob crossed his arms and placed his right hand upon Ephraim's head and his left upon Manasseh's to declare the blessing. This matter displeased Joseph. However, Jacob refused to switch his hands. Jacob declared that Massesseh's younger brother would be greater than he and that Ephraim's seed would become a multitude of

358

nations. Jacob called upon the One *"who redeemed him from all evil [to] bless the lads"* (Gen. 48:16). This is the first mention of Joseph expecting God to work according to human protocol, but God has already shown in this book that He normally works by unconventional means; in this way there is no question of His presence, and in the end, He achieves the greatest glory. We must remember *"For as the heavens are higher than the earth, so are My ways higher than your ways, and My thoughts than your thoughts"* (Isa. 55:9).

God is viewed, from human reasoning, as unconventional in bestowing blessing to the younger brother instead of the first born son and in opting to use unlikely methods rather than those already naturally proven to be successful. For example, Adam was revealed first and brought judgment to the human race, but the last Adam – Christ – brought peace to humanity (Rom. 5:12-21). Cain was presented first, but it was righteous Abel that pleased God. Then, the ungodly line of Cain was revealed prior to the godly line of Seth (Gen. 4 and 5). Isaac was chosen and not Ishmael. Jacob was chosen for God's purpose, not Esau. Now Joseph, not Reuben, was to get the double blessing (two sons – two tribes – double inheritances) allotted to the first born. Israel was first revealed, but it will be a Gentile Church that will rule and reign with Christ. God does this in order to show His greatness in bringing about redemption and the foremost blessing possible to all that will receive it. Jacob now trusts God fully and verbally declares his faith in whatever way God deems best when he says, *"I know it my son, I know it."* He understood Joseph's quandary over God's plan, but he had learned just to trust, because God's way always worked out to be the best!

Jacob concluded his conversation with Joseph by informing him that he was near death and that he was bestowing upon Joseph an extra portion of blessing above his brothers. This was the right of the oldest son, but Jacob viewed his beloved son Joseph, the first born of Rachel, as the one who deserved it. Jacob had taken the hill country of the Amorites through conquest and was now giving it to Joseph. Interestingly, the Hebrew word for "portion" is *sekem*. This is apparently a word play on the town of "Shechem," which was an enormous city in the land Jacob was giving to Joseph. Later, Joseph

Seeds of Destiny

would be buried at "Shechem" (Josh. 24:32). He would be with his descendants when the resurrection occurred.

Joseph got a double portion of the Promised Land – thus, the double blessing. Both Ephraim and Manasseh became heads of tribes; thus, each got a portion in Canaan when it was divided. Although the division of the land was decided by lot, Ephraim and Manasseh received the very land that Jacob had given to Joseph – the foothills and plain of Samaria (Josh. 16-17). Shechem was directly in the middle of this region. Was Jacob just babbling vain prophecies? Apparently not. Everything he spoke to Joseph concerning his boys came true. Years later, Ephraim would become the leading tribe of the Northern Kingdom and hold a position of superiority over Manasseh. Eventually, Ephraim and Manasseh would be awarded, by lot, the very land Jacob promised Joseph now. God is in control! God is in control! Let us not forget God is in control of every aspect of our lives.

> All praise to Him who reigns above, In majesty supreme,
> Who gave His Son for man to die, That He might man redeem.
> His name above all names shall stand, Exalted more and more,
> At God the Father's own right hand, Where angel hosts adore.
> His name shall be the Counselor, The mighty Prince of Peace;
> Of all earth's kingdoms Conqueror, Whose reign shall never cease.
>
> W. H. Clark

Jacob's Family Prophecies
Genesis 49

Jacob's blessings continued from Genesis 48 into Genesis 49. Now that the birthright blessing and double portion had been given to Joseph (i.e. his two sons), Jacob would gather and bless his other eleven sons also. However, these blessings are prophetic in nature. The phrase *"the last days"* is first mentioned in the Bible here; thus, the principle of "first mention" in Scripture is invoked.

The clause "the last days" is also translated in various locations in the Bible as the "latter days" and the "last times." In general context and given the precedence of Genesis 49, these terms all describe a period of time in which God will be drawing together for conclusion the purpose of a particular group or nation of people. For the nation of Israel, this expression is synonymous with the yet future conclusion of the rule of Gentile authority over Israel. This period of time will also include Israel's final rebellion against God and, consequently, God's judgment upon His adulterous wife (Israel) during the Tribulation Period (Deut. 4:30, 31:29, Ezek. 36:17-19). Yet, in Genesis 49, the focus is more upon individual tribes and their future destinies than the nation as a whole.

For some of these tribes, their destinies reflected the moral inclinations and characteristics of their tribal heads. For example, Reuben, although he was firstborn and should have been the leading tribe, had an adulterous relationship with Bilhah (Gen. 35:22) which led to his loss of that birthright position. His lusts and impulses were as turbulent as boiling water and, thus, would make him a failure as a leader. In the time of the Judges, the tribe of Reuben was characterized by indecision and a lack of resolve to be used by God to vanquish the Canaanites (Jud. 5:15-16). There are many Christians like Reuben. They know what God's will is but linger between action and slumber.

Seeds of Destiny

Some say, "I want to pray about this matter for a while." Obedience does not need prayer; it requires action!

Simeon and Levi were men of violence, referring to the time they slaughtered the Shechemites (Gen. 34:25-29) to avenge their sister Dinah's defilement. Because of their cruelty, they would be divided and scattered in Israel. By the second census of the children of Israel in Numbers, the tribes of Simeon and Levi are recorded as the smallest two in size. Simeon was mostly absorbed into the land of Judah and lost distinction. Because the tribe of Levi later sided with Moses while others were worshipping the golden calf, God gave them a special service in conducting worship for the nation and a portion in forty-eight cities after coming into Canaan. The descendants of Levi were scattered among these cities.

The prestige of the prophetic blessings was bestowed on Judah. Through Judah, kings would rule over Israel. One day the scepter "would come to the one it belongs" (the literal meaning of *"until Shiloh come"*), and it would never depart. This clearly speaks of the kingdom of the Lord Jesus, which will endure forever once He receives it. Then, the manifold abundance of this kingdom is described in Genesis 49:11-12.

A wondrous scene graces heaven's throne room just prior to the Tribulation Period according to Revelation 5:5: *"Behold, the Lion of the tribe of Judah, the Root of David, hath prevailed to open the [scroll]."* In Revelation 5:6, the Lion of the tribe of Judah is identified as a Lamb standing amidst the throngs of heaven as though it had been slain (indicating that the Lord Jesus will bear the scars of Calvary forever). The Lord Jesus, the sacrificial Lamb that took away the sins of the world, was now a Lion ready to unleash fury and wrath upon those who had crucified Him (the Jews) and the wicked upon the earth. The Tribulation Period begins in Revelation 6:1 when He opens the first seal of the scroll and allows the anti-Christ a short dominion over the world.

What emotions will engulf us as we gaze upon the thorn-scarred brow and the nail-torn hands of the blessed Savior for the first time? Will we weep, or perhaps, be speechless in His presence? A missionary made an initial visit to a remote African village many years ago. There he met a boy with terrible scars on his legs and wrists. Curious about the scars he inquired of the lad how he received such marring wounds. The boy explained that while swimming in the river, a large crocodile had grabbed him by the legs and pulled him under. "What about your wrists?" the missionary inquired. The boy smiled and said, "Those are my love scars." His mother, despite the danger, had waded into the river and grabbed the boy's wrists. The boy continued, "She pulled harder than the crocodile, which left these scars of love!" One day, our emotions will be completely undone as we gaze upon the Lord of Glory who bears those precious scars of love.

Thy form was scarred, Thy visage marred, Now cloudless peace for me,

Ann R. Cousins

Jacob further prophesied that Zebulun would be enriched by sea trade and that Issachar would be compelled to work for others. After arriving in Canaan, Issachar dwelled in the plain of Esdraelon. Because of the flatness of land, they often fell prey to invading armies. Dan, whose name means "judge," was going to be as treacherous as a snake by the roadside instead of being righteous and providing justice to Israel. This tribe was the first to engage in mass idolatry (Judg. 18:30).

Gad, whose name means "the good fortune of a troop," would not experience good fortune but would be attacked by others. Because Gad settled east of the Jordan, apart from the land specifically given to Israel to inhabit at that time, their bordering enemies were constantly raiding them. Naphtali would enjoy the peace of the high hill country in Israel. For Joseph, Jacob had only kind words of fruitfulness, prosperity and victory over enemies. It is noted that several key leaders and military victors during the time of the Canaan conquest and the period of the Judges came from Joseph. Joshua, Deborah, and Samuel came from Ephraim, and Jephthah and Gideon were from the tribe of Manasseh. Finally, Benjamin is described as a tribe that would be as violent in spirit as a ravenous wolf devouring its prey. This prophecy was clearly seen in the wickedness of the tribe of Benjamin in Judges 19 and 20, and in their refusal to repent but rather to war against all the other tribes of Israel, which nearly resulted in their doom.

God exposes a fundamental principle of His working in our lives and the lives of our descendants in this chapter. The principle is that the

Seeds of Destiny

behavior and actions of fathers (parents) affect their children for years to come. Sometimes, the effect and consequences of sin and rebellion are felt for four generations (Ex. 34:7). A parental bent of lying or uncontrolled anger is learned by children and passed along to reap a future harvest of corruption and heartache. A man cheats on his wife and unknowingly contracts an incurable venereal disease, which lies dormant for years. Unknowingly, he passes the disease to his wife and to his children, who then suffer years of misery because of their father's sin. The message to parents is – live Spirit-controlled lives, and your children will not reap the consequences of your ungodly behavior.

Before Jacob died, he again made the request that he be buried in the cave of Machpelah, which is where his parents and grandparents and his wife Leah were buried.

> Crown Him with many crowns, the Lamb upon His throne;
> Hark! How the heavenly anthem drowns all music but its own!
> Awake, my soul, and sing of Him who died for thee;
> And hail Him as thy matchless King through all eternity.
>
> Matthew Bridges

Devotions in Genesis

Dead in the World
Genesis 50

The closing chapter of Genesis contains one of the most elaborate funeral processions and burials in the Bible. This chapter symbolizes the completion of God's great plan to restore and bless the only creation to bear His image – man. Together we have traveled from the dawn of time, observed the birth pangs of the world, witnessed the fall of man, and have been awestruck by the unveiling of God's dazzling plan of redemption. Through the keys contained in New Testament Scripture, we are able to unlock the meaning of "types," "shadows," "symbols" and "analogies," which encode God's plan for man and allow us to appreciate the prophetic seeds planted in Genesis.

Thus, the book of Genesis contains the whole timeline from creation to new creation – from the fall of man to the uplifting of Christ and those in Him unto everlasting life and felicity. God has repeatedly shown that He uses the weakest and least likely people and methods to bestow the greatest blessing to mankind. In doing so, He obtains the most glory and affords man the opportunity to witness how inferior his own wisdom, strength, and capabilities are compared to God's.

The embalming of Jacob's body took forty days. All of Egypt mourned with Joseph over the death of his beloved father for seventy days, then an enormous funeral procession carried Jacob's body back to Hebron for burial. They mourned seven more days after arriving at the cave of Machpelah, then they buried Jacob and returned to Egypt. The multitude that came out of Egypt to bury Jacob was so great and the lamenting so strong for Jacob that even the inhabitants of Canaan were disturbed. They renamed the place "Abelmizraim," which means "mourning of the Egyptians."

Joseph's brothers again feared that Joseph would recompense them for selling him into slavery. Herein Joseph's serene faith in God's plan is again expressed. He understood that the life-preserving blessings to many were only possible through the ill experiences of one man – himself.

Before Joseph himself died, he beseeched his brethren to not abandon his bones in Egypt when God brought them again into Canaan. The children of Israel kept this promise years later when they exited Egypt (Ex. 13:19), and Joseph was finally laid to rest in Shechem in the land given to his two sons (Josh. 24:32).

Genesis 50 transports us from the blessings of the Kingdom Age when God the Father and the Son will be dwelling in peace with restored Israel and the Church to the harsh spiritual reality of man's present existence. The last verse of Genesis is the key to this chapter: *"So Joseph died ... and they embalmed him, and he was put in a coffin in Egypt."* Although God has shown how He will bring about His plan of redemption, this verse calls our attention back to the fact that man is spiritually dead in the world – "in a coffin in Egypt." The key words in this chapter are "mourning," "weeping" and "lamentation" (seven times). These words capture the anguish of God over the fallen spiritual condition of man. Man was created to bring Him pleasure and fellowship, but His Holiness precludes close fellowship with a rebellious and self-willed race.

The Lord Jesus was exceedingly sorrowful in His soul as He contemplated the judgment that awaited Him at Calvary (Mk. 14:34). However, His grief over His fallen creation was more sorrowful for Him; therefore, He was determined to suffer the greatest agony the world has ever know. The Lord Jesus was forward thinking, *"Looking unto Jesus, the Author and Finisher of our faith, Who for the joy that was set before Him endured the cross, despising the shame, and is set down at the right hand of the throne of God"* (Heb. 12:2). For the joy of pleasing the Father primarily, but also for the joy of receiving back His glory and for the joy of having eternal fellowship with His virgin bride – the Church, He endured the cross.

The book of Genesis has demonstrated that God is in control, He is longsuffering and patient to bring about His purposes, and He is faithful to His promises! *"The Lord is not slack concerning His promise, as some men count slackness, but is longsuffering toward us, not willing that any should perish, but that all should come to repentance"* (2 Pet. 3:9).

We will allow F. W. Grant to conclude our study of Genesis by once again gazing on the Lord of glory – the Lord Jesus:

> Genesis closes with the vision of the glory of the Lord, suffering and exalted, the government laid upon His shoulder, the true Zaphnath-paaneah, revealer of the secrets of His Father's heart, Bridegroom of His Gentile Bride, Saviour of the world. Where He fills the eye and occupies the heart, all else finds its just place and completest harmony; communion with the Father is the portion of the soul, the power of the living Spirit realized. And here what limit of attainment is imposed, save that which we may impose? The study of these Genesis-pictures will have done nothing for us, if it does not invite our hearts more than ever into the King's banqueting-house, where the everlasting arms inclose and uphold us, and "His banner" over us is "love."[1]

"Abba, Father," we approach Thee in our Saviour's precious name.
We, Thy children, here assembling, access to Thy presence claim.
Once as prodigals we wandered, in our folly, far from Thee:
But Thy grace, o'er sin abounding, rescued us from misery.

James G. Deck

Appendix A

Appendix A

Viewpoints on Creation (Gen. 1)

There are three prevalent views (each having several variations) of when the Genesis 1 account of creation occurred: Young Earth Creationism, Old Earth Creationism, and Theistic Evolution.

Young Earth Creationism has God creating the entire universe approximately 6,000 to 10,000 years ago. According to the young earth view, the global flood in Noah's day explains why the earth may appear older than it is.

Old Earth Creationism places the creation of the universe 10 to 15 billion years ago. This date is established by astronomical evidence of an expanding universe, fossil dating and geological discoveries. Some holding this view believe that the "days" of Genesis 1 were long periods of time, while others think that God created in literal 24 hour days with long gaps of time between the days.

Theistic Evolution teaches that the creation account of Genesis 1 is figurative and that God created all living things, including man, through evolution and natural selection.

So, which is correct? Through the centuries social, religious, and scientific means have all proven effective in swaying the church from one view to another. The early church fathers generally favored Old Earth Creationism, while Darwin's evolutionary theories of the 19th century caused many to embrace Theistic Evolution. Through his Study Bible, C. I. Scofield popularized the gap theory – a version of the Old Earth view in the early 20th century. However, this view was actually first publicized in 1814 by a Scottish theologian named Thomas Chalmers. The rapid advancement of instrumentation and science

Seeds of Destiny

sophistication in the 20th and 21st centuries has supplied many startling discoveries to support a Young Earth viewpoint.

As none of us were present when the world was created, I would suggest that Christians lock in on the clear absolutes of Scripture and keep an open mind as to how God actually created the universe. It probably occurred in a way quite different than anything man has devised through scientific theories.

The English word "day" in Genesis 1 is translated from the Hebrew word *"yom"* and can mean a 24-hour day or a period of creative time. However, whenever *"yom"* occurs in Scripture proceeded by an ordinal (such as 1st, 2nd, etc.), it means a literal 24-hour day. Therefore, the "days" in Genesis 1 are not periods of evolutionary development, or long periods of time, but are literal 24-hour days. Why would God need time to create? He created time!

God declares in Genesis 1:27 that He created man, not that man evolved. The Lord Jesus said God made male and female from the beginning (Matt. 19:4). Therefore, "theistic evolution" is not sound. Besides this, the literal 24-hour day becomes a building block for a seven-day week, which God used as a foundation for directing human affairs and declaring Bible prophecy. It is noted that the "beginning" spoken of by the Lord Jesus in Matthew 19:4 is the specific beginning of the world as it pertains to man, and not the beginning of all physical and spiritual assets of the universe. John uses the same terminology in 1 John 1:1 to speak of the beginning of the Lord's ministry on earth – it was the only beginning related to his message – the life and sacrifice of Christ.

We learn from Job 38:4-7 that *all* the angels shouted for joy and praised God when the original foundations of the earth were created (This is not a reference to land appearing on day three, but the initial creation of the world.). Thus, angels were created prior to any physical reality of creation, and secondly, Lucifer's rebellion in heaven would have occurred after initial creation. Lucifer praised God during the initial acts of creation (Job 38:7).

Some holding the gap theory believe that angels inhabited the earth and that when Lucifer rebelled, God destroyed the earth with a flood (thus the scene of Genesis 1:2). However, Scripture and logic refute this scenario, for a flood would not destroy angelic creatures. Also, the

Appendix A

site of Lucifer's rebellion, as recorded in Isaiah 14:12-15, was God's heavenly throne, not an earthly habitation. Before the earth was created, God's throne existed in heaven (Ps. 103:19), and the angels were ministering before Him (Ps. 103:20-22). Thus, Satan was not on earth when he rebelled against God's order for he drew a third of the angels out of heaven (Rev. 12:4). Jude 6 informs us that there are evil angels who are chained and awaiting the final judgment because they left their first estate (position in created order) and their habitation (heaven).

The gap theory inserts a gap of unknown years between Genesis 1:1 and 1:2. The gap theory draws a distinction between the origin of creation (Gen. 1:1) and the literal six-day re-creation account in the remainder of Genesis 1. Geological ages, dinosaurs, fossils, etc. are seen as contemporaries of this huge gap prior to re-creation. The majority of Christians holding to an Old Earth view or the variation *gap* idea would flatly reject evolutionary thinking. According to the gap thinking, Genesis 1:1 informs us that God created the heavens and the earth in perfection (Isa. 45:18), but after the fall of Lucifer, all creation was adversely affected, and the earth was made void and uninhabitable. Now, these rebellious spiritual beings are intent on causing disorder to God's created order. Satan's insurrection brought chaos to God's perfect creation just as man's rebellion in the garden brought judgment upon a newly created earth (Gen. 3). Because of sin, all creation groans and is waiting for Christ to put again all things in perfect order (Rom. 8:22).

It seems unreasonable to think that any event other than spiritual rebellion could cause such chaos in God's perfect universe, if indeed there was an interval between Genesis 1:1 and 1:2. Satan's rebellion, whenever it did occur, had devastating consequences throughout creation. Possibly Job made a reference to this degradation when he noted that neither the heavens nor the stars were pure in God's sight (Job 15:15, 25:5).

The Young Earth thinking views the Genesis account as literal. The creation of all that God created occurred in six 24-hour days some 6 to 10 thousand years ago. God created time, space, and matter (including energy) out of nothing in Genesis 1:1 and then, differentiated these basic elements and resources to specific purposes to bring order to all things. The initial creation of Genesis 1:1 was not perfect in the sense of being complete, but it was perfect for that first stage of God's planned six days of creation. This two step process is apparent when God formed Adam; He made dust first and formed Adam from that dust then gave him life. It is obvious that before God said *"Let there be ...,"* there already were some basic resources He was working with (Gen. 1:2).

Those holding a literal six-day creation view of Genesis 1 would argue against the *gap* theory in several ways. Although the Hebrew word *hayetha*, translated *"was without form,"* in Genesis 1:2, may be translated "had become without form" it is not normally applied in this way. It is translated simply as "was" in 98 percent of the Old Testament occurrences (i.e. where no change of state is occurring).

Secondly, death came into the world only after the fall of Adam (Rom. 5:12; 1 Cor. 15:21). Others see that the affect of death pertains only to that portion of creation which God has revealed to us in Genesis 1 – that which pertains directly to man. When Adam fell, death came upon mankind and curses upon the earth, the earth God had just created or re-created. This new earth was God's stage for accomplishing redemption to save a creation that bore his image. The benefit of Calvary only reaches back to Adam, where death entered the new world. Christ's blood was shed only for sins of mankind, the only earthly creation bearing His image.

Thirdly, the young earth creationist would see Isaiah 45:18 simply referring to the fact that God formed the earth to be inhabited, that He did not form it without purpose.

Perhaps there is not much difference between the gap and young earth creation views. Given the gap viewpoint, as explained above, it is not likely that it took Lucifer long to rebel against his Creator after being created. Why would God leave the earth waste (as a testimony of Lucifer's rebellion) or wait to recreate the earth, in order to place a special creation bearing His Own image there? If a gap did exist between original creation and reconstruction of the earth it would likely be relatively short. Thus, perhaps the gap thinking really leans more to a young earth view than an old earth view. Yet, Scripture is silent, and this is just fallible human reasoning.

Appendix B

Appendix B
Four Hundred Year Prophecy (Gen. 15)

God told Abram in a vision that his future descendants would be strangers sojourning in a land and that that nation would make them servants and severely trouble them (Gen. 15:13-15). The duration of this prophecy is 400 years (Gen. 15:13; Acts 7:6) and would span four generations (Gen. 15:16). How was this prophecy fulfilled? Some believe that the 400 years began with Jacob's arrival at Goshen, where the descendants of Abram sojourned in peace for a time and then were placed in bondage for a total duration of 430 years before being delivered (see Ex.12:40-41 and Gal. 3:17, where Gen. 15:13 and Acts 7:6 speak of 400 years, these may be rounded figures).

Yet, this understanding does not explain the deliverance and return of the Jewish nation in the fourth generation of captivity unless you assume generations were not named. This is unlikely considering these were the glory days of Israel's expansion. The four generations probably referred to the generations from Levi to Moses the deliverer. We read that Kohath, the son of Levi, was already born when Jacob's family arrived in Egypt (Gen. 46:11). Kohath had a son named Amram, and Amram had a son named Moses. Kohath lived only 133 years; Amram lived 137 years (Ex. 6:18-20), and Moses was 80 years old when he was sent as God's deliverer (Ex. 7:7). It is noted that Amram was the first of four sons born to Kohath. So, even if Kohath and Amram had both married late in life and had children late in life (which is not apparent because each had several children), it would "practically speaking" be difficult to have more than 275 years between Kohath's coming into Egypt and Moses' delivering of the children of Israel.

It is my **opinion** that the best fit of all Scripture would initiate the 400 years, or more specifically, the 430-year duration of sojourning with the

Seeds of Destiny

covenant with Abram in Genesis 12. Abram then traveled to Egypt and sojourned there for a time to escape a famine soon after arriving in Canaan. Sir Robert Anderson's *Bible Chronology* places this covenant in the year 2055 BC.

With this assumption, we may figure periods of time based on this covenant event to obtain a close approximation of how long the Israelites were actually in Egypt. Abraham was 75 years old when the covenant was made (Gen. 12:4). Then, 25 years later, Isaac was born (Gen. 21:5); 60 years later Jacob was born to Isaac, and we know that Jacob was 130 years old when he went to Egypt (Gen. 47:9). If we use the total time of 430 years that the descendants sojourned in Egypt (Ex. 12:40-41) and subtract the years known to exist between the covenant and Jacob's entrance into Egypt, we can surmise the total time the descendants of Jacob were in Egypt to be 215 years (430 – 25 – 60 – 130 = 215).

How does this fit with the fourth generation prophecy? If we assume Kohath and Amram were about halfway through their life span before having children (say ages 65 to 70 respectively), 215 years between arriving at Egypt and deliverance from Egypt would be observed (133 – 65 {for Kohath} + 137 –70 {Amram}+80 {for Moses} = 215 years). It is noted that Isaac was 60 before Jacob was born (Gen. 25:26), and Jacob was in his early eighties before having children.

How long were the Israelites slaves and not just sojourners? We cannot definitely say, but we do know that they were not slaves while Joseph was alive. Joseph was 39 years old when Jacob came to Egypt (Gen. 41:45-53, 45:6), and Joseph died at 110 years of age (Gen. 50:26). Therefore, we can subtract another 71 years (110 – 39) from the 215 number to represent the time after Jacob arrived in Egypt to the death of Joseph. The result would be 144 years. It would be safe to assume that the descendants of Abraham were not enslaved while Joseph was alive and, therefore, were not enslaved more than 144 years.

The prophecy states the Abraham's descendants *"shall be a sojourner in a land that is not theirs, and shall serve them; and they shall afflict them four hundred years"* (Gen. 15:13). It would seem events unfold according to the order revealed – sojourning to suffering. Perhaps, one could say Abraham suffered somewhat in Egypt when Pharaoh took Sarah into his harem. Certainly, the Hebrews suffered verbal abuse in those early years in Egypt due to the fact that Egyptians

Appendix B

despised shepherds. The cruelty of the Egyptians seems to have increased over time to enslaving them, then to the point that innocent children were being murdered in an attempt to control the exploding slave population.

End Notes

Why is Genesis so Important?
1. John Darby, *Synopsis of the Books of the Bible Vol. 1* (Stow Hill Bible and Tract Depot, Kingston, ON: 1948), p. 7
2. H. A. Ironside, *Holiness – The False and the True* (Loizeaux, Neptune, NJ: 1912), p. 33
3. A. W. Pink, *Gleanings in Genesis* (Moody Press, Chicago: 1922), p. 343
4. J. Boyd Nicholson, *Counsel Magazine* Vol. 24: Num. 3 (Gospel Folio Press, Grand Rapids, MI: May 1994), p. 3

A Book of Beginning
1. J. Wesley Ferguson, *What the Bible Teaches* (John Ritchie Ltd., Kilmarnock, Scotland: 2000), p. 24

The First Workweek
1. John Darby, op. cit., p. 8

Three in One
1. B. H. Carroll, Studies in Genesis (Broadman Press, Nashville, TN: 1937), p. 11

God's Icon
1. Matthew Henry, *Matthew Henry's Commentary on the Whole Bible* (Electronic Edition STEP Files Copyright © 1998, Parsons Technology, Inc.), Genesis 1

Creating or Making?
1. John Darby, op. cit., p. 8
2. William Kelly, Lectures on the Pentateuch (Heijkoop, Winschoten/Netherlands: reprinted 1970), pp. 8-9
3. David Bercot, *A Dictionary of Early Christian Beliefs* (Hendrickson Publishers, Peabody, MA: 1998), p. 180

Seeds of Destiny

Is Seeing Believing?
1. Henry M. Morris, *The Genesis Record* (Baker Book House, Grand Rapids: 1976), p. 45
2. Sir Robert Anderson, *The Coming Prince* (16th Edition; Kregel Publications, Grand Rapids, MI: 1967), p. 246
3. Albert Edersheim, Bible History Old Testament (Hendrickson Publishing, Peabody: 1995), p. 12

The Gift of Rest
1. William MacDonald, *Believer's Bible Commentary* (Thomas Nelson Publishers, Nashville: 1989), p. 109

A Price to be Paid
1. C. H. Mackintosh, op. cit., p. 21
2. Henry M. Morris, op. cit., p. 102

The First Question
1. F. W. Grant, *Genesis in the Light – The Serious Christian Series* (Loizeaux Brothers, Inc., Neptune, NJ), p. 39

Lost in Eden
1. William Kelly, op. cit., p. 22

Curses
1. Francis A. Schaeffer, *Genesis in Space and Time* (InterVarsity Press, Downers Grove, IL: 1972), p. 96
2. F. W. Grant, op. cit., p. 49

The Way of Cain
1. Albert Edersheim, op. cit. p. 18

The Second Murder
1. F. W. Grant, op. cit., p. 60
2. Derek Kidner, *Genesis An Introduction and Commentary* (Inter-Varsity Press, Downers Grove, IL: 1967), p. 76
3. A. W. Pink, op. cit., p. 67

Unnatural Unions
1. H. C. Leupold, *Exposition of Genesis Vol. 1* (Baker Book House, Grand Rapids, MI: 1942), p. 256
2. J. Wesley Ferguson, op. cit., p. 60

End Notes

Unnatural Unions (cont.)
3. Henry M. Morris, op. cit., p. 166
4. C. H. Mackintosh, op. cit., p. 47

When It Comes
1. B. H. Carroll, op. cit., p. 61

The Gift of Hope
1. William Lincoln from A.W. Pink, op. cit., p. 108

An Offering and A Promise
1. Henry M. Morris, op. cit., p. 215

A Rebel
1. James G. Murphy, *A Commentary on the Book of Genesis* (Baker Book House, Grand Rapids, MI, reprinted from 1873 edition), p. 239

A Pagan named Abram
1. Sir Robert Anderson, op. cit., p. 246

No More Delays
1. F. W. Grant, op. cit., p. 78
2. Matthew Henry, *Matthew Henry Commentary* (MacDonald Pub. Co., Mclean, VA), p. 83
3. Herbert Taylor, *Abraham My Friend* (Loizeaux Brothers, Bible Truth Depot, New York, NY), p. 16

The Promise of a New World
1. Hamilton Smith, *Abraham the Friend of God* (Gospel Folio Press, Grand Rapids, MI), p. 20

The Tent and the Altar
1. William Kelly, op. cit., pp. 54-55
2. Hamilton Smith, op. cit., p. 27

A Trial for Abram
1. Ridout from A.W. Pink, op. cit., p. 145
2. C. H. Mackintosh, op. cit., pp. 64-65
3. J. N. Darby from Hamilton Smith, op. cit., p. 29
4. Herbert Taylor, op. cit., pp. 18-19

Too Much Stuff
1. F. W. Grant, op. cit., p. 85
2. Hamilton Smith, op. cit., p. 33

Abram the Hebrew
1. Herbert Taylor, op. cit. pp. 26-27
2. B. H. Carroll, op. cit., p. 73

A Priest Intervenes
1. William Kelly, op. cit., p. 60

Faith That Obeys
1. Herbert Taylor, op. cit., p. 49

God Needs Help Again?
1. Matthew Henry, op. Cit., Genesis 16

A Well for Hagar
1. C. H. Waller, Shadows of Redemption (Gospel Folio Press, Grand Rapids, MI; 1881, reprinted 1999), p. 31

New Names
1. A. W. Pink, op. cit., p. 187

Abraham the Intercessor
1. S. Emery, Treasury of Bible Doctrine (Precious Seed Magazine, UK: 1977), p. 210
2. James Gunn, *Christ The Fullness of the Godhead* (Loizeaux Brothers, Neptune, NJ: 1982), p. 167

Immersed in the World
1. Henry M. Morris, op. cit., p. 347

A Man Without Respect
1. Delitzsch from H. C. Leupold, op. cit., p. 559
2. F. W. Grant, op. cit., pp. 118-119

Remember Lot's Wife
1. H. C. Leupold, op. cit., p. 571

End Notes

After These Things
1. F. W. Grant, op. cit., p. 138

The Father Offers His Son
1. A. P. Gibbs, *Worship – The Christian's Highest Occupation* (2nd Edition, Walterick Publishers, Kansas City, KS), p. 19
2. C. H. Mackintosh, op. cit., p. 96

God Will Provide a Lamb
1. Hamilton Smith, op. cit., p. 112
2. Herbert Taylor, op. cit., p. 66

The Father Departs the Mount
1. F. W. Grant, op. cit., p. 146

A Bride Sought for Isaac
1. Matthew Henry, op. cit., Genesis 24

A Bride Bought for Isaac
1. B. H. Carroll, op. cit., p. 89

A Bride Brought to Isaac
1. Hamilton Smith, op. cit., pp. 126-127

Obey My Voice!
1. David Augsburger, *When Caring is Not Enough* (Ventura, Calif. Regal Books:1983), pp. 5-7
2. Henry M. Morris, op. cit., p. 435

A Special Son is Born
1. Henry M. Morris, op. cit., p. 468

The Shepherd is Blessed
1. Andrew Fuller from A. W. Pink, op. cit., p. 273
2. J. N. Darby from A. W. Pink, op. cit., p. 273

The Shepherd Leads
1. A. W. Pink, op. cit., p. 274

All Alone
1. C. H. Mackintosh, op. cit., p. 122

The Beginning of Edom
1. C. I. Scofield, *The New Scofield Study Bible* (Oxford University Press, New York: 1967), p. 53

A Special Son Dies?
1. Knapp from A. W. Pink, op. cit., p. 354
2. F. W. Grant, op. cit., pp. 174-175
3. C. H. Mackintosh, op. cit., p. 127
4. William MacDonald, op. cit., pp. 70-71

Temptation, Accusation, and Unjust Punishment
1. Henry M. Morris, op. cit., p. 559
2. Sara McLanahan, *November 1998 Reader's Digest* (Reader's Digest Association Inc. Marion, Ohio) p. 178

Joseph Forgotten
1. Matthew Henry, op. cit., Genesis 40

The Final Test
1. F. W. Grant, op. cit., pp. 183-184

Dead In the World
1. F. W. Grant, op. cit., p. 188